Android Recipes

A Problem-Solution Approach

Dave Smith
Jeff Friesen

Apress®

Android Recipes: A Problem-Solution Approach

ISBN-13 (pbk): 978-1-4302-3413-5

ISBN-13 (electronic): 978-1-4302-3414-2

Trademarked names, logos, and images may appear in this book. Rather than use a trademark symbol with every occurrence of a trademarked name, logo, or image we use the names, logos, and images only in an editorial fashion and to the benefit of the trademark owner, with no intention of infringement of the trademark.

The use in this publication of trade names, trademarks, service marks, and similar terms, even if they are not identified as such, is not to be taken as an expression of opinion as to whether or not they are subject to proprietary rights.

President and Publisher: Paul Manning
Lead Editor: Tom Welsh
Technical Reviewer: Paul Connolly
Editorial Board: Steve Anglin, Mark Beckner, Ewan Buckingham, Gary Cornell, Jonathan Gennick, Jonathan Hassell, Michelle Lowman, Matthew Moodie, Jeff Olson, Jeffrey Pepper, Frank Pohlmann, Douglas Pundick, Ben Renow-Clarke, Dominic Shakeshaft, Matt Wade, Tom Welsh
Coordinating Editor: Corbin Collins
Copy Editor: Tracy Brown
Compositor: MacPS, LLC
Indexer: BIM Indexing & Proofreading Services
Artist: April Milne
Cover Designer: Anna Ishchenko

Distributed to the book trade worldwide by Springer Science+Business Media, LLC., 233 Spring Street, 6th Floor, New York, NY 10013. Phone 1-800-SPRINGER, fax (201) 348-4505, e-mail orders-ny@springer-sbm.com, or visit www.springeronline.com.

For information on translations, please e-mail rights@apress.com, or visit www.apress.com.

Apress and friends of ED books may be purchased in bulk for academic, corporate, or promotional use. eBook versions and licenses are also available for most titles. For more information, reference our Special Bulk Sales–eBook Licensing web page at www.apress.com/info/bulksales.

The information in this book is distributed on an "as is" basis, without warranty. Although every precaution has been taken in the preparation of this work, neither the author(s) nor Apress shall have any liability to any person or entity with respect to any loss or damage caused or alleged to be caused directly or indirectly by the information contained in this work.

The source code for this book is available to readers at www.apress.com.

Contents at a Glance

Contents

Foreword

Dave Smith and Jeff Friesen have taken on a daunting task in writing this book. Knowing Dave for a long time in the mobile development community, I know he labored over every chapter, debating the best advice to give. How do I know this? Because I have the pleasure to work with Dave on a daily basis, and he brings a methodical, measured, deliberative approach to the problems we solve shipping Android software.

With the explosion of Android-powered devices in a very short period of time, a unique opportunity to shape the future of mobile computing has arisen. Android powers phones, tablets, industrial appliances, and in the future devices we have not yet imagined. This broad range of devices running on a common platform allows software developers to write once and run everywhere. Within, Dave and Jeff present examples that they have learned writing real-world Android applications to start you on your journey. Now, take this information and build quality mobile experiences. When your app is launched, these devices become your application. With the flood of mobile devices will come with it a flood of software, much of which will be crap. Put yourself in the users' shoes, solve a problem they have, and create something to be proud of. Obsess on the details, your users will appreciate it — and remember, "Real Artists Ship."

—Ben Reubenstein (@benr75)
benr@xcellentcreations.com
Xcellent Creations, Inc.

About the Authors

 **Dave Smith** has been developing hardware and software for embedded platforms since graduating from Colorado School of Mines in 2006 with degrees in Electrical Engineering and Computer Science. Dave now focuses his engineering efforts full-time in the mobile space, working as a consultant in Denver, CO. Since 2009, Dave has worked on developing at all levels of the Android platform, from writing user applications using the SDK to building and customizing the Android source code. His favorite Android projects are those that integrated custom hardware with consumer devices, or include building Android for custom embedded platforms. In addition, Dave regularly communicates via his development blog (blog.wiresareobsolete.com) and Twitter stream (@devunwired).

 **Jeff Friesen** is a freelance tutor and software developer with an emphasis on Java (and now Android). In addition to writing this book, Jeff has written numerous articles on Java and other technologies for *JavaWorld* (www.javaworld.com), *informIT* (www.informit.com), *java.net*, and *DevSource* (www.devsource.com). Jeff can be contacted via his website at tutortutor.ca.

About the Technical Reviewer

 **Paul Connolly** is the Director of Engineering for Atypon Systems' RightSuite product line. RightSuite is an enterprise access-control and commerce solution used by many of the world's largest publishing and media companies. Paul enjoys designing and implementing high-performance, enterprise-class software systems. He is also an active contributor in the open-source community.

Prior to joining Atypon Systems, Paul worked as a senior software engineer at Standard & Poor's, where he architected and developed key communications systems. Paul is a Sun Certified Java Programmer, Sun Certified Business Component Developer, and a Sun Certified Web Component Developer. Paul lives in New York City with his wife Marina and daughter Olivia.

Acknowledgments

First and foremost, I would like to thank my wife, Lorie, for her eternal patience and support during the long hours I spent compiling and constructing the materials for this book. Next, many thanks to my coauthor, Jeff Friesen, whose willingness to explore new options and paths to Android development have given this book a diverse flavor that makes it great. To my friend and colleague, Ben Reubenstein: thank you for taking time to provide the Foreword for the book, and for making the intial introductions between myself and the team here at Apress. Finally, I send a huge thank you to the team that Apress brought together to work with Jeff and me and make the book the best it could possibly be: Steve Anglin, Corbin Collins, Tom Welsh, Paul Connolly, and everyone else. Without your time and effort, this project would not even exist.

—Dave Smith

I thank Steve Anglin for contacting me to write this book, Corbin Collins for guiding me through the various aspects of this project, Tom Welsh for helping me with the development of my chapters, and Paul Connolly for his diligence in catching various flaws that would otherwise have made it into this book. I also thank my coauthor Dave Smith for making a fantastic contribution to this book.

—Jeff Friesen

Preface

Welcome to Android Recipes!

If you are reading this book, you probably don't need to be told of the immense opportunity that mobile devices represent for software developers and users. In recent years, Android has become one of the top mobile platforms for device users. This means that you, as a developer, must know how to harness Android so you can stay connected to this market and the potential that it offers. But any new platform brings with it uncertainty about best practices or solutions to common needs and problems.

What we aim to do with *Android Recipes* is give you the tools to write applications for the Android platform through direct examples targeted at the specific problems you are trying to solve. This book is not a deep dive into the Android SDK, NDK, or any of the other tools. We don't weigh you down with all the details and theory behind the curtain. That's not to say that those details aren't interesting or important. You should take the time to learn them, as they may save you from making future mistakes. However, more often than not they are simply a distraction when you are just looking for a solution to an immediate problem.

This book is not meant to teach you Java programming or even the building blocks of an Android application. You won't find many basic recipes in this book (such as how to display text with TextView, for instance), as we feel these are tasks easily remembered once learned. Instead, we set out to address tasks that developers, once comfortable with Android, need to do often, but that are too complex to remember or accomplish with a few lines of code.

Treat *Android Recipes* as a reference to consult, a resource-filled cookbook that you can always open to find the pragmatic advice you need to get the job done quickly and well.

What Will You Find in the Book?

Although this book is not a beginner's guide to Android, Chapter 1 offers an overview of those Android fundamentals that are necessary for understanding the rest of the book's content. Chapter 1 also shows you how to set up your environment so that you can develop Android apps. Specifically, it shows you how to install the Android SDK and Eclipse with the ADT Plugin.

As you become a seasoned Android app developer, you're going to want to save time by not reinventing the wheel. Instead, you'll want to create and use your own libraries of reusable code, or use the libraries that others have created. Chapter 7 shows you how to create and use your own library code in the form of JAR-based libraries and Android library projects. In addition to creating your own libraries, we'll introduce a couple of Java libraries outside the Android SDK that your applications can make use of.

In the intervening chapters, we dive into using the Android SDK to solve real problems. You will learn tricks for effectively creating a user interface that runs well across device boundaries. You will become a master of incorporating the collection of hardware (radios, sensors, and cameras) that makes mobile devices such a unique platform. We'll even discuss how to make the system work for you, integrating with the services and applications provided by Google and the various device manufacturers. Along the way, you'll be introduced to some tools developed by the community to help making development and testing of your applications easier.

Are you interested in scripting languages (such as Python or Ruby)? If so, you'll want to check out Appendix A, which introduces you to Scripting Layer for Android. This special app lets you install scripting language interpreters and scripts on a device, and then run these scripts, which can speed up development.

Performance matters if you want your apps to succeed. Most of the time, this isn't a problem because (as of version 2.2) Android's Dalvik virtual machine features a Just-In-Time compiler that compiles Dalvik bytecode to the device's native code. However, if this isn't enough, you'll need to leverage the Android NDK to boost performance. Appendix B offers you an introduction to the NDK and demonstrates its usefulness in the context of an OpenGL example.

When creating apps, you need to ensure that they are performant, responsive, and seamless. Apps that perform well drain less power from the battery, responsive apps avoid the dreaded *Application Not Responding* dialog box, and seamless apps interact properly with other apps so as not to annoy or confuse the user. Additionally, when you publish your app to Google's Android Market, you don't want the app to be visible to incompatible devices. Instead, you want Android Market to filter your app so that users of these incompatible devices cannot download (or even see) the app. Appendix C rounds out the book by offering you guidelines for creating performant, responsive, and seamless apps; and for taking advantage of filtering so that an app can be downloaded (from Android Market) only by those users whose devices are compatible with the app.

Keep a Level Eye on the Target

Throughout the book, you will see that we have marked most recipes with the minimum API Level that is required to support it. Most of the recipes in this book are marked API Level 1, meaning that the code used can be run in applications targeting any version of Android since 1.0. However, where necessary we make use of APIs introduced in later versions. Pay close attention to the API Level marking of each recipe to ensure that you are not using code that doesn't match up with the version of Android your application is targeted to support.

Chapter 1

Getting Started with Android

Android is hot, and many people are developing Android applications (apps for short). Perhaps you would also like to develop apps, but are unsure about how to get started. Although you could study Google's online *Android Developer's Guide* (http://developer.android.com/guide/index.html) to acquire the needed knowledge, you might be overwhelmed by the vast amount of information that this guide presents. In contrast, this chapter provides just enough theory to help you understand the basics of Android. This theory is followed by several recipes that teach you how to develop apps and prepare them for publication to Google's Android Market.

What Is Android?

The *Android Developer's Guide* defines Android as a *software stack* – a set of software subsystems needed to deliver a fully functional solution – for mobile devices. This stack includes an operating system (a modified version of the Linux kernel), *middleware* (software that connects the low-level operating system to high-level apps) that's partly based on Java, and key apps (written in Java) such as a web browser (known as Browser) and a contact manager (known as Contacts).

Android offers the following features:

- Application framework enabling reuse and replacement of app components (discussed later in this chapter)

- Bluetooth, EDGE, 3G, and WiFi support (hardware dependent)

- Camera, GPS, compass, and accelerometer support (hardware dependent)

- Dalvik Virtual Machine (DVM) optimized for mobile devices

- GSM Telephony support (hardware dependent)

- Integrated browser based on the open source WebKit engine

- Media support for common audio, video, and still image formats (MPEG4, H.264, MP3, AAC, AMR, JPG, PNG, GIF)

- Optimized graphics powered by a custom 2D graphics library; 3D graphics based on the OpenGL ES 1.0 specification (hardware acceleration optional)

- SQLite for structured data storage

Although not part of an Android device's software stack, Android's rich development environment (including a device emulator and a plugin for the Eclipse IDE) could also be considered an Android feature.

History of Android

Contrary to what you might expect, Android did not originate with Google. Instead, Android was initially developed by Android, Inc., a small Palo Alto, California-based startup company. Google bought this company in July 2005 and released a preview version of the Android SDK in November 2007.

In mid-August, 2008, Google released the Android 0.9 SDK beta, and subsequently released the Android 1.0 SDK one month later. Table 1–1 outlines subsequent SDK update releases. (Starting with version 1.5, each major release comes under a code name that's based on a dessert item.)

Table 1–1. *Android Update Releases*

SDK Update	Release Date and Changes
1.1	Google released SDK 1.1 on February 9, 2009. Changes included paid apps (via Android Market) and "search by voice" support.
1.5 (Cupcake) Based on Linux Kernel 2.6.27	Google released SDK 1.5 on April 30, 2009. Changes included the ability to record and watch videos through camcorder mode, the ability to upload videos to YouTube and pictures to Picasa, the ability to populate the home screen with widgets, and animated screen transitions.
1.6 (Donut) Based on Linux Kernel 2.6.29	Google released SDK 1.6 on September 15, 2009. Changes included an improved Android Market experience, an integrated camera/camcorder/gallery interface, updated "search by voice" with speed and other improvements, and an updated search experience.
2.0/2.1 (Eclair) Based on Linux Kernel 2.6.29	Google released SDK 2.0 on October 26, 2009. Changes included a revamped user interface, a new contacts list, support for Microsoft Exchange, digital zoom, improved Google Maps (version 3.1.2), HTML5 support for the Browser app, live wallpapers, and Bluetooth 2.1 support. Google subsequently released SDK update 2.0.1 on December 3, 2009, and SDK update 2.1 on January 12, 2010.

SDK Update	Release Date and Changes
2.2 (Froyo) Based on Linux Kernel 2.6.32	Google released SDK 2.2 on May 20, 2009. Changes included the integration of Chrome's V8 JavaScript engine into the Browser app, voice dialing and contact sharing over Bluetooth, Adobe Flash 10.1 support, additional app speed improvements courtesy of a JIT implementation, and USB tethering and WiFi hotspot functionality.
2.3 (Gingerbread) Based on Linux Kernel 2.6.35.7	Google released SDK 2.3 on December 6, 2010. Changes included a new concurrent garbage collector that improves an app's responsiveness, support for gyroscope sensing, support for WebM video playback and other video improvements, support for near field communication, and improved social networking features. This book focuses on Android 2.3. Google subsequently released SDK 2.3.1 to fix some bugs, and SDK 2.3.3, a small feature release that adds several improvements and APIs to the Android 2.3 platform.
3.0 (Honeycomb) Based on Linux 2.6.36	Google released SDK 3.0 on February 22, 2011. Unlike previous releases, version 3.0 focuses exclusively on tablets, such as Motorola Zoom, the first tablet to be released (on February 24, 2011). In addition to an improved user interface, version 3.0 improves multitasking, supports multicore processors, supports hardware acceleration, and provides a 3D desktop with redesigned widgets.

Android Architecture

The Android software stack consists of apps at the top, middleware (consisting of an application framework, libraries, and the Android runtime) in the middle, and a Linux kernel with various drivers at the bottom. Figure 1–1 shows this layered architecture.

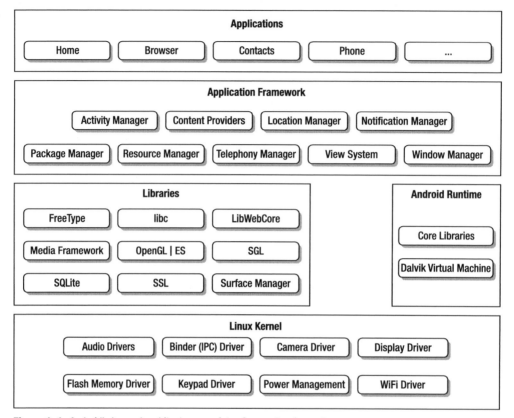

Figure 1–1. *Android's layered architecture consists of several major parts.*

Users care about apps, and Android ships with a variety of useful core apps, which include Browser, Contacts, and Phone. All apps are written in the Java programming language. Apps form the top layer of Android's architecture.

Directly beneath the app layer is the *application framework*, a set of high-level building blocks for creating apps. The application framework is preinstalled on Android devices and consists of the following components:

- *Activity Manager*: This component provides an app's *lifecycle* and maintains a shared activity stack for navigating within and among apps. Both topics are discussed later in this chapter.

- *Content Providers*: These components encapsulate data (such as the Browser app's bookmarks) that can be shared among apps.

- *Location Manager*: This component makes it possible for an Android device to be aware of its physical location.

- *Notification Manager*: This component lets an app notify the user of a significant event (such as a message's arrival) without interrupting what the user is currently doing.

- *Package Manager*: This component lets an app learn about other app packages that are currently installed on the device. (App packages are discussed later in this chapter.)

- *Resource Manager*: This component lets an app access its resources, a topic that's briefly discussed in Recipe 1–5.

- *Telephony Manager*: This component lets an app learn about a device's telephony services. It also handles making and receiving phone calls.

- *View System*: This component manages user interface elements and user interface-oriented event generation. (These topics are briefly discussed in Recipe 1–5.)

- *Window Manager*: This component organizes the screen's real estate into windows, allocates drawing surfaces, and performs other window-related jobs.

The components of the application framework rely on a set of C/C++ libraries to perform their jobs. Developers interact with the following libraries by way of framework APIs:

- *FreeType*: This library supports bitmap and vector font rendering.

- *libc*: This library is a BSD-derived implementation of the standard C system library, tuned for embedded Linux-based devices.

- *LibWebCore*: This library offers a modern and fast web browser engine that powers the Android browser and an embeddable web view. It's based on WebKit (http://en.wikipedia.org/wiki/WebKit) and is also used by the Google Chrome and Apple Safari browsers.

- *Media Framework*: These libraries, which are based on PacketVideo's OpenCORE, support the playback and recording of many popular audio and video formats, as well as working with static image files. Supported formats include MPEG4, H.264, MP3, AAC, AMR, JPEG, and PNG.

- *OpenGL | ES*: These 3D graphics libraries provide an OpenGL implementation based on OpenGL | ES 1.0 APIs. They use hardware 3D acceleration (where available) or the included (and highly optimized) 3D software rasterizer.

- *SGL*: This library provides the underlying 2D graphics engine.

- *SQLite*: This library provides a powerful and lightweight relational database engine that's available to all apps, and that's also used by Mozilla Firefox and Apple's iPhone for persistent storage.

- *SSL*: This library provides secure sockets layer-based (SSL-based) security for network communication.

- *Surface Manager*: This library manages access to the display subsystem, and seamlessly composites 2D and 3D graphic layers from multiple apps.

Android provides a runtime environment that consists of core libraries (implementing a subset of the Apache Harmony Java version 5 implementation) and the Dalvik Virtual Machine (DVM), a non-Java virtual machine that's based on processor registers instead of being stack-based.

> **NOTE:** Google's Dan Bornstein created Dalvik and named this virtual machine after an Icelandic fishing village where some of his ancestors lived.

Each Android app defaults to running in its own Linux process, which hosts an instance of Dalvik. This virtual machine has been designed so that devices can run multiple virtual machines efficiently. This efficiency is largely due to Dalvik executing Dalvik Executable (DEX)-based files – DEX is a format that's optimized for a minimal memory footprint.

> **NOTE:** Android starts a process when any of part of the app needs to execute, and shuts down the process when it's no longer needed and system resources are required by other apps.

Perhaps you're wondering how it's possible to have a non-Java virtual machine run Java code. The answer is that Dalvik doesn't run Java code. Instead, Android transforms compiled Java classfiles into the DEX format, and it's this resulting code that gets executed by Dalvik.

Finally, the libraries and Android runtime rely on the Linux kernel (version 2.6) for underlying core services such as threading, low-level memory management, a network stack, process management, and a driver model. Furthermore, the kernel acts as an abstraction layer between the hardware and the rest of the software stack.

ANDROID SECURITY MODEL

Android's architecture includes a security model that prevents apps from performing operations considered harmful to other apps, Linux, or users. This security model, which is mostly based on process level enforcement via standard Linux features (such as user and group IDs), places processes in a security sandbox.

By default, the sandbox prevents apps from reading or writing the user's private data (such as contacts or emails), reading or writing another app's files, performing network access, keeping the device awake, accessing the camera, and so on. Apps that need to access the network or perform other sensitive operations must first obtain permission to do so.

Android handles permission requests in various ways, typically by automatically allowing or disallowing the request based upon a certificate, or by prompting the user to grant or revoke the permission. Permissions required by an app are declared in the app's manifest file (discussed later in this chapter) so that they are known to Android when the app is installed. These permissions won't subsequently change.

App Architecture

The architecture of an Android app differs from desktop application architecture. App architecture is based upon components that communicate with each other by using intents that are described by a manifest and that are stored in an app package.

Components

An app is a collection of *components* (activities, services, content providers, and broadcast receivers) that run in a Linux process and that are managed by Android. These components share a set of resources, including databases, preferences, a filesystem, and the Linux process.

> **NOTE:** Not all of these components need to be present in an app. For example, one app might consist of activities only, whereas another app might consist of activities and a service.

This component-oriented architecture lets an app reuse the components of other apps, provided that those other apps permit reuse of their components. Component reuse reduces overall memory footprint, which is very important for devices with limited memory.

To make the reuse concept concrete, suppose you're creating a drawing app that lets users choose a color from a palette, and suppose that another app has developed a suitable color chooser and permits this component to be reused. In this scenario, the drawing app can call upon that other app's color chooser to have the user select a color rather than provide its own color chooser. The drawing app doesn't contain the other app's color chooser or even link to this other app. Instead, it starts up the other app's color chooser component when needed.

Android starts a process when any part of the app (such as the aforementioned color chooser) is needed, and instantiates the Java objects for that part. This is why Android's apps don't have a single entry point (no C-style `main()` function, for example). Instead, apps use components that are instantiated and run as needed.

Activities

An *activity* is a component that presents a user interface so that the user can interact with an app. For example, Android's Contacts app includes an activity for entering a new contact, its Phone app includes an activity for dialing a phone number, and its Calculator app includes an activity for performing basic calculations (see Figure 1–2).

Figure 1–2. *The main activity of Android's Calculator app lets the user perform basic calculations.*

Although an app can include a single activity, it's more typical for apps to include multiple activities. For example, Calculator also includes an "advanced panel" activity that lets the user calculate square roots, perform trigonometry, and carry out other advanced mathematical operations.

Services

A *service* is a component that runs in the background for an indefinite period of time, and which doesn't provide a user interface. As with an activity, a service runs on the process's main thread; it must spawn another thread to perform a time-consuming operation. Services are classified as local or remote.

- A *local service* runs in the same process as the rest of the app. Such services make it easy to implement background tasks.

- A *remote service* runs in a separate process. Such services let you perform interprocess communications.

NOTE: A service is not a separate process, although it can be specified to run in a separate process. Also, a service is not a thread. Instead, a service lets the app tell Android about something it wants to be doing in the background (even when the user is not directly interacting with the app), and lets the app expose some of its functionality to other apps.

Consider a service that plays music in response to a user's music choice via an activity. The user selects the song to play via this activity, and a service is started in response to the selection. The service plays the music on another thread to prevent the *Application Not Responding* dialog box (discussed in Appendix C) from appearing.

NOTE: The rationale for using a service to play the music is that the user expects the music to keep playing even after the activity that initiated the music leaves the screen.

Broadcast Receivers

A *broadcast receiver* is a component that receives and reacts to broadcasts. Many broadcasts originate in system code; for example, an announcement is made to indicate that the timezone has been changed or the battery power is low.

Apps can also initiate broadcasts. For example, an app may want to let other apps know that some data has finished downloading from the network to the device and is now available for them to use.

Content Providers

A *content provider* is a component that makes a specific set of an app's data available to other apps. The data can be stored in the Android filesystem, in an SQLite database, or in any other manner that makes sense.

Content providers are preferable to directly accessing raw data because they decouple component code from raw data formats. This decoupling prevents code breakage when formats change.

Intents

Intents are messages that describe operations to perform (such as "send an email" or "choose a photo"), or in the case of broadcasts, provide descriptions of external events that have occurred (a device's camera being activated, for example) and are being announced.

Because nearly everything in Android involves intents, there are many opportunities to replace existing components with your own components. For example, Android provides the intent for sending an email. Your app can send that intent to activate the standard mail app, or it can register an activity that responds to the "send an email" intent, effectively replacing the standard mail app with its own activity.

These messages are implemented as instances of the `android.content.Intent` class. An `Intent` object describes a message in terms of some combination of the following items:

- *Action*: A string naming the action to be performed or, in the case of broadcast intents, the action that took place and is being reported. Actions are described by `Intent` constants such as `ACTION_CALL` (initiate a phone call), `ACTION_EDIT` (display data for the user to edit), and `ACTION_MAIN` (start up as the initial activity). You can also define your own action strings for activating the components in your app. These strings should include the app package as a prefix (`"com.example.project.SELECT_COLOR"`, for example).

- *Category*: A string that provides additional information about the kind of component that should handle the intent. For example, CATEGORY_LAUNCHER means that the calling activity should appear in the device's app launcher as a top-level app. (The app launcher is briefly discussed in Recipe 1–4.)

- *Component name*: A string that specifies the fully qualified name (package plus name) of a component class to use for the intent. The component name is optional. If set, the Intent object is delivered to an instance of the designated class. If not set, Android uses other information in the Intent object to locate a suitable target.

- *Data*: The uniform resource identifier of the data on which to operate (such as a person record in a contacts database).

- *Extras*: A set of key-value pairs providing additional information that should be delivered to the component handling the intent. For example, given an action for sending an email, this information could include the message's subject, body, and so on.

- *Flags:* Bit values that instruct Android on how to launch an activity (for example, which task the activity should belong to – tasks are discussed later in this chapter) and how to treat the activity after launch (for example, whether the activity can be considered a recent activity). Flags are represented by constants in the Intent class; for example, FLAG_ACTIVITY_NEW_TASK specifies that this activity will become the start of a new task on this activity stack. The activity stack is discussed later in this chapter.

- *Type*: The MIME type of the intent data. Normally, Android infers a type from the data. By specifying a type, you disable that inference.

Intents can be classified as explicit or implicit. An *explicit intent* designates the target component by its name (the previously mentioned component name item is assigned a value). Because component names are usually unknown to the developers of other apps, explicit intents are typically used for app-internal messages (such as an activity that launches another activity located within the same app). Android delivers an explicit intent to an instance of the designated target class. Only the Intent object's component name matters for determining which component should get the intent.

An *implicit intent* doesn't name a target (the component name is not assigned a value). Implicit intents are often used to start components in other apps. Android searches for the best component (a single activity or service to perform the requested action) or components (a set of broadcast receivers to respond to the broadcast announcement) to handle the implicit intent. During the search, Android compares the contents of the Intent object to *intent filters*, manifest information associated with components that can potentially receive intents.

Filters advertise a component's capabilities and identify only those intents that the component can handle. They open up the component to the possibility of receiving implicit intents of the advertised type. If a component has no intent filters, it can receive only explicit intents. In contrast, a component with filters can receive explicit and implicit intents. Android consults an Intent object's action, category, data, and type when comparing the intent against an intent filter. It doesn't take extras and flags into consideration.

Manifest

Android learns about an app's various components (and more) by examining the app's XML-structured manifest file, AndroidManifest.xml. For example, Listing 1–1 shows how this file might declare an activity component.

Listing 1–1. *A Manifest File Declaring an Activity*

```xml
<?xml version="1.0" encoding="utf-8"?>
<manifest xmlns:android="http://schemas.android.com/apk/res/android"
          package="com.example.project" android:versionCode="1"
          android:versionName="1.0">
   <application android:label="@string/app_name" android:icon="@drawable/icon">
      <activity android:name=".MyActivity" android:label="@string/app_name">
         <intent-filter>
            <action android:name="android.intent.action.MAIN" />
            <category android:name="android.intent.category.LAUNCHER" />
         </intent-filter>
      </activity>
   </application>
</manifest>
```

Listing 1–1 begins with the necessary <?xml version="1.0" encoding="utf-8"?> prolog, which identifies this file as an XML version 1.0 file, whose content is encoded according to the UTF-8 encoding standard.

Listing 1–1 next presents a <manifest> tag, which is this XML document's root element; android identifies the Android namespace, package identifies the app's Java package, and versionCode/versionName identify version information.

Nested within <manifest> is <application>, which is the parent of app component tags. The icon and label attributes refer to icon and label resources that Android devices display to represent the app. (Resources are briefly discussed in Recipe 1–5.)

> **NOTE:** Resources are identified by the @ prefix, followed by a resource category name (such as string or drawable), /, and the resource ID (such as app_name or icon).
>
> The <application> tag's icon and label attributes specify defaults that are inherited by components whose tags don't specify these attributes.

Nested within <application> is <activity>, which describes an activity component. This tag's name attribute identifies a class (MyActivity) that implements the activity. This name begins with a period character to imply that it's relative to com.example.project.

> **NOTE:** The period is not present when `AndroidManifest.xml` is created at the command line. However, this character is present when this file is created from within Eclipse (discussed in Recipe 1–10). Regardless, `MyActivity` is relative to `<manifest>`'s package value (`com.example.project`).

Nested within `<activity>` is `<intent-filter>`. This tag declares the capabilities of the component described by the enclosing tag. For example, it declares the capabilities of the activity component via its nested `<action>` and `<category>` tags.

- `<action>` identifies the action to perform. This tag's `android:name` attribute is assigned `"android.intent.action.MAIN"` to identify the activity as the app's entry point.

- `<category>` identifies a component category. This tag's `android:name` attribute is assigned `"android.intent.category.LAUNCHER"` to identify the activity as needing to be displayed in the app launcher.

> **NOTE:** Other components are similarly declared. For example, services are declared via `<service>` tags, broadcast receivers are declared via `<receiver>` tags, and content providers are declared via `<provider>` tags. Except for broadcast receivers, which can be created at runtime, components not declared in the manifest are not created by Android.

The manifest may also contain `<uses-permission>` tags to identify permissions that the app needs. For example, an app that needs to use the camera would specify the following tag: `<uses-permission android:name="android.permission.CAMERA" />`.

> **NOTE:** `<uses-permission>` tags are nested within `<manifest>` tags. They appear at the same level as the `<application>` tag.

At app-install time, permissions requested by the app (via `<uses-permission>`) are granted to it by Android's package installer, based upon checks against the digital signatures of the apps declaring those permissions and/or interaction with the user.

No checks with the user are done while an app is running. It was granted a specific permission when installed and can use that feature as desired, or the permission was not granted and any attempt to use the feature will fail without prompting the user.

> **NOTE:** `AndroidManifest.xml` provides additional information, such as naming any libraries that the app needs to be linked against (besides the default Android library), and identifying all app-enforced permissions (via `<permission>` tags) to other apps, such as controlling who can start the app's activities.

App Package

Android apps are written in Java. The compiled Java code for an app's components is further transformed into Dalvik's DEX format. The resulting code files along with any other required data and resources are subsequently bundled into an *App PacKage (APK)*, a file identified by the `.apk` suffix.

An APK is not an app, but is used to distribute an app and install it on a mobile device. It's not an app because its components may reuse another APK's components, and (in this situation) not all of the app would reside in a single APK. However, it's common to refer to an APK as representing a single app.

An APK must be signed with a certificate (which identifies the app's author) whose private key is held by its developer. The certificate doesn't need to be signed by a certificate authority. Instead, Android allows APKs to be signed with self-signed certificates, which is typical. (APK signing is discussed in Recipe 1–8.)

APK FILES, USER IDS, AND SECURITY

Each APK installed on an Android device is given its own unique Linux user ID, and this user ID remains unchanged for as long as the APK resides on that device.

Security enforcement occurs at the process level, so the code contained in any two APKs cannot normally run in the same process, because each APK's code needs to run as a different Linux user.

However, you can have the code in both APKs run in the same process by assigning the same name of a user ID to the `<manifest>` tag's `sharedUserId` attribute in each APK's `AndroidManifest.xml` file.

When you make these assignments, you tell Android that the two packages are to be treated as being the same app, with the same user ID and file permissions.

In order to retain security, only two APKs signed with the same signature (and requesting the same `sharedUserId` value in their manifests) will be given the same user ID.

Activities in Depth

Activities are described by subclasses of the `android.app.Activity` class, which is an indirect subclass of the abstract `android.content.Context` class.

> **NOTE:** `Context` is an abstract class whose methods let apps access global information about their environments (such as their resources and filesystems), and allow apps to perform contextual operations, such as launching activities and services, broadcasting intents, and opening private files.

`Activity` subclasses override various `Activity` *lifecycle callback methods* that Android calls during the life of an activity. For example, the `SimpleActivity` class in Listing 1–2 extends `Activity` and also overrides the `void onCreate(Bundle bundle)` and `void onDestroy()` lifecycle callback methods.

Listing 1–2. *A Skeletal Activity*

```
import android.app.Activity;
import android.os.Bundle;

public class SimpleActivity extends Activity
{
    @Override
    public void onCreate(Bundle savedInstanceState)
    {
        super.onCreate(savedInstanceState); // Always call superclass method first.
        System.out.println("onCreate(Bundle) called");
    }
    @Override
    public void onDestroy()
    {
        super.onDestroy(); // Always call superclass method first.
        System.out.println("onDestroy() called");
    }
}
```

The overriding `onCreate(Bundle)` and `onDestroy()` methods in Listing 1–2 first invoke their superclass counterparts, a pattern that must be followed when overriding the `void onStart()`, `void onRestart()`, `void onResume()`, `void onPause()`, and `void onStop()` lifecycle callback methods.

- `onCreate(Bundle)` is called when the activity is first created. This method is used to create the activity's user interface, create background threads as needed, and perform other global initialization. `onCreate()` is passed an `android.os.Bundle` object containing the activity's previous state, if that state was captured; otherwise, the null reference is passed. Android always calls the `onStart()` method after calling `onCreate(Bundle)`.

- `onStart()` is called just before the activity becomes visible to the user. Android calls the `onResume()` method after calling `onStart()` when the activity comes to the foreground, and calls the `onStop()` method after `onStart()` when the activity becomes hidden.

- `onRestart()` is called after the activity has been stopped, just prior to it being started again. Android always calls `onStart()` after calling `onRestart()`.

- `onResume()` is called just before the activity starts interacting with the user. At this point, the activity has the focus and user input is directed to the activity. Android always calls the `onPause()` method after calling `onResume()`, but only when the activity must be paused.

- onPause() is called when Android is about to resume another activity. This method is typically used to persist unsaved changes, stop animations that might be consuming processor cycles, and so on. It should perform its job quickly, because the next activity won't be resumed until it returns. Android calls onResume() after calling onPause() when the activity starts interacting with the user, and calls onStop() when the activity becomes invisible to the user.

- onStop() is called when the activity is no longer visible to the user. This may happen because the activity is being destroyed, or because another activity (either an existing one or a new one) has been resumed and is covering the activity. Android calls onRestart() after calling onStop(), when the activity is coming back to interact with the user, and calls the onDestroy() method when the activity is going away.

- onDestroy() is called before the activity is destroyed, unless memory is tight and Android is forced to kill the activity's process. In this scenario, onDestroy() is never called. If onDestroy() is called, it will be the final call that the activity ever receives.

NOTE: Android can kill the process hosting the activity at any time after onPause(), onStop(), or onDestroy() returns. An activity is in a killable state from the time onPause() returns until the time onResume() is called. The activity won't again be killable until onPause() returns.

These seven methods define an activity's entire lifecycle and describe the following three nested loops:

- The *entire lifetime* of an activity is defined as everything from the first call to onCreate(Bundle) through to a single final call to onDestroy(). An activity performs all of its initial setup of "global" state in onCreate(Bundle), and releases all remaining resources in onDestroy(). For example, if the activity has a thread running in the background to download data from the network, it might create that thread in onCreate(Bundle) and stop the thread in onDestroy().

- The *visible lifetime* of an activity is defined as everything from a call to onStart() through to a corresponding call to onStop(). During this time, the user can see the activity onscreen, although it might not be in the foreground interacting with the user. Between these two methods, the activity can maintain resources that are needed to show itself to the user. For example, it can register a broadcast receiver in onStart() to monitor for changes that impact its user interface, and unregister this object in onStop() when the user can no longer see what the activity is displaying. The onStart() and onStop() methods can be called multiple times, as the activity alternates between being visible to and being hidden from the user.

- The *foreground lifetime* of an activity is defined as everything from a call to onResume() through to a corresponding call to onPause(). During this time, the activity is in front of all other activities onscreen and is interacting with the user. An activity can frequently transition between the resumed and paused states; for example, onPause() is called when the device goes to sleep or when a new activity is started, and onResume() is called when an activity result or a new intent is delivered. The code in these two methods should be fairly lightweight.

> **NOTE:** Each lifecycle callback method is a hook that an activity can override to perform appropriate work. All activities must implement onCreate(Bundle) to carry out the initial setup when the activity object is first instantiated. Many activities also implement onPause() to commit data changes and otherwise prepare to stop interacting with the user.

Figure 1–3 illustrates an activity's lifecycle in terms of these seven methods.

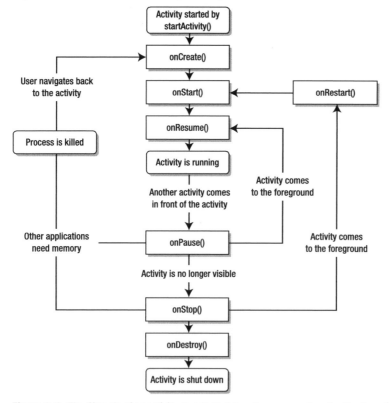

Figure 1–3. *The lifecycle of an activity reveals that there's no guarantee of onDestroy() being called.*

Because onDestroy() might not be called, you should not count on using this method as a place for saving data. For example, if an activity is editing a content provider's data, those edits should typically be committed in onPause().

In contrast, onDestroy() is usually implemented to free resources (such as threads) that are associated with an activity so that a destroyed activity doesn't leave such things around while the rest of its app is still running.

Figure 1–3 reveals that an activity is started by calling startActivity(). More specifically, the activity is started by creating an Intent object describing an explicit or implicit intent, and by passing this object to Context's void startActivity(Intent intent) method (launch a new activity; no result is returned when it finishes).

Alternatively, the activity could be started by calling Activity's void startActivityForResult(Intent intent, int requestCode) method. The specified int result is returned to Activity's void onActivityResult(int requestCode, int resultCode, Intent data) callback method as an argument.

> **NOTE:** The responding activity can look at the initial intent that caused it to be launched by calling Activity's Intent getIntent() method. Android calls the activity's void onNewIntent(Intent intent) method (also located in the Activity class) to pass any subsequent intents to the activity.

Suppose that you've created an app named SimpleActivity, and that this app consists of SimpleActivity (described in Listing 1–2) and SimpleActivity2 classes. Now suppose that you want to launch SimpleActivity2 from SimpleActivity's onCreate(Bundle) method. The following code fragment shows you how to start SimpleActivity2:

```
Intent intent = new Intent(SimpleActivity.this, SimpleActivity2.class);
SimpleActivity.this.startActivity(intent);
```

The first line creates an Intent object that describes an explicit intent. It initializes this object by passing the current SimpleActivity instance's reference and SimpleActivity2's Class instance to the Intent(Context packageContext, Class<?> cls) constructor.

The second line passes this Intent object to startActivity(Intent), which is responsible for launching the activity described by SimpleActivity2.class. If startActivity(Intent) was unable to find the specified activity (which shouldn't happen), it would throw an android.content.ActivityNotFoundException instance.

Activities must be declared in the app's AndroidManifest.xml file or they cannot be started (because they are invisible to Android). For example, the AndroidManifest.xml file in Listing 1–3 declares SimpleActivity and SimpleActivity2 – the ellipsis refers to content not relevant to this discussion.

Listing 1–3. *SimpleActivity's Manifest File*

```xml
<?xml version="1.0" encoding="utf-8"?>
<manifest xmlns:android="http://schemas.android.com/apk/res/android"
          package="com.example.project" ...>
    <application ...>
        <activity android:name=".SimpleActivity" ...>
            <intent-filter ...>
                <action android:name="android.intent.action.MAIN" />
                <category android:name="android.intent.category.LAUNCHER" />
            </intent-filter>
        </activity>
        <activity android:name=".SimpleActivity2" ...>
            <intent-filter ...>
                <action android:name="android.intent.action.VIEW" />
                <data android:mimeType="image/jpeg" />
                <category android:name="android.intent.category.DEFAULT" />
            </intent-filter>
        </activity>
        ...
    </application>
</manifest>
```

Listing 1–3 reveals that each of SimpleActivity and SimpleActivity2 is associated with an intent filter via an <intent-filter> tag that's nested within <activity>. SimpleActivity2's <intent-filter> tag helps Android determine that this activity is to be launched when the Intent object's values match the following tag values:

- <action>'s android:name attribute is assigned "android.intent.action.VIEW"

- <data>'s android:mimeType attribute is assigned "image/jpeg" MIME type – additional attributes (such as android:path) would typically be present to locate the data to be viewed

- <category>'s android:name attribute is assigned "android.intent.category.DEFAULT" to allow the activity to be launched without explicitly specifying its component.

The following code fragment shows you how to start SimpleActivity2 implicitly:

```java
Intent intent = new Intent();
intent.setAction("android.intent.action.VIEW");
intent.setType("image/jpeg");
intent.addCategory("android.intent.category.DEFAULT");
SimpleActivity.this.startActivity(intent);
```

The first four lines create an Intent object describing an implicit intent. Values passed to Intent's Intent setAction(String action), Intent setType(String type), and Intent addCategory(String category) methods specify the intent's action, MIME type, and category. They help Android identify SimpleActivity2 as the activity to be launched.

ACTIVITIES, TASKS, AND THE ACTIVITY STACK

Android refers to a sequence of related activities as a *task* and provides an *activity stack* (also known as *history stack* or *back stack*) to remember this sequence. The activity starting the task is the initial activity pushed onto the stack and is known as the *root activity*. This activity is typically the activity selected by the user via the device's app launcher. The activity that's currently running is located at the top of the stack.

When the current activity starts another, the new activity is pushed onto the stack and takes focus (becomes the running activity). The previous activity remains on the stack, but is stopped. When an activity stops, the system retains the current state of its user interface.

When the user presses the device's BACK key, the current activity is popped from the stack (the activity is destroyed), and the previous activity resumes operation as the running activity (the previous state of its user interface is restored).

Activities in the stack are never rearranged, only pushed and popped from the stack. Activities are pushed onto the stack when started by the current activity, and popped off the stack when the user leaves them using the BACK key. As such, the stack operates as a "last in, first out" object structure.

Each time the user presses BACK, an activity in the stack is popped off to reveal the previous activity. This continues until the user returns to the home screen or to whichever activity was running when the task began. When all activities are removed from the stack, the task no longer exists.

Check out the "Tasks and Back Stack" section in Google's online Android documentation to learn more about activities and tasks:
http://developer.android.com/guide/topics/fundamentals/tasks-and-back-stack.html.

Services in Depth

Services are described by subclasses of the abstract android.app.Service class, which is an indirect subclass of Context.

Service subclasses override various Service lifecycle callback methods that Android calls during the life of a service. For example, the SimpleService class in Listing 1–4 extends Service and also overrides the void onCreate() and void onDestroy() lifecycle callback methods.

Listing 1–4. *A Skeletal Service, Version 1*

```
import android.app.Service;

public class SimpleService extends Service
{
   @Override
   public void onCreate()
   {
      System.out.println("onCreate() called");
   }
   @Override
   public void onDestroy()
   {
```

```
        System.out.println("onDestroy() called");
    }
    @Override
    public IBinder onBind(Intent intent)
    {
        System.out.println("onBind(Intent) never called");
        return null;
    }
}
```

onCreate() is called when the service is initially created, and onDestroy() is called when the service is being removed. Because it is abstract, the IBinder onBind(Intent intent) lifecycle callback method (described later in this section) must always be overridden, even if only to return null, which indicates that this method is ignored.

> **NOTE:** Service subclasses typically override onCreate() and onDestroy() to perform initialization and cleanup. Unlike Activity's onCreate(Bundle) and onDestroy() methods, Service's onCreate() method isn't repeatedly called and its onDestroy() method is always called.
>
> A service's lifetime happens between the time onCreate() is called and the time onDestroy() returns. As with an activity, a service initializes in onCreate() and cleans up in onDestroy(). For example, a music playback service could create the thread that plays music in onCreate() and stop the thread in onDestroy().

Local services are typically started via Context's ComponentName startService(Intent intent) method, which returns an android.content.ComponentName instance that identifies the started service component, or the null reference if the service doesn't exist. Furthermore, startService(Intent) results in the lifecycle shown in Figure 1–4.

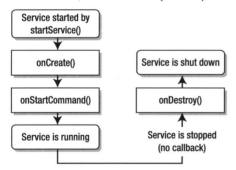

Figure 1–4. *The lifecycle of a service that's started by* startService(Intent) *features a call to* onStartCommand(Intent, int, int).

The call to startService(Intent) results in a call to onCreate(), followed by a call to int onStartCommand(Intent intent, int flags, int startId). This latter lifecycle callback method, which replaces the deprecated void onStart(Intent intent, int startId) method, is called with the following arguments:

- intent is the Intent object passed to startService(Intent).

- flags can provide additional data about the start request, but are often set to 0.

- startID is a unique integer that describes this start request. A service can pass this value to Service's boolean stopSelfResult(int startId) method to stop itself.

onStartCommand(Intent, int, int) processes the Intent object, and typically returns the constant Service.START_STICKY to indicate that the service is to continue running until explicitly stopped. At this point, the service is running and will continue to run until one of the following events occurs:

- Another component stops the service by calling Context's boolean stopService(Intent intent) method. Only one stopService(Intent) call is needed no matter how often startService(Intent) was called.

- The service stops itself by calling one of Service's overloaded stopSelf() methods, or by calling Service's stopSelfResult(int) method.

After stopService(Intent), stopSelf(), or stopSelfResult(int) has been called, Android calls onDestroy() to let the service perform cleanup tasks.

> **NOTE:** When a service is started by calling startService(Intent), onBind(Intent) is not called.

Listing 1–5 presents a skeletal service class that could be used in the context of the startService(Intent) method.

Listing 1–5. *A Skeletal Service, Version 2*

```
import android.app.Service;

public class SimpleService extends Service
{
   @Override
   public void onCreate()
   {
      System.out.println("onCreate() called");
   }
   @Override
   public int onStartCommand(Intent intent, int flags, int startId)
   {
      System.out.println("onStartCommand(Intent, int, int) called");
      return START_STICKY;
   }
   @Override
   public void onDestroy()
   {
      System.out.println("onDestroy() called");
   }
```

```
    @Override
    public IBinder onBind(Intent intent)
    {
        System.out.println("onBind(Intent) never called");
        return null;
    }
}
```

The following code fragment, which is assumed to be located in the onCreate() method of Listing 1–2's SimpleActivity class, employs startService(Intent) to start an instance of Listing 1–5's SimpleService class via an explicit intent:

```
Intent intent = new Intent(SimpleActivity.this, SimpleService.class);
SimpleActivity.this.startService(intent);
```

Remote services are started via Context's boolean bindService(Intent service, ServiceConnection conn, int flags) method, which connects to a running service, creating the service if necessary, and which returns 'true' when successfully connected. bindService(Intent, ServiceConnection, int) results in the lifecycle illustrated by Figure 1–5.

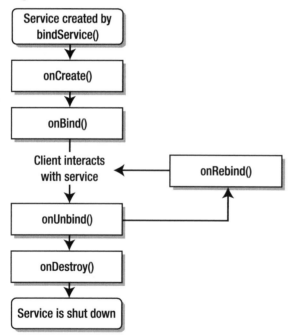

Figure 1–5. *The lifecycle of a service started by* bindService(Intent, ServiceConnection, int) *doesn't include a call to* onStartCommand(Intent, int, int).

The call to bindService(Intent, ServiceConnection, int) results in a call to onCreate() followed by a call to onBind(Intent), which returns the *communications channel* (an instance of a class that implements the android.os.IBinder interface) that clients use to interact with the service.

The client interacts with the service as follows:

1. The client subclasses `android.content.ServiceConnection` and overrides this class's abstract void `onServiceConnected(ComponentName className, IBinder service)` and void `onServiceDisconnected(ComponentName name)` methods in order to receive information about the service as the service is started and stopped. When `bindService(Intent, ServiceConnection, int)` returns true, the former method is called when a connection to the service has been established; the `IBinder` argument passed to this method is the same value returned from `onBind(Intent)`. The latter method is called when a connection to the service has been lost.

   Lost connections typically occur when the process hosting the service has crashed or has been killed. The `ServiceConnection` instance itself is not removed – the binding to the service will remain active, and the client will receive a call to `onServiceConnected(ComponentName, IBinder)` when the service is next running.

2. The client passes the `ServiceConnection` subclass object to `bindService(Intent, ServiceConnection, int)`.

A client disconnects from a service by calling `Context`'s void `unbindService(ServiceConnection conn)` method. This component no longer receives calls as the service is restarted. If no other components are bound to the service, the service is allowed to stop at any time.

Before the service can stop, Android calls the service's boolean `onUnbind(Intent intent)` lifecycle callback method with the `Intent` object that was passed to `unbindService(ServiceConnection)`. Assuming that `onUnbind(Intent)` doesn't return 'true,' which tells Android to call the service's void `onRebind(Intent intent)` lifecycle callback method each time a client subsequently binds to the service, Android calls `onDestroy()` to destroy the service.

Listing 1–6 presents a skeletal service class that could be used in the context of the `bindService(Intent, ServiceConnection, int)` method.

Listing 1–6. *A Skeletal Service, Version 3*

```
import android.app.Service;

public class SimpleService extends Service
{
    public class SimpleBinder extends Binder
    {
        SimpleService getService()
        {
            return SimpleService.this;
        }
    }
    private final IBinder binder = new SimpleBinder();
    @Override
```

```
    public IBinder onBind(Intent intent)
    {
        return binder;
    }
    @Override
    public void onCreate()
    {
        System.out.println("onCreate() called");
    }
    @Override
    public void onDestroy()
    {
        System.out.println("onDestroy() called");
    }
}
```

Listing 1–6 first declares a SimpleBinder inner class that extends the android.os.Binder class. SimpleBinder declares a single SimpleService getService() method that returns an instance of the SimpleService subclass.

> **NOTE:** Binder works with the IBinder interface to support a remote procedure call mechanism for communicating between processes. Although this example assumes that the service is running in the same process as the rest of the app, Binder and IBinder are still required.

Listing 1–6 next instantiates SimpleBinder and assigns the instance's reference to the private binder field. This field's value is returned from the subsequently overriding onBind(Intent) method.

Let's assume that the SimpleActivity class in Listing 1–2 declares a private SimpleService field named ss (private SimpleService ss;). Continuing, let's assume that the following code fragment is contained in SimpleActivity's onCreate(Bundle) method:

```
ServiceConnection sc = new ServiceConnection()
{
    public void onServiceConnected(ComponentName className, IBinder service)
    {
        ss = ((SimpleService.SimpleBinder) service).getService();
        System.out.println("Service connected");
    }
    public void onServiceDisconnected(ComponentName className)
    {
        ss = null; System.out.println("Service disconnected");
    }
};
bindService(new Intent(SimpleActivity.this, SimpleService.class), sc,
            Context.BIND_AUTO_CREATE);
```

This code fragment first instantiates a ServiceConnection subclass. The overriding onServiceConnected(ComponentName, IBinder) method concerns itself with using the service argument to call SimpleBinder's getService() method and save the result.

Although it must be present, the overriding onServiceDisconnected(ComponentName) method should never be called, because SimpleService runs in the same process as SimpleActivity.

The code fragment next passes the ServiceConnection subclass object, along with an intent identifying SimpleService as the intent's target and Context.BIND_AUTO_CREATE (create a persistent connection), to bindService(Intent, ServiceConnection, int).

> **NOTE:** A service can be started (with startService(Intent)) and have connections bound to it (with bindService(Intent, ServiceConnection, int). In this situation, Android keeps the service running as long as it's started, or one or more connections with the BIND_AUTO_CREATE flag have been made to the service. Once neither of these situations holds, the service's onDestroy() method is called and the service is terminated. All cleanup work, such as stopping threads or unregistering broadcast receivers, should be finished upon returning from onDestroy().

Regardless of how you start the service, the app's AndroidManifest.xml file must have an entry for this component. The following entry declares SimpleService:

```
<service android:name=".SimpleService">
</service>
```

> **NOTE:** Although the previous example used bindService(Intent, ServiceConnection, int) to start a local service, it's more typical to use this method to start a remote service. Chapter 5 introduces you to remote services.

Broadcast Receivers in Depth

Broadcast receivers are described by classes that subclass the abstract android.content.BroadcastReceiver class and override BroadcastReceiver's abstract void onReceive(Context context, Intent intent) method. For example, the SimpleBroadcastReceiver class in Listing 1–7 extends BroadcastReceiver and overrides this method.

Listing 1–7. *A Skeletal Broadcast Receiver*

```
public class SimpleBroadcastReceiver extends BroadcastReceiver
{
    @Override
    public void onReceive(Context context, Intent intent)
    {
        System.out.println("onReceive(Context, Intent) called");
    }
}
```

You start a broadcast receiver by creating an Intent object and passing this object to any of Context's broadcast methods (such as Context's overloaded sendBroadcast() methods), which broadcast the message to all interested broadcast receivers.

The following code fragment, which is assumed to be located in the onCreate() method of Listing 1–2's SimpleActivity class, starts an instance of Listing 1–7's SimpleBroadcastReceiver class:

```
Intent intent = new Intent(SimpleActivity.this, SimpleBroadcastReceiver.class);
intent.putExtra("message", "Hello, broadcast receiver!");
SimpleActivity.this.sendBroadcast(intent);
```

Intent's Intent putExtra(String name, String value) method is called to store the message as a key/value pair. As with Intent's other putExtra() methods, this method returns a reference to the Intent object so that method calls can be chained together.

Unless you create a broadcast receiver dynamically, AndroidManifest.xml must have an entry for this component. The following entry declares SimpleBroadcastReceiver:

```
<receiver android:name=".SimpleBroadcastReceiver">
</receiver>
```

Content Providers in Depth

Content providers are described by classes that subclass the abstract android.content.ContentProvider class and override ContentProvider's abstract methods (such as String getType(Uri uri)). For example, the SimpleContentProvider class in Listing 1–8 extends ContentProvider and overrides these methods.

Listing 1–8. *A Skeletal Content Provider*

```
public class SimpleContentProvider extends ContentProvider
{
    @Override
    public int delete(Uri uri, String selection, String[] selectionArgs)
    {
        System.out.println("delete(Uri, String, String[]) called");
        return 0;
    }
    @Override
    public String getType(Uri uri)
    {
        System.out.println("getType(Uri) called");
        return null;
    }
    @Override
    public Uri insert(Uri uri, ContentValues values)
    {
        System.out.println("insert(Uri, ContentValues) called");
        return null;
    }
    @Override
    public boolean onCreate()
    {
        System.out.println("onCreate() called");
```

```
        return false;
    }
    @Override
    public Cursor query(Uri uri, String[] projection, String selection,
                        String[] selectionArgs, String sortOrder)
    {
        System.out.println("query(Uri, String[], String, String[], String) called");
        return null;
    }
    @Override
    public int update(Uri uri, ContentValues values, String selection,
                      String[] selectionArgs)
    {
        System.out.println("update(Uri, ContentValues, String, String[]) called");
        return 0;
    }
}
```

Clients don't instantiate SimpleContentProvider and call these methods directly. Rather, they instantiate a subclass of the abstract android.content.ContentResolver class and call its methods (such as public final Cursor query(Uri uri, String[] projection, String selection, String[] selectionArgs, String sortOrder)).

> **NOTE:** A ContentResolver instance can talk to any content provider; it cooperates with the provider to manage any interprocess communication that's involved.

AndroidManifest.xml must have to an entry for this component. The following entry declares SimpleContentProvider:

```
<provider android:name=".SimpleContentProvider">
</provider>
```

1–1. Installing the Android SDK

Problem

You've read the previous introduction to Android and are eager to develop your first Android app. However, you must install Android SDK 2.3 before you can develop apps.

Solution

Google provides an Android SDK 2.3 distribution file for each of the Windows, Intel-based Mac OS X, and Linux operating systems. Download and unarchive the appropriate file for your platform and move its unarchived home directory to a convenient location. You might also want to update your PATH environment variable so that you can access the SDK's command-line tools from anywhere in your filesystem.

Before downloading and installing this file, you must be aware of SDK requirements. You cannot use the SDK if your development platform doesn't meet these requirements.

Android SDK 2.3 supports the following operating systems:

- Windows XP (32-bit), Vista (32- or 64-bit), or Windows 7 (32- or 64-bit)

- Mac OS X 10.5.8 or later (x86 only)

- Linux (tested on Ubuntu Linux, Lucid Lynx): GNU C Library (glibc) 2.11 or later is required. 64-bit distributions must be able to run 32-bit applications. To learn how to add support for 32-bit applications, see the Ubuntu Linux installation notes at `http://developer.android.com/sdk/installing.html#troubleshooting`.

You'll quickly discover that Android SDK 2.3 is organized into various components: SDK tools, SDK Platform tools, different versions of the *Android platform* (also known as the Android software stack), SDK add-ons, USB driver for Windows, samples, and offline documentation. Each component requires a minimum amount of disk storage space; the total required amount of space depends upon which components you choose to install:

- *SDK Tools*: The SDK's tools require approximately 35MB of disk storage space and must be installed.

- *SDK Platform Tools*: The SDK's platform tools require approximately 6MB of disk storage space and must be installed.

- *Android platform*: Each Android platform corresponds to a specific version of Android and requires approximately 150MB of disk storage space. At least one Android platform must be installed.

- *SDK Add-on*: Each optional SDK add-on (such as Google APIs or a third-party vendor's API libraries) requires approximately 100MB of disk storage space.

- *USB Driver for Windows*: The optional USB driver for the Windows platform requires approximately 10MB of disk storage space. If you're developing on Mac OS X or Linux, you don't need to install the USB driver.

- *Samples*: Each Android platform's optional app examples require approximately 10MB of disk storage space.

- *Offline documentation*: Instead of having to be online to access the Android documention, you can choose to download the documentation so that you can view it even when not connected to the Internet. The offline documentation requires approximately 250MB of disk storage space.

Finally, you should ensure that the following additional software is installed:

- *JDK 5 or JDK 6*: You need to install one of these Java Development Kits (JDKs) to compile Java code. It's not sufficient to have only a Java Runtime Environment (JRE) installed.

■ *Apache Ant*: You need to install Ant version 1.6.5 or later for Linux and Mac, and Ant version 1.7 or later for Windows so that you can build Android projects.

NOTE: If a JDK is already installed on your development platform, take a moment to ensure that it meets the previously listed version requirement (5 or 6). Some Linux distributions may include JDK 1.4, which is not supported for Android development. Also, Gnu Compiler for Java is not supported.

How It Works

Point your browser to http://developer.android.com/sdk/index.html and download one of android-sdk_r08-windows.zip (Windows), android-sdk_r08-mac_86.zip (Mac OS X), and android-sdk_r08-linux_86.tgz (Linux).

NOTE: Windows developers have the option of downloading and running installer_r08-windows.exe. This tool automates must of the installation process.

For example, if you run Windows XP, download android-sdk_r08-windows.zip. After unarchiving this file, move the unarchived android-windows-sdk home directory to a convenient location in your filesystem; for example, you might move the unarchived C:\unzipped\android-sdk_r08-windows\android-sdk-windows home directory to the root directory on your C: drive, resulting in C:\android-sdk-windows.

NOTE: To complete installation, add the tools subdirectory to your PATH environment variable so that you can access the SDK's command-line tools from anywhere in your filesystem.

A subsequent examination of android-windows-sdk shows that this home directory contains the following subdirectories and files:

■ *add-ons*: This initially empty directory stores add-ons from Google and other vendors; for example, the Google APIs add-on is stored here.

■ *platforms*: This initially empty directory stores Android platforms in separate subdirectories. For example, Android 2.3 would be stored in one platforms subdirectory, whereas Android 2.2 would be stored in another platforms subdirectory.

■ *tools*: This directory contains a set of platform-independent development and profiling tools. The tools in this directory may be updated at any time, independent of Android platform releases.

■ *SDK Manager.exe*: A special tool that launches the Android SDK and AVD Manager tool, which you use to add components to your SDK.

- *SDK Readme.txt*: Tells you how to perform the initial setup of your SDK, including how to launch the Android SDK and AVD Manager tool on all platforms.

The `tools` directory contains a variety of useful tools, including the following:

- *android*: Creates and updates Android projects; updates the Android SDK with new platforms, add-ons, and documentation; and creates, deletes, and views Android Virtual Devices (discussed in Recipe 1–3).

- *emulator*: Runs a full Android software stack down to the kernel level, and includes a set of preinstalled apps (such as Browser) that you can access.

- *sqlite3*: Manages SQLite databases created by Android apps.

- *zipalign*: Performs archive alignment optimization on APK files.

1–2. Installing an Android Platform

Problem

Installing the Android SDK is insufficient for developing Android apps; you must also install at least one Android platform.

Solution

Use the `SDK Manager` tool to install an Android platform.

How It Works

Run `SDK Manager`. This tool presents the *Android SDK and AVD Manager* dialog box, followed by the *Refresh Sources* and *Choose Packages to Install* dialog boxes.

Android SDK and AVD Manager identifies virtual devices, installed packages, and available packages. It also lets you configure proxy server and other settings.

When this dialog box appears, the Installed packages entry in the list appearing on the right side of the dialog box is highlighted, and the pane to the right of that list identifies all packages that have been installed. If you're installing Android for the first time, this pane reveals that only the Android SDK tools (revision 8) component has been installed.

> **NOTE:** You can also use the `android` tool to display the *Android SDK and AVD Manager* dialog box. Accomplish this task by specifying `android` by itself on the command line. When displayed in this manner, *Android SDK and AVD Manager* highlights Virtual devices instead of Installed packages.

After presenting this dialog box, SDK Manager scans Google's servers for available component packages to install. The *Refresh Sources* dialog box reveals its progress.

After SDK Manager finishes its scan, it presents the *Choose Packages to Install* dialog box (see Figure 1–6) to let you choose those SDK components you want to install.

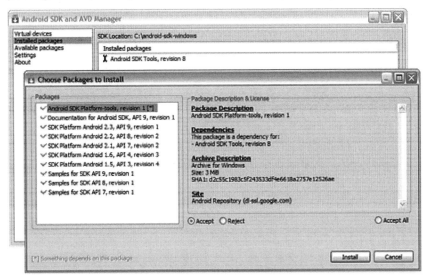

Figure 1–6. *The Packages list identifies those packages that can be installed.*

NOTE: Google recommends that you disable any active antivirus software before installing SDK components. Otherwise, you'll probably encounter an *SDK Manager: failed to install* dialog box telling you that a folder could not be renamed or moved, and telling you to momentarily disable your antivirus software before clicking the dialog box's Yes button to try again.

The *Choose Packages to Install* dialog box shows a Packages list that identifies those packages that can be installed. It displays checkmarks beside packages that have been accepted for installation, and displays Xs beside those packages that have been rejected for installation.

For the highlighted package, Package Description & License presents a package description, a list of other packages that are dependent on this package being installed, information about the archive that houses the package, and additional information. Also, you can select a radio button to accept or reject the package.

NOTE: In some cases, an SDK component may require a specific minimum revision of another component or SDK tool. In addition to Package Description & License documenting these dependencies, the development tools will notify you with debug warnings if there's a dependency that you need to address.

Because this book focuses on Android 2.3, the only packages that you need to install are Android SDK Platform-tools, revision 1 and SDK Platform Android 2.3, API 9, revision 1. All other checked package entries can be unchecked by clicking the Reject radio button on their respective panes.

NOTE: If you plan to develop apps that will run on devices with earlier versions of Android, you might want to leave the checkmarks beside those versions. However, it's not necessary to do so at this point; you can always come back later and add those versions via SDK Manager.

After making sure that only these entries are checked, click the Install button to begin installation. Figure 1–7 shows you the resulting *Installing Archives* dialog box.

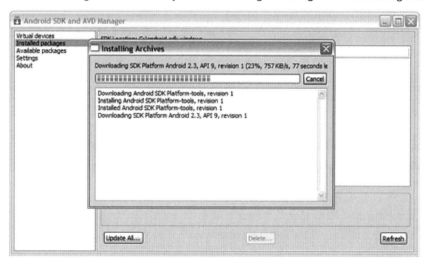

Figure 1–7. *The Installing Archives dialog box reveals the progress of downloading and installing each selected package archive.*

You'll probably encounter the *ADB Restart* dialog box, which tells you that a package dependent on Android Debug Bridge (ADB) has been updated, and asking you whether you want to restart ADB now. Click the Yes button, which closes *ADB Restart*, then click Close on the *Installing Archives* dialog box.

You should now observe the Android SDK and AVD Manager's Installed packages pane also displaying Android SDK Platform-tools, revision 1 and SDK Platform Android 2.3,

API 9, revision 1 in addition to Android SDK Tools, revision 8. You should also observe the following new subdirectories:

- platform-tools (in android-sdk-windows)
- android-9 (in android-sdk-windows/platforms)

platform-tools contains development tools that may be updated with each platform release. Its tools include aapt (Android Asset Packaging Tool – view, create, and update Zip-compatible archives (.zip, .jar, .apk); and compile resources into binary assets), adb (Android Debug Bridge – manage the state of an emulator instance or an Android-powered device), and dx (Dalvik Executable – generate Android bytecode from Java .class files). android-9 stores Android 2.3 data and user interface-oriented files.

> **TIP** You might want to add platform-tools to your PATH environment variable so that you can access these tools from anywhere in your filesystem.

AVAILABLE PACKAGES AND COMPONENT UPDATES DETECTION

The pane corresponding to Available packages presents packages that are available for installation. It defaults to offering packages from Google's Android respository and third-party add-ons (from Google and Samsung), but you can add other websites that host their own Android SDK add-ons, and then download the SDK add-ons from those websites.

For example, suppose that a mobile carrier or device manufacturer offers additional API libraries that are supported by their own Android-powered devices. In order to use its libraries to assist in developing apps, you must install the carrier's/device manufacturer's Android SDK add-on.

If the carrier or device manufacturer has hosted an SDK add-on repository file on its website, you must follow these steps to add the website to SDK Manager:

1. Select Available packages from the listbox.

2. Click the Add Add-on Site button on the resulting pane and enter the URL of the website's repository.xml file into the resulting dialog box's textfield. Click OK.

Any SDK components that are available from the website will appear under Available Packages.

New revisions of existing SDK components are occasionally released and made available through the SDK repository. In most cases, assuming that you have those components installed in your environment, you'll want to download the new revisions as soon as possible.

The easiest way to learn about component updates is to visit the Available Packages pane. When you discover that a new revision is available, use SDK Manager to download and install it to your environment, and in the same manner as used to install the Android 2.3 platform. The new component is installed in place of the old component, but in such a manner as to not impact your apps.

1–3. Creating an Android Virtual Device

Problem

After installing the Android SDK and an Android platform, you're ready to start creating Android apps. However, you won't be able to run those apps via the emulator tool until you create an *Android Virtual Device (AVD)*, a device configuration that represents an Android device.

Solution

Use the SDK Manager tool to create an AVD.

How It Works

Run SDK Manager if necessary. Click the *Android SDK and AVD Manager* dialog box's Virtual devices entry in the list on the left. You should see the pane shown in Figure 1–8.

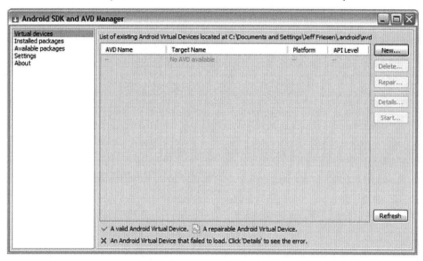

Figure 1–8. *No AVDs are initially installed.*

Click the New button. Figure 1–9 shows you the resulting *Create new Android Virtual Device (AVD)* dialog box.

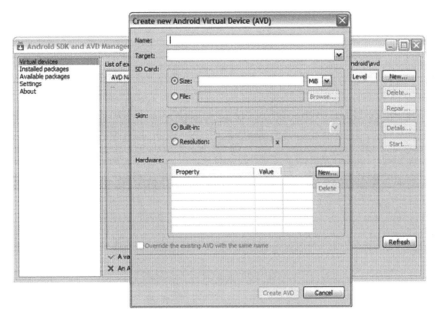

Figure 1–9. *An AVD consists of a name, a target platform, an SD Card, a skin, and hardware properties.*

Figure 1–9 reveals that an AVD has a name, targets a specific Android platform, can emulate an SD card, and provides a skin with a certain screen resolution. Enter `test_AVD` for the name, select `Android 2.3 - API Level 9` for the target platform, and enter `100` into the Size field for the SD card. Selecting `Android 2.3 - API Level 9` results in `Default (HVGA)` being selected for the skin with an `Abstracted LCD density` property set to 160 dots per inch (dpi).

> **NOTE:** If you've installed Android 2.3.1, selecting `Android 2.3.1 - API Level 9` results in `Default (WVGA800)` being selected for the skin with an `Abstracted LCD density` property set to 240 dpi. Furthermore, a `Max VM application heap size` property set to 24 megabytes is also present.

After entering the previous values and keeping the screen defaults, finish AVD creation by clicking Create AVD. The AVD pane in Figure 1–8 will now include an entry for `test_AVD`.

> **CAUTION:** When creating an AVD that you plan to use to test compiled apps, make sure that the target platform has an API level greater than or equal to the API level required by your app. In other words, if you plan to test your app on the AVD, your app cannot access platform APIs that are more recent than those APIs supported by the AVD's API level.

Although it's easier to use SDK Manager to create an AVD, you can also accomplish this task via the android tool by specifying android create avd -n *name* -t *targetID* [-option *value*].... Given this syntax, *name* identifies the device configuration (such as target_AVD), *targetID* is an integer ID that identifies the targeted Android platform (you can obtain this integer ID by executing android list targets), and [-option *value*]... identifies a series of options (such as SD card size).

If you don't specify sufficient options, android prompts to create a custom hardware profile. Press the Enter key if you don't want a custom hardware profile and prefer to use the default hardware emulation options. For example, the android create avd -n test_AVD -t 1 command line causes an AVD named test_AVD to be created. This command line assumes that 1 corresponds to the Android 2.3 platform and prompts to create a custom hardware profile.

> **NOTE:** Each AVD functions as an independent device with its own private storage for user data, its own SD card, and so on. When you launch the emulator tool with an AVD, this tool loads user data and SD card data from the AVD's directory. By default, emulator stores user data, SD card data, and a cache in the directory assigned to the AVD.

1–4. Starting the AVD

Problem

You must start the AVD, which can take a few minutes to get started, before you can install and run apps on it, and want to know how to accomplish this task.

Solution

Use the SDK Manager tool to start the AVD. Or, start the AVD by using the emulator tool.

How It Works

Refer to Figure 1–8 and you'll notice a disabled Start button. This button is no longer disabled after an AVD entry is created. Click Start to run the emulator tool with the highlighted AVD entry as the emulator's device configuration.

A *Launch Options* dialog box appears. This dialog box identifies the AVD's skin and screen density. It also provides unchecked checkboxes for scaling the resolution of the emulator's display to match the physical device's screen size, and for wiping user data.

NOTE: As you update your apps, you'll periodically package and install them on the emulator, which preserves the apps and their state data across AVD restarts in a user-data disk partition. To ensure that an app runs properly as you update it, you might need to delete the emulator's user-data partition, which is accomplished by checking Wipe user data.

Click the Launch button to launch the emulator with the AVD. SDK Manager responds by briefly displaying a *Starting Android Emulator* dialog box, followed by command windows (on Windows XP), and by finally displaying the emulator window.

The emulator window is divided into a left pane that displays the Android logo on a black background followed by the home screen, and a right pane that displays phone controls and a keyboard. Figure 1–10 shows these panes for the test_AVD device.

Figure 1–10. *The emulator window presents the home screen on the left, and phone controls and a keyboard on the right.*

If you've previously used an Android device, you're probably familiar with the home screen, the phone controls, and the keyboard. If not, there are a few items to keep in mind:

- The *home screen* is a special app that serves as a starting point for using an Android device.

■ A status bar appears above the home screen (and every app screen). The *status bar* presents the current time, amount of battery power remaining, and other information; and also provides access to notifications.

■ The home screen presents a wallpaper background. Click the MENU button in the phone controls followed by Wallpaper in the popup menu to change the wallpaper.

■ The home screen presents the Google Search widget near the top. A *widget* is a miniature app view that can be embedded in the home screen and other apps, and receives periodic updates.

■ The home screen presents the *app launcher* near the bottom. The launcher presents icons for launching the commonly used Phone and Browser apps, and for displaying a rectangular grid of all installed apps, which are subsequently launched by double-clicking their icons.

■ The home screen consists of multiple panes. Click the dots on either side of the app launcher to replace the current pane with the next pane to the left or right – the number of dots indicate the number of panes remaining to be visited to the left or right. Or, press and hold down the mouse pointer over the middle icon on the app launcher to bring up a list of miniature pane icons; click one of these icons to display the corresponding home screen pane.

■ The house icon phone control button takes you from wherever you are to the home screen.

■ The MENU phone control button presents a menu of app-specific choices for the currently running app.

■ The curved arrow icon phone control button takes you back to the previous activity in the activity stack.

While the AVD is running, you can interact with it by using your mouse to "touch" the touchscreen and your keyboard to "press" the AVD keys. Table 1–2 shows you the mappings between AVD keys and keyboard keys.

Table 1–2. *Mappings Between AVD Keys and Keyboard Keys*

AVD Key	Keyboard Key
Home	HOME
Menu (left softkey)	F2 or Page Up
Star (right softkey)	Shift-F2 or Page Down
Back	ESC
Call/dial button	F3
Hangup/end call button	F4
Search	F5
Power button	F7
Audio volume up button	KEYPAD_PLUS, Ctrl-5
Audio volume down button	KEYPAD_MINUS, Ctrl-F6
Camera button	Ctrl-KEYPAD_5, Ctrl-F3
Switch to previous layout orientation (portrait or landscape)	KEYPAD_7, Ctrl-F11
Switch to next layout orientation	KEYPAD_9, Ctrl-F12
Toggle cell networking on/off	F8
Toggle code profiling	F9 (only with -trace startup option)
Toggle fullscreen mode	Alt-Enter
Toggle trackball mode	F6
Enter trackball mode temporarily (while key is pressed)	Delete
DPad left/up/right/down	KEYPAD_4/8/6/2
DPad center click	KEYPAD_5
Onion alpha increase/decrease	KEYPAD_MULTIPLY(*) / KEYPAD_DIVIDE(/)

> **TIP:** You must first disable NumLock on your development computer before you can use keypad keys.

Table 1–2 refers to the -trace startup option in the context of toggle code profiling. This option lets you store profiling results in a file when starting the AVD via the emulator tool.

For example, emulator -avd test_AVD -trace results.txt starts the emulator for device configuration test_AVD, and also stores profiling results in results.txt when you press F9. Press F9 again to stop code profiling.

Figure 1–10 displays 5554:test_AVD in the titlebar. The 5554 value identifies a console port that you can use to dynamically query and otherwise control the environment of the AVD.

> **NOTE:** Android supports up to 16 concurrently executing AVDs. Each AVD is assigned an even-numbered console port number starting with 5554.

You can connect to the AVD's console by specifying telnet localhost *console-port*. For example, specify telnet localhost 5554 to connect to test_AVD's console. Figure 1–11 shows you the resulting command window on Windows XP.

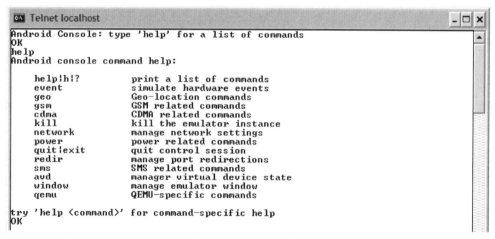

Figure 1–11. *Type a command name by itself for command-specific help.*

1–5. Introducing UC

Problem

Now that you've installed the Android SDK, installed an Android platform, and created and started an AVD, you're ready to create an app, and install and run this app on the AVD. Although you could create an app based on Listing 1–2's `SimpleActivity` class, you'll probably find this recipe's UC app to be more interesting (and useful).

Solution

UC (an acronym for Units Converter) is an app that lets you convert between types of units. For example, you can convert a specific number of degrees Celsius to its equivalent number of degrees Fahrenheit, a specific number of pounds to its equivalent number of kilograms, and so on.

How It Works

UC consists of a single activity (also named UC) that presents a user interface (revealed in Recipe 1–7) consisting of an input/output textfield for entering the number of units to convert and displaying the conversion result, a spinner for choosing a conversion, and buttons for clearing the textfield, performing the conversion, and closing the app.

Listing 1–9 presents the UC activity's source code.

Listing 1–9. *An Activity for Performing Unit Conversions*

```java
// UC.java

package com.apress.uc;

import android.app.Activity;

import android.os.Bundle;

import android.text.Editable;
import android.text.TextWatcher;

import android.view.View;

import android.widget.AdapterView;
import android.widget.ArrayAdapter;
import android.widget.Button;
import android.widget.EditText;
import android.widget.Spinner;

public class UC extends Activity
{
   private int position = 0;

   private double[] multipliers =
```

```
{
    0.0015625,          // Acres to square miles
    101325.0,           // Atmospheres to Pascals
    100000.0,           // Bars to Pascals
    0,                  // Degrees Celsius to Degrees Fahrenheit (placeholder)
    0,                  // Degrees Fahrenheit to Degrees Celsius (placeholder)
    0.00001,            // Dynes to Newtons
    0.3048,             // Feet/Second to Metres/Second
    0.0284130625,       // Fluid Ounces (UK) to Litres
    0.0295735295625,    // Fluid Ounces (US) to Litres
    746.0,              // Horsepower (electric) to Watts
    735.499,            // Horsepower (metric) to Watts
    1/1016.0469088,     // Kilograms to Tons (UK or long)
    1/907.18474,        // Kilograms to Tons (US or short)
    1/0.0284130625,     // Litres to Fluid Ounces (UK)
    1/0.0295735295625,  // Litres to Fluid Ounces (US)
    331.5,              // Mach Number to Metres/Second
    1/0.3048,           // Metres/Second to Feet/Second
    1/331.5,            // Metres/Second to Mach Number
    0.833,              // Miles/Gallon (UK) to Miles/Gallon (US)
    1/0.833,            // Miles/Gallon (US) to Miles/Gallon (UK)
    100000.0,           // Newtons to Dynes
    1/101325.0,         // Pascals to Atmospheres
    0.00001,            // Pascals to Bars
    640.0,              // Square Miles to Acres
    1016.0469088,       // Tons (UK or long) to Kilograms
    907.18474,          // Tons (US or short) to Kilograms
    1/746.0,            // Watts to Horsepower (electic)
    1/735.499           // Watts to Horsepower (metric)
};

@Override
public void onCreate(Bundle savedInstanceState)
{
    super.onCreate(savedInstanceState);
    setContentView(R.layout.main);

    final EditText etUnits = (EditText) findViewById(R.id.units);

    final Spinner spnConversions = (Spinner) findViewById(R.id.conversions);
    ArrayAdapter<CharSequence> aa;
    aa = ArrayAdapter.
            createFromResource(this, R.array.conversions,
                                android.R.layout.simple_spinner_item);
    aa.setDropDownViewResource(android.R.layout.simple_spinner_item);
    spnConversions.setAdapter(aa);

    AdapterView.OnItemSelectedListener oisl;
    oisl = new AdapterView.OnItemSelectedListener()
    {
        @Override
        public void onItemSelected(AdapterView<?> parent, View view,
                                    int position, long id)
        {
            UC.this.position = position;
        }
```

```java
    @Override
    public void onNothingSelected(AdapterView<?> parent)
    {
        System.out.println("nothing");
    }
};
spnConversions.setOnItemSelectedListener(oisl);

final Button btnClear = (Button) findViewById(R.id.clear);
AdapterView.OnClickListener ocl;
ocl = new AdapterView.OnClickListener()
{
    @Override
    public void onClick(View v)
    {
        etUnits.setText("");
    }
};
btnClear.setOnClickListener(ocl);
btnClear.setEnabled(false);

final Button btnConvert = (Button) findViewById(R.id.convert);
ocl = new AdapterView.OnClickListener()
{
    @Override
    public void onClick(View v)
    {
        String text = etUnits.getText().toString();
        double input = Double.parseDouble(text);
        double result = 0;
        if (position == 3)
            result = input*9.0/5.0+32; // Celsius to Fahrenheit
        else
        if (position == 4)
            result = (input-32)*5.0/9.0; // Fahrenheit to Celsius
        else
            result = input*multipliers[position];
        etUnits.setText(""+result);
    }
};
btnConvert.setOnClickListener(ocl);
btnConvert.setEnabled(false);

Button btnClose = (Button) findViewById(R.id.close);
ocl = new AdapterView.OnClickListener()
{
    @Override
    public void onClick(View v)
    {
        finish();
    }
};
btnClose.setOnClickListener(ocl);

TextWatcher tw;
tw = new TextWatcher()
{
```

```
    @Override
    public void afterTextChanged(Editable s)
    {
    }

    @Override
    public void beforeTextChanged(CharSequence s, int start, int count,
                                  int after)
    {
    }

    @Override
    public void onTextChanged(CharSequence s, int start, int before,
                              int count)
    {
        if (etUnits.getText().length() == 0)
        {
            btnClear.setEnabled(false);
            btnConvert.setEnabled(false);
        }
        else
        {
            btnClear.setEnabled(true);
            btnConvert.setEnabled(true);
        }
    }
};
etUnits.addTextChangedListener(tw);
    }
}
```

Listing 1–9 begins with a comment that conveniently identifies the source file (UC.java) describing the activity. This listing next presents a package statement that names the package (com.apress.uc), in which the source file's UC class is stored, followed by a series of import statements that import various Android API types.

> **TIP:** You should familiarize yourself with the Android API's package organization so that you can quickly find API types in Google's Android API reference (http://developer.android.com/reference/packages.html). You'll want to locate documentation on these types quickly as you dig deeper into Android app development.

Listing 1–9 next describes the UC class, which extends Activity. This class first declares position and multipliers fields:

- position stores the zero-based index of the conversion selected via the spinner, and defaults to 0 (the first conversion displayed by the spinner). Storing the spinner's position in this field simplifies choosing an appropriate conversion to perform.

- multipliers stores an array of multiplier values, with each entry corresponding to a spinner value. A conversion is performed by multiplying the input value by multipliers[position]. However, there are two exceptions: Celsius-to-Fahrenheit and Fahrenheit-to-Celsius. These conversions are handled separately, because they also require an addition or a subtraction operation.

All of the app's work takes place in the overriding onCreate(Bundle) method: no other methods are required, which helps to keep this app simple.

onCreate(Bundle) first invokes its same-named superclass method, a rule that must be followed by all overriding activity methods.

This method then executes setContentView(R.layout.main) to establish the app's user interface.

R.layout.main identifies a *resource*, a piece of data required by an app's code, and which you maintain independently of the code by storing it in a separate file.

NOTE: Resources simplify app maintenance, make it easier to adapt a user interface to different screen sizes, and facilitate adapting an app to different languages.

You interpret this resource ID as follows:

- R is the name of a class that's generated (by the aapt tool) when the app is being built. This class is named R because its content identifies various kinds of resources (such as layouts, images, strings, and colors).

- layout is the name of a class that's nested within R. All resources whose IDs are stored in this class describe specific layout resources. Each kind of resource is associated with a nested class that's named in a similar fashion. For example, string identifies string resources.

- main is the name of an int constant declared within layout. This resource ID identifies the main layout resource. Specifically, main refers to a main.xml file that stores the main screen's layout information. main is UC's only layout resource.

R.layout.main is passed to Activity's void setContentView(int layoutResID) method to tell Android to create a user interface screen using the layout information stored in main.xml. Behind the scenes, Android creates the user interface components described in main.xml and positions them on the screen as specified by main.xml's layout data.

This user interface is based on *views* (abstractions of user interface components) and *view groups* (views that group related user interface components). Views are instances of classes that subclass the android.view.View class and are analogous to Java components. View groups are instances of classes that subclass the abstract android.view.ViewGroup class and are analogous to Java containers. Android refers to specific views (such as buttons or spinners) as *widgets*.

Continuing, onCreate(Bundle) executes final EditText etUnits = (EditText) findViewById(R.id.units);. This statement first calls View's View findViewById(int id) method to find the EditText view declared in main.xml and identified as units, and instantiate android.widget.EditText and initialize it to this view's declarative information, and then saves this object's reference in local variable etUnits. This variable is final because it's subsequently accessed from an anonymous inner class.

In a similar manner, final Spinner spnConversions = (Spinner) findViewById(R.id.conversions); instantiates the android.widget.Spinner class using the declarative information that's stored in main.xml, and saves the resulting object reference for subsequent access.

onCreate(Bundle) next addresses the spinner object having no text to display, by first calling the android.widget.ArrayAdapter class's ArrayAdapter<CharSequence> createFromResource(Context context, int textArrayResId, int textViewResId) method, which returns an array adapter that supplies text messages to the spinner:

- context requires a Context instance that identifies the current app component, which happens to be the current activity as specified by keyword this.

- textArrayResId requires the ID of an array resource that stores strings (such as "Degrees Celsius to Degrees Fahrenheit"), which happen to identify different kinds of conversions. The R.array.conversions argument passed to this parameter identifies conversions as the name of an array resource containing conversion strings and specified in a file named arrays.xml (described later in this recipe).

- textViewResId requires the ID of the layout resource used to create the spinner's look. The android.R.layout.simple_spinner_item argument passed to this parameter is a predefined ID stored in the android package's R class's nested layout class. simple_spinner_item describes a spinner that looks something like a Java Swing combobox.

After calling createFromResource(Context, int, int), onCreate(Bundle) calls ArrayAdapter's void setDropDownViewResource(int resource) method with android.R.layout.simple_spinner_item as the argument. This method call creates the dropdown view portion of the spinner.

Now that the array adapter has been created and initialized with the appropriate unit conversion strings and layout information, onCreate(Bundle) attaches this information to the spinner by calling spnConversions.setAdapter(aa);. This method call allows the spinner widget to access this information and present a list of conversions to the user.

> **NOTE:** Spinner inherits the void setAdapter(T) method from its abstract android.widget.AdapterView<T extends Adapter> ancestor class.

UC needs to keep track of the currently selected spinner item so that it can perform the appropriate conversion. onCreate(Bundle) makes this possible by registering a listener with the spinner that responds to item-selected events by assigning the spinner's position to the (previously mentioned) position variable.

onCreate(Bundle) first instantiates an anonymous class that implements ArrayAdapter's nested OnItemSelectedListener interface, and then registers this instance with the spinner by calling AdapterView's void setOnItemSelectedListener(AdapterView.OnItemSelectedListener listener) method.

OnItemSelectedListener's void onItemSelected(AdapterView<?> parent, View view, int position, long id) method is invoked whenever the user selects a new item, and is the perfect place to save the position. Although not needed, the companion void onNothingSelected(AdapterView<?> parent) method must also be implemented.

With the spinner out of the way, onCreate(Bundle) turns its attention to creating the Clear, Convert, and Close buttons. For each button, it invokes findByViewId(int) to obtain the button information from main.xml, and then instantiate the android.widget.Button class.

AdapterView's nested onClickListener interface is then employed to create listener objects, whose void onClick(View v) methods are invoked whenever the user clicks a button. Each listener is registered with its Button object by calling AdapterView's void setOnItemClickListener(AdapterView.OnItemClickListener listener) method.

The Clear button's click listener simply executes etUnits.setText("") to clear user input or a conversion result from the etUnits textfield. The Close button's click listener is equally simple; it invokes finish() to terminate the current activity and UC app. In contrast, the Convert button's click listener has more work to accomplish:

1. Obtain the contents of the etUnits textfield as a String object: String text = etUnits.getText().toString();.

2. Parse this String object into a double precision floating-point value: double input = Double.parseDouble(text);.

3. Perform the conversion and save the result based on position's value:
    result = input*9.0/5.0+32;, result = (input-32)*5.0/9.0;, or result
    = input*multipliers[position];.

4. Update etUnits with the result: etUnits.setText(""+result);.

There's one more task for onCreate(Bundle) to perform: make sure that the Clear and
Convert buttons are disabled when etUnits is empty. After all, there's no point clearing
an empty textfield, and parseDouble() throws an exception when attempting to parse an
empty textfield.

onCreate(Bundle) accomplishes this task by registering a *textwatcher* (an object whose
class implements the android.text.TextWatcher interface) with the etUnits textfield, via
android.widget.TextView's void addTextChangedListener(TextWatcher watcher)
method. TextView is EditText's superclass.

TextWatcher declares void afterTextChanged(Editable s), void
beforeTextChanged(CharSequence s, int start, int count, int after), and void
onTextChanged(CharSequence s, int start, int before, int count) methods. Only
the latter method is overridden to enable or disable the Clear and Convert buttons.

onTextChanged(s, int, int, int) first evaluates etUnits.getText().length(), which
returns the textfield's length. If the length is 0 (empty textfield), the buttons are disabled
via btnClear.setEnabled(false); and btnConvert.setEnabled(false);. Otherwise,
they're enabled via btnClear.setEnabled(true); and btnConvert.setEnabled(true);.

Most of UC's resources are stored in XML files. For example, UC's widget and layout
information is stored in main.xml, which Listing 1–10 presents.

Listing 1–10. *The* main.xml *File Storing Widget and Layout Information*

```xml
<?xml version="1.0" encoding="utf-8"?>
<LinearLayout xmlns:android="http://schemas.android.com/apk/res/android"
    android:orientation="vertical"
    android:layout_width="fill_parent"
    android:layout_height="fill_parent"
    android:gravity="center_vertical"
    android:background="@drawable/gradientbg"
    android:padding="5dip">
    <LinearLayout android:layout_width="fill_parent"
        android:layout_height="wrap_content">
        <TextView android:layout_width="wrap_content"
            android:layout_height="wrap_content"
            android:layout_marginRight="10dip"
            android:text="@string/units"
            android:textColor="#000000"
            android:textSize="15sp"
            android:textStyle="bold"/>
        <EditText android:id="@+id/units"
            android:layout_width="fill_parent"
            android:layout_height="wrap_content"
            android:hint="type a number"
            android:inputType="numberDecimal|numberSigned"
            android:maxLines="1"/>
    </LinearLayout>
```

```
    <Spinner android:id="@+id/conversions"
        android:layout_width="fill_parent"
        android:layout_height="wrap_content"
        android:prompt="@string/prompt"/>
    <LinearLayout android:layout_width="fill_parent"
        android:layout_height="wrap_content">
        <Button android:id="@+id/clear"
            android:layout_width="fill_parent"
            android:layout_height="wrap_content"
            android:layout_weight="1"
            android:text="@string/clear"/>
        <Button android:id="@+id/convert"
            android:layout_width="fill_parent"
            android:layout_height="wrap_content"
            android:layout_weight="1"
            android:text="@string/convert"/>
        <Button android:id="@+id/close"
            android:layout_width="fill_parent"
            android:layout_height="wrap_content"
            android:layout_weight="1"
            android:text="@string/close"/>
    </LinearLayout>
</LinearLayout>
```

Listing 1–10 begins by declaring a `<LinearLayout>` tag that specifies a *layout* (a view group that arranges contained views on an Android device's screen in some manner) for arranging contained widgets and nested layouts either horizontally or vertically across the screen.

The `<LinearLayout>` tag specifies several attributes for controlling this linear layout. These attributes include the following:

- `orientation` identifies the linear layout as horizontal or vertical. The default orientation is horizontal. `"horizontal"` and `"vertical"` are the only legal values that can be assigned to this attribute.

- `layout_width` identifies the width of the layout. Legal values include `"fill_parent"` (occupy the entire width) and `"wrap_content"` (occupy only the width required by the view). `fill_parent` was renamed to `match_parent` in Android 2.2, but is still supported and widely used.

- `layout_height` identifies the height of the layout. Legal values include `"fill_parent"` (occupy the entire height) and `"wrap_content"` (occupy only the height required by the view). `fill_parent` was renamed to `match_parent` in Android 2.2, but is still supported and widely used.

- `gravity` identifies how the layout is positioned relative to the screen. For example, `"center_vertical"` specifies that the layout should be centered vertically on the screen.

- `background` identifies a background image or gradient via a *resource reference* (special syntax beginning with the @ character). For example, `"@drawable/gradientbg"` references a *drawable resource* (an image or a graphic) named `gradientbg`.

- padding identifies space to add to the layout to provide a boundary between itself and the screen's edges. "5dip" refers to five *density-independent pixels*, virtual pixel units that apps can use to express layout dimensions/positions in a screen density-independent way.

> **NOTE:** A density-independent pixel is equivalent to one physical pixel on a 160-dpi screen, the baseline density assumed by Android. At run time, Android transparently handles any scaling of the required dip units, based on the actual density of the screen in use. Dip units are converted to screen pixels via equation pixels = dips * (density / 160). For example, on a 240-dpi screen, 1 dip equals 1.5 physical pixels. Google recommends using dip units to define your app's user interface to ensure proper display of the UI on different screens.

A second linear layout has been nested inside the first linear layout. Because no orientation attribute is specified, this layout lays out its widgets horizontally. As with the parent layout, layout_width is assigned "fill_parent". However, layout_height is assigned "wrap_content" to prevent this nested layout from occupying the entire screen.

The nested linear layout encapsulates textview and edittext elements. The textview element describes a widget that serves as a label for the widget described by the edittext element. The <textview> tag presents the following attributes in addition to layout_width and layout_height:

- layout_marginRight specifies the amount of space to reserve on the right side of the textview widget; 10 density-independent pixels have been selected as the space amount.

- text identifies the text that this widget displays. The text is identified via @string/units, a string resource reference to the units entry in the standard strings.xml resource file (see Listing 1–12). This entry's value is the text.

- textColor identifies the color of the text. The color is specified in *#RRGGBB* format – #00000 identifies black.

- textSize identifies the text's size. The size is specified as "15sp", which is interpreted as 15 scale-independent pixels (the user selects the scaling via a device setting). Google recommends specifying scale-independent pixels (to let the user scale text) or device-independent pixels (to prevent the user from scaling text).

- textStyle identifies the text styling, such as bold or italic. The style is set to "bold" to emphasize the text so that it stands out on the screen.

The `<edittext>` tag provides the following attributes:

- `id` identifies this widget element so that it can be referenced from code. The resource identifier is specifed by using a special syntax that begins with the `@+id` prefix. For example, `"@+id/units"` identifies this edittext widget as `units`; this widget resource is referenced from code by specifying `R.id.units`.

- `hint` identifies a string that appears in the textfield when nothing has been entered. It serves as a hint to the user about what kind of data to enter into the textfield. Instead of assigning a string resource reference to this attribute, the `"type a number"` literal string was assigned to make the following point: although you can embed literal string values in the resources (or even code), you really should store them in the separate `strings.xml` resource file to facilitate localization of the app to a different language, such as French or German.

- `inputType` identifies the kind of data that you want the user to enter. By default, any character can be entered. Because this is unacceptable when a number is required, `"numberDecimal|numberSigned"` is assigned to `inputType`. This string specifies that only decimal numbers can be entered. Furthermore, these numbers can be negative.

- `maxLines` restricts the number of lines of text that can be entered into a textfield. The `"1"` assignment indicates that only a single line of text can be entered.

Below the linear layout element lies a spinner element named `conversions`. This element is declared to fill the screen's width, but not the screen's height. Futhermore, its `prompt` attribute is assigned `"@string/prompt"` to prompt the user (on the dropdown view, which is shown in Figure 1–15) to select a conversion.

Below the spinner element lies another nested linear layout, encapsulating the Clear, Convert, and Close buttons. Each button is assigned a unique ID so it can be referenced from code. Its `layout_weight` attribute is assigned the same value as the other buttons' `layout_weight` attributes so that each button has the same width (it looks nicer).

Android let you declare shape resources (such as rectangles or ovals) as XML files. These shapes can be declared with straight or rounded corners, with gradient backgrounds, and with other attributes. For example, Listing 1–11 introduces a rectangle shape with a gradient background.

Listing 1–11. *The* `gradientbg.xml` *File Storing a Gradient Shape to Color the Activity's Background*

```xml
<?xml version="1.0" encoding="utf-8"?>
<shape xmlns:android="http://schemas.android.com/apk/res/android">
    <gradient android:startColor="#fccb06"
        android:endColor="#fd6006"
        android:angle="270"/>
    <corners android:radius="10dp"/>
</shape>
```

The `<shape>` tag introduces a shape via its shape attribute. If this attribute is not present, the shape defaults to a rectangle.

The nested `<gradient>` tag defines the shape's color in terms of a gradient, which is specified via startColor, endColor, and angle attributes. The angle attribute specifies the direction that the gradient sweeps across the rectangle. If angle is not present, the angle defaults to 0 degrees.

The nested `<corners>` tag determines whether or not a rectangle shape has corners. If this tag is present, its attributes identify the degree of roundness for each or all corners. For example, the radius attribute in Listing 1–11 specifies that each corner has a radius of 10 density-independent pixels – dp is a synonym for dip.

Strings should be stored separately to facilitate localization of text. Android mandates that strings be stored in a file named `strings.xml`, which Listing 1–12 presents.

Listing 1–12. *The* `strings.xml` *File Storing the App's Strings*

```
<?xml version="1.0" encoding="utf-8"?>
<resources>
    <string name="app_name">Units Converter</string>
    <string name="clear">Clear</string>
    <string name="close">Close</string>
    <string name="convert">Convert</string>
    <string name="prompt">Select a conversion</string>
    <string name="units">Units</string>
</resources>
```

The `strings.xml` file stores its strings as a sequence of string elements that are nested in a resources element. Each `<string>` tag requires a unique name attribute whose content identifies the string, and which is referenced from code or some other resource. The string text is placed between the `<string>` and `</string>` tags.

Finally, the array of conversion strings is stored in `arrays.xml`. Listing 1–13 reveals this standard file's contents.

Listing 1–13. *The* `arrays.xml` *File Storing an Array of Conversion Strings*

```
<?xml version="1.0" encoding="utf-8"?>
<resources>
    <string-array name="conversions">
        <item>Acres to Square Miles</item>
        <item>Atmospheres to Pascals</item>
        <item>Bars to Pascals</item>
        <item>Degrees Celsius to Degrees Fahrenheit</item>
        <item>Degrees Fahrenheit to Degrees Celsius</item>
        <item>Dynes to Newtons</item>
        <item>Feet/Second to Metres/Second</item>
        <item>Fluid Ounces (UK) to Litres</item>
        <item>Fluid Ounces (US) to Litres</item>
        <item>Horsepower (electric) to Watts</item>
        <item>Horsepower (metric) to Watts</item>
        <item>Kilograms to Tons (UK or long)</item>
        <item>Kilograms to Tons (US or short)</item>
        <item>Litres to Fluid ounces (UK)</item>
        <item>Litres to Fluid ounces (US)</item>
```

```
    <item>Mach Number to Metres/Second</item>
    <item>Metres/Second to Feet/Second</item>
    <item>Metres/Second to Mach Number</item>
    <item>Miles/Gallon (UK) to Miles/Gallon (US)</item>
    <item>Miles/Gallon (US) to Miles/Gallon (UK)</item>
    <item>Newtons to Dynes</item>
    <item>Pascals to Atmospheres</item>
    <item>Pascals to Bars</item>
    <item>Square Miles to Acres</item>
    <item>Tons (UK or long) to Kilograms</item>
    <item>Tons (US or short) to Kilograms</item>
    <item>Watts to Horsepower (electric)</item>
    <item>Watts to Horsepower (metric)</item>
  </string-array>
</resources>
```

Android lets you store arrays with different types of data in `arrays.xml`. For example, `<string-array>` indicates that the array contains strings. This tag requires a name attribute whose value uniquely identifies this array. Each array item is specified by placing its content between `<item>` and `</item>` tags.

1–6. Creating UC

Problem

You want to learn how to create UC using the Android SDK's command-line tools, but are not sure how to accomplish this task.

Solution

Use the `android` tool to create UC, and then use `ant` to build this project.

How It Works

Your first step in creating UC is to use the `android` tool to create a project. When used in this way, `android` requires you to adhere to the following syntax (which is spread across multiple lines for readability):

```
android create project --target target_ID
                       --name your_project_name
                       --path /path/to/your/project/project_name
                       --activity your_activity_name
                       --package your_package_namespace
```

Except for `--name` (or `-n`), which specifies the project's name (if provided, this name will be used for the resulting `.apk` filename when you build your app), all of the following options are required:

- The --target (or -t) option specifies the app's build target. The *target_ID* value is an integer value that identifies an Android platform. You can obtain this value by invoking android list targets. If you've only installed the Android 2.3 platform, this command should output a single Android 2.3 platform target identified as integer ID 1.

- The --path (or -p) option specifies the project directory's location. The directory is created if it doesn't exist.

- The --activity (or -a) option specifies the name for the default activity class. The resulting classfile is created inside */path/to/your/project/project_name/src/your_package_namespace/*, and is used as the .apk filename if --name (or -n) isn't specified.

- The --package (or -k) option specifies the project's package namespace, which must follow the rules for packages that are specified in the Java language.

Assuming a Windows XP platform, and assuming a C:\prj\dev hierarchy where the UC project is to be stored in C:\prj\dev\UC, invoke the following command from anywhere in the filesystem to create UC:

```
android create project -t 1 -p C:\prj\dev\UC -a UC -k com.apress.uc
```

This command creates various directories and adds files to some of these directories. It specifically creates the following file and directory structure within C:\prj\dev\UC:

- AndroidManifest.xml is the manifest file for the app being built. This file is synchronized to the Activity subclass previously specified via the --activity or -a option.

- bin is the output directory for the Apache Ant build script.

- build.properties is a customizable properties file for the build system. You can edit this file to override default build settings used by Apache Ant, and provide a pointer to your keystore and key alias so that the build tools can sign your app when built in release mode (discussed in Recipe 1–8).

- build.xml is the Apache Ant build script for this project.

- default.properties is the default properties file for the build system. Don't modify this file.

- libs contains private libraries, when required.

- local.properties contains the location of the Android SDK home directory.

- proguard.cfg contains configuration data for *ProGuard*, an SDK tool that lets developers obfuscate their code (making it very difficult to reverse engineer the code) as an integrated part of a release build.

- res contains project resources.

- `src` contains the project's source code.

`res` contains the following directories:

- `drawable-hdpi` contains drawable resources (such as icons) for high-density screens.

- `drawable-ldpi` contains drawable resources for low-density screens.

- `drawable-mdpi` contains drawable resources for medium-density screens. The `gradientbg.xml` file in Listing 1–11 is stored in this directory.

- `layout` contains layout files. The `main.xml` file in Listing 1–10 is stored in this directory.

- `values` contains value files. Listing 1–12's `strings.xml` and Listing 1–13's `arrays.xml` files are stored in this directory.

Also, `src` contains the `com\apress\uc` directory structure, and the final `uc` subdirectory contains a skeletal `UC.java` source file. This skeletal file's contents are replaced with Listing 1–9.

Assuming that `C:\prj\dev\UC` is current, build this app with the help of Apache's ant tool, which defaults to processing this directory's `build.xml` file. At the command line, specify ant followed by `debug` or `release` to indicate the build mode:

- *Debug mode*: Build the app for testing and debugging. The build tools sign the resulting APK with a debug key and optimize the APK with `zipalign`. Specify `ant debug`.

- *Release mode*: Build the app for release to users. You must sign the resulting APK with your private key, and then optimize the APK with `zipalign`. (I discuss these tasks later in this chapter.) Specify `ant release`.

Build UC in debug mode by invoking `ant debug` from the `C:\prj\dev\UC` directory. This command creates a gen subdirectory containing the ant-generated `R.java` file (in a `com\apress\uc` directory hierarchy), and stores the created `UC-debug.apk` file in the `bin` subdirectory.

1–7. Installing and Running UC

Problem

You want to install the `UC-debug.apk` package file that you just created on the previously started AVD and run this app.

Solution

Use the adb tool to install UC. Navigate to the app launcher screen to run UC.

How It Works

Assuming that the AVD is still running, execute adb install C:\prj\dev\UC\bin\UC-debug.apk to install UC-debug.apk on the AVD. After a few moments, you should see several messages similar to the following:

```
411 KB/s (19770 bytes in 0.046s)
        pkg: /data/local/tmp/UC-debug.apk
Success
```

From the home screen, click the app launcher icon (the rectangular grid icon centered at the bottom of the home screen) and scroll down on the result screen's list of app icons. Figure 1–12 shows you the Units Converter app entry.

Figure 1–12. *The highlighted Units Converter app entry displays a custom icon (in an* icon.png *file, which is included in this book's code) that's also stored in* drawable-mdpi.

Click the Units Converter icon and you should see the screen shown in Figure 1–13.

Figure 1–13. *The Units textfield prompts the user to type a number.*

Enter **37** into the Units textfield and you'll see the screen shown in Figure 1–14.

Figure 1–14. *The Clear and Convert buttons are no longer disabled.*

Click the spinner and you'll see the screen shown in Figure 1–15.

Figure 1–15. *The spinner displays the prompt at the top of its drop-down list of conversion names.*

Select "Degrees Celsius to Degrees Fahrenheit" and you'll see a screen similar to Figure 1–16.

Figure 1–16. *The Units textfield displays the conversion result after clicking Convert.*

Click Close to terminate the app and return to the launcher screen shown in Figure 1–12.

> **NOTE:** Although UC appears to run correctly, its (and any other app's) code should be unit tested to verify that the code is correct before publishing the app. Google's online Android Developer's Guide delves into this topic in its "Testing" section at
> `http://developer.android.com/guide/topics/testing/index.html`.

1–8. Preparing UC for Publishing

Problem

You're satisfied that UC works properly, and now you want to prepare it for publishing to Google's Android Market or another publishing service.

Solution

Before you can publish an app such as UC, you should version the app. You then build the app in release mode, and sign and align its app package.

How It Works

Google's online *Android Developer's Guide* (http://developer.android.com/guide/index.html) provides extensive information on publishing an app. Rather than repeat the guide's information, this recipe presents the steps that are necessary to prepare UC for publishing.

Version UC

Android lets you add version information to your app by specifying this information in AndroidManifest.xml's <manifest> tag via its versionCode and versionName attributes.

versionCode is assigned an integer value that represents the version of the app's code. The value is an integer so that other apps can programmatically evaluate it to check an upgrade or downgrade relationship, for example. Although you can set the value to any desired integer, you should ensure that each successive release of your app uses a greater value. Android doesn't enforce this behavior, but increasing the value in successive releases is normative.

versionName is assigned a string value that represents the release version of the app's code, and should be shown to users (by the app). This value is a string so that you can describe the app version as a *<major>*.*<minor>*.*<point>* string, or as any other type of absolute or relative version identifier. As with android:versionCode, Android doesn't use this value for any internal purpose. Publishing services may extract the versionName value for display to users.

The <manifest> tag in UC's AndroidManifest.xml file includes a versionCode attribute initialized to "1" and a versionName attribute initialized to "1.0".

Build UC in Release Mode

Assuming Windows XP, the previous C:\prj\dev\UC directory, and that this directory is current, execute the following command line:

```
ant release
```

This command line generates UC-unsigned.apk and stores this file in the bin directory. It also outputs a message stating that this APK must be signed and aligned with zipalign.

Sign UC's App Package

Android requires that all installed apps be digitally signed with a certificate whose private key is held by the app's developer. Android uses the certificate as a means of identifying the app's author and establishing trust relationships between apps; it doesn't use the certificate to control which apps can be installed by the user. Certificates don't need to be signed by certificate authorities: it's perfectly allowable, and typical, for Android apps to use self-signed certificates.

> **NOTE:** Android tests a signer certificate's expiration date only at install time. If an app's signer certificate expires after the app is installed, the app will continue to function normally.

Before you can sign UC-unsigned.apk, you must obtain a suitable private key. A private key is suitable if it meets the following criteria:

- The key represents the personal, corporate, or organizational entity to be identified with the app.

- The key has a validity period that exceeds the expected lifespan of the app. Google recommends a validity period of more than 25 years. If you plan to publish the app on Android Market, keep in mind that a validity period ending after October 22, 2033 is a requirement. You cannot upload an app if it's signed with a key whose validity expires before that date.

- The key is not the debug key generated by the Android SDK tools.

The JDK's keytool tool is used to create a suitable private key. The following command line (split over two lines for readability) uses keytool to generate this key:

```
keytool -genkey -v -keystore uc-release-key.keystore -alias uc_key -keyalg RSA
        -keysize 2048 -validity 10000
```

The following command-line arguments are specified:

- -genkey causes keytool to generate a public and a private key (a key pair).

- -v enables verbose output.

- -keystore identifies the *keystore* (a file) that stores the private key; the keystore is named uc-release-key.keystore in the command line.

- -alias identifies an alias for the key (only the first eight characters are used when the alias is specified during the actual signing operation); the alias is named uc_key in the command line.

- `-keyalg` specifies the encryption algorithm to use when generating the key; although DSA and RSA are supported, RSA is specified in the command line.

- `-keysize` specifies the size of each generated key (in bits); 2048 is specified in the command line because Google recommends using a key size of 2048 bits or higher (the default size is 1024 bits).

- `-validity` specifies the period (in days) in which the key remains valid (Google recommends a value of 10000 or greater); 10000 is specified in the command line.

keytool prompts you for a password (to protect access to the keystore), and to reenter the same password. It then prompts for your first and last name, your organizational unit name, the name of your organization, the name of your city or locality, the name of your state or province, and a two-letter country code for your organizational unit.

keytool subsequently prompts you to indicate whether or not this information is correct (by typing yes and pressing Enter, or by pressing Enter for no). Assuming you entered yes, keytool lets you choose a different password for the key, or use the same password as that of the keystore.

> **CAUTION:** Keep your private key secure. Fail to do so, and your app authoring identity and user trust could be compromised. Here are some tips for keeping your private key secure:
>
> * Select strong passwords for the keystore and key.
>
> * When you generate your key with `keytool`, don't supply the `-storepass` and `-keypass` options at the command line. If you do so, your passwords will be available in your shell history, which any user on your computer could access.
>
> * When signing your apps with `jarsigner`, don't supply the `-storepass` and `-keypass` options at the command line (for the same reason as mentioned in the previous tip).
>
> * Don't give or lend anyone your private key, and don't let unauthorized persons know your keystore and key passwords.

keytool creates `uc-release-key.keystore` in the current directory. You can view this keystore's information by executing the following command line:

```
keytool -list -v -keystore uc-release-key.keystore
```

After requesting the keystore password, keytool outputs the number of entries in the keystore (which should be one) and certificate information.

The JDK's jarsigner tool is used to sign UC-unsigned.apk. Assuming that `C:\prj\dev\UC` is the current directory, this directory contains the keytool-created `uc-release-key.keystore` file, and this directory contains a `bin` subdirectory that contains `UC-unsigned.apk`, execute the following command line to sign this file:

```
jarsigner -verbose -keystore uc-release-key.keystore bin/UC-unsigned.apk uc_key
```

The following command-line arguments are specified:

- -verbose enables verbose output.

- -keystore identifies the keystore that stores the private key; uc-release-key.keystore is specified in the command line.

- bin/UC-unsigned.apk identifies the location and name of the APK being signed.

- uc-key identifies the previously created alias for the private key.

jarsigner prompts you to enter the keystore password that you previously specified via keytool. This tool then outputs messages similar to the following:

```
 adding: META-INF/MANIFEST.MF
 adding: META-INF/UC_KEY.SF
 adding: META-INF/UC_KEY.RSA
signing: res/layout/main.xml
signing: AndroidManifest.xml
signing: resources.arsc
signing: res/drawable-hdpi/icon.png
signing: res/drawable-ldpi/icon.png
signing: res/drawable-mdpi/gradientbg.xml
signing: res/drawable-mdpi/icon.png
signing: classes.dex
```

Execute jarsigner -verify bin/UC-unsigned.apk to verify that UC-unsigned.apk has been signed.

Assuming success, you should notice a single "jar verified." message. Assuming failure, you should notice the following messages:

```
no manifest.
jar is unsigned. (signatures missing or not parsable)
```

Align UC's App Package

As a performance optimization, Android requires that a signed APK's uncompressed content be aligned relative to the start of the file, and supplies the zipalign SDK tool for this task. According to Google's documentation, all uncompressed data within the APK, such as images or raw files, is aligned on 4-byte boundaries.

zipalign requires the following syntax to align an input APK to an output APK:

```
zipalign [-f] [-v] <alignment> infile.apk outfile.apk
```

The following command-line arguments are specified:

- -f forces outfile.apk to be overwritten if it exists.

- -v enables verbose output.

- alignment specifies that the APK content is to be aligned on this number of bytes boundary; it appears that zipalign ignores any value other than 4.

- infile.apk identifies the signed APK file to be aligned.

- outfile.apk identifies the resulting signed and aligned APK file.

Assuming that C:\prj\dev\UC\bin is the current directory, execute the following command line to align UC-unsigned.apk to UC.apk:

```
zipalign -f -v 4 UC-unsigned.apk UC.apk
```

zipalign requires the following syntax to verify that an existing APK is aligned:

```
zipalign -c -v <alignment> existing.apk
```

The following command-line arguments are specified:

- -c confirms the alignment of existing.apk.

- -v enables verbose output.

- alignment specifies that the APK content is aligned on this number of bytes boundary; it appears that zipalign ignores any value other than 4.

- infile.apk identifies the signed APK file to be aligned.

Execute the following command line to verify that UC.apk is aligned:

```
zipalign -c -v 4 UC.apk
```

zipalign presents a list of APK entries, indicating which are compressed and which are not, followed by a verification successful or a verification failed message.

1–9. Migrating to Eclipse

Problem

You prefer to develop apps using the Eclipse IDE.

Solution

To develop apps with Eclipse, you need to install an IDE such as Eclipse Classic 3.6.1. Furthermore, you need to install the ADT Plugin.

How It Works

Before you can develop Android apps with Eclipse, you must complete at least the first two of the following three tasks:

1. Install the Android SDK and at least one Android platform (see Recipes 1–1 and 1–2). JDK 5 or JDK 6 must also be installed.

2. Install a version of Eclipse that's compatible with the Android SDK and the Android Development Tools (ADT) Plugin for the Eclipse IDE.

3. Install the ADT Plugin.

You should complete these tasks in the order presented. You cannot install the ADT Plugin before installing Eclipse, and you cannot configure or use the ADT Plugin before installing the Android SDK and at least one Android platform.

THE BENEFICIAL ADT PLUGIN

Although you can develop Android apps in Eclipse without using the ADT Plugin, it's much faster and easier to create, debug, and otherwise develop these apps with this plugin.

The ADT Plugin offers the following features:

- It gives you access to other Android development tools from inside the Eclipse IDE. For example, ADT lets you access the many capabilities of the Dalvik Debug Monitor Server (DDMS) tool, allowing you to take screenshots, manage port-forwarding, set breakpoints, and view thread and process information directly from Eclipse.

- It provides a New Project Wizard, which helps you quickly create and setup all of the basic files you'll need for a new Android app.

- It automates and simplifies the process of building your Android app.

- It provides an Android code editor that helps you write valid XML for your Android manifest and resource files.

- It lets you export your project into a signed APK, which can be distributed to users.

You'll learn how to install the ADT Plugin after learning how to install Eclipse.

The Eclipse.org website makes available for download several IDE packages that meet different requirements. Google places several stipulations and recommendations on which IDE package you should download and install:

- Install an Eclipse 3.4 (Ganymede) or greater IDE package.

- Make sure that the Eclipse package being downloaded includes the Eclipse JDT (Java Development Tools) Plugin. Most packages include this plugin.

- You should install one of the Eclipse Classic (versions 3.5.1 and higher), Eclipse IDE for Java Developers, or Eclipse IDE for Java EE Developers packages.

Complete the following steps to install Eclipse Classic 3.6.1:

1. Point your browser to the Eclipse Classic 3.6.1 page at
   `www.eclipse.org/downloads/packages/eclipse-classic-361/heliossr1`.

2. Select the appropriate distribution file by clicking one of the links in the
   Download Links box on the right side of this page. For example, you
   might click Windows 32-bit platform.

3. Click a download link and save the distribution file to your harddrive. For
   example, you might save `eclipse-SDK-3.6.1-win32.zip` to your
   harddrive.

4. Unarchive the distribution file and move the `eclipse` home directory to a
   convenient location. For example, you might move `eclipse` to your
   `C:\Program Files` directory.

5. You might also want to create a desktop shortcut to the `eclipse`
   application located in the `eclipse` home directory.

Complete the following steps to install the latest revision of the ADT Plugin:

1. Start Eclipse.

2. The first time you start Eclipse, you will discover a *Workspace Launcher*
   dialog box following the splash screen. You can use this dialog box to
   select a workspace folder in which to store your projects. You can also
   tell Eclipse to not display this dialog box on subsequent startups.
   Change or keep the default folder setting and click OK.

3. Once Eclipse displays its main window, select Install New Software from
   the Help menu.

4. Click the Add button on the resulting *Install* dialog box's Available
   Software pane.

5. On the resulting *Add Repository* dialog box, enter a name for the remote
   site (for example, **Android Plugin**) in the Name field, and enter
   https://dl-ssl.google.com/android/eclipse/ into the Location field.
   Click OK.

6. You should now see Developer Tools in the list that appears in the
   middle of the *Install* dialog box.

7. Check the checkbox next to Developer Tools, which will automatically
   check the nested Android DDMS, Android Development Tools, and
   Android Hierarchy Viewer checkboxes. Click Next.

8. The resulting Install Details pane lists Android DDMS, Android Development Tools, and Android Hierarchy Viewer. Click Next to read and accept the license agreement and install any dependencies, and then click Finish.

9. An *Installing Software* dialog box appears and takes care of installation. If you encounter a *Security Warning* dialog box, click OK.

10. Finally, Eclipse presents a *Software Updates* dialog box that prompts you to restart this IDE. Click the Restart Now button to restart.

> **TIP:** If you have trouble acquiring the plugin in Step 5, try specifying http instead of https (https is preferred for security reasons) in the Location field.

To complete the installation of the ADT Plugin, you must configure this plugin by modifying the ADT preferences in Eclipse to point to the Android SDK home directory. Accomplish this task by completing the following steps:

1. Select Preferences from the Window menu to open the Preferences panel. For Mac OS X, select Preferences from the Eclipse menu.

2. Select Android from the left panel.

3. Click the Browse button beside the SDK Location textfield and locate your downloaded SDK's home directory (such as C:\android-sdk-windows, for example).

4. Click Apply followed by OK.

> **NOTE:** For more information on installing the ADT Plugin, along with helpful information in case of difficulty, please review the ADT Plugin for Eclipse page (http://developer.android.com/sdk/eclipse-adt.html) in Google's online *Android Developer's Guide*.

1–10. Developing UC with Eclipse

Problem

Now that you've installed Eclipse Classic 3.6.1 and the ADT Plugin, you want to learn how to use this IDE/Plugin to develop UC.

Solution

You first need to create an Android Eclipse project named UC. You then introduce various source files and drag resources to various directories. Finally, you execute UC by selecting Run from the menubar.

How It Works

The first task in developing UC with Eclipse is to create a new Android project. Complete the following steps to create this project:

1. Start Eclipse if not running.

2. Select New from the File menu, and select Project from the resulting popup menu.

3. On the *New Project* dialog box, expand the Android node in the wizard tree, select the Android Project branch below this node, and click the Next button.

4. On the resulting *New Android Project* dialog box, enter UC into the Project name textfield. This entered name identifies the folder in which the UC project is stored.

5. Select the Create new project in workspace radio button if not selected.

6. Under Build Target, select the checkbox of the appropriate Android target to be used as UC's build target. This target specifies which Android platform you'd like your application to be built against. Assuming that you've installed only the Android 2.3 platform, only this build target should appear and should already be checked.

7. Under Properties, enter **Units Converter** into the Application name textfield. This human-readable title will appear on the Android device. Continuing, enter **com.apress.uc** into the Package name textfield. This value is the package namespace (following the same rules as for packages in the Java programming language) where all your source code will reside. Check the Create Activity checkbox if not checked and enter UC as the name of the app's starting activity in the textfield that appears beside this checkbox. The textfield is disabled when this checkbox is not checked. Finally, enter **integer 9** into the Min SDK Version textfield to identify the minimum API Level required to properly run UC on the Android 2.3 platform.

8. Click Finish.

Eclipse responds by creating a UC directory with the following subdirectories and files within your Eclipse workspace directory:

- *.settings*: This directory contains an `org.eclipse.jdt.core.prefs` file that records project-specific settings.

- *assets*: This directory is used to store an unstructured hierarchy of files. Anything stored in this directory can later be retrieved by an app via a raw byte stream.

- *bin*: Your APK file is stored here.

- *gen*: The generated `R.java` file is stored within a subdirectory structure that reflects the package hierarchy (such as `com\apress\uc`).

- *res*: App resources are stored in various subdirectories.

- *src*: App source code is stored according to a package hierarchy.

- *.classpath*: This file stores the project's classpath information so that external libraries on which the project depends can be located.

- *.project*: This file contains important project information such as the kind of project it is, what builders it contains, and what linked resources are attached to the project.

- *AndroidManifest.xml*: This file contains UC's manifest information.

- *default.properties*: This file contains project settings.

- *Proguard.cfg*: This file contains ProGuard configuration data.

Close the Welcome tab. Eclipse presents the user interface that's shown in Figure 1–17.

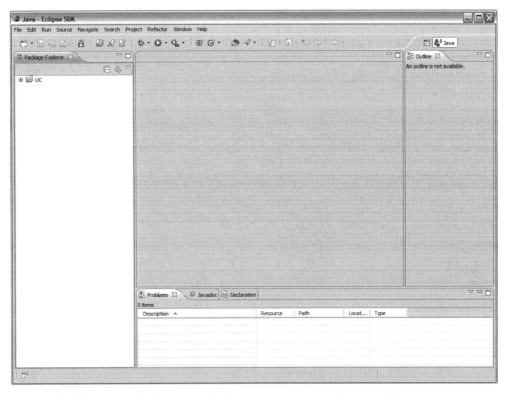

Figure 1–17. *Eclipse's user interface is organized around a menubar, a toolbar, several windows (such as Package Explorer and Outline), a statusbar, and a blank area that's reserved for editor windows.*

This user interface is known as the *workbench*. The Package Explorer window appears on the left and presents an expandable list of nodes that identify the various projects in the current workspace and their components. Figure 1–17 reveals that UC is the only project in the workspace.

To learn how Eclipse organizes the UC project, click the + icon to the left of this node. Figure 1–18 reveals an expanded project hierarchy.

UC
src
ca.mb.javajeff.uc
UC.java
UC
onCreate(Bundle) : void
gen [Generated Java Files]
ca.mb.javajeff.uc
R.java
R
attr
drawable
layout
string
Android 2.3
android.jar
assets
res
drawable-hdpi
drawable-ldpi
drawable-mdpi
icon.png
layout
main.xml
values
strings.xml
AndroidManifest.xml
default.properties
proguard.cfg

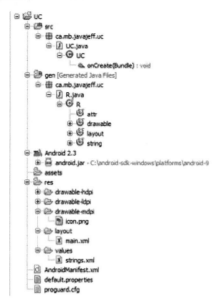

Figure 1–18. *Additional + icons have been clicked to reveal more of UC's file organization.*

Double-click the `UC.java` node. Eclipse responds by presenting the `UC.java` window that's revealed in Figure 1–19.

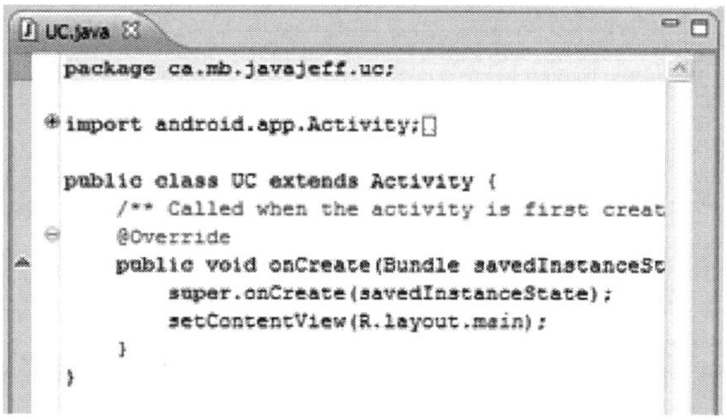

UC.java
package ca.mb.javajeff.uc;
import android.app.Activity;
public class UC extends Activity {
/** Called when the activity is first creat
@Override
public void onCreate(Bundle savedInstanceSt
super.onCreate(savedInstanceState);
setContentView(R.layout.main);
}
}

Figure 1–19. *UC.java reveals skeletal content.*

Replace `UC.java`'s skeletal content with Listing 1–9 and disregard the errors that Eclipse reports. You'll correct these errors later.

Complete the following steps to introduce the necessary resources to this project:

1. Double-click the `main.xml` node. Eclipse presents a main.xml editor window in graphical layout mode.
2. Click the `main.xml` tab below the window to switch to text mode. Replace window content with Listing 1–10.

3. Double-click the `strings.xml` node. Eclipse presents a `strings.xml` editor window in resources mode.

4. Click the strings.xml tab below the window to switch to text mode. Replace window content with Listing 1–12.

5. Right-click the values node and select New followed by Other from the popup menus. A *New* dialog box appears.

6. Expand the XML node in the wizards list, select XML File, and click Next. On the next pane, replace `NewFile.xml` with `arrays.xml` in the File Name field; click Finish.

7. Eclipse presents an arrays.xml editor window in design mode. Click the Source tab below the window to switch to text mode. Replace window content with Listing 1–13.

8. Right-click the `drawable-mdpi` node and select New followed by Other from the popup menus. A *New* dialog box appears.

9. Expand the XML node in the wizards list, select XML File, and click Next. On the next pane, replace `NewFile.xml` with `gradientbg.xml` in the File Name field; click Finish.

10. Eclipse presents a `gradientbg.xml` editor window in design mode. Click the Source tab below the window to switch to text mode. Replace window content with Listing 1–11.

11. Right-click the `icon.png` node underneath `drawable-mdpi`. Select Delete from the popup menu and delete this node.

12. Copy the `icon.png` file from this chapter's section in this book's code archive to the clipboard. Right-click `drawable-mdpi` and select Paste from the popup menu.

Select Run from the menubar, and select Run from the resulting dropdown menu. On the resulting *Run As* dialog box, select Android Application and click OK.

If all goes well, Eclipse launches the `emulator` tool with the `test_AVD` device, installs the UC app, and causes this app to start running (see Figure 1–13).

NOTE: Eclipse provides much more support for Android app development than can be covered in this recipe. For example, if you need to debug a failing Android app, you can start the Dalvik Debug Monitor Service by selecting Open Perspective from the Window menu, followed by Other from the popup menu, followed by DDMS from the *Open Perspective* dialog box. To learn about DDMS, check out J Beer's "How-to use Dalvik Debug Monitor Service (DDMS) Tool With Google Android" tutorial (www.brighthub.com/mobile/google-android/articles/25023.aspx) and James Sugrue's "Debugging Android: Using DDMS To Look Under The Hood" tutorial (http://java.dzone.com/articles/debugging-android-using-ddms).

For additional insight into developing Android apps via Eclipse/ADT Plugin, check out Lars Vogel's "Android Development Tutorial – Gingerbread" tutorial (www.vogella.de/articles/Android/article.html).

Summary

Android has excited many people who are developing (and even selling) apps for this platform. It's not too late to join in the fun, and this chapter showed you how by taking you on a rapid tour of key Android concepts and development tools.

You first learned that Android is a software stack for mobile devices, and that this stack consists of apps, middleware, and the Linux operating system. You then learned about Android's history, including the various SDK updates that have been made available.

You next encountered Android's layered architecture, which includes apps at the top; an application framework, C/C++ libraries, and the Dalvik virtual machine as middleware; and a modified version of the Linux kernel at the bottom.

Continuing, you encountered app architecture, which is based upon components (activities, services, broadcast receivers, and content providers) that communicate with each other by using intents, that are described by a manifest, and that are stored in an app package.

You then learned how to implement activities by subclassing the android.app.Activity class, services by subclassing the abstract android.app.Service class, broadcast receivers by subclassing the abstract android.content.BroadcastReceiver class, and content providers by subclassing the abstract android.content.ContentProvider class.

At this point, Chapter 1 moved away from this essential theory and focused on practical matters via a series of recipes. Initial recipes focused on installing the Android SDK and an Android platform, creating an AVD, and starting the emulator with this AVD.

The next batch of recipes introduced you to a sample Units Converter app. They also showed you how to create this app, install it on the emulator, run it from the emulator, and how to prepare a release version for publication to Google's Android Market.

Working with command-line tools in a command-line environment can be tedious. For this reason, the final two recipes focused on migrating to the Eclipse IDE, and showed you how to develop Units Converter in the context of this graphical environment.

While exploring the Units Converter app, you were introduced to some user interface concepts. Chapter 2 builds upon these concepts by presenting recipes that focus on various Android user interface technologies.

User Interface Recipes

The Android platform is designed to operate on a variety of different device types, screen sizes, and screen resolutions. To assist developers in meeting this challenge, Android provides a rich toolkit of user interface components to utilize and customize to the needs of their specific application. Android also relies very heavily on an extensible XML framework and set resource qualifiers to create liquid layouts that can adapt to these environmental changes. In this chapter, we take a look at some practical ways to shape this framework to fit your specific development needs.

2–1. Customizing the Window

Problem

The default window elements are not satisfactory for your application.

Solution

(API Level 1)

Customize the window attributes and features using themes and the `WindowManager`. Without any customization, an Activity in an Android application will load with the default system theme, looking something like Figure 2–1.

The window color will be black, with a title bar (often grey) at the top of the Activity. The status bar is visible above everything, with a slight shadow effect underneath it. These are all customizable aspects of the application that are controlled by the Window, and can be set for the entire application or for specific Activities.

Figure 2–1. *A bare-bones Activity*

How It Works

Customize Window Attributes with a Theme

A Theme in Android is a type of appearance style that is applicable to an entire application or Activity. There are two choices when applying a theme: use a system theme or create a custom one. In either case, a theme is applied in the AndroidManifest.xml file as shown in Listing 2–1.

Listing 2–1. *AndroidManifest.xml*

```xml
<?xml version="1.0" encoding="utf-8"?>
<manifest xmlns:android="http://schemas.android.com/apk/res/android"
    …>
    <!-Apply to the application tag for a global theme -->
    <application android:theme="THEME_NAME"
        …>
        <!-Apply to the activity tag for an individual theme -->
        <activity android:name=".Activity" android:theme="THEME_NAME"
            …>
            <intent-filter>
                …
            </intent-filter>
        </activity>
    </application>
</manifest>
```

System Themes

The styles.xml packaged with the Android framework includes a few options for themes with some useful custom properties set. Referencing R.style in the SDK documentation will provide the full list, but here are a few useful examples:

- Theme.NoTitleBar: Remove the title bar from components with this theme applied.

- Theme.NoTitleBar.Fullscreen: Remove the title bar and status bar, filling the entire screen.

- Theme.Dialog: A useful theme to make an Activity look like a dialog.

- Theme.Wallpaper **(API Level 5):** Apply the user's wallpaper choice as the window background.

Listing 2–2 is an example of a system theme applied to the entire application by setting the android:theme attribute in the AndroidManifest.xml file:

Listing 2–2. *Manifest with Theme Set on Application*

```
<?xml version="1.0" encoding="utf-8"?>
<manifest xmlns:android="http://schemas.android.com/apk/res/android"
    …>
    <!–Apply to the application tag for a global theme -->
    <application android:theme="Theme.NoTitleBar"
        …>
        …
    </application>
</manifest>
```

Custom Themes

Sometimes the provided system choices aren't enough. After all, some of the customizable elements in the window are not even addressed in the system options. Defining a custom theme to do the job is simple.

If there is not one already, create a styles.xml file in the res/values path of the project. Remember, themes are just styles applied on a wider scale, so they are defined in the same place. Theme aspects related to window customization can be found in the R.attr reference of the SDK, but here are the most common items:

- android:windowNoTitle
  - Governs whether to remove the default title bar.
  - Set to true to remove the title bar.
- android:windowFullscreen
  - Governs whether to remove the system status bar.
  - Set to true to remove the status bar and fill the entire screen.
- android:windowBackground

- ■ Color or drawable resource to apply as a background

- ■ Set to color or drawable value or resource

- ■ android:windowContentOverlay

  - ■ Drawable placed over the window content foreground. By default, this is a shadow below the status bar.

  - ■ Set to any resource to use in place of the default status bar shadow, or null (@null in XML) to remove it.

- ■ android:windowTitleBackgroundStyle

  - ■ Style to apply to the window's title view

  - ■ Set to any style resource.

- ■ android:windowTitleSize

  - ■ Height of the window's title view

  - ■ Set to any dimension or dimension resource

- ■ android:windowTitleStyle

  - ■ Style to apply to the window's title text

  - ■ Set to any style resource

Listing 2–3 is an example of a styles.xml file that creates two custom themes:

- ■ MyTheme.One: No title bar and the default status bar shadow removed

- ■ MyTheme.Two: Fullscreen with a custom background image

Listing 2–3. *res/values/styles.xml with Two Custom Themes*

```
<?xml version="1.0" encoding="utf-8"?>
<resources>
    <style name="MyTheme.One" parent="@android:style/Theme">
        <item name="android:windowNoTitle">true</item>
        <item name="android:windowContentOverlay">@null</item>
    </style>
    <style name="MyTheme.Two" parent="@android:style/Theme">
        <item name="android:windowBackground">@drawable/window_bg</item>
        <item name="android:windowFullscreen">true</item>
    </style>
</resources>
```

Notice that a theme (or style) may also indicate a parent from which to inherit properties, so the entire theme need not be created from scratch. In the example, we chose to inherit from Android's default system theme, customizing only the properties that we needed to differentiate. All platform themes are defined in res/values/themes.xml of the Android package. Refer to the SDK documentation on styles and themes for more details.

Listing 2–4 shows how to apply these themes to individual Activity instances in the AndroidManifest.xml:

Listing 2–4. *Manifest with Themes Set on Each Activity*

```xml
<?xml version="1.0" encoding="utf-8"?>
<manifest xmlns:android="http://schemas.android.com/apk/res/android"
    ...>
    <!-Apply to the application tag for a global theme -->
    <application
        ...>
        <!-Apply to the activity tag for an individual theme -->
        <activity android:name=".ActivityOne" android:theme="MyTheme.One"
            ...>
            <intent-filter>
                ...
            </intent-filter>
        </activity>
        <activity android:name=".ActivityTwo" android:theme="MyTheme.Two"
            ...>
            <intent-filter>
                ...
            </intent-filter>
        </activity>

    </application>
</manifest>
```

Customizing Window Features in Code

In addition to using style XML, window properties may also be customized from the Java code in an Activity. This method opens up a slightly different feature set to the developer for customization, although there is some overlap with the XML styling.

Customizing the window through code involves making requests of the system using the `Activity.requestWindowFeature()` method for each feature change prior to setting the content view for the Activity.

> **NOTE:** All requests for extended window features with
> `Activity.requestWindowFeature()` must be made PRIOR to calling
> `Activity.setContentView()`. Any changes made after this point will not take place.

The features you can request from the window, and their meanings, are defined in the following:

■ `FEATURE_CUSTOM_TITLE`: Set a custom layout resource as the Activity title view.

■ `FEATURE_NO_TITLE`: Remove the title view from Activity.

■ `FEATURE_PROGRESS`: Utilize a determinate (0–100%) progress bar in the title.

- FEATURE_INDETERMINATE_PROGRESS: Utilize a small indeterminate (circular) progress indicator in the title view.

- FEATURE_LEFT_ICON: Include a small title icon on the left side of the title view.

- FEATURE_RIGHT_ICON: Include a small title icon on the right side of the title view.

FEATURE_CUSTOM_TITLE

Use this window feature to replace the standard title with a completely custom layout resource (see Listing 2–5).

Listing 2–5. *Activity Setting a Custom TitleLlayout*

```
protected void onCreate(Bundle savedInstanceState) {
    super.onCreate(savedInstanceState);
    //Request window features before setContentView
    requestWindowFeature(Window.FEATURE_CUSTOM_TITLE);
    setContentView(R.layout.main);

    //Set the layout resource to use for the custom title
    getWindow().setFeatureInt(Window.FEATURE_CUSTOM_TITLE, R.layout.custom_title);

}
```

NOTE: Because this feature completely replaces the default title view, it cannot be combined with any of the other window feature flags.

FEATURE_NO_TITLE

Use this window feature to remove the standard title view (see Listing 2–6).

Listing 2–6. *Activity Removing the Standard Title View*

```
protected void onCreate(Bundle savedInstanceState) {
    super.onCreate(savedInstanceState);
    //Request window features before setContentView
    requestWindowFeature(Window.FEATURE_NO_TITLE);
    setContentView(R.layout.main);

}
```

NOTE: Because this feature completely removes the default title view, it cannot be combined with any of the other window feature flags.

FEATURE_PROGRESS

Use this window feature to access a determinate progress bar in the window title. The progress can be set to any value from 0 (0%) to 10000 (100%) (see Listing 2–7.)

Listing 2–7. *Activity Using Window's Progress Bar*

```
protected void onCreate(Bundle savedInstanceState) {
    super.onCreate(savedInstanceState);
    //Request window features before setContentView
    requestWindowFeature(Window.FEATURE_PROGRESS);
    setContentView(R.layout.main);

    //Set the progress bar visibility
    setProgressBarVisibility(true);
    //Control progress value with setProgress
    setProgress(0);
    //Setting progress to 100% will cause it to disappear
    setProgress(10000);

}
```

FEATURE_INDETERMINATE_PROGRESS

Use this window feature to access an indeterminate progress indicator to show background activity. Since this indicator is indeterminate, it can only be shown or hidden (see Listing 2–8).

Listing 2–8. *Activity Using Window's Indeterminate Progress Bar*

```
protected void onCreate(Bundle savedInstanceState) {
    super.onCreate(savedInstanceState);
    //Request window features before setContentView
    requestWindowFeature(Window.FEATURE_INDETERMINATE_PROGRESS);
    setContentView(R.layout.main);

    //Show the progress indicator
    setProgressBarIndeterminateVisibility(true);

    //Hide the progress indicator
 setProgressBarIndeterminateVisibility(false);
}
```

FEATURE_LEFT_ICON

Use this window feature to place a small drawable icon on the left side of the title view (see Listing 2–9).

Listing 2–9. *Activity Using Feature Icon*

```
protected void onCreate(Bundle savedInstanceState) {
    super.onCreate(savedInstanceState);
    //Request window features before setContentView
    requestWindowFeature(Window.FEATURE_LEFT_ICON);
    setContentView(R.layout.main);

    //Set the layout resource to use for the custom title
```

```
    setFeatureDrawableResource(Window.FEATURE_LEFT_ICON, R.drawable.icon);
}
```

FEATURE_RIGHT_ICON

Use this window feature to place a right-aligned small drawable icon (see Listing 2–10).

Listing 2–10. *Activity Using Feature Icon*

```
protected void onCreate(Bundle savedInstanceState) {
    super.onCreate(savedInstanceState);
    //Request window features before setContentView
    requestWindowFeature(Window.FEATURE_RIGHT_ICON);
    setContentView(R.layout.main);

    //Set the layout resource to use for the custom title
    setFeatureDrawableResource(Window.FEATURE_RIGHT_ICON, R.drawable.icon);
}
```

NOTE: FEATURE_RIGHT_ICON does NOT necessarily mean the icon will be placed on the right side of the title text.

Figure 2–2 shows an Activity with all the icon and progress features enabled simultaneously. Note the locations of all the elements relative to each other in this view.

Figure 2–2. *Window features enabled in a pre-Froyo Activity (left) and an Activity from Froyo and later (right)*

Notice that in API Levels prior to 8 (Froyo), the layout of the RIGHT feature icon was still on the left-hand side of the title text. API Levels 8 and higher corrected this issue, and now display the icon on the right side of the view, although still to the left of the indeterminate progress indicator, if it is visible.

2–2. Creating and Displaying Views

Problem

The application needs view elements to display information and interact with the user.

Solution

(API Level 1)

Whether using one of the many views and widgets available in the Android SDK or creating a custom display, all applications need views to interact with the user. The preferred method for creating user interfaces in Android is to define them in XML and inflate them at runtime.

The view structure in Android is a tree, with the root typically being the Activity or Window's content view. ViewGroups are special views that manage the display of one or more child views, of which could be another ViewGroup, and the tree continues to grow. All the standard layout classes descend from ViewGroup, and are the most common choices for the root node of the XML layout file.

How It Works

Let's define a layout with two Button instances, and an EditText to accept user input. We can define a file in res/layout/ called main.xml with the following contents (see Listing 2–11).

Listing 2–11. *res/layout/main.xml*

```xml
<LinearLayout xmlns:android="http://schemas.android.com/apk/res/android"
    android:layout_width="fill_parent"
    android:layout_height="fill_parent"
    android:orientation="vertical">
  <EditText
    android:id="@+id/editText"
    android:layout_width="fill_parent"
    android:layout_height="wrap_content"
  />
  <LinearLayout
    android:layout_width="fill_parent"
    android:layout_height="wrap_content"
    android:orientation="horizontal">
    <Button
      android:id="@+id/save"
      android:layout_width="wrap_content"
```

```
      android:layout_height="wrap_content"
      android:text="Save"
    />
    <Button
      android:id="@+id/cancel"
      android:layout_width="wrap_content"
      android:layout_height="wrap_content"
      android:text="Cancel"
    />
  </LinearLayout>
</LinearLayout>
```

LinearLayout is a ViewGroup that lays out its elements one after the other in either a horizontal or vertical fashion. In main.xml, the EditText and inner LinearLayout are laid out vertically in order. The contents of the inner LinearLayout (the buttons) are laid out horizontally. The view elements with an android:id value are elements that will need to be referenced in the Java code for further customization or display.

To make this layout the display contents of an Activity, it must be inflated at runtime. The Activity.setContentView() method is overloaded with a convenience method to do this for you, only requiring the layout ID value. In this case, setting the layout in the Activity is as simple as this:

```
public void onCreate(Bundle savedInstanceState) {
    super.onCreate(savedInstanceState);
    setContentView(R.layout.main);
    //Continue Activity initialization
}
```

Nothing beyond supplying the ID value (main.xml automatically has an ID of R.layout.main) is required. If the layout needs a little more customization before it is attached to the window, you can inflate it manually and do some work before adding it as the content view. Listing 2–12 inflates the same layout and adds a third button before displaying it.

Listing 2–12. *Layout Modification Prior to Display*

```
public void onCreate(Bundle savedInstanceState) {
    super.onCreate(savedInstanceState);
    //Inflate the layout file
    LinearLayout layout = (LinearLayout)getLayoutInflater().inflate(R.layout.main,
null);
    //Add a new button
    Button reset = new Button(this);
    reset.setText("Reset Form");
    layout.addView(reset,
        new LinearLayout.LayoutParams(LayoutParams.FILL_PARENT,
LayoutParams.WRAP_CONTENT));

    //Attach the view to the window
    setContentView(layout);
}
```

In this instance the XML layout is inflated in the Activity code using a LayoutInflater, whose inflate() method returns a handle to the inflated View. Since

LayoutInflater.inflate() returns a View, we must cast it to the specific subclass in the XML in order to do more than just attach it to the window.

> **NOTE:** The root element in the XML layout file is the View element returned from
> LayoutInflater.inflate().

2–3. Monitoring Click Actions

Problem

The Application needs to do some work when the user taps on a View.

Solution

(API Level 1)

Ensure that the view object is clickable, and attach a View.OnClickListener to handle the event. By default, many widgets in the SDK are already clickable, such as Button, ImageButton, and CheckBox. However, any View can be made to receive click events by setting android:clickable="true" in XML or by calling View.setClickable(true) from code.

How It Works

To receive and handle the click events, create an OnClickListener and attach it to the view object. In this example, the view is a button defined in the root layout like so:

```
<Button
    android:id="@+id/myButton"
    android:layout_width="wrap_content"
    android:layout_height="wrap_content"
    android:text="My Button"
/>
```

In the Activity code, the button is retrieved by its android:id value and the listener attached (see Listing 2–13).

Listing 2–13. *Setting Listener on a Button*

```
public void onCreate(Bundle savedInstanceState) {
    super.onCreate(savedInstanceState);
    //Retrieve the button object
    Button myButton = (Button)findViewById(R.id.myButton);
    //Attach the listener
    myButton.setOnClickListener(clickListener);
}

//Listener object to handle the click events
View.OnClickListener clickListener = new View.OnClickListener() {
```

```
public void onClick(View v) {
    //Code to handle the click event
    {
};
```

(API Level 4)

Starting with API Level 4, there is a more efficient way to attach basic click listeners to view widgets. View widgets can set the android:onClick attribute in XML, and the runtime will user Java Reflection to call the required method when events occur. If we modify the previous example to use this method, the button's XML will become the following:

```
<Button
  android:layout_width="wrap_content"
  android:layout_height="wrap_content"
  android:text="My Button"
  android:onClick="onMyButtonClick"
/>
```

The android:id attribute is no longer required in this example since the only reason we referenced it in code was to add the listener. This simplifies the Java code as well to look like Listing 2–14.

Listing 2–14. *Listener Attached in XML*

```
public void onCreate(Bundle savedInstanceState) {
    super.onCreate(savedInstanceState);
    //No code required here to attach the listener
}

public void onMyButtonClick(View v) {
    //Code to handle the click event
}
```

2–4. Resolution-Independent Assets

Problem

Your application uses graphic assets that do not scale well using Android's traditional mechanism for scaling images up on higher resolution screens.

Solution

(API Level 4)

Use resource qualifiers and supply multiple sizes of each asset. The Android SDK has defined four types of screen resolutions, or densities, listed here:

- Low (ldpi): 120dpi
- Medium (mdpi): 160dpi

- High (hdpi): 240dpi

- Extra High (xhdpi): 320dpi (Added in **API Level 8**)

By default, an Android project may only have one `res/drawable/` directory where all graphic assets are stored. In this case, Android will take those images to be 1:1 in size on medium resolution screens. When the application is run on a higher resolution screen, Android will scale up the image to 150% (200% for xhdpi), which can result in loss of quality.

How It Works

To avoid this issue, it is recommended that you provide multiple copies of each image resource at different resolutions and place them into resource qualified directory paths.

- `res/drawable-ldpi/`

  - 75% of the size at mdpi

- `res/drawable-mdpi/`

  - Noted as the original image size

- `res/drawable-hdpi/`

  - 150% of the size at mdpi

- `res/drawable-xhdpi/`

  - 200% of the size at mdpi

  - Only if application supports API Level 8 as the minimum target

The image must have the same file name in all directories. For example, if you had left the default icon value in AndroidManifest.xml (i.e. `android:icon="@drawable/icon"`), then you would place the following resource files in the project.

`res/drawable-ldpi/icon.png` (36x36 pixels)

`res/drawable-mdpi/icon.png` (48x48 pixels)

`res/drawable-hdpi/icon.png` (72x72 pixels)

`res/drawable-xhdpi/icon.png` (96x96 pixels, if supported)

Android will select the asset that fits the device resolution and display it as the application icon on the Launcher screen, resulting in no scaling and no loss of image quality.

As another example, a logo image is to be displayed several places throughout an application, and is 200x200 pixels on a medium-resolution device. That image should be provided in all supported sizes using resource qualifiers.

`res/drawable-ldpi/logo.png` (150x150 pixels)

`res/drawable-mdpi/logo.png` (200x200 pixels)

`res/drawable-hdpi/logo.png` (300x300 pixels)

This application doesn't support extra-high resolution displays, so we only provide three images. When the time comes to reference this resource, simply use `@drawable/logo` (from XML) or `R.drawable.logo` (from Java code), and Android will display the appropriate resource.

2–5. Locking Activity Orientation

Problem

A certain Activity in your application should not be allowed to rotate, or rotation requires more direct intervention from the application code.

Solution

(API Level 1)

Using static declarations in the AndroidManifest.xml file, each individual Activity can be modified to lock into either portrait or landscape orientation. This can only be applied to the `<activity>` tag, so it cannot be done once for the entire application scope. Simply add `android:screenOrientation="portrait"` or `android:screenOrientation="landscape"` to the `<activity>` element and they will always display in the specified orientation, regardless of how the device is positioned.

There is also an option you can pass in the XML entitled "behind." If an Activity element has `android:screenOrientation="behind"` set, it will take it's settings from the previous Activity in the stack. This can be a useful way for an Activity to match the locked orientation of its originator for some slightly more dynamic behavior.

How It Works

The example AndroidManifest.xml depicted in Listing 2–15 has three Activities. Two of them are locked into portrait orientation (MainActivity and ResultActivity), while the UserEntryActivity is allowed to rotate, presumably because the user may want to rotate and use a physical keyboard.

Listing 2–15. *Manifest with Some Activities Locked in Portrait*

```
<?xml version="1.0" encoding="utf-8"?>
<manifest xmlns:android="http://schemas.android.com/apk/res/android"
    package="com.examples.rotation"
    android:versionCode="1"
    android:versionName="1.0">
  <application android:icon="@drawable/icon" android:label="@string/app_name">
    <activity android:name=".MainActivity"
        android:label="@string/app_name"
        android:screenOrientation="portrait">
        <intent-filter>
```

```
                <action android:name="android.intent.action.MAIN" />
                <category android:name="android.intent.category.LAUNCHER" />
            </intent-filter>
        </activity>
        <activity android:name=".ResultActivity"
            android:screenOrientation="portrait" />
        <activity android:name=".UserEntryActivity" />
    </application>
</manifest>
```

2–6. Dynamic Orientation Locking

Problem

Conditions exist during which the screen should not rotate, but the condition is temporary, or dependant on user wishes.

Solution

(API Level 1)

Using the requested orientation mechanism in Android, an application can adjust the screen orientation used to display the Activity, fixing it to a specific orientation or releasing it to the device to decide. This is accomplished through the use of the `Activity.setRequestedOrientation()` method, which takes an integer constant from the `ActivityInfo.screenOrientation` attribute grouping.

By default, the requested orientation is set to `SCREEN_ORIENTATION_UNSPECIFIED`, which allows the device to decide for itself which orientation should be used. This is a decision typically based on the physical orientation of the device. The current requested orientation can be retrieved at any time as well using `Activity.getRequestedOrientation()`.

How It Works

User Rotation Lock Button

As an example of this, let's create a ToggleButton instance that controls whether or not to lock the current orientation, allowing the user to control at any point whether or not the Activity should change orientation.

Somewhere in the main.xml layout, a ToggleButton instance is defined:

```
<ToggleButton
    android:id="@+id/toggleButton"
    android:layout_width="wrap_content"
    android:layout_height="wrap_content"
    android:textOff="Lock"
    android:textOn="LOCKED"
/>
```

In the Activity code, we will create a listener to the button's state that locks and releases the screen orientation based on its current value (see Listing 2–16).

Listing 2–16. *Activity to Dynamically Lock/Unlock Screen Orientation*

```java
public class LockActivity extends Activity {

    protected void onCreate(Bundle savedInstanceState) {
        super.onCreate(savedInstanceState);
        setContentView(R.layout.main);

        //Get handle to the button resource
        ToggleButton toggle = (ToggleButton)findViewById(R.id.toggleButton);
        //Set the default state before adding the listener
        if( getRequestedOrientation() != ActivityInfo.SCREEN_ORIENTATION_UNSPECIFIED ) {
            toggle.setChecked(true);
        } else {
            toggle.setChecked(false);
        }
        //Attach the listener to the button
        toggle.setOnCheckedChangeListener(listener);
    }

    OnCheckedChangeListener listener = new OnCheckedChangeListener() {
        public void onCheckedChanged(CompoundButton buttonView, boolean isChecked) {
            int current = getResources().getConfiguration().orientation;
            if(isChecked) {
                switch(current) {
                case Configuration.ORIENTATION_LANDSCAPE:
                    setRequestedOrientation(ActivityInfo.SCREEN_ORIENTATION_LANDSCAPE);
                    break;
                case Configuration.ORIENTATION_PORTRAIT:
                    setRequestedOrientation(ActivityInfo.SCREEN_ORIENTATION_PORTRAIT);
                    break;
                default:
                    setRequestedOrientation(ActivityInfo.SCREEN_ORIENTATION_UNSPECIFIED);
                }
            } else {
                setRequestedOrientation(ActivityInfo.SCREEN_ORIENTATION_UNSPECIFIED);
            }
        }
    }

}
```

The code in the listener is the key ingredient to this recipe. If the user presses the button and it toggles to the ON state, the current orientation is read by storing the `orientation` parameter from `Resources.getConfiguration()`. The Configuration object and the requested orientation use different constants to map the states, so we switch on the current orientation and call `setRequestedOrientation()` with the appropriate constant.

> **NOTE:** If an orientation is requested that is different from the current state, and your Activity is in the foreground, the Activity will change immediately to accommodate the request.

If the user presses the button and it toggles to the OFF state, we no longer want to lock the orientation, so setRequestedOrientation() is called with the SCREEN_ORIENTATION_UNSPECIFIED constant again to return control back to the device. This may also cause an immediate change to occur if the device orientation dictates that the Activity be different than where the application had it locked.

> **NOTE:** Setting a request orientation does *not* keep the default Activity lifecycle from occurring. If a device configuration change occurs (keyboard slides out or device orientation changes), the Activity will still be destroyed and recreated, so all rules about persisting Activity state still apply.

2–7. Manually Handling Rotation

Problem

The default behavior destroying and recreating an Activity during rotation causes an unacceptable performance penalty in the application.

Without customization, Android will respond to configuration changes by finishing the current Activity instance and creating a new one in its place, appropriate for the new configuration. This can cause undue performance penalties since the UI state must be saved, and the UI completely rebuilt.

Solution

(API Level 1)

Utilize the android:configChanges manifest parameter to instruct Android that a certain Activity will handle rotation events without assistance from the runtime. This not only reduces the amount of work required from Android, destroying and recreating the Activity instance, but also from your application. With the Activity instance intact, the application does not have to necessarily spend time to save and restore the current state in order to maintain consistency to the user.

An Activity that registers for one or more configuration changes will be notified via the Activity.onConfigurationChanged() callback method, where it can perform any necessary manual handling associated with the change.

There are two configuration change parameters the Activity should register for in order to handle rotation completely: orientation and keyboardHidden. The orientation parameter registers the Activity for any event when the device orientation changes. The keyboardHidden parameter registers the Activity for the event when the user slides a physical keyboard in or out. While the latter may not be directly of interest, if you do not register for these events Android will recreate your Activity when they occur, which may subvert your efforts in handling rotation in the first place.

How It Works

These parameters are added to any <activity> element in AndroidManifest.xml like so:

```
<activity android:name=".MyActivity" android:configChanges="orientation|keyboardHidden"
/>
```

Multiple changes can be registered in the same assignment statement, using a pipe "|" character between them. Because these parameters cannot be applied to an <application> element, each individual Activity must register in the AndroidManifest.xml.

With the Activity registered, a configuration change results in a call to the Activity's onConfigurationChanged() method. Listing 2–17 is a simple Activity definition that can be used to handle the callback received when the changes occur.

Listing 2–17. *Activity to Manage Rotation Manually*

```java
public class MyActivity extends Activity {

    @Override
    protected void onCreate(Bundle savedInstanceState) {
        //Calling super is required
        super.onCreate(savedInstanceState);
        //Load view resources
        loadView();
    }

    @Override
    public void onConfigurationChanged(Configuration newConfig) {
        //Calling super is required
        super.onConfigurationChanged(newConfig);
        //Store important UI state
        saveState();
        //Reload the view resources
        loadView();
    }

    private void saveState() {
        //Implement any code to persist the UI state
    }

    private void loadView() {
        setContentView(R.layout.main);

        //Handle any other required UI changes upon a new configuration
        //Including restoring and stored state
    }
}
```

NOTE: Google does not recommend handling rotation in this fashion unless it is necessary for the application's performance. All configuration-specific resources must be loaded manually in response to each change event.

It is worth noting that Google recommends allowing the default recreation behavior on Activity rotation unless the performance of your application requires circumventing it. Primarily, this is because you lose all assistance Android provides for loading alternative resources if you have them stored in resource qualified directories (such as res/layout-land/ for landscape layouts).

In the example Activity, all code dealing with the view layout is abstracted to a private method, loadView(), called from both onCreate() and onConfigurationChanged(). In this method, code like setContentView() is placed to ensure that the appropriate layout is loaded to match the configuration.

Calling setContentView() will completely reload the view, so any UI state that is important still needs to be saved, and without the assistance of lifecycle callbacks like onSaveInstanceState() and onRestoreInstanceState(). The example implements a method called saveState() for this purpose.

2–8. Creating Pop-Up Menu Actions

Problem

You want to provide the user with multiple actions to take as a result of them selecting some part of the user interface.

Solution

(API Level 1)

Display a ContextMenu or AlertDialog in response to the user action.

How It Works

ContextMenu

Using a ContextMenu is a useful solution, particularly when you want to provide a list of actions based on an item click in a ListView or other AdapterView. This is because the ContextMenu.ContextMenuInfo object provides useful information about the specific item that was selected, such as id and position, which may be helpful in constructing the menu.

First, create an XML file in res/menu/ to define the menu itself; we'll call this one contextmenu.xml (see Listing 2–18).

Listing 2–18. *res/menu/contextmenu.xml*

```
<?xml version="1.0" encoding="utf-8"?>
<menu xmlns:android="http://schemas.android.com/apk/res/android">
  <item
    android:id="@+id/menu_delete"
```

```
    android:title="Delete Item"
  />
  <item
    android:id="@+id/menu_copy"
    android:title="Copy Item"
  />
  <item
    android:id="@+id/menu_edit"
    android:title="Edit Item"
  />
</menu>
```

Then, utilize onCreateContextMenu() and onContextItemSelected() in the Activity to inflate the menu and handle user selection (see Listing 2–19).

Listing 2–19. *Activity Utilizing Custom Menu*

```
@Override
public void onCreateContextMenu(ContextMenu menu, View v, ContextMenu.ContextMenuInfo
menuInfo) {
    super.onCreateContextMenu(menu, v, menuInfo);
    getMenuInflater().inflate(R.menu.contextmenu, menu);
    menu.setHeaderTitle("Choose an Option");
}

@Override
public boolean onContextItemSelected(MenuItem item) {
    //Switch on the item's ID to find the action the user selected
    switch(item.getItemId()) {
    case R.id.menu_delete:
        //Perform delete actions
        return true;
    case R.id.menu_copy:
        //Perform copy actions
        return true;
    case R.id.menu_edit:
        //Perform edit actions
        return true;
    }
    return super.onContextItemSelected(item);
}
```

In order for these callback methods to fire, you must register the view that will trigger the menu. In effect, this sets the View.OnCreateContextMenuListener for the view to the current Activity:

```
@Override
protected void onCreate(Bundle savedInstanceState) {
    super.onCreate(savedInstanceState);
    //Register a button for context events
    Button button = new Button(this);
    registerForContextMenu(button);

    setContentView(button);
}
```

The key ingredient to this recipe is calling the Activity.openContextMenu() method to manually trigger the menu at any time. The default behavior in Android is for many views to show a ContextMenu when a long-press occurs as an alternate to the main click action. However, in this case we want the menu to be the main action, so we call openContextMenu() from the action listener method:

```
public void onClick(View v) {
    openContextMenu(v);
}
```

Tying all the pieces together, we have a simple Activity that registers a button to show our menu when tapped (see Listing 2–20).

Listing 2–20. *Activity Utilizing Context Action Menu*

```
public class MyActivity extends Activity {

    protected void onCreate(Bundle savedInstanceState) {
        super.onCreate(savedInstanceState);
        //Register a button for context events
        Button button = new Button(this);
        button.setText("Click for Options");
        button.setOnClickListener(listener);
        registerForContextMenu(button);

        setContentView(button);
    }

    View.OnClickListener listener = new View.OnClickListener() {
        public void onClick(View v) {
            openContextMenu(v);
        }
    };

    @Override
    public void onCreateContextMenu(ContextMenu menu, View v,
                ContextMenu.ContextMenuInfo menuInfo) {
        super.onCreateContextMenu(menu, v, menuInfo);
        getMenuInflater().inflate(R.menu.contextmenu, menu);
        menu.setHeaderTitle("Choose an Option");
    }

    @Override
    public boolean onContextItemSelected(MenuItem item) {
        //Switch on the item's ID to find the action the user selected
        switch(item.getItemId()) {
        case R.id.menu_delete:
            //Perform delete actions
            return true;
        case R.id.menu_copy:
            //Perform copy actions
            return true;
        case R.id.menu_edit:
            //Perform edit actions
            return true;
        }
        return super.onContextItemSelected(item);
    }

}
```

The resulting application is shown in Figure 2–3.

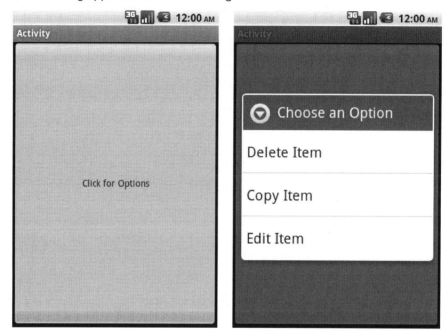

Figure 2–3. *Context action menu*

AlertDialog

Using an `AlertDialog.Builder` a similar AlertDialog can be constructed, but with some additional options. AlertDialog is a very versatile class for creating simple pop-ups to get feedback from the user. With AlertDialog.Builder, a single or multi-choice list, buttons, and a message string can all be easily added into one compact widget.

To illustrate this, let's create the same pop-up selection as before using an AlertDialog. This time, we will add a cancel button to the bottom of the options list (see Listing 2–21).

Listing 2–21. *Action Menu Using AlertDialog*

```
public class MyActivity extends Activity {

    AlertDialog actions;

    @Override
    protected void onCreate(Bundle savedInstanceState) {
        super.onCreate(savedInstanceState);
        setTitle("Activity");
        Button button = new Button(this);
        button.setText("Click for Options");
        button.setOnClickListener(buttonListener);


        AlertDialog.Builder builder = new AlertDialog.Builder(this);
```

```
        builder.setTitle("Choose an Option");
        String[] options = {"Delete Item","Copy Item","Edit Item"};
        builder.setItems(options, actionListener);
        builder.setNegativeButton("Cancel", null);
        actions = builder.create();

        setContentView(button);
    }

    //List selection action handled here
    DialogInterface.OnClickListener actionListener =
            new DialogInterface.OnClickListener() {
        @Override
        public void onClick(DialogInterface dialog, int which) {
            switch(which) {
            case 0: //Delete
                break;
            case 1: //Copy
                break;
            case 2: //Edit
                break;
            default:
                break;
            }
        }
    };

    //Button action handled here (pop up the dialog)
    View.OnClickListener buttonListener = new View.OnClickListener() {
        @Override
        public void onClick(View v) {
            actions.show();
        }
    };
}
```

In this example, we create a new AlertDialog.Builder instance and use its convenience
methods to add:

- A title, using setTitle()

- The selectable list of options, using setItems() with an array of strings
  (also works with array resources)

- A Cancel button, using setNegativeButton()

The listener that we attach to the list items returns which list item was selected as a
zero-based index into the array we supplied, so the switch statement checks for each of
the three cases that apply. We pass in null for the Cancel button's listener, because in
this instance we just want cancel to dismiss the dialog. If there is some important work
to be done on cancel, another listener could be passed in to the setNegativeButton()
method.

The resulting application now looks like Figure 2–4 when the button is pressed.

Figure 2–4. *AlertDialog action menu*

2–9. Customizing Options Menu

Problem

Your application needs to do something beyond displaying a standard menu when the user presses the hardware MENU button.

Solution

(API Level 1)

Intercept the KeyEvent for the menu button and present a custom view instead.

How It Works

Intercepting this event can be done inside of an Activity or View by overriding the onKeyDown() or onKeyUp() method:

```
@Override
public boolean onKeyUp(int keyCode, KeyEvent event) {
    if(keyCode == KeyEvent.KEYCODE_MENU) {
        //Create and display a custom menu view
```

```
        //Return true to consume the event
        return true;
    }
    //Pass other events along their way up the chain
    return super.onKeyUp(keyCode, event);
}
```

> **NOTE:** `Activity.onKeyDown()` and `Activity.onKeyUp()` are only called if none if its child views handle the event first. It is important that you return a true value when consuming these events so they don't get improperly handed up the chain.

The next example illustrates an `Activity` that displays a custom set of buttons wrapped in a simple `AlertDialog` in place of the traditional options menu when the user presses the MENU key. In Listing 2–22, we will create a layout for our buttons in res/layout/ and call it custommenu.xml.

Listing 2–22. *res/layout/custommenu.xml*

```xml
<?xml version="1.0" encoding="utf-8"?>
<LinearLayout xmlns:android="http://schemas.android.com/apk/res/android"
  android:layout_width="fill_parent"
  android:layout_height="wrap_content"
  android:orientation="horizontal">
  <ImageButton
    android:layout_width="fill_parent"
    android:layout_height="wrap_content"
    android:layout_weight="1"
    android:src="@android:drawable/ic_menu_send"
  />
  <ImageButton
    android:layout_width="fill_parent"
    android:layout_height="wrap_content"
    android:layout_weight="1"
    android:src="@android:drawable/ic_menu_save"
  />
  <ImageButton
    android:layout_width="fill_parent"
    android:layout_height="wrap_content"
    android:layout_weight="1"
    android:src="@android:drawable/ic_menu_search"
  />
  <ImageButton
    android:layout_width="fill_parent"
    android:layout_height="wrap_content"
    android:layout_weight="1"
    android:src="@android:drawable/ic_menu_preferences"
  />
</LinearLayout>
```

This is a layout with four buttons of equal weight (so the space evenly across the screen), displaying some of the default menu images in Android. In Listing 2–23, we can inflate this layout and apply it as the view to an `AlertDialog`.

Listing 2–23. *Activity Overriding Menu Action*

```java
public class MyActivity extends Activity {

MenuDialog menuDialog;
private class MenuDialog extends AlertDialog {

    public MenuDialog(Context context) {
        super(context);
        setTitle("Menu");
        View menu = getLayoutInflater().inflate(R.layout.custommenu, null);
        setView(menu);
    }

    @Override
    public boolean onKeyUp(int keyCode, KeyEvent event) {
        if(keyCode == KeyEvent.KEYCODE_MENU) {
            dismiss();
            return true;
        }
        return super.onKeyUp(keyCode, event);
    }
}

@Override
public boolean onKeyUp(int keyCode, KeyEvent event) {
    if(keyCode == KeyEvent.KEYCODE_MENU) {
        if(menuDialog == null) {
            menuDialog = new MenuDialog(this);
        }
        menuDialog.show();
        return true;
    }
    return super.onKeyUp(keyCode, event);
}

}
```

Here we choose to monitor the `Activity.onKeyUp()` method, and handle the event if it was a MENU press by creating and displaying a custom subclass of `AlertDialog`.

This example creates a custom class for the dialog so we can extend the `AlertDialog.onKeyUp()` method to dismiss the custom menu when the user presses the MENU button again. We cannot handle this event in the `Activity`, because the `AlertDialog` consumes all key events while it is in the foreground. We do this so we match the existing functionality of Android's standard menu, and thus don't disrupt the user's expectation of how the application should behave.

When the previous Activity is loaded, and the MENU button pressed, we get something like Figure 2–5.

Figure 2–5. *Custom Options menu*

2–10. Customizing Back Button

Problem

Your application needs to handle the user pressing the hardware BACK button in a custom manner.

Solution

(API Level 1)

Similar to overriding the function of the MENU button, the hardware BACK button sends a KeyEvent to your Activity that can be intercepted and handled in your application code.

How It Works

In the same fashion as Recipe 2–9, overriding onKeyDown() will give you the control:

```
@Override
public boolean onKeyDown(int keyCode, KeyEvent event) {
    if(keyCode == KeyEvent.KEYCODE_BACK) {
        //Implement a custom back function
```

```
        //Return true to consume the event
        return true;
    }
    //Pass other events along their way up the chain
    return super.onKeyDown(keyCode, event);
}
```

> **CAUTION:** Overriding hardware button events should be done with care. All hardware buttons have consistent functionality across the Android system, and adjusting the functionality to work outside these bounds will be confusing and upsetting to users.

Unlike the previous example, you can not reliably use onKeyUp(),because the default behavior (such as finishing the current Activity) occurs when the key is pressed, as opposed to when it is released. For this reason, onKeyUp() will often never get called for the BACK key.

(API Level 5)

Starting with Eclair, the SDK included the `Activity.onBackPressed()` callback method. This method can be overridden to perform custom processing if your application is targeting SDK Level 5 or higher.

```
@Override
public void onBackPressed() {
    //Custom back button processing
    //Must manually finish when complete
    finish();
}
```

The default implementation of this method simply calls `finish()` for you, so if you want the Activity to close after your processing is complete, the implementation will need to call `finish()` directly.

2–11. Emulating the Home Button

Problem

Your application needs to take the same action as if the user pressed the hardware HOME button.

Solution

(API Level 1)

The act of the user hitting the HOME button sends an `Intent` to the system telling it to load the Home Activity. This is no different from starting any other Activity in your application; you just have to construct the proper Intent to get the effect.

How It Works

Add the following lines wherever you want this action to occur in your Activity:

```
Intent intent = new Intent(Intent.ACTION_MAIN);
intent.addCategory(Intent.CATEGORY_HOME);
startActivity(intent);
```

A common use of this function is to override the back button to go home instead of to the previous Activity. This is useful in cases where everything underneath the foreground Activity may be protected (a login screen, for instance), and letting the default back button behavior occur could allow unsecured access to the system. Here is an example of using the two in concert to make a certain Activity bring up the home screen when back is pressed:

```
@Override
public boolean onKeyDown(int keyCode, KeyEvent event) {
    if(keyCode == KeyEvent.KEYCODE_BACK) {
        Intent intent = new Intent(Intent.ACTION_MAIN);
        intent.addCategory(Intent.CATEGORY_HOME);
        startActivity(intent);
        return true;
    }
    return super.onKeyDown(keyCode, event);
}
```

2–12. Monitoring TextView Changes

Problem

Your application needs to continuously monitor for text changes in a TextView widget (like EditText).

Solution

(API Level 1)

Implement the android.text.TextWatcher interface. TextWatcher provides three callback methods during the process of updating text:

```
public void beforeTextChanged(CharSequence s, int start, int count, int after);
public void onTextChanged(CharSequence s, int start, int before, int count);
public void afterTextChanged(Editable s);
```

The beforeTextChanged() and onTextChanged() methods are provided mainly as notifications, as you cannot actually make changes to the CharSequence in either of these methods. If you are attempting to intercept the text entered into the view, changes may be made when afterTextChanged() is called.

How It Works

To register a `TextWatcher` instance with a `TextView`, call the
`TextView.addTextChangedListener()` method. Notice from the syntax that more than
one `TextWatcher` can be registered with a `TextView`.

Character Counter Example

A simple use of TextWatcher is to create a live character counter that follows an EditText
as the user types or deletes information. Listing 2–24 is an example Activity that
implements TextWatcher for this purpose, registers with an EditText widget, and prints
the character count in the Activity title.

Listing 2–24. *Character Counter Activity*

```java
public class MyActivity extends Activity implements TextWatcher {

EditText text;
int textCount;

    @Override
    protected void onCreate(Bundle savedInstanceState) {
        super.onCreate(savedInstanceState);
        //Create an EditText widget and add the watcher
        text = new EditText(this);
        text.addTextChangedListener(this);

        setContentView(text);
    }

    /* TextWatcher Implementation Methods */
    public void beforeTextChanged(CharSequence s, int start, int count, int after) { }

    public void onTextChanged(CharSequence s, int start, int before, int end) {
        textCount = text.getText().length();
        setTitle(String.valueOf(textCount));
    }

    public void afterTextChanged(Editable s) { }

}
```

Because our needs do not include modifying the text being inserted, we can read the
count from onTextChanged(), which happens as soon as the text change occurs. The
other methods are unused and left empty.

Currency Formatter Example

The SDK has a handful of predefined TextWatcher instances to format text input;
PhoneNumberFormattingTextWatcher is one of these. Their job is to apply standard
formatting for the user while they type, reducing the number of keystrokes required to
enter legible data.

In Listing 2–25, we create a CurrencyTextWatcher to insert the currency symbol and separator point into a TextView.

Listing 2–25. *Currency Formatter*

```java
public class CurrencyTextWatcher implements TextWatcher {

    boolean mEditing;

    public CurrencyTextWatcher() {
        mEditing = false;
    }

    public synchronized void afterTextChanged(Editable s) {
        if(!mEditing) {
            mEditing = true;

            //Strip symbols
            String digits = s.toString().replaceAll("\\D", "");
            NumberFormat nf = NumberFormat.getCurrencyInstance();
            try{
                String formatted = nf.format(Double.parseDouble(digits)/100);
                s.replace(0, s.length(), formatted);
            } catch (NumberFormatException nfe) {
                s.clear();
            }

            mEditing = false;
        }
    }

    public void beforeTextChanged(CharSequence s, int start, int count, int after) { }

    public void onTextChanged(CharSequence s, int start, int before, int count) { }

}
```

> **NOTE:** Making changes to the Editable value in afterTextChanged() will cause the TextWatcher methods to be called again (after all, you just changed the text). For this reason, custom TextWatcher implementations that edit should use a boolean or some other tracking mechanism to track where the editing is coming from, or you may create an infinite loop.

We can apply this custom text formatter to an EditText in an Activity (see Listing 2–26).

Listing 2–26. *Activity Using Currency Formatter*

```java
public class MyActivity extends Activity {

    EditText text;

    @Override
    protected void onCreate(Bundle savedInstanceState) {
        super.onCreate(savedInstanceState);
        text = new EditText(this);
        text.addTextChangedListener(new CurrencyTextWatcher());
```

```
        setContentView(text);
    }

}
```

It is very handy if you are formatting user input with this formatter to define the EditText in XML so you can apply the `android:inputType` and `android:digits` constraints to easily protect the field against entry errors. In particular, adding `android:digits="0123456789."` (notice the period at the end for a decimal point) to the EditText will protect this formatter as well as the user.

2–13. Scrolling TextView Ticker

Problem

You want to create a "ticker" view that continuously scrolls its contents across the screen.

Solution

(API Level 1)

Use the built-in marquee feature of `TextView`. When the content of a `TextView` is too large to fit within it bounds, the text is truncated by default. This truncation can be configured using the `android:ellipsize` attribute, which can be set to one of the following options:

- none
  - Default.
  - Truncate the end of the text with no visual indicator.
- start
  - Truncate the start of the text with an ellipsis at the beginning of the view.
- middle
  - Truncate the middle of the text with an ellipsis in the middle of the view.
- end
  - Truncate the end of the text with an ellipsis at the end of the view.
- marquee
  - Do not ellipsize; animate and scroll the text while selected.

> **NOTE:** The marquee feature is designed to only animate and scroll the text when the `TextView` is selected. Setting the `android:ellipsize` attribute to marquee alone will not animate the view.

How It Works

In order to create an automated ticker that repeats indefinitely, we add a TextView to an XML layout that looks like this:

```
<TextView
  android:id="@+id/ticker"
  android:layout_width="fill_parent"
  android:layout_height="wrap_content"
  android:singleLine="true"
  android:scrollHorizontally="true"
  android:ellipsize="marquee"
  android:marqueeRepeatLimit="marquee_forever"
/>
```

The key attributes to configuring this view are the last four. Without `android:singleLine` and `android:scrollHorizontally`, the TextView will not properly lay itself out to allow for the text to be longer than the view (a key requirement for ticker scrolling). Setting the `android:ellipsize` and `android:marqueeRepeatLimit` allow the scrolling to occur, and for an indefinite amount of time. The repeat limit can be set to any integer value as well, which will repeat the scrolling animation that many times and then stop.

With the TextView attributes properly set in XML, the Java code must set the selected state to true, which enables the scrolling animation:

```
TextView ticker = (TextView)findViewById(R.id.ticker);
ticker.setSelected(true);
```

If you need to have the animation start and stop based on certain events in the user interface, just call `setSelected()` each time with either true or false, respectively.

2–14. Animating a View

Problem

Your application needs to animate a view object, either as a transition or for effect.

Solution

(API Level 1)

An `Animation` object can be applied to any view and run using the `View.startAnimation()` method; this will run the animation immediately. You may also use `View.setAnimation()` to schedule an animation and attach the object to a view but not run it immediately. In this case, the `Animation` must have its start time parameter set.

How It Works

System Animations

For convenience, the Android SDK provides a handful of transition animations that you can apply to views, which can be loaded at runtime using the `AnimationUtils` class:

- Slide and Fade In
  - `AnimationUtils.makeInAnimation()`
  - Use the boolean parameter to determine if the slide is left or right.
- Slide Up and Fade In
  - `AnimationUtils.makeInChildBottomAnimation()`
  - View always slides up from the bottom.
- Slide and Fade Out
  - `AnimationUtils.makeOutAnimation()`
  - Use the boolean parameter to determine if the slide is left or right.
- Fade Out
  - `AnimationUtils.loadAnimation()`
  - Set the int parameter to `android.R.anim.fade_out`.
- Fade In
  - `AnimationUtils.loadAnimation()`
  - Set the int parameter to `android.R.anim.fade_in`.

> **NOTE:** These transition animations only temporarily change how the view is drawn. The visibility parameter of the view must also be set if you mean to permanently add or remove the object.

Listing 2–27 animates the appearance and disappearance of a View with each Button click event.

Listing 2–27. *res/layout/main.xml*

```xml
<?xml version="1.0" encoding="utf-8"?>
<LinearLayout xmlns:android="http://schemas.android.com/apk/res/android"
  android:orientation="vertical"
  android:layout_width="fill_parent"
  android:layout_height="fill_parent">
  <Button
    android:id="@+id/toggleButton"
```

```
    android:layout_width="fill_parent"
    android:layout_height="wrap_content"
    android:text="Click to Toggle"
  />
  <View
    android:id="@+id/theView"
    android:layout_width="fill_parent"
    android:layout_height="wrap_content"
    android:background="#AAA"
  />
</LinearLayout>
```

In Listing 2–28 each user action on the Button toggles the visibility of the grey View below it with an animation.

Listing 2–28. *Activity Animating View Transitions*

```java
public class AnimateActivity extends Activity implements View.OnClickListener {

    View viewToAnimate;

    @Override
    public void onCreate(Bundle savedInstanceState) {
        super.onCreate(savedInstanceState);
        setContentView(R.layout.main);

        Button button = (Button)findViewById(R.id.toggleButton);
        button.setOnClickListener(this);

        viewToAnimate = findViewById(R.id.theView);
    }

    @Override
    public void onClick(View v) {
        if(viewToAnimate.getVisibility() == View.VISIBLE) {
            //If the view is visible already, slide it out to the right
            Animation out = AnimationUtils.makeOutAnimation(this, true);
            viewToAnimate.startAnimation(out);
            viewToAnimate.setVisibility(View.INVISIBLE);
        } else {
            //If the view is hidden, do a fade_in in-place
            Animation in = AnimationUtils.loadAnimation(this, android.R.anim.fade_in);
            viewToAnimate.startAnimation(in);
            viewToAnimate.setVisibility(View.VISIBLE);
        }
    }
}
```

The view is hidden by sliding off to the right and fading out simultaneously, whereas the view simple fades into place when it is shown. We chose a simple View as the target here to demonstrate that any UI element (since they all subclass from View) can be animated in this way.

Custom Animations

Creating custom animations to add effect to views by scaling, rotation, and transforming them can provide invaluable additions to a user interface as well. In Android, we can create the following Animation elements:

- AlphaAnimation
    - Animate changes to a view's transparency.
- RotateAnimation
    - Animate changes to a view's rotation.
    - The point about which rotation occurs is configurable. The top, left corner is chosen by default.
- ScaleAnimation
    - Animate changes to a view's scale (size).
    - The center point of the scale change is configurable. The top, left corner is chosen by default.
- TranslateAnimation
    - Animate changes to a view's position.

Let's illustrate how to construct and add a custom animation object by creating a sample application that creates a "coin flip" effect on an image (see Listing 2–30).

Listing 2–29. *res/layout/main.xml*

```xml
<?xml version="1.0" encoding="utf-8"?>
<RelativeLayout xmlns:android="http://schemas.android.com/apk/res/android"
  android:layout_width="fill_parent"
  android:layout_height="fill_parent">
  <ImageView
    android:id="@+id/flip_image"
    android:layout_width="wrap_content"
    android:layout_height="wrap_content"
    android:layout_centerInParent="true"
  />
</RelativeLayout>
```

Listing 2–30. *Activity with Custom Animations*

```java
public class Flipper extends Activity {

    boolean isHeads;
    ScaleAnimation shrink, grow;
    ImageView flipImage;

    @Override
    public void onCreate(Bundle savedInstanceState) {
        super.onCreate(savedInstanceState);
        setContentView(R.layout.main);

        flipImage = (ImageView)findViewById(R.id.flip_image);
```

```java
        flipImage.setImageResource(R.drawable.heads);
        isHeads = true;

        shrink = new ScaleAnimation(1.0f, 0.0f, 1.0f, 1.0f,
                        ScaleAnimation.RELATIVE_TO_SELF, 0.5f,
                        ScaleAnimation.RELATIVE_TO_SELF, 0.5f);
        shrink.setDuration(150);
        shrink.setAnimationListener(new Animation.AnimationListener() {
            @Override
            public void onAnimationStart(Animation animation) {}

            @Override
            public void onAnimationRepeat(Animation animation) {}

            @Override
            public void onAnimationEnd(Animation animation) {
                if(isHeads) {
                    isHeads = false;
                    flipImage.setImageResource(R.drawable.tails);
                } else {
                    isHeads = true;
                    flipImage.setImageResource(R.drawable.heads);
                }
                flipImage.startAnimation(grow);
            }
        });
        grow = new ScaleAnimation(0.0f, 1.0f, 1.0f, 1.0f,
                        ScaleAnimation.RELATIVE_TO_SELF, 0.5f,
                        ScaleAnimation.RELATIVE_TO_SELF, 0.5f);
        grow.setDuration(150);
    }

    @Override
    public boolean onTouchEvent(MotionEvent event) {
        if(event.getAction() == MotionEvent.ACTION_DOWN) {
            flipImage.startAnimation(shrink);
            return true;
        }
        return super.onTouchEvent(event);
    }
}
```

This example includes the following pertinent components:

- Two image resources for the coin's head and tail (we named them heads.png and tails.png).

    - These images may be any two-image resources placed in res/drawable. The ImageView defaults to displaying the heads image.

- Two ScaleAnimation objects

    - Shrink: Reduce the image width from full to nothing about the center.

- Grow: Increase the image width from nothing to full about the center.

- Anonymous AnimationListener to link the two animations in sequence

Custom animation objects can be defined either in XML or in code. In the next section we will look at making the animations as XML resources. Here we created the two ScaleAnimation objects using the following constructor:

```
ScaleAnimation(
  float fromX,
  float toX,
  float fromY,
  float toY,
  int pivotXType,
  float pivotXValue,
  int pivotYType,
  float pibotYValue
)
```

The first four parameters are the horizontal and vertical scaling factors to apply. Notice in the example the X went from 100–0% to shrink and 0–100% to grow, while leaving the Y alone at 100% always.

The remaining parameters define an anchor point for the view while the animation occurs. In this case, we are telling the application to anchor the midpoint of the view, and bring both sides in toward the middle as the view shrinks. The reverse is true for expanding the image: the center stays in place and the image grows outward towards its original edges.

Android does not inherently have a way to link multiple animation objects together in a sequence, so we use an Animation.AnimationListener for this purpose. The listener has methods to notify when an animation begins, repeats, and completes. In this case, we are only interested in the latter so that when the shrink animation is done, we can automatically start the grow animation after it.

The final method used in the example is to setDuration() method to set the animation duration of time. The value supplied here is in milliseconds, so our entire coin flip would take 300ms to complete, 150ms apiece for each ScaleAnimation.

AnimationSet

Many times the custom animation you are searching to create requires a combination of the basic types described previously; this is where AnimationSet becomes useful. AnimationSet defines a group of animations that should be run simultaneously. By default, all animations will be started together, and complete at their respective durations.

In this section we will also expose how to define custom animations using Android's preferred method of XML resources. XML animations should be defined in the res/anim/ folder of a project. The following tags are supported, and all of them can be either the root or child node of an animation:

- ■ `<alpha>`: An AlphaAnimation object

- ■ `<rotate>`: A RotateAnimation object

- ■ `<scale>`: A ScaleAnimation object

- ■ `<translate>`: A TranslateAnimation object

- ■ `<set>`: An AnimationSet

Only the `<set>` tag, however, can be a parent and contain other animation tags.

In this example, let's take our coin flip animations and add another dimension. We will pair each ScaleAnimation with a TranslateAnimation as a set. The desired effect will be for the image to slide up and down the screen as it "flips." To do this, in Listings 2–31 and 2–32 we will define our animations in two XML files and place them in res/anim/. The first will be grow.xml.

Listing 2–31. *res/anim/grow.xml*

```
<?xml version="1.0" encoding="utf-8"?>
<set xmlns:android="http://schemas.android.com/apk/res/android">
  <scale
    android:duration="150"
    android:fromXScale="0.0"
    android:toXScale="1.0"
    android:fromYScale="1.0"
    android:toYScale="1.0"
    android:pivotX="50%"
    android:pivotY="50%"
  />
<translate
    android:duration="150"
    android:fromXDelta="0%"
    android:toXDelta="0%"
    android:fromYDelta="50%"
    android:toYDelta="0%"
  />
</set>
```

Followed by shrink.xml:

Listing 2–32. *res/anim/shrink.xml*

```
<?xml version="1.0" encoding="utf-8"?>
<set xmlns:android="http://schemas.android.com/apk/res/android">
<scale
    android:duration="150"
    android:fromXScale="1.0"
    android:toXScale="0.0"
    android:fromYScale="1.0"
    android:toYScale="1.0"
    android:pivotX="50%"
    android:pivotY="50%"
  />
  <translate
    android:duration="150"
    android:fromXDelta="0%"
    android:toXDelta="0%"
```

```
      android:fromYDelta="0%"
      android:toYDelta="50%"
  />
</set>
```

Defining the scale values isn't any different than previously when using the constructor in code. One thing to make note of, however, is the definition style of units for the pivot parameters. All animation dimensions that can be defined as ABSOLUTE, RELATIVE_TO_SELF, or RELATIVE_TO_PARENT use the following XML syntax:

- ABSOLUTE: Use a float value to represent an actual pixel value (e.g., "5.0").

- RELATIVE_TO_SELF: Use a percent value from 0–100 (e.g., "50%").

- RELATIVE_TO_PARENT: Use a percent value with a 'p' suffix (e.g., "25%p").

With these animation files defined, we can modify the previous example to now load these sets (see Listings 2–33 and 2–34).

Listing 2–33. *res/layout/main.xml*

```xml
<?xml version="1.0" encoding="utf-8"?>
<RelativeLayout xmlns:android="http://schemas.android.com/apk/res/android"
  android:layout_width="fill_parent"
  android:layout_height="fill_parent">
  <ImageView
    android:id="@+id/flip_image"
    android:layout_width="wrap_content"
    android:layout_height="wrap_content"
    android:layout_centerInParent="true"
  />
</RelativeLayout>
```

Listing 2–34. *Activity Using Animation Sets*

```java
public class Flipper extends Activity {

    boolean isHeads;
    Animation shrink, grow;
    ImageView flipImage;

    @Override
    public void onCreate(Bundle savedInstanceState) {
        super.onCreate(savedInstanceState);
        setContentView(R.layout.main);

        flipImage = (ImageView)findViewById(R.id.flip_image);
        flipImage.setImageResource(R.drawable.heads);
        isHeads = true;

        shrink = AnimationUtils.loadAnimation(this, R.anim.shrink);
        shrink.setAnimationListener(new Animation.AnimationListener() {
            @Override
            public void onAnimationStart(Animation animation) {}

            @Override
```

```
            public void onAnimationRepeat(Animation animation) {}

            @Override
            public void onAnimationEnd(Animation animation) {
                if(isHeads) {
                    isHeads = false;
                    flipImage.setImageResource(R.drawable.tails);
                } else {
                    isHeads = true;
                    flipImage.setImageResource(R.drawable.heads);
                }
                flipImage.startAnimation(grow);
            }
        });
        grow = AnimationUtils.loadAnimation(this, R.anim.grow);
    }

    @Override
    public boolean onTouchEvent(MotionEvent event) {
        if(event.getAction() == MotionEvent.ACTION_DOWN) {
            flipImage.startAnimation(shrink);
            return true;
        }
        return super.onTouchEvent(event);
    }
}
```

The result is a coin that flips, but also slides down and up the y-axis of the screen slightly with each flip.

2–15. Creating Drawables as Backgrounds

Problem

Your application needs to create custom backgrounds with gradients and rounded corners, and you don't want to waste time scaling lots of image files.

Solution

(API Level 1)

Use Android's most powerful implementation of the XML resources system: creating shape drawables. When you are able to do so, creating these views as an XML resource makes sense because they are inherently scalable, and they will fit themselves to the bounds of the view when set as a background.

When defining a drawable in XML using the <shape> tag, the actual result is a GradientDrawable object. You may define objects in the shape of a rectangle, oval, line, or ring; although the rectangle is the most commonly used for backgrounds. In particular, when working with the rectangle the following parameters can be defined for the shape:

- Corner radius
    - Define the radius to use for rounding all four corners, or individual radii to round each corner differently
- Gradient
    - Linear, radial, or sweep
    - Two or Three color values
    - Orientation on any multiple of 45 degrees (0 is left to right, 90 bottom to top, and so on.)
- Solid Color
    - Single color to fill the shape
    - Doesn't play nice with gradient also defined
- Stroke
    - Border around shape
    - Define width and color
- Size and Padding

How It Works

Creating static background images for views can be tricky, given that the image must often be created in multiple sizes to display properly on all devices. This issue is compounded if it is expected that the size of the view may dynamically change based on its contents.

To avoid this problem, we create an XML file in res/drawable to describe a shape that we can apply as the android:background attribute of any View.

Gradient ListView Row

Our first example for this technique will be to create a gradient rectangle that is suitable to be applied as the background of individual rows inside of a ListView. The XML for this shape is defined in Listing 2–35.

Listing 2–35. *res/drawable/backgradient.xml*

```
<?xml version="1.0" encoding="utf-8"?>
<shape xmlns:android="http://schemas.android.com/apk/res/android"
  android:shape="rectangle">
  <gradient
    android:startColor="#EFEFEF"
    android:endColor="#989898"
    android:type="linear"
    android:angle="270"
  />
</shape>
```

Here we chose a linear gradient between two shades of grey, moving from top to bottom. If we wanted to add a third color to the gradient, we would add an android:middleColor attribute to the <gradient> tag.

Now, this drawable can be referenced by any view or layout used to create the custom items of your ListView (we will discusss more about creating these views in Recipe 2–23). The drawable would be added as the background by including the attribute android:background="@drawable/backgradient" to the view's XML, or calling View.setBackgroundResource(R.drawable.backgradient) in Java code.

> **ADVANCED TIP:** The limit on colors in XML is three, but the constructor for GradientDrawable takes an int[] parameter for colors, and you may pass as many as you like.

When we apply this drawable as the background to rows in a ListView, the result will be similar to Figure 2–6.

Figure 2–6. *Gradient drawable as row background*

Rounded View Group

Another popular use of XML drawables is to create a background for a layout that visually groups a handful of widgets together. For style, rounded corners and a thin border are often applied as well. This shape defined in XML would look like Listing 2–36.

Listing 2–36. *res/drawable/roundback.xml*

```xml
<?xml version="1.0" encoding="utf-8"?>
<shape xmlns:android="http://schemas.android.com/apk/res/android"
  android:shape="rectangle">
  <solid
    android:color="#FFF"
  />
  <corners
    android:radius="10dip"
  />
  <stroke
    android:width="5dip"
    android:color="#555"
  />
</shape>
```

In this case, we chose white for the fill color and grey for the border stroke. As mentioned in the previous example, this drawable can be referenced by any view or layout as the background by including the attribute `android:background="@drawable/roundback"` to the view's XML, or calling `View.setBackgroundResource(R.drawable.roundback)` in Java code.

When applied as the background to a view, the result is shown in Figure 2–7.

Figure 2–7. *Rounded rectangle with border as view background*

2–16. Creating Custom State Drawables

Problem

You want to customize an element such as a `Button` or `CheckBox` that has multiple states (default, pressed, selected, and so on).

Solution

(API Level 1)

Create a state-list drawable to apply to the element. Whether you have defined your drawable graphics yourself in XML, or you are using images, Android provides the means via another XML element, the `<selector>`, to create a single reference to multiple images and the conditions under which they should be visible.

How It Works

Let's take a look at an example state-list drawable, and the discuss its parts:

```xml
<?xml version="1.0" encoding="utf-8"?>
<selector xmlns:android="http://schemas.android.com/apk/res/android">
  <item android:state_enabled="false" android:drawable="@drawable/disabled" />
  <item android:state_pressed="true" android:drawable="@drawable/selected" />
  <item android:state_focused="true" android:drawable="@drawable/selected" />
  <item android:drawable="@drawable/default" />
</selector>
```

> **NOTE:** The `<selector>` is order specific. Android will return the drawable of the first state it matches completely as it traverses the list. Bear this in mind when determining which state attributes to apply to each item.

Each item in the list identifies the state(s) that must be in effect for the referenced drawable to be the one chosen. Multiple state parameters can be added for one item if multiple state values need to be matched. Android will traverse the list and pick the first state that matches all criteria of the current view the drawable is attached to. For this reason, it is considered good practice to put your normal, or default state at the bottom of the list with no criteria attached.

Here is a list of the most commonly useful state attributes. All of these are boolean values:

- `state_enabled`
  - Value the view would return from `isEnabled()`.
- `state_pressed`
  - View is pressed by the user on the touch screen.

- state_focused
  - View has focus.
- state_selected
  - View is selected by the user using keys or a D-pad.
- state_checked
  - Value a checkable view would return from isChecked().

Now, let's look at how to apply these state-list drawables to different views.

Button and Clickable Widgets

Widgets like Button are designed to have their background drawable change when the view moves through the above states. As such, the android:background attribute in XML, or the View.setBackgroundDrawable() method are the proper method for attaching the state-list. Listing 2–37 is an example with a file defined in res/drawable/ called button_states.xml:

Listing 2–37. *res/drawable/button_states.xml*

```
<?xml version="1.0" encoding="utf-8"?>
<selector xmlns:android="http://schemas.android.com/apk/res/android">
  <item android:state_enabled="false" android:drawable="@drawable/disabled" />
  <item android:state_pressed="true" android:drawable="@drawable/selected" />
  <item android:drawable="@drawable/default" />
</selector>
```

The three @drawable resources listed here are images in the project that the selector is meant to switch between. As we mentioned in the previous section, the last item will be returned as the default if no other items include matching states to the current view, therefore we do not need to include a state to match on that item. Attaching this to a view defined in XML looks like the following:

```
<Button
  android:layout_width="wrap_content"
  android:layout_height="wrap_content"
  android:text="My Button"
  android:background="@drawable/button_states"
/>
```

CheckBox and Checkable Widgets

Many of the widgets that implement the Checkable interface, like CheckBox and other subclasses of CompoundButton, have a slightly different mechanism for changing state. In these cases, the background is not associated with the state, and customizing the drawable to represent the "checked" states is done through another attribute called the button. In XML, this is the android:button attribute, and in code the CompoundButton.setButtonDrawable() method should do the trick.

Listing 2–38 is an example with a file defined in res/drawable/ called check_states.xml. Again, the @drawable resources listed are meant to reference images in the project to be switched.

Listing 2–38. *res/drawable/check_states.xml*

```xml
<?xml version="1.0" encoding="utf-8"?>
<selector xmlns:android="http://schemas.android.com/apk/res/android">
  <item android:state_enabled="false" android:drawable="@drawable/disabled" />
  <item android:state_checked="true" android:drawable="@drawable/checked" />
  <item android:drawable="@drawable/unchecked" />
</selector>
```

And attached to a CheckBox in XML:

```xml
<CheckBox
  android:layout_width="wrap_content"
  android:layout_height="wrap_content"
  android:button="@drawable/check_states"
/>
```

2–17. Applying Masks to Images

Problem

You need to apply one image or shape as a clipping mask to define the visible boundaries of second image in your application.

Solution

(API Level 1)

Using 2D Graphics and a PorterDuffXferMode, you can apply any arbitrary mask (in the form of another Bitmap) to a Bitmap image. The basic steps to this recipe are as follows:

1. Create a mutable Bitmap (blank), and a Canvas to draw into it.

2. Draw the mask pattern into onto the Canvas first.

3. Apply a PorterDuffXferMode to the Paint.

4. Draw the source image on the Canvas using the transfer mode.

They key ingredient being the PorterDuffXferMode, which considers the current state of both the source and destination objects during a paint operation. The destination is the existing Canvas data, and the source is the graphic data being applied in the current operation.

There are many mode parameters that can be attached to this, which create varying effects on the result, but for masking we are interested in using the PorterDuff.Mode.SRC_IN mode. This mode will only draw at locations where the source and destination overlap, and the pixels drawn will be from the source; in other words, the source is clipped by the bounds of the destination.

How It Works

Rounded Corner Bitmap

One extremely common use of this technique is to apply rounded corners to a Bitmap image before displaying it in an ImageView. For this example, Figure 2–8 is the original image we will be masking.

Figure 2–8. *Original source image*

We will first create a rounded rectangle on our canvas with the required corner radius, and this will serve as our "mask" for the image. Then, applying the PorterDuff.Mode.SRC_IN transform as we paint the source image into the same canvas, the result will be the source image with rounded corners.

This is because the SRC_IN transfer mode tells the paint object to only paint pixels on the canvas locations where there is overlap between the source and destination (the rounded rectangle we already drew), and the pixels that get drawn come from the source. Listing 2–39 is the code inside an Activity.

Listing 2–39. *Activity Applying Rounded Rectangle Mask to Bitmap*

```
public class MaskActivity extends Activity {
    /** Called when the activity is first created. */
    @Override
    public void onCreate(Bundle savedInstanceState) {
        super.onCreate(savedInstanceState);
        ImageView iv = new ImageView(this);

        //Create and load images (immutable, typically)
        Bitmap source = BitmapFactory.decodeResource(getResources(), R.drawable.dog);

        //Create a *mutable* location, and a canvas to draw into it
        Bitmap result = Bitmap.createBitmap(source.getWidth(), source.getHeight(),
            Config.ARGB_8888);
```

```
        Canvas canvas = new Canvas(result);
        Paint paint = new Paint(Paint.ANTI_ALIAS_FLAG);

        //Create and draw the rounded rectangle "mask" first
        RectF rect = new RectF(0,0,source.getWidth(),source.getHeight());
        float radius = 25.0f;
        paint.setColor(Color.BLACK);
        canvas.drawRoundRect(rect, radius, radius, paint);
        //Switch over and paint the source using the transfer mode
        paint.setXfermode(new PorterDuffXfermode(Mode.SRC_IN));
        canvas.drawBitmap(source, 0, 0, paint);
        paint.setXfermode(null);

        iv.setImageBitmap(result);
        setContentView(iv);
    }
}
```

The result for your efforts are shown in Figure 2–9.

Figure 2–9. *Image with rounded rectangle mask applied*

Arbitrary Mask Image

Let's looks at an example that's a little more interesting. Here we take two images, the source image and an image representing the mask we want to apply – in this case, and upside-down triangle (see Figure 2–10).

Figure 2–10. *Original source image (left) and arbitrary mask image to apply (right)*

The chosen mask image does not have to conform to the style chosen here, with black pixels for the mask and transparent everywhere else. However, it is the best choice to guarantee that the system draws the mask exactly as you expect it to be. Listing 2–40 is the simple Activity code to mask the image and display it in a view.

Listing 2–40. *Activity Applying Arbitrary Mask to Bitmap*

```java
public class MaskActivity extends Activity {

@Override
    public void onCreate(Bundle savedInstanceState) {
        super.onCreate(savedInstanceState);
        ImageView iv = new ImageView(this);

        //Create and load images (immutable, typically)
        Bitmap source = BitmapFactory.decodeResource(getResources(), R.drawable.dog);
        Bitmap mask = BitmapFactory.decodeResource(getResources(), R.drawable.triangle);

        //Create a *mutable* location, and a canvas to draw into it
        Bitmap result = Bitmap.createBitmap(source.getWidth(), source.getHeight(),
            Config.ARGB_8888);
        Canvas canvas = new Canvas(result);
        Paint paint = new Paint(Paint.ANTI_ALIAS_FLAG);

        //Draw the mask image first, then paint the source using the transfer mode
        canvas.drawBitmap(mask, 0, 0, paint);
        paint.setXfermode(new PorterDuffXfermode(Mode.SRC_IN));
        canvas.drawBitmap(source, 0, 0, paint);
        paint.setXfermode(null);

        iv.setImageBitmap(result);
        setContentView(iv);
    }
}
```

As with before, we draw the mask onto the canvas first and then draw the source image in using the `PorterDuff.Mode.SRC_IN` mode to only paint the source pixels where they overlap the existing mask pixels. The result looks something like Figure 2–11.

Figure 2–11. *Image with mask applied*

Please Try This At Home

Applying the `PorterDuffXferMode` in this fashion to blend two images can create lots of interesting results. Try taking this same example code, but changing the `PorterDuff.Mode` parameter to one of the many other options. Each of the modes will blend the two Bitmaps in a slightly different way. Have fun with it!

2–18. Creating Dialogs that Persist

Problem

You want to create a user dialog that has multiple input fields or some other set of information that needs to be persisted if the device is rotated.

Solution

(API Level 1)

Don't use a dialog at all; create an Activity with the Dialog theme. Dialogs are managed objects that must be handled properly when the device rotates while they are visible, otherwise they will cause a leaked reference in the window manager. You can mitigate this issue by having your Activity manage the dialog for you using methods like

`Activity.showDialog()` and `Activity.dismissDialog()` to present it, but that only solves one problem.

The Dialog does not have any mechanism of its own to persist state through a rotation, and this job (by design) falls back to the Activity that presented it. This results in extra required effort to ensure that the Dialog can pass back or persist any values entered into it before it is dismissed.

If you have an interface to present to the user that will need to persist state and stay front facing through rotation, a better solution is to make it an Activity. This allows that object access to the full set of lifecycle callback methods for saving/restoring state. Plus, as an Activity, it does not have to be managed to dismiss and present again during rotation, which removes the worry of leaking references. You can still make the Activity behave like a Dialog from the user's perspective using the `Theme.Dialog` system theme.

How It Works

Listing 2–41 is an example of a simple Activity that has a title and some text in a TextView.

Listing 2–41. *Activity to be Themed As a Dialog*

```
public class DialogActivity extends Activity {
    @Override
    public void onCreate(Bundle savedInstanceState) {
        super.onCreate(savedInstanceState);
        setTitle("Activity");
        TextView tv = new TextView(this);
        tv.setText("I'm Really An Activity!");
        //Add some padding to keep the dialog borders away
        tv.setPadding(15, 15, 15, 15);
        setContentView(tv);
    }
}
```

We can apply the Dialog theme to this Activity in the AndroidManifest.xml file for the application (see Figure 2–42).

Listing 2–42. *Manifest Setting the Above Activity with the Dialog Theme*

```
<?xml version="1.0" encoding="utf-8"?>
<manifest xmlns:android="http://schemas.android.com/apk/res/android"
    package="com.examples.dialogs"
    android:versionCode="1"
    android:versionName="1.0">
    <application android:icon="@drawable/icon" android:label="@string/app_name">
        <activity android:name=".DialogActivity"
                android:label="@string/app_name"
                android:theme="@android:style/Theme.Dialog">
            <intent-filter>
                <action android:name="android.intent.action.MAIN" />
                <category android:name="android.intent.category.LAUNCHER" />
            </intent-filter>
        </activity>
    </application>
</manifest>
```

Note the `android:theme="@android:style/Theme.Dialog"` parameter, which creates the look and feel of a Dialog, with all the benefits of a full-blown Activity. When you run this application, you will see a screen like that shown in Figure 2–12.

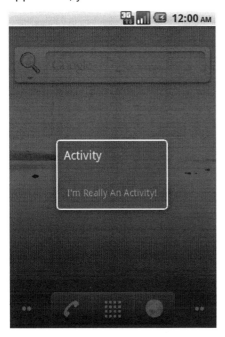

Figure 2–12. *Applying Dialog theme to an Activity*

Notice that, even though this is an Activity for all intents and purposes, it can act as a Dialog inside of your user interface, partially covering the Activity underneath it (in this case, the Home screen).

2–19. Implementing Situation-Specific Layouts

Problem

Your application must be universal, running on different screen sizes and orientations. You need to provide different layout resources for each of these instances.

Solution

(API Level 4)

Build multiple layout files, and use resource qualifiers to let Android pick what's appropriate. We will look at using resources to create resources specific for different screen orientations and sizes.

How It Works

Orientation-Specific

In order to create different resources for an Activity to use in portrait versus landscape, use the following qualifiers:

- *resource*-land
- *resource*-port

This works for all resource types, but the most common in this case is to do this with layouts. Therefore, instead of a res/layout/ directory in the project, there would be a res/layout-port/ and a res/layout-land/ directory.

> **NOTE:** It is good practice to include a default resource directory without a qualifier. This gives Android something to fall back on if it is running on a device that doesn't match any of the specific criteria you list.

Size-Specific

There are also screen size qualifiers (physical size, not to be confused with pixel density) that we can use to target large screen devices like tablets. In most cases, a single layout will suffice for all physical screen sizes of mobile phone. However, you may want to add more features to a tablet layout to assist in filling the noticeably more screen real estate the user has to operate. The following resource qualifiers are acceptable for physical screen size:

- *resource*-small
- *resource*-medium
- *resource*-large

So, to include a tablet-only layout to a universal application we could add a res/layout-large/directory as well.

Example

Let's look at a quick example that puts this into practice. We'll define a single Activity, that loads a single layout resource in code. However, this layout will be define three times in the resources to produce different results in portrait, landscape, and on a tablet. First, the Activity, which is shown in Listing 2–43.

Listing 2–43. *Simple Activity Loading One Layout*

```
public class UniversalActivity extends Activity {

    @Override
    public void onCreate(Bundle savedInstanceState) {
        super.onCreate(savedInstanceState);
        setContentView(R.layout.main);
    }
}
```

We'll now define a default/portrait layout in res/layout/main.xml (see Listing 2–44).

Listing 2–44. *res/layout/main.xml*

```
<?xml version="1.0" encoding="utf-8"?>
<!-- PORTRAIT/DEFAULT LAYOUT -->
<LinearLayout xmlns:android="http://schemas.android.com/apk/res/android"
  android:orientation="vertical"
  android:layout_width="fill_parent"
  android:layout_height="fill_parent">
  <TextView
    android:layout_width="fill_parent"
    android:layout_height="wrap_content"
    android:text="This is a vertical layout for PORTRAIT"
  />
  <Button
    android:layout_width="wrap_content"
    android:layout_height="wrap_content"
    android:text="Button One"
  />
  <Button
    android:layout_width="wrap_content"
    android:layout_height="wrap_content"
    android:text="Button Two"
  />
</LinearLayout>
```

And a landscape version in res/layout-land/main.xml (see Figure 2–45).

Listing 2–45. *res/layout-land/main.xml*

```
<?xml version="1.0" encoding="utf-8"?>
<!-- LANDSCAPE LAYOUT -->
<LinearLayout xmlns:android="http://schemas.android.com/apk/res/android"
  android:orientation="horizontal"
  android:layout_width="fill_parent"
  android:layout_height="fill_parent">
  <TextView
    android:layout_width="wrap_content"
    android:layout_height="wrap_content"
    android:text="The is a horizontal layout for LANDSCAPE"
  />
  <Button
    android:layout_width="wrap_content"
    android:layout_height="wrap_content"
    android:text="Button One"
  />
  <Button
    android:layout_width="wrap_content"
```

```
      android:layout_height="wrap_content"
      android:text="Button Two"
  />
</LinearLayout>
```

We have now reordered our layout to be horizontal on a landscape screen.

The tablet version in res/layout-large/main.xml (see Figure 2–46).

Listing 2–46. *res/layout-large/main.xml*

```
<?xml version="1.0" encoding="utf-8"?>
<!-- LARGE LAYOUT -->
<LinearLayout xmlns:android="http://schemas.android.com/apk/res/android"
  android:orientation="vertical"
  android:layout_width="fill_parent"
  android:layout_height="fill_parent">
  <TextView
    android:layout_width="fill_parent"
    android:layout_height="wrap_content"
    android:text="This is the layout for TABLETS"
  />
  <Button
    android:layout_width="wrap_content"
    android:layout_height="wrap_content"
    android:text="Button One"
  />
  <Button
    android:layout_width="wrap_content"
    android:layout_height="wrap_content"
    android:text="Button Two"
  />
  <Button
    android:layout_width="wrap_content"
    android:layout_height="wrap_content"
    android:text="Button Three"
  />
  <Button
    android:layout_width="wrap_content"
    android:layout_height="wrap_content"
    android:text="Button Four"
  />
</LinearLayout>
```

Since we have more screen real estate to work with, there are a couple extra buttons for the user to interact with.

Now, when we run the application, you can see how Android selects the appropriate layout to match our configuration, whether it is portrait and landscape on the phone (see Figure 2–13), or running on a larger tablet screen (see Figure 2–14).

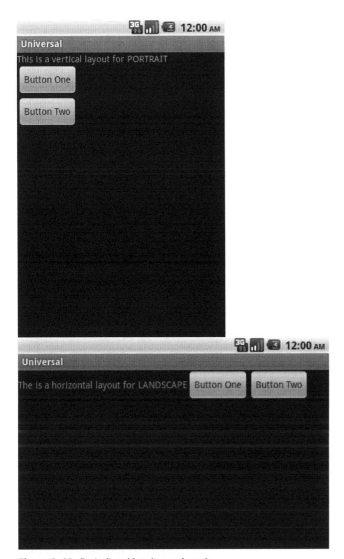

Figure 2–13. *Portrait and Landscape layouts*

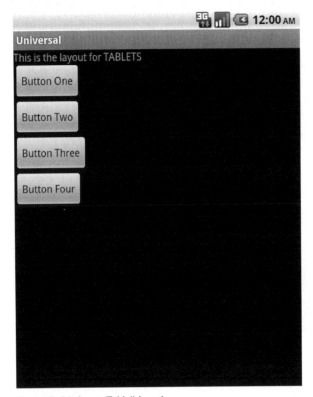

Figure 2–14. *Large (Tablet) layout*

Late Additions

In API Level 9 (Android 2.3), one more resource qualifier was added to support "extra large" screens:

- *resource*-xlarge

According to the SDK documentation, a traditionally "large" screen is one in the range of approximately 5 to 7 inches. The new qualifier for "extra large" covers screens roughly 7 to 10+ inches in size.

If your application is built against API Level 9, you should include your tablet layouts in the res/layout-xlarge/ directory as well. Keeping in mind that tables running Android 2.2 or earlier will only recognize res/layout-large/ as a valid qualifier.

2–20. Customizing Keyboard Actions

Problem

You want to customize the appearance of the soft keyboard's enter key, the action that occurs when a user tap it, or both.

Solution

(API Level 3)

Customize the Input Method (IME) options for the widget in which the keyboard is entering data.

How It Works

Custom Enter Key

When the keyboard is visible on screen, the text on the return key typically has an action based on the order of focusable items in the view. While unspecified, the keyboard will display a "next" action if there are more focusables in the view to move to, or a "done" action if the last item is currently focused on. This value is customizable, however, for each input view by setting the `android:imeOptions` value in the view's XML. The values you may set to customize the return key are listed here:

- actionUnspecified: Default. Display action of the device's choice
    - Action event will be IME_NULL
- actionGo: Display "Go" as the return key
    - Action event will be IME_ACTION_GO
- actionSearch: Display a search glass as the return key
    - Action event will be IME_ACTION_SEARCH
- actionSend: Display "Send" as the return key
    - Action event will be IME_ACTION_SEND
- actionNext: Display "Next" as the return key
    - Action event will be IME_ACTION_NEXT
- actionDone: Display "Done" as the return key
    - Action event will be IME_ACTION_DONE

Let's look at an example layout with two editable text fields, shown in Listing 2–47. The first will display the search glass on the return key, and the second will display "Go."

Listing 2–47. *Layout with Custom Input Options on EditText Widgets*

```
<LinearLayout xmlns:android="http://schemas.android.com/apk/res/android"
  android:layout_width="fill_parent"
  android:layout_height="fill_parent"
  android:orientation="vertical">
  <EditText
    android:id="@+id/text1"
    android:layout_width="fill_parent"
    android:layout_height="wrap_content"
```

```
    android:imeOptions="actionSearch"
  />
  <EditText
    android:id="@+id/text2"
    android:layout_width="fill_parent"
    android:layout_height="wrap_content"
    android:imeOptions="actionGo"
  />
</LinearLayout>
```

The resulting display of the keyboard will vary somewhat as some manufacturer specific UI kits include different keyboards, but the results on a pure Google UI will show up like in Figure 2–15.

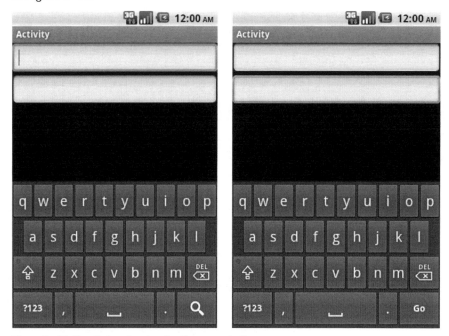

Figure 2–15. *Result of custom input options on enter key*

> **NOTE:** Custom editor options only apply to the soft input methods. Changing this value will not affect the events that get generated when the user presses return on a physical hardware keyboard.

Custom Action

Customizing what happens when the user presses the enter key can be just as important as adjusting its display. Overriding the default behavior of any action simply requires that a TextView.OnEditorActionListener be attached to the view of interest. Let's continue with the example layout above, and this time add a custom action to both views (see Listing 2–48).

Listing 2–48. *Activity Implementing a Custom Keyboard Action*

```
public class MyActivity extends Activity implements OnEditorActionListener {

    @Override
    public void onCreate(Bundle savedInstanceState) {
        super.onCreate(savedInstanceState);
        setContentView(R.layout.main);

        //Add the listener to the views
        EditText text1 = (EditText)findViewById(R.id.text1);
        text1.setOnEditorActionListener(this);
        EditText text2 = (EditText)findViewById(R.id.text2);
        text2.setOnEditorActionListener(this);
    }

    @Override
    public boolean onEditorAction(TextView v, int actionId, KeyEvent event) {
        if(actionId == IME_ACTION_SEARCH) {
            //Handle search key click
            return true;
        }
        if(actionId == IME_ACTION_GO) {
            //Handle go key click
            return true;
        }
        return false;
    }
}
```

The boolean return value of onEditorAction() tells the system whether your implementation has consumed the event or whether it should be passed on to the next possible responder, if any. It is important for you to return true when your implementation handles the event so no other processing occurs. However, it is just as important for you to return false when you are not handling the event so your application does not steal key events from the rest of the system.

2–21. Dismissing Soft Keyboard

Problem

You need an event on the user interface to hide or dismiss the soft keyboard from the screen.

Solution

(API Level 3)

Tell the Input Method Manager explicitly to hide any visible Input Methods using the `InputMethodManager.hideSoftInputFromWindow()` method.

How It Works

Here is an example of how to call this method inside of a `View.OnClickListener`:

```
public void onClick(View view) {
    InputMethodManager imm = (InputMethodManager)getSystemService(
            Context.INPUT_METHOD_SERVICE);
    imm.hideSoftInputFromWindow(view.getWindowToken(), 0);
}
```

Notice the `hideSoftInputFromWindow()` take an IBinder window token as a parameter. This can be retrieved from any View object currently attached to the window via `View.getWindowToken()`. In most cases, the callback method for the specific event will either have a reference to the TextView where the editing is taking place, or the View that was tapped to generate the event (like a Button). These views are the most convenient objects to call on to get the window token and pass it to the `InputMethodManager`.

2–22. Customizing AdapterView Empty Views

Problem

You want to display a custom view when an AdapterView (ListView, GridView, and the like) has an empty data set.

Solution

(API Level 1)

Lay out the view you would like displayed in the same tree as the AdapterView and call `AdapterView.setEmptyView()` to have the AdapterView manage it. The AdapterView will switch the visibility parameters between itself and its empty view based on the result of the attached ListAdapter's `isEmpty()` method.

> **IMPORTANT:** Be sure to include both the AdapterView and the empty view in your layout. The AdapterView ONLY changes the visibility parameters on the two objects; it does not insert or remove them in the layout tree.

How It Works

Here is how this would look with a simple TextView used as the empty. First, a layout that includes both views, shown in Listing 2–49.

Listing 2–49. *Layout Containing AdapterView and an Empty View*

```xml
<?xml version="1.0" encoding="utf-8"?>
<FrameLayout xmlns:android="http://schemas.android.com/apk/res/android"
  android:layout_width="fill_parent"
  android:layout_height="fill_parent">
  <TextView
    android:id="@+id/myempty"
    android:layout_width="fill_parent"
    android:layout_height="wrap_content"
    android:text="No Items to Display"
  />
  <ListView
    android:id="@+id/mylist"
    android:layout_width="fill_parent"
    android:layout_height="fill_parent"
  />
</FrameLayout>
```

Then, in the Activity, give the ListView a reference to the empty view so it can be managed (see Listing 2–50).

Listing 2–50. *Activity Connecting the Empty View to the List*

```java
public void onCreate(Bundle savedInstanceState) {
    super.onCreate(savedInstanceState);
    ListView list = (ListView)findViewById(R.id.mylist);
    TextView empty = (TextView)findViewById(R.id.myempty);
    //Attach the reference
    list.setEmptyView(empty);

    //Continue adding adapters and data to the list

}
```

Make Empty Interesting

Empty views don't have to be simple and boring like the single TextView. Let's try to make things a little more useful for the user and add a refresh button when the list is empty (see Listing 2–51).

Listing 2–51. *Interactive Empty Layout*

```xml
<?xml version="1.0" encoding="utf-8"?>
<FrameLayout xmlns:android="http://schemas.android.com/apk/res/android"
  android:layout_width="fill_parent"
  android:layout_height="fill_parent">
  <LinearLayout
    android:id="@+id/myempty"
    android:layout_width="fill_parent"
    android:layout_height="wrap_content"
    android:orientation="vertical">
```

```
    <TextView
      android:layout_width="fill_parent"
      android:layout_height="wrap_content"
      android:text="No Items to Display"
    />
    <Button
      android:layout_width="fill_parent"
      android:layout_height="wrap_content"
      android:text="Tap Here to Refresh"
    />
  </LinearLayout>
  <ListView
    android:id="@+id/mylist"
    android:layout_width="fill_parent"
    android:layout_height="fill_parent"
  />
</FrameLayout>
```

Now, with the same Activity code from before, we have set an entire layout as the empty view, and added the ability for the user to do something about their lack of data.

2–23. Customizing ListView Rows

Problem

Your application needs to use a more customized look for each row in a ListView.

Solution

(API Level 1)

Create a custom XML layout and pass it to one of the common adapters, or extend your own. You can then apply custom state drawables for overriding the background and selected states of each row.

How It Works

Simply Custom

If your needs are simple, create a layout that can connect to an existing ListAdapter for population; we'll use ArrayAdapter as an example. The ArrayAdapter can take parameters for a custom layout resource to inflate and the ID of one TextView in that layout to populate with data. Let's create some custom drawables for the background and a layout that meets these requirements (see Listings 2–52 through 2–54).

Listing 2–52. *res/drawable/row_background_default.xml*

```
<?xml version="1.0" encoding="utf-8"?>
<shape xmlns:android="http://schemas.android.com/apk/res/android"
  android:shape="rectangle">
```

```
  <gradient
    android:startColor="#EFEFEF"
    android:endColor="#989898"
    android:type="linear"
    android:angle="270"
  />
</shape>
```

Listing 2–53. *res/drawable/row_background_pressed.xml*

```
<?xml version="1.0" encoding="utf-8"?>
<shape xmlns:android="http://schemas.android.com/apk/res/android"
  android:shape="rectangle">
  <gradient
    android:startColor="#0B8CF2"
    android:endColor="#0661E5"
    android:type="linear"
    android:angle="270"
  />
</shape>
```

Listing 2–54. *res/drawable/row_background.xml*

```
<?xml version="1.0" encoding="utf-8"?>
<selector xmlns:android="http://schemas.android.com/apk/res/android">
  <item android:state_pressed="true" android:drawable="@drawable/row_background_pressed"/>
  <item android:drawable="@drawable/row_background_default"/>
</selector>
```

Listing 2–55 shows a custom layout with the text fully centered in the row instead of aligned to the left.

Listing 2–55. *res/layout/custom_row.xml*

```
<?xml version="1.0" encoding="utf-8"?>
<LinearLayout xmlns:android="http://schemas.android.com/apk/res/android"
  android:layout_width="fill_parent"
  android:layout_height="wrap_content"
  android:padding="10dip"
  android:background="@drawable/row_background">
  <TextView
    android:id="@+id/line1"
    android:layout_width="wrap_content"
    android:layout_height="wrap_content"
    android:layout_gravity="center"
  />
</LinearLayout>
```

This layout has the custom gradient state-list set as its background; setting up the default and pressed states for each item in the list. Now, since we have defined a layout that matches up with what an ArrayAdapter expects, we can create one and set it on our list without any further customization (see Listing 2–56).

Listing 2–56. *Activity Using the Custom Row Layout*

```
public void onCreate(Bundle savedInstanceState) {
    super.onCreate(savedInstanceState);
    ListView list = new ListView(this);
    ArrayAdapter<String> adapter = new ArrayAdapter<String>(this,
```

```
                      R.layout.custom_row,
                      R.id.line1,
                      new String[] {"Bill","Tom","Sally","Jenny"});
        list.setAdapter(adapter);

        setContentView(list);
}
```

Adapting to a More Complex Choice

Sometimes customizing the list rows means extending a ListAdapter as well. This is usually the case if you have multiple pieces of data in a single row, or if any of them are not text. In this example, let's utilize the custom drawables again for the background, but make the layout a little more interesting (see Listing 2–57).

Listing 2–57. *res/layout/custom_row.xml Modified*

```xml
<?xml version="1.0" encoding="utf-8"?>
<RelativeLayout xmlns:android="http://schemas.android.com/apk/res/android"
  android:layout_width="fill_parent"
  android:layout_height="wrap_content"
  android:orientation="horizontal"
  android:padding="10dip">
  <ImageView
    android:id="@+id/leftimage"
    android:layout_width="32dip"
    android:layout_height="32dip"
  />
  <ImageView
    android:id="@+id/rightimage"
    android:layout_width="32dip"
    android:layout_height="32dip"
    android:layout_alignParentRight="true"
  />

  <TextView
    android:id="@+id/line1"
    android:layout_width="fill_parent"
    android:layout_height="wrap_content"
    android:layout_toLeftOf="@id/rightimage"
    android:layout_toRightOf="@id/leftimage"
    android:layout_centerVertical="true"
    android:gravity="center_horizontal"
  />
</RelativeLayout>
```

This layout contains the same centered TextView, but bordered with an ImageView on each side. In order to apply this layout to the ListView, we will need to extend one of the ListAdapters in the SDK. Which one you extend is dependent on the data source you are presenting in the list. If the data is still just a simple array of strings, and extension of ArrayAdapter is sufficient. If the data is more complex, a full extension of the abstract BaseAdapter may be necessary. The only required method to extend is getView(), which governs how each row in the list is presented.

In our case, the data is a simple array of strings, so we will create a simple extension of ArrayAdapter (see Listing 2–58).

Listing 2–58. *Activity and Custom ListAdapter to Display the New Layout*

```
public class MyActivity extends Activity {

    public void onCreate(Bundle savedInstanceState) {
        super.onCreate(savedInstanceState);
        ListView list = new ListView(this);
        setContentView(list);

        CustomAdapter adapter = new CustomAdapter(this,
                    R.layout.custom_row,
                    R.id.line1,
                    new String[] {"Bill","Tom","Sally","Jenny"});
        list.setAdapter(adapter);

    }

    private class CustomAdapter extends ArrayAdapter<String> {

        public CustomAdapter(Context context, int layout, int resId, String[] items) {
            //Call through to ArrayAdapter implementation
            super(context, layout, resId, items);
        }

        @Override
        public View getView(int position, View convertView, ViewGroup parent) {
            View row = convertView;
            //Inflate a new row if one isn't recycled
            if(row == null) {
                row = getLayoutInflater().inflate(R.layout.custom_row, parent, false);
            }

            String item = getItem(position);
            ImageView left = (ImageView)row.findViewById(R.id.leftimage);
            ImageView right = (ImageView)row.findViewById(R.id.rightimage);
            TextView text = (TextView)row.findViewById(R.id.line1);

            left.setImageResource(R.drawable.icon);
            right.setImageResource(R.drawable.icon);
            text.setText(item);

            return row;
        }
    }
}
```

Notice that we use the same constructor to create an instance of the adapter as before, since it is inherited from ArrayAdapter. Because we are overriding the view display mechanism of the adapter, the only reason the R.layout.custom_row and R.id.line1 are now passed into the constructor is that they are required parameters of the constructor; they don't serve a useful purpose in this example anymore.

Now, when the ListView wants to display a row it will call getView() on its adapter, which we have customized so we can control how each row returns. The getView()

method is passed a parameter called the convertView, which is very important for performance. Layout inflation from XML is an expensive process, and to minimize its impact on the system, ListView recycles views as the list scrolls. If a recycled view is available to be reused, it is passed into getView() as the convertView. Whenever possible, reuse these views instead of inflating new ones to keep the scrolling performance of the list fast and responsive.

In this example, call getItem() to get the current value at that position in the list (our array of Strings), and then later on set that value on the TextView for that row. We can also set the images in each row to something significant for the data, although here they are set to the app icon for simplicity.

2–24. Making ListView Section Headers

Problem

You want to create a list with multiple sections, each with a header at the top.

Solution

(API Level 1)

Use the SimplerExpandableListAdapter code defined here and an ExpandableListView. Android doesn't officially have an extensible way to create sections in a list, but it does offer the ExpandableListView widget and associated adapters designed to handle a two-dimensional data structure in a sectioned list. The drawback is that the adapters provided with the SDK to handle this data are cumbersome to work with for simple data structures.

How It Works

Enter the SimplerExpandableListAdapter (see Listing 2–59), an extension of the BaseExpandableListAdapter that, as an example, handles an Array of string arrays, with a separate string array for the section titles.

Listing 2–59. *SimplerExpandableListAdapter*

```
public class SimplerExpandableListAdapter extends BaseExpandableListAdapter {
    private Context mContext;
    private String[][] mContents;
    private String[] mTitles;

    public SimplerExpandableListAdapter(Context context, String[] titles, String[][]
contents) {
        super();
        //Check arguments
        if(titles.length != contents.length) {
            throw new IllegalArgumentException("Titles and Contents must be the same
size.");
```

```java
    }

    mContext = context;
    mContents = contents;
    mTitles = titles;
}

//Return a child item
@Override
public String getChild(int groupPosition, int childPosition) {
    return mContents[groupPosition][childPosition];
}

//Return a item's id
@Override
public long getChildId(int groupPosition, int childPosition) {
    return 0;
}

//Return view for each item row
@Override
public View getChildView(int groupPosition, int childPosition,
        boolean isLastChild, View convertView, ViewGroup parent) {
    TextView row = (TextView)convertView;
    if(row == null) {
        row = new TextView(mContext);
    }
    row.setText(mContents[groupPosition][childPosition]);
    return row;
}

//Return number of items in each section
@Override
public int getChildrenCount(int groupPosition) {
    return mContents[groupPosition].length;
}

//Return sections
@Override
public String[] getGroup(int groupPosition) {
    return mContents[groupPosition];
}

//Return the number of sections
@Override
public int getGroupCount() {
    return mContents.length;
}

//Return a section's id
@Override
public long getGroupId(int groupPosition) {
    return 0;
}

//Return a view for each section header
@Override
```

```
    public View getGroupView(int groupPosition, boolean isExpanded,
            View convertView, ViewGroup parent) {
        TextView row = (TextView)convertView;
        if(row == null) {
            row = new TextView(mContext);
        }
        row.setTypeface(Typeface.DEFAULT_BOLD);
        row.setText(mTitles[groupPosition]);
        return row;
    }

    @Override
    public boolean hasStableIds() {
        return false;
    }

    @Override
    public boolean isChildSelectable(int groupPosition, int childPosition) {
        return true;
    }

}
```

Now we can create a simple data structure and use it to populate an
ExpandableListView in an example Activity (see Listing 2–60).

Listing 2–60. *Activity Using the SImplerExpandableListAdapter*

```
public void onCreate(Bundle savedInstanceState) {
    super.onCreate(savedInstanceState);
    //Set up an expandable list
    ExpandableListView list = new ExpandableListView(this);
    list.setGroupIndicator(null);
    list.setChildIndicator(null);
    //Set up simple data and the new adapter
    String[] titles = {"Fruits","Vegetables","Meats"};
    String[] fruits = {"Apples","Oranges"};
    String[] veggies = {"Carrots","Peas","Broccoli"};
    String[] meats = {"Pork","Chicken"};
    String[][] contents = {fruits,veggies,meats};
    SimplerExpandableListAdapter adapter = new SimplerExpandableListAdapter(this,
        titles, contents);

    list.setAdapter(adapter);
    setContentView(list);
}
```

That Darn Expansion

There is one catch to utilizing ExpandableListView in this fashion: it expands.
ExpandableListView is designed to expand and collapse the child data underneath the
group heading when the heading it tapped. Also, by default all the groups are collapsed,
so you can only see the header items.

In some cases this may be desirable behavior, but often it is not if you just want to add
section headers. In that case, there are two addition steps to take:

1. In the Activity code, expand all the groups. Something like

```
for(int i=0; i < adapter.getGroupCount(); i++) {
    list.expandGroup(i);
}
```

2. In the Adapter, override onGroupCollapsed() to force re-expansion. This
    will require adding a reference to the list widget to the adapter.

```
@Override
public void onGroupCollapsed(int groupPosition) {
    list.expandGroup(groupPosition);
}
```

2–25. Creating Compound Controls

Problem

You need to create a custom widget that is a collection of existing elements.

Solution

(API Level 1)

Create a custom widget by extending a common ViewGroup and adding functionality.
One of the simplest, and most powerful ways to create custom or reusable user
interface elements is to create compound controls leveraging the existing widgets
provided by the Android SDK.

How It Works

ViewGroup, and its subclasses LinearLayout, RelativeLayout, and so on, give you the
tools to make this simple by assisting you with component placement, so you can be
more concerned with the added functionality.

TextImageButton

Let's create an example by making a widget that the Android SDK does not have
natively: a button containing either an image or text as its content. To do this, we are
going to create the TextImageButton class, which is an extension of FrameLayout. It will
contain a TextView to handle text content, and an ImageView for image content (see
Listing 2–61).

Listing 2–61. *Custom TextImageButton Widget*

```
public class TextImageButton extends FrameLayout {

    private ImageView imageView;
    private TextView textView;
```

```java
/* Constructors */
public TextImageButton(Context context) {
    this(context, null);
}

public TextImageButton(Context context, AttributeSet attrs) {
    this(context, attrs, 0);
}

public TextImageButton(Context context, AttributeSet attrs, int defaultStyle) {
    super(context, attrs, defaultStyle);
    imageView = new ImageView(context, attrs, defaultStyle);
    textView = new TextView(context, attrs, defaultStyle);
    //create layout parameters
    FrameLayout.LayoutParams params = new FrameLayout.LayoutParams(
                LayoutParams.FILL_PARENT, LayoutParams.FILL_PARENT);
    //Add the views
    this.addView(imageView, params);
    this.addView(textView, params);

    //Make this view interactive
    setClickable(true);
    setFocusable(true);
    //Set the default system button background
    setBackgroundResource(android.R.drawable.btn_default);

    //If image is present, switch to image mode
    if(imageView.getDrawable() != null) {
        textView.setVisibility(View.GONE);
        imageView.setVisibility(View.VISIBLE);
    } else {
        textView.setVisibility(View.VISIBLE);
        imageView.setVisibility(View.GONE);
    }
}

/* Accessors */
public void setText(CharSequence text) {
    //Switch to text
    textView.setVisibility(View.VISIBLE);
    imageView.setVisibility(View.GONE);
    //Apply text
    textView.setText(text);
}

public void setImageResource(int resId) {
    //Switch to image
    textView.setVisibility(View.GONE);
    imageView.setVisibility(View.VISIBLE);
    //Apply image
    imageView.setImageResource(resId);
}

public void setImageDrawable(Drawable drawable) {
    //Switch to image
    textView.setVisibility(View.GONE);
    imageView.setVisibility(View.VISIBLE);
```

```
        //Apply image
        imageView.setImageDrawable(drawable);
    }
}
```

All of the widgets in the SDK have three constructors. The first constructor takes only Context as a parameter and is generally used to create a new view in code. The remaining two are used when a view is inflated from XML, where the attributes defined in the XML file are passed in as the AttributeSet parameter. Here we use Java's this() notation to drill the first two constructors down to the one that really does all the work. Building the custom control in this fashion ensures that we can still define this view in XML layouts. Without implementing the attributed constructors, this would not be possible.

The constructor creates a TextView and ImageView, and places them inside the layout. FrameLayout is not an interactive view by default, so the constructor makes the control clickable and focusable so it can handle user interaction events; we also set the system's default button background on the view as a cue to the user that this widget is interactive. The remaining code sets the default display mode (either text or image) based on the data that was passed in as attributes.

The accessor functions are added as a convenience to later switch the button contents. These functions are also tasked with switching between text and image mode if the content change warrants it.

Because this custom control is not in the android.view or android.widget packages, we must use the fully qualified name when it is used in an XML layout. Listings 2–62 and 2–63 show an example Activity display the custom widget.

Listing 2–62. *res/layout/main.xml*

```xml
<?xml version="1.0" encoding="utf-8"?>
<LinearLayout xmlns:android="http://schemas.android.com/apk/res/android"
  android:layout_width="fill_parent"
  android:layout_height="fill_parent"
  android:orientation="vertical">
  <com.examples.customwidgets.TextImageButton
    android:layout_width="wrap_content"
    android:layout_height="wrap_content"
    android:textColor="#000"
    android:text="Click Me!"
  />
  <com.examples.customwidgets.TextImageButton
    android:layout_width="wrap_content"
    android:layout_height="wrap_content"
    android:src="@drawable/icon"
  />
</LinearLayout>
```

Listing 2–63. *Activity Using the New Custom Widget*

```java
public class MyActivity extends Activity {

    @Override
    public void onCreate(Bundle savedInstanceState) {
        super.onCreate(savedInstanceState);
```

```
        setContentView(R.layout.main);
    }
}
```

Notice that we can still use traditional attributes to define properties like the text or image to display. This is due to the fact that we construct each item (the FrameLayout, TextView, and ImageView) with the attributed constructors, so each view sets the parameters it is interested in, and ignores the rest.

If we define an Acitivity to use this layout, the results look like Figure 2–16.

Figure 2–16. *TextImageButton displayed in both text and image modes*

Useful Tools to Know: DroidDraw

Chapter 1 introduced a units-conversion Android app named UC. In addition to exploring UC's source code, this chapter explored this app's resources, starting with the `main.xml` layout file that describes how the app's main screen is laid out.

Coding layout and other resource files by hand is at best a tedious undertaking, even for advanced developers. For this reason, Professor Brendan Burns created a tool named DroidDraw.

DroidDraw is a Java-based tool that facilitates building an Android app's user interface. This tool does not generate app logic. Instead, it generates XML layout and other resource information that can be merged into another development tool's app project.

Obtaining and Launching DroidDraw

DroidDraw is hosted at the `droiddraw.org` web site. From this web site's main page, you can try out DroidDraw as a Java applet, or you can download the DroidDraw application for the Mac OS X, Windows, and Linux platforms.

For example, click the main page's Windows link and download `droiddraw-r1b18.zip` to obtain DroidDraw for Windows. (Release 1, Build 18 is the latest DroidDraw version at time of writing.)

Unarchive `droiddraw-r1b18.zip` and you'll discover `droiddraw.exe` and `droiddraw.jar` (an executable JAR file) for launching DroidDraw. From the Windows Explorer, double-click either filename to launch this tool.

TIP: Specify `java -jar droiddraw.jar` to launch DroidDraw at the command line via the JAR file.

Figure 2–17 presents DroidDraw's user interface.

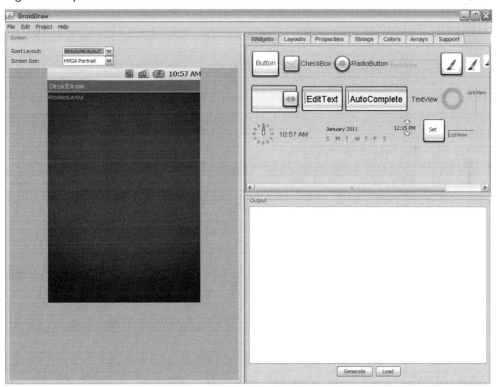

Figure 2–17. *DroidDraw's user interface reveals a mockup of an Android device screen.*

Exploring DroidDraw's User Interface

Figure 2–17 reveals a simple user interface consisting of a menubar, a screen area, a tabbed area, and an output area. You can drag each area's border by a small amount to enlarge or shrink that area.

The menubar consists of File, Edit, Properties, and Help menus. File presents the following menu items:

- *Open*: Open an Android layout file (such as `main.xml`)

- *Save*: Save the current layout information to the last opened layout file. A dialog box is displayed if no layout file has been opened.

- *Save As*: Display a dialog box that prompts the user for the name of a layout file and saves the current layout information to this file.

- *Quit*: Exit DroidDraw. Unsaved changes will be lost.

The Edit menu presents the following menu items:

- *Cut*: Remove the selected text plus the character to the right of the selected text from the output area.

- *Copy*: Copy the selected text from the output area to the clipboard.

- *Paste*: Paste the contents of the clipboard over the current selection or at the current caret position in the output area.

- *Select All*: Select the entire contents of the output area.

- *Clear Screen*: Remove all widgets and layout information from the user interface displayed in the screen area.

- *Set Ids from Labels*: Instead of assigning text such as `"@+id/widget29"` to a widget's `android:id` XML attribute, assign a widget's value (such as a button's OK text) to `android:id`; `"@+id/Ok"`, for example. This text is displayed in the output area the next time the XML layout information is generated.

Unlike the File and Edit menus, the menu items for the Project menu don't appear to be fully implemented.

The Help menu presents the following menu items:

- *Tutorial*: Point the default browser to `http://www.droiddraw.org/tutorial.html` to explore some interesting DroidDraw tutorials.

- *About*: Present a simple about dialog box without any version information.

- *Donate*: Point the default browser to the PayPal web site to make a donation that supports continued DroidDraw development.

The screen area presents visual feedback for the Android screen being built. It also provides Root Layout and Screen Size dropdown listboxes for choosing which layout serves as the ultimate parent layout (choices include AbsoluteLayout, LinearLayout, RelativeLayout, ScrollView, and TableLayout), and for choosing the target screen size so you'll know what the user interface looks like when displayed on that screen (choices include QVGA Landscape, QVGA Portrait, HVGA Landscape, and HVGA Portrait).

The tabbed area provides a Widgets tab whose widgets can be dragged to the screen, a Layouts tab whose layouts can be dragged to the screen, a Properties tab for entering values for the selected widget's/layout's properties, Strings/Colors/Arrays tabs for entering these resources, and a Support tab for making a donation.

Finally, the output area presents a textarea that displays the XML equivalent of the displayed screen when you click its Generate button. The Load button doesn't appear to accomplish anything useful (although it appears to undo a clear screen operation).

Creating a Simple Screen

Suppose you're building an app that displays (via a textview component) a randomly selected famous quotation in response to a button click. You decide to use DroidDraw to build the app's single screen.

Start DroidDraw, leave HVGA Portrait as the screen size, and replace AbsoluteLayout with LinearLayout as the root layout in order to present the textview and button components in a vertical column.

> **NOTE:** Unlike Android, which chooses horizontal as the default orientation for `LinearLayout`, DroidDraw chooses vertical as the default orientation.

On the Widgets tab, select TextView and drag it to the screen. Select the Properties tab, and enter `fill_parent` into the Width textfield, 100px into the Height textfield, and `Quotation` into the Text textfield. Click Apply; Figure 2–18 shows the resulting screen.

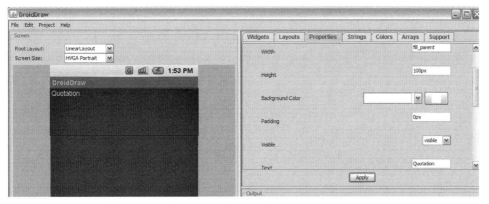

Figure 2–18. *The textview component appears at the top of the screen.*

On the Widgets tab, select Button and drag it to the screen. Select the Properties tab, and enter `fill_parent` into the Width textfield and `Get Quote` into the Text textfield. Click Apply; Figure 2–19 shows the resulting screen.

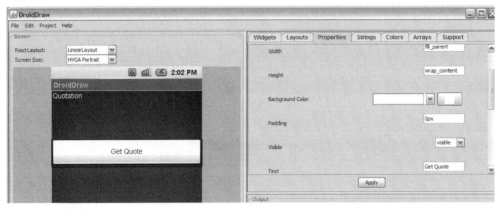

Figure 2–19. *The button component appears underneath the textview component.*

Select Save As from the File menu to save this screen's XML to a resource file named `main.xml`. As you learned in Chapter 1, this file is ultimately placed in the `layout` subdirectory of an Android project's `res` directory.

Alternatively, you could click the Generate button (at the bottom of the Output area) to generate the screen's XML (see Listing 2–64), select this text (via Edit's Select All menu item), and copy it to the clipboard (via Edit's Copy menu item) for later use.

Listing 2–64. *main.xml*

```xml
<?xml version="1.0" encoding="utf-8"?>
<LinearLayout
  android:id="@+id/widget27"
  android:layout_width="fill_parent"
  android:layout_height="fill_parent"
  xmlns:android="http://schemas.android.com/apk/res/android"
  android:orientation="vertical"
  >
<TextView
  android:id="@+id/widget29"
  android:layout_width="fill_parent"
  android:layout_height="100px"
  android:text="Quotation"
  >
</TextView>
<Button
  android:id="@+id/widget30"
  android:layout_width="fill_parent"
  android:layout_height="wrap_content"
  android:text="Get Quote"
  >
</Button>
</LinearLayout>
```

DroidDraw assigns text to XML properties rather than employing resource references. For example, Listing 2–64 assigns "Quotation" instead of "@string/quotation" to the TextView element's android:text property.

Although embedding strings is inconvenient from a maintenance perspective, you can use the Strings tab to enter string resource name/value pairs and click the Save button to save these resources to a strings.xml file, and manually enter the references later.

Summary

As you have seen, Android provides some very flexible and extensible user interface tools in the provided SDK. Properly leveraging these tools means you can be free of worrying whether or not your application will look and feel the same across the broad range of devices running Android today.

In this chapter, we have explored how to use Android's resource framework to supply resources for multiple devices. You saw techniques for manipulating static images as well as creating drawables of your own. We looked at overriding the default behavior of the window decorations as well as system input methods. We looked at ways to add user value through animating views. Finally we extended the default toolkit by creating new custom controls and customizing the AdapterViews used to display sets of data.

In the next chapter, we will look at using the SDK to communicate with the outside world; accessing network resources and talking to other devices.

Chapter 3

Communications and Networking

The key to many successful mobile applications is their ability to connect and interact with remote data sources. Web services and APIs are abundant in today's world, allowing an application to interact with just about any service, from weather forecasts to personal financial information. Bringing this data into the palm of a user's hand and making it accessible from anywhere is one of the greatest powers of the mobile platform. Android builds on the Web foundations that Google is known for and provides a rich toolset for communicating with the outside world.

3–1. Displaying Web Information

Problem

HTML or image data from the Web needs to be presented in the application without any modification or processing.

Solution

(API Level 1)

Display the information in a `WebView`. `WebView` is a view widget that can be embedded in any layout to display Web content, both local and remote, in your application. `WebView` is based on the same open source WebKit technology that powers the Android Browser application; affording applications the same level of power and capability.

How It Works

`WebView` has some very desirable properties when displaying assets downloaded from the Web , not the least of which are two-dimensional scrolling (horizontal and vertical at the same time), and zoom controls. A WebView can be the perfect place to house a large image, such as a stadium map, that the user may want to pan and zoom around. Here we will discuss how to do this with assets both local and remote.

Display a URL

The simplest case is displaying an HTML page or image by supplying the URL of the resource to the WebView. The following are a handful of practical uses for this technique in your applications:

- Provide access to your corporate site without leaving the application

- Display a page of live content from a web server, such as an FAQ section, that can be changed without requiring an upgrade to the application.

- Display a large image resource that the user would want to interact with using pan/zoom.

Let's take a look at a simple example that loads a very popular web page, but inside the content view of an Activity instead of opening the Browser (see Listings 3–1 and 3–2).

Listing 3–1. *Activity Containing a WebView*

```
public class MyActivity extends Activity {
    @Override
    public void onCreate(Bundle savedInstanceState) {
        super.onCreate(savedInstanceState);

        WebView webview = new WebView(this);
        //Enable JavaScript support
        webview.getSettings().setJavaScriptEnabled(true);
        webview.loadUrl("http://www.google.com/");

        setContentView(webview);
    }
}
```

> **NOTE:** By default, WebView has JavaScript support disabled. Be sure to enable JavaScript in the WebView.WebSettings object if the content you are displaying requires it.

Listing 3–2. *AndroidManifest.xml Setting Required Permissions*

```
<?xml version="1.0" encoding="utf-8"?>
<manifest xmlns:android="http://schemas.android.com/apk/res/android"
      package="com.examples.webview"
      android:versionCode="1"
      android:versionName="1.0">
    <application android:icon="@drawable/icon" android:label="@string/app_name">
        <activity android:name=".MyActivity">
            <intent-filter>
                <action android:name="android.intent.action.MAIN" />
                <category android:name="android.intent.category.LAUNCHER" />
            </intent-filter>
```

```
      </activity>
    </application>
    <uses-permission android:name="android.permission.INTERNET" />
</manifest>
```

> **IMPORTANT:** If the content you are loading into WebView is remote, AndroidManifest.xml must declare that it uses the android.permission.INTERNET permission.

The result displays the HTML page in your Activity (see Figure 3–1).

Sign in

iGoogle   Settings   Help

View Google in: **Mobile** | Classic

Figure 3–1. *HTML Page in a WebView*

Local Assets

WebView is also quite useful in displaying local content to take advantage of either HTML/CSS formatting or the pan/zoom behavior it provides to its contents. You may use the assets directory of your Android project to store resources you would like to display in a WebView, such as large images or HTML files. To better organize the assets, you may also create directories under assets to store files in.

WebView.loadUrl() can display stored under assets by using the *file:///android_asset/<resource path>* URL schema. For example, if the file android.jpg was placed into the assets directory, it could be loaded into a WebView using

```
file:///android_asset/android.jpg
```

If that same file were placed in a directory named `images` under assets, `WebView` could load it with the URL

```
file:///android_asset/images/android.jpg
```

In addition, `WebView.loadData()` will load raw HTML stored in a String resource or variable into the view. Using this technique, preformatted HTML text could be stored in `res/values/strings.xml` or downloaded from a remote API and displayed in the application.

Listings 3–3 and 3–4 show an example Activity with two `WebView` widgets stacked vertically on top of one another. The upper view is displaying a large image file stored in the assets directory, and the lower view is displaying an HTML string stored in the applications string resources.

Listing 3–3. *res/layout/main.xml*

```
<LinearLayout xmlns:android="http://schemas.android.com/apk/res/android"
  android:layout_width="fill_parent"
  android:layout_height="fill_parent"
  android:orientation="vertical">
  <WebView
    android:id="@+id/upperview"
    android:layout_width="fill_parent"
    android:layout_height="fill_parent"
    android:layout_weight="1"
  />
  <WebView
    android:id="@+id/lowerview"
    android:layout_width="fill_parent"
    android:layout_height="fill_parent"
    android:layout_weight="1"
  />
</LinearLayout>
```

Listing 3–4. *Activity to Display Local Web Content*

```
public class MyActivity extends Activity {
    @Override
    public void onCreate(Bundle savedInstanceState) {
        super.onCreate(savedInstanceState);
        setContentView(R.layout.main);

        WebView upperView = (WebView)findViewById(R.id.upperview);
        //Zoom feature must be enabled
        upperView.getSettings().setBuiltInZoomControls(true);
        upperView.loadUrl("file:///android_asset/android.jpg");

        WebView lowerView = (WebView)findViewById(R.id.lowerview);
        String htmlString =
            "<h1>Header</h1><p>This is HTML text<br /><i>Formatted in italics</i></p>";
        lowerView.loadData(htmlString, "text/html", "utf-8");
    }
}
```

When the Activity is displayed, each WebView occupies half of the screen's vertical space. The HTML string is formatted as expected, while the large image can be scrolled both horizontally and vertically; the user may even zoom in or out (see Figure 3–2).

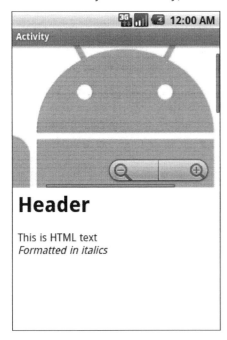

Figure 3–2. *Two WebViews displaying local resources*

3–2. Intercepting WebView Events

Problem

Your application is using a WebView to display content, but also needs to listen and respond to users clicking links on the page.

Solution

(API Level 1)

Implement a WebViewClient and attach it to the WebView. WebViewClient and WebChromeClient are two WebKit classes that allow an application to get event callbacks and customize the behavior of the WebView. By default, WebView will pass a URL to the ActivityManager to be handled if no WebViewClient is present, which usually results in any clicked link loading in the Browser application instead of the current WebView.

How It Works

In Listing 3–5, we create an Activity with a WebView that will handle its own URL loading.

Listing 3–5. *Activity with a WebView That Handles URLs*

```
public class MyActivity extends Activity {
    @Override
    public void onCreate(Bundle savedInstanceState) {
        super.onCreate(savedInstanceState);

        WebView webview = new WebView(this);
        webview.getSettings().setJavaScriptEnabled(true);
        //Add a client to the view
        webview.setWebViewClient(new WebViewClient());
        webview.loadUrl("http://www.google.com");
        setContentView(webview);
    }
}
```

In this example, simply providing a plain vanilla WebViewClient to WebView allows it to handle any URL requests itself, instead of passing them up to the ActivityManager, so clicking on a link will load the requested page inside the same view. This is because the default implementation simply returns false for shouldOverrideUrlLoading(), which tells the client to pass the URL to the WebView and not the application.

In this next case, we will take advantage of the WebViewClient.shouldOverrideUrlLoading() callback to intercept and monitor user activity (see Listing 3–6).

Listing 3–6. *Activity That Intercepts WebView URLs*

```
public class MyActivity extends Activity {
    @Override
    public void onCreate(Bundle savedInstanceState) {
        super.onCreate(savedInstanceState);

        WebView webview = new WebView(this);
        webview.getSettings().setJavaScriptEnabled(true);
        //Add a client to the view
        webview.setWebViewClient(mClient);
        webview.loadUrl("http://www.google.com");
        setContentView(webview);
    }

    private WebViewClient mClient = new WebViewClient() {
        @Override
        public boolean shouldOverrideUrlLoading(WebView view, String url) {
            Uri request = Uri.parse(url);

            if(TextUtils.equals(request.getAuthority(), "www.google.com")) {
                //Allow the load
                return false;
            }

            Toast.makeText(MyActivity.this, "Sorry, buddy", Toast.LENGTH_SHORT).show();
            return true;
```

```
        }
    };
}
```

In this example, `shouldOverrideUrlLoading()` determines whether to load the content back in this `WebView` based on the url it was passed, keeping the user from leaving Google's site. `Uri.getAuthority()` returns the hostname portion of a URL, and we use that to check if the link the user clicked is on Google's domain (www.google.com). If we can verify the link is to another Google page, returning false allows the `WebView` to load the content. If not, we notify the user and returning true tell the `WebViewClient` that the application has taken care of this URL, and not to allow the `WebView` to load it.

This technique can be more sophisticated, where the application actually handles the URL by doing something interesting. A custom schema could even be developed to create a full interface between your application and the `WebView` content.

3–3. Accessing WebView with JavaScript

Problem

Your application needs access to the raw HTML of the current contents displayed in a `WebView`, either to read or modify specific values.

Solution

(API Level 1)

Create a JavaScript interface to bridge between the `WebView` and application code.

How It Works

`WebView.addJavascriptInterface()` binds a Java object to JavaScript so that its methods can then be called within the `WebView`. Using this interface, JavaScript can be used to marshal data between your application code and the `WebView`'s HTML.

> **CAUTION:** Allowing JavaScript to control your application can inherently present a security threat, allowing remote execution of application code. This interface should be utilized with that possibility in mind.

Let's look at an example of this in action. Listing 3–7 presents a simple HTML form to be loaded into the WebView from local assets. Listing 3–8 is an Activity that uses two JavaScript functions to exchange data between the Activity preferences and content in a WebView.

Listing 3–7. *assets/form.html*

```html
<!DOCTYPE HTML PUBLIC "-//W3C//DTD HTML 4.01//EN"
    "http://www.w3.org/TR/html4/strict.dtd">
<html>
<form name="input" action="form.html" method="get">
Enter Email: <input type="text" id="emailAddress" />
<input type="submit" value="Submit" />
</form>
</html>
```

Listing 3–8. *Activity with JavaScript Bridge Interface*

```java
public class MyActivity extends Activity {
    @Override
    public void onCreate(Bundle savedInstanceState) {
        super.onCreate(savedInstanceState);

        WebView webview = new WebView(this);
        webview.getSettings().setJavaScriptEnabled(true);
        webview.setWebViewClient(mClient);
        //Attach the custom interface to the view
        webview.addJavascriptInterface(new MyJavaScriptInterface(), "BRIDGE");

        setContentView(webview);
        //Load the form
        webview.loadUrl("file:///android_asset/form.html");
    }

    private static final String JS_SETELEMENT =
        "javascript:document.getElementById('%s').value='%s'";
    private static final String JS_GETELEMENT =
        "javascript:window.BRIDGE.storeElement('%s',document.getElementById('%s').value)";
    private static final String ELEMENTID = "emailAddress";

    private WebViewClient mClient = new WebViewClient() {
        @Override
        public boolean shouldOverrideUrlLoading(WebView view, String url) {
            //Before leaving the page, attempt to retrieve the email using JavaScript
            view.loadUrl(String.format(JS_GETELEMENT, ELEMENTID, ELEMENTID));
            return false;
        }

        @Override
        public void onPageFinished(WebView view, String url) {
            //When page loads, inject address into page using JavaScript
            SharedPreferences prefs = getPreferences(Activity.MODE_PRIVATE);
            view.loadUrl(String.format(JS_SETELEMENT, ELEMENTID,
                prefs.getString(ELEMENTID, "")));
        }
    };

    private class MyJavaScriptInterface {
        //Store an element in preferences
        @SuppressWarnings("unused")
        public void storeElement(String id, String element) {
            SharedPreferences.Editor edit =
                getPreferences(Activity.MODE_PRIVATE).edit();
            edit.putString(id, element);
```

```
            edit.commit();
            //If element is valid, raise a Toast
            if(!TextUtils.isEmpty(element)) {
                Toast.makeText(MyActivity.this, element, Toast.LENGTH_SHORT).show();
            }
        }
    }
}
```

In this somewhat contrived example, a single element form is created in HTML and displayed in a WebView. In the Activity code, we look for a form value in the WebView with the id of "emailAddress," and save its value to SharedPreferences every time a link is clicked on the page (in this case, the submit button of the form) through the shouldOverrideUrlLoading() callback. Whenever the page finished loading (i.e., onPageFinished() is called), we attempt to inject the current value from SharedPreferences back into the web form.

A Java class is created called MyJavaScriptInterface, which defines the method storeElement(). When the view is created, we call the WebView.addJavascriptInterface() method to attach this object to the view, and give it the name BRIDGE. When calling this method, the String parameter is a name used to reference the interface inside of JavaScript code.

We have defined two JavaScript methods as constant Strings here, JS_GETELEMENT and JS_SETELEMENT. These methods are executed on the WebView by being passed to. loadUrl() Notice that JS_GETELEMENT is a reference to calling our custom interface function (referenced as BRIDGE.storeElement), which will call that method on MyJavaScripInterface and store the form element's value in preferences. If the value retrieved from the form is not blank, a Toast will also be raised.

Any JavaScript may be executed on the WebView in this manner, and it does not need to be a method included as part of the custom interface. JS_SETELEMENT, for example, uses pure JavaScript to set the value of the form element on the page.

One popular application of this technique is to remember form data that a user may need to enter in the application, but the form must be Web-based, such as a reservation form or payment form for a Web application that doesn't have a lower-level API to access.

3–4. Downloading an Image File

Problem

Your application needs to download and display an image from the Web or other remote server.

Solution

(API Level 3)

Use AsyncTask to download the data in a background thread. AsyncTask is a wrapper class that makes threading long-running operations into the background painless and simple; as well as managing concurrency with an internal thread pool. In addition to handling the background threading, callback methods are also provided before, during, and after the operation executes, allowing you to make any updates required on the main UI thread.

How It Works

In the context of downloading an image, let's create a subclass of ImageView called WebImageView, which will lazily load an image from a remote source and display it as soon as it is available. The downloading will be performed inside of an AsyncTask operation (see Listing 3–9).

Listing 3–9. *WebImageView*

```
public class WebImageView extends ImageView {

    private Drawable mPlaceholder, mImage;

    public WebImageView(Context context) {
        this(context, null);
    }

    public WebImageView(Context context, AttributeSet attrs) {
        this(context, attrs, 0);
    }

    public WebImageView(Context context, AttributeSet attrs, int defaultStyle) {
        super(context, attrs, defaultStyle);
    }

    public void setPlaceholderImage(Drawable drawable) {
        mPlaceholder = drawable;
        if(mImage == null) {
            setImageDrawable(mPlaceholder);
        }
    }

    public void setPlaceholderImage(int resid) {
        mPlaceholder = getResources().getDrawable(resid);
        if(mImage == null) {
            setImageDrawable(mPlaceholder);
        }
    }

    public void setImageUrl(String url) {
        DownloadTask task = new DownloadTask();
        task.execute(url);
```

```
            }
    private class DownloadTask extends AsyncTask<String, Void, Bitmap> {
        @Override
        protected Bitmap doInBackground(String... params) {
            String url = params[0];
            try {
                URLConnection connection = (new URL(url)).openConnection();
                InputStream is = connection.getInputStream();
                BufferedInputStream bis = new BufferedInputStream(is);

                ByteArrayBuffer baf = new ByteArrayBuffer(50);
                int current = 0;
                while ((current = bis.read()) != -1) {
                    baf.append((byte)current);
                }
                byte[] imageData = baf.toByteArray();
                return BitmapFactory.decodeByteArray(imageData, 0, imageData.length);
            } catch (Exception exc) {
                return null;
            }
        }

        @Override
        protected void onPostExecute(Bitmap result) {
            mImage = new BitmapDrawable(result);
            if(mImage != null) {
                setImageDrawable(mImage);
            }
        }
    };
}
```

As you can see, WebImageView is a simple extension of the Android ImageView widget. The setPlaceholderImage() methods allow a local drawable to be set as the display image until the remote content is finished downloading. The bulk of the interesting work begins once the view has been given a remote URL using setImageUrl(), at which point the custom AsyncTask begins work.

Notice that an AsyncTask is strongly typed with three values for the input parameter, progress value, and result. In this case, a String is passed in to the task's execute method and the background operation should return a Bitmap. The middle value, the progress, we are not using in this example, so it is set as Void. When extending AsyncTask, the only required method to implement is doInBackground(), which defines the chunk of work to be run on a background thread. In the previous example, this is where a connection is made to the remote URL provided and the image data is downloaded. Upon completion, we attempt to create a Bitmap from the downloaded data. If an error occurs at any point, the operation will abort and return null.

The other callback methods defined in AsyncTask, such as onPreExecute(), onPostExecute(), and onProgressUpdate(), are called on the main thread for the purposes of updating the user interface. In the previous example, onPostExecute() is used to update the view's image with the result data.

> **IMPORTANT:** Android UI classes are not thread-safe. Be sure to use one of the callback methods that occur on the main thread to make any updates to the UI. Do not update views from within `doInBackground()`.

Listings 3–10 and 3–11 show a simple example of using this class in an Activity. Since this class is not part of the `android.widget` or `android.view` packages, we must user the fully qualified package name when using it in XML.

Listing 3–10. *res/layout/main.xml*

```xml
<?xml version="1.0" encoding="utf-8"?>
<LinearLayout xmlns:android="http://schemas.android.com/apk/res/android"
  android:layout_width="fill_parent"
  android:layout_height="fill_parent"
  android:orientation="vertical">
  <com.examples.WebImageView
    android:id="@+id/webImage"
    android:layout_width="wrap_content"
    android:layout_height="wrap_content"
  />
</LinearLayout>
```

Listing 3–11. *Example Activity*

```java
public class WebImageActivity extends Activity {
    @Override
    public void onCreate(Bundle savedInstanceState) {
        super.onCreate(savedInstanceState);
        setContentView(R.layout.main);

        WebImageView imageView = (WebImageView)findViewById(R.id.webImage);
        imageView.setPlaceholderImage(R.drawable.icon);
        imageView.setImageUrl("http://apress.com/resource/weblogo/Apress_120x90.gif");
    }
}
```

In this example we first set a local image (the application icon) as the `WebImageView` placeholder. This image is displayed immediately to the user. We then tell the view to fetch an image of the Apress logo from the Web. As noted previously, this downloads the image in the background and, when it is complete, replaces the placeholder image in the view. It is this simplicity in creating background operations that had lead the Android team to refer to `AsyncTask` as "Painless Threading".

3–5. Downloading Completely in the Background

Problem

The application must download a large resource to the device, such as a movie file, that must not require the user to keep the application active.

Solution

(API Level 9)

Use the `DownloadManager` API. The `DownloadManager` is a service added to the SDK with API Level 9 that allows a long-running downloads to be handed off and managed completely by the system. The primary advantage of using this service is that `DownloadManager` will continue attempting to download the resource through failures, connection changes, and even device reboots.

How It Works

Listing 3–12 is a sample Activity that makes use of DownloadManager to handle the download of a large image file. When complete, the image is displayed in an ImageView. Whenever you utilize DownloadManager to access content from the Web , be sure to declare you are using the `android.permission.INTERNET` in the application's manifest.

Listing 3–12. *DownloadManager Sample Activity*

```java
public class DownloadActivity extends Activity {

    private static final String DL_ID = "downloadId";
    private SharedPreferences prefs;

    private DownloadManager dm;
    private ImageView imageView;

    @Override
    public void onCreate(Bundle savedInstanceState) {
        super.onCreate(savedInstanceState);
        imageView = new ImageView(this);
        setContentView(imageView);

        prefs = PreferenceManager.getDefaultSharedPreferences(this);
        dm = (DownloadManager)getSystemService(DOWNLOAD_SERVICE);
    }

    @Override
    public void onResume() {
        super.onResume();

        if(!prefs.contains(DL_ID)) {
            //Start the download
            Uri resource = Uri.parse("http://www.bigfoto.com/dog-animal.jpg");
            DownloadManager.Request request = new DownloadManager.Request(resource);
            request.setAllowedNetworkTypes(Request.NETWORK_MOBILE |
                Request.NETWORK_WIFI);
            request.setAllowedOverRoaming(false);
            //Display in the notification bar
            request.setTitle("Download Sample");
            long id = dm.enqueue(request);
            //Save the unique id
            prefs.edit().putLong(DL_ID, id).commit();
        } else {
            //Download already started, check status
```

```java
            queryDownloadStatus();
        }

        registerReceiver(receiver,
            new IntentFilter(DownloadManager.ACTION_DOWNLOAD_COMPLETE));
    }

    @Override
    public void onPause() {
        super.onPause();
        unregisterReceiver(receiver);
    }

    private BroadcastReceiver receiver = new BroadcastReceiver() {
        @Override
        public void onReceive(Context context, Intent intent) {
            queryDownloadStatus();
        }
    };

    private void queryDownloadStatus() {
        DownloadManager.Query query = new DownloadManager.Query();
        query.setFilterById(prefs.getLong(DL_ID, 0));
        Cursor c = dm.query(query);
        if(c.moveToFirst()) {
            int status = c.getInt(c.getColumnIndex(DownloadManager.COLUMN_STATUS));
            switch(status) {
            case DownloadManager.STATUS_PAUSED:
            case DownloadManager.STATUS_PENDING:
            case DownloadManager.STATUS_RUNNING:
                //Do nothing, still in progress
                break;
            case DownloadManager.STATUS_SUCCESSFUL:
                //Done, display the image
                try {
                    ParcelFileDescriptor file =
                        dm.openDownloadedFile(prefs.getLong(DL_ID, 0));
                    FileInputStream fis =
                        new ParcelFileDescriptor.AutoCloseInputStream(file);
                    imageView.setImageBitmap(BitmapFactory.decodeStream(fis));
                } catch (Exception e) {
                    e.printStackTrace();
                }
                break;
            case DownloadManager.STATUS_FAILED:
                //Clear the download and try again later
                dm.remove(prefs.getLong(DL_ID, 0));
                prefs.edit().clear().commit();
                break;
            }
        }
    }

}
```

> **IMPORTANT:** As of this book's publishing date, there is a bug in the SDK that throws an Exception claiming `android.permission.ACCESS_ALL_DOWNLOADS` is required to use DownloadManager. This Exception is actually thrown when `android.permission.INTERNET` is not in your manifest.

This example does all of its useful work in the `Activity.onResume()` method so the application can determine the status of the download each time the user returns to the Activity. Downloads within the manager can be references using a long ID value that is returned when `DownloadManager.enqueue()` is called. In the example, we persist that value in the application's preferences in order to monitor and retrieve the downloaded content at any time.

On first launch of the example application, a `DownloadManager.Request` object is created to represent the content to download. At a minimum, this request needs the `Uri` of the remote resource. However, there are many useful properties to set on the request as well to control its behavior. Some of the useful properties include:

- `Request.setAllowedNetworkTypes()`
- Set specific network types over which the download may be retrieved.
- `Request.setAllowedOverRoaming()`
- Set if the download is allowed to occur while the device is on a roaming connection.
- `Request.setTitle()`
- Set a title to be displayed in the system notification for the download.
- `Request.setDescription()`
- Set a description to be displayed in the system notification for the download.

Once an ID has been obtained, the application uses that value to check the status of the download. By registering a `BroadcastReceiver` to listen for the `ACTION_DOWNLOAD_COMPLETE` broadcast, the application will react to the download finishing by setting the image file on the Activity's ImageView. If the Activity is paused while the download completes, upon the next resume the status will be checked and the ImageView content will be set.

It is important to note that the `ACTION_DOWNLOAD_COMPLETE` is a broadcast sent by the `DownloadManager` for every download it may be managing. Because of this, we still much check that the download ID we are interested in is really ready.

Destinations

In the Listing 3–12 example, we never told the `DownloadManager` where to place the file. Instead, when we wanted to access the file we used the

DownloadManager.openDownloadedFile() method with the ID value stored in preferences to get a ParcelFileDescriptor, which can be turned into a stream the application can read from. This is a simple and straightforward way to gain access to the downloaded content, but it has some caveats to be aware of.

Without a specific destination, files are downloaded to the shared download cache, where the system retains the right to delete them at any time to reclaim space. Because of this, downloading in this fashion is a convenient way to get data quickly, but if your needs for the download are more long term, a permanent destination should be specific on external storage using one of the DownloadManager.Request methods:

- Request.setDestinationUri()
    - Set the destination to a file Uri located on external storage.
- Request.setDestinationInExternalFilesDir()
    - Set the destination to a hidden directory on external storage.
- Request.setDestinationInExternalPublicDir()
    - Set the destination to a public directory on external storage.

> **NOTE:** All destination methods writing to external storage will require your application to declare use of android.permission.WRITE_EXTERNAL_STORAGE in the manifest.

Files without an explicit destination also often get removed when DownloadManager.remove() gets called to clear the entry from the manager list or the user clears the downloads list; files downloaded to external storage will not be removed by the system under these conditions.

3–6. Accessing a REST API

Problem

Your application needs to access a RESTful API over HTTP to interact with the web services of a remote host.

Solution

(API Level 3)

Use the Apache HTTP classes inside of an AsyncTask. Android includes the Apache HTTP components library, which provides a robust method of creating connections to remote APIs. The Apache library includes classes to create GET, POST, PUT, and DELETE requests with ease, as well as providing support for SSL, cookie storage, authentication, and other HTTP requirements that your specific API may have in its HttpClient.

REST stands for Representational State Transfer, and is a common architectural style for web services today. RESTful APIs are typically built using standard HTTP verbs to create requests of the remote resource and the responses are typically returned in a structured document format, such as XML, JSON, or comma separated values (CSV).

How It Works

Listing 3–13 is an AsyncTask that can process any HttpUriRequest and return the string response.

Listing 3–13. *AsyncTask Processing HttpRequest*

```java
public class RestTask extends AsyncTask<HttpUriRequest, Void, String> {

    public static final String HTTP_RESPONSE = "httpResponse";

    private Context mContext;
    private HttpClient mClient;
    private String mAction;

    public RestTask(Context context, String action) {
        mContext = context;
        mAction = action;
        mClient = new DefaultHttpClient();
    }

    public RestTask(Context context, String action, HttpClient client) {
        mContext = context;
        mAction = action;
        mClient = client;
    }

    @Override
    protected String doInBackground(HttpUriRequest... params) {
        try{
            HttpUriRequest request = params[0];
            HttpResponse serverResponse = mClient.execute(request);

            BasicResponseHandler handler = new BasicResponseHandler();
            String response = handler.handleResponse(serverResponse);
            return response;
        } catch (Exception e) {
            e.printStackTrace();
            return null;
        }
    }

    @Override
    protected void onPostExecute(String result) {
        Intent intent = new Intent(mAction);
        intent.putExtra(HTTP_RESPONSE, result);
        //Broadcast the completion
        mContext.sendBroadcast(intent);
    }

}
```

The RestTask can be constructed with or without an HttpClient parameter. The reason for allowing this is so multiple requests can use the same client object. This is extremely useful if your API requires cookies to maintain a session or if there is a specific set of required parameters that are easier to set up once (like SSL stores). The task takes an HttpUriRequest parameter to process (of which HttpGet, HttpPost, HttpPut, and HttpDelete are all subclasses) and executes it.

A BasicResponseHandler processes the response, which is a convenience class that abstracts our task from needing to check the response for errors. BasicResponseHandler will return the HTTP response as a string if the response code is 1XX or 2XX, but throw an HttpResponseException if the response code was 300 or greater.

The final important piece of this class exists in onPostExecute(), after the interaction with the API is complete. When constructed, the RestTask takes a String parameter to be the action of an Intent that is broadcast back to all listeners with the API response encapsulated as an extra. This broadcast is the notification mechanism back to the caller of the API that the data is ready for processing.

Now let's use this powerful new tool to create some basic API requests. In the following examples we utilize the Yahoo! Search REST API. This API only has two required parameters for each request:

- appid
- Unique value to identify that application making the request
- query
- String representing the search query you want to execute

Visit http://developer.yahoo.com/search to find more information about this API.

GET Example

A GET request is the simplest and most common request in many public APIs. Parameters that must be sent with the request are encoded into the URL string itself, so no additional data must be provided. Let's create a GET request to search for "Android" (see Listing 3–14).

Listing 3–14. *Activity Executing API GET Request*

```
public class SearchActivity extends Activity {

    private static final String SEARCH_ACTION = "com.examples.rest.SEARCH";
    private static final String SEARCH_URI =
            "http://search.yahooapis.com/WebSearchService/V1/webSearch?appid=%s&query=%s";

    private TextView result;
    private ProgressDialog progress;

    @Override
    public void onCreate(Bundle savedInstanceState) {
        super.onCreate(savedInstanceState);
```

```
        result = new TextView(this);
        setContentView(result);

        //Create the search request
        try{
            String url = String.format(SEARCH_URI, "YahooDemo","Android");
            HttpGet searchRequest = new HttpGet( new URI(url) );

            RestTask task = new RestTask(this,SEARCH_ACTION);
            task.execute(searchRequest);
            //Display progress to the user
            progress = ProgressDialog.show(this, "Searching", "Waiting For Results...",
                true);
        } catch (Exception e) {
            e.printStackTrace();
        }
    }

    @Override
    public void onResume() {
        super.onResume();
        registerReceiver(receiver, new IntentFilter(SEARCH_ACTION));
    }

    @Override
    public void onPause() {
        super.onPause();
        unregisterReceiver(receiver);
    }

    private BroadcastReceiver receiver = new BroadcastReceiver() {
        @Override
        public void onReceive(Context context, Intent intent) {
            //Clear progress indicator
            if(progress != null) {
                progress.dismiss();
            }
            String response = intent.getStringExtra(RestTask.HTTP_RESPONSE);
            //Process the response data (here we just display it)
            result.setText(response);
        }
    };
}
```

In the example, we create the type of HTTP request that we need with the URL that we want to connect to (in this case, a GET request to search.yahooapis.com). The URL is stored as a constant format string, and the required parameters for the Yahoo! API (appid and query) are added at runtime just before the request is created.

A RestTask is created with a unique action string to be broadcast upon completion, and the task is executed. The example also defines a BroadcastReceiver and registers it for the same action that was sent to the RestTask. When the task is complete, this receiver will catch the broadcast and the API response can be unpacked and processed. We will discuss parsing structured XML and JSON responses like this one in Recipes 3–7 and 3–8, so for now the example simply displays the raw response to the user interface.

POST Example

Many times, APIs require that you provide some data as part of the request, perhaps an authentication token or the contents of a search query. The API will require you to send the request over HTTP POST so these values may be encoded into the request body instead of the URL. Let's run our search for "Android" again, but using a POST this time (see Listing 3–15).

Listing 3–15. *Activity Executing API POST Request*

```java
public class SearchActivity extends Activity {

    private static final String SEARCH_ACTION = "com.examples.rest.SEARCH";
    private static final String SEARCH_URI =
            "http://search.yahooapis.com/WebSearchService/V1/webSearch";
    private static final String SEARCH_QUERY = "Android";

    private TextView result;
    private ProgressDialog progress;

    @Override
    public void onCreate(Bundle savedInstanceState) {
        super.onCreate(savedInstanceState);
        setTitle("Activity");
        result = new TextView(this);
        setContentView(result);

        //Create the search request
        try{
            HttpPost searchRequest = new HttpPost( new URI(SEARCH_URI) );
            List<NameValuePair> parameters = new ArrayList<NameValuePair>();
            parameters.add(new BasicNameValuePair("appid","YahooDemo"));
            parameters.add(new BasicNameValuePair("query",SEARCH_QUERY));
            searchRequest.setEntity(new UrlEncodedFormEntity(parameters));

            RestTask task = new RestTask(this,SEARCH_ACTION);
            task.execute(searchRequest);
            //Display progress to the user
            progress = ProgressDialog.show(this, "Searching", "Waiting For Results...",
true);
        } catch (Exception e) {
            e.printStackTrace();
        }
    }

    @Override
    public void onResume() {
        super.onResume();
        registerReceiver(receiver, new IntentFilter(SEARCH_ACTION));
    }

    @Override
    public void onPause() {
        super.onPause();
        unregisterReceiver(receiver);
    }
```

```
    private BroadcastReceiver receiver = new BroadcastReceiver() {
        @Override
        public void onReceive(Context context, Intent intent) {
            //Clear progress indicator
            if(progress != null) {
                progress.dismiss();
            }
            String response = intent.getStringExtra(RestTask.HTTP_RESPONSE);
            //Process the response data (here we just display it)
            result.setText(response);
        }
    };
}
```

Notice in this example that the required parameters passed to the API to execute the search are encoded into an HttpEntity instead of passed directly in the request URL. The request created in this case was an HttpPost instance, which is still a subclass of HttpUriRequest (like HttpGet), so we can use the same RestTask to run the operation. As with the GET example, we will discuss parsing structured XML and JSON responses like this one in Recipes 3–7 and 3–8, so for now the example simply displays the raw response to the user interface.

> **NOTE:** The Apache library bundled with the Android SDK does not include support for Multipart HTTP POSTs. However, MultipartEntity, from the publicly available org.apache.http.mime library, is compatible and can be brought in to your project as an external source.

Basic Authentication

Another common requirement for working with an API is some form of authentication. Standards are emerging for REST API authentication such as OAuth 2.0, but the most common authentication method is still basic username and password authentication over HTTP. In Listing 3–16, we modify the RestTask to enable authentication in the HTTP header per request.

Listing 3–16. *RestTask with Basic Authentication*

```
public class RestAuthTask extends AsyncTask<HttpUriRequest, Void, String> {

    public static final String HTTP_RESPONSE = "httpResponse";

    private static final String AUTH_USER = "user@mydomain.com";
    private static final String AUTH_PASS = "password";

    private Context mContext;
    private AbstractHttpClient mClient;
    private String mAction;

    public RestAuthTask(Context context, String action, boolean authenticate) {
        mContext = context;
        mAction = action;
```

```
        mClient = new DefaultHttpClient();
        if(authenticate) {
            UsernamePasswordCredentials creds =
                    new UsernamePasswordCredentials(AUTH_USER, AUTH_PASS);
            mClient.getCredentialsProvider().setCredentials(AuthScope.ANY, creds);
        }
    }

    public RestAuthTask(Context context, String action, AbstractHttpClient client) {
        mContext = context;
        mAction = action;
        mClient = client;
    }

    @Override
    protected String doInBackground(HttpUriRequest... params) {
        try{
            HttpUriRequest request = params[0];
            HttpResponse serverResponse = mClient.execute(request);

            BasicResponseHandler handler = new BasicResponseHandler();
            String response = handler.handleResponse(serverResponse);
            return response;
        } catch (Exception e) {
            e.printStackTrace();
            return null;
        }
    }

    @Override
    protected void onPostExecute(String result) {
        Intent intent = new Intent(mAction);
        intent.putExtra(HTTP_RESPONSE, result);
        //Broadcast the completion
        mContext.sendBroadcast(intent);
    }

}
```

Basic authentication is added to the `HttpClient` in the Apache paradigm. Since our example task allows for a specific client object to be passed in for use, which may already have the necessary authentication credentials, we have only modified the case where a default client is created. In this case, a `UsernamePasswordCredentials` instance is created with the username and password strings, and then set on the client's `CredentialsProvider`.

3–7. Parsing JSON

Problem

Your application needs to parse responses from an API or other source that are formatted in JavaScript Object Notation (JSON).

Solution

(API Level 1)

Use the org.json parser classes that are baked into Android. The SDK comes with a very efficient set of classes for parsing JSON formatted strings in the org.json package. Simply create a new JSONObject or JSONArray from the formatted string data and you'll be armed with a set of accessor methods to get primitive data or nested JSONObjects and JSONArrays from within.

How It Works

This JSON parser is strict by default, meaning that it will halt with an Exception when encountering invalid JSON data or an invalid key. Accessor methods that prefix with "get" will throw a JSONException if the requested value is not found. In some cases this behavior is not ideal, and for the there is a companion set of methods that are prefixed with "opt". These methods will return null instead of throwing an exception when a value for the requested key is not found. In addition, many of them have an overloaded version that also takes a fallback parameter to return instead of null.

Let's look at an example of how to parse a JSON string into useful pieces. Consider the JSON in Listing 3–17.

Listing 3–17. *Example JSON*

```
{
    "person": {
        "name": "John",
        "age": 30,
        "children": [
            {
                "name": "Billy"
                "age": 5
            },
            {
                "name": "Sarah"
                "age": 7
            },
            {
                "name": "Tommy"
                "age": 9
            }
        ]
    }
}
```

This defines a single object with three values: name (String), age (Integer), and children. The parameter entitled "children" is an array of three more objects, each with their own name and age. If we were to use org.json to parse this data and display some elements in TextViews, it would look like the examples in Listings 3–18 and 3–19.

Listing 3–18. *res/layout/main.xml*

```
<?xml version="1.0" encoding="utf-8"?>
<LinearLayout xmlns:android="http://schemas.android.com/apk/res/android"
  android:layout_width="fill_parent"
  android:layout_height="fill_parent"
  android:orientation="vertical">
  <TextView
    android:id="@+id/line1"
    android:layout_width="fill_parent"
    android:layout_height="wrap_content"
  />
  <TextView
    android:id="@+id/line2"
    android:layout_width="fill_parent"
    android:layout_height="wrap_content"
  />
  <TextView
    android:id="@+id/line3"
    android:layout_width="fill_parent"
    android:layout_height="wrap_content"T
  />
</LinearLayout>
```

Listing 3–19. *Sample JSON Parsing Activity*

```
public class MyActivity extends Activity {
    private static final String JSON_STRING =
        "{\"person\":{\"name\":\"John\",\"age\":30,\"children\":
        [{\"name\":\"Billy\",\"age\":5}," + "\"name\":\"Sarah\",\"age\":7},
        {\"name\":\"Tommy\",\"age\":9}]}}";

    @Override
    public void onCreate(Bundle savedInstanceState) {
        super.onCreate(savedInstanceState);
        setContentView(R.layout.main);

        TextView line1 = (TextView)findViewById(R.id.line1);
        TextView line2 = (TextView)findViewById(R.id.line2);
        TextView line3 = (TextView)findViewById(R.id.line3);
        try {
            JSONObject person = (new JSONObject(JSON_STRING)).getJSONObject("person");
            String name = person.getString("name");
            line1.setText("This person's name is " + name);
            line2.setText(name + " is " + person.getInt("age") + " years old.");
            line3.setText(name + " has " + person.getJSONArray("children").length()
                + " children.");
        } catch (JSONException e) {
            e.printStackTrace();
        }
    }
}
```

For this example, the JSON string has been hard-coded as a constant. When the
Activity is created, the string is turned into a JSONObject, at which point all its data can
be accessed as key-value pairs, just as if it were stored in a Map or Dictionary. All the
business logic is wrapped in a try/catch statement since we are using the strict methods
for accessing data.

Functions like JSONObject.getString() and JSONObject.getInt() are used to reads primitive data out and place it in the TextView; the getJSONArray() method pulls out the nested "children" array. JSONArray has the same set of accessor methods as JSONObject to read data, but they take an index into the array as a parameter instead of the name of the key. In addition, a JSONArray can return its length, which we used in the example to display how many children the person had.

The result of the sample application is shown in Figure 3–3.

Figure 3–3. *Display of parsed JSON data in Activity*

Debugging Trick

JSON is a very efficient notation; however, it can be difficult for humans to read a raw JSON string, which can make it hard to debug parsing issues. Quite often the JSON you are parsing is coming from a remote source or is not completely familiar to you, and you need to display it for debugging purposes. Both JSONObject and JSONArray have an overloaded toString() method that takes an integer parameter for pretty-printing the data in a returned and indented fashion, making it easier to decipher. Often adding something like myJsonObject.toString(2) to a troublesome section can save time and headache.

3–8. Parsing XML

Problem

Your application needs to parse responses from an API or other source that are formatted as XML.

Solution

(API Level 1)

Implement a subclass of `org.xml.sax.helpers.DefaultHandler` to parse the data using event-based SAX. Android has three primary methods you can use to parse XML data: DOM, SAX, and Pull. The simplest to implement, and most memory-efficient, of these is the SAX parser. SAX parsing works by traversing the XML data and generating callback events at the beginning and end of each element.

How It Works

To describe this further, let's look at the format of the XML that is returned when requesting an RSS/ATOM news feed (see Listing 3–20).

Listing 3–20. *RSS Basic Structure*

```
<rss version="2.0">
  <channel>
    <item>
      <title></title>
      <link></link>
      <description></description>
    </item>
    <item>
      <title></title>
      <link></link>
      <description></description>
    </item>
    <item>
      <title></title>
      <link></link>
      <description></description>
    </item>
    ...
  </channel>
</rss>
```

Between each of the <title>, <link>, and <description> tags is the value associated with each item. Using SAX, we can parse this data out into an array of items that the application could then display to the user in a list (see Listing 3–21).

Listing 3–21. *Custom Handler to Parse RSS*

```java
public class RSSHandler extends DefaultHandler {

    public class NewsItem {
        public String title;
        public String link;
        public String description;

        @Override
        public String toString() {
            return title;
        }
    }

    private StringBuffer buf;
    private ArrayList<NewsItem> feedItems;
    private NewsItem item;

    private boolean inItem = false;

    public ArrayList<NewsItem> getParsedItems() {
        return feedItems;
    }

    //Called at the head of each new element
    @Override
    public void startElement(String uri, String name, String qName, Attributes atts) {
        if("channel".equals(name)) {
            feedItems = new ArrayList<NewsItem>();
        } else if("item".equals(name)) {
            item = new NewsItem();
            inItem = true;
        } else if("title".equals(name) && inItem) {
            buf = new StringBuffer();
        } else if("link".equals(name) && inItem) {
            buf = new StringBuffer();
        } else if("description".equals(name) && inItem) {
            buf = new StringBuffer();
        }
    }

    //Called at the tail of each element end
    @Override
    public void endElement(String uri, String name, String qName) {
        if("item".equals(name)) {
            feedItems.add(item);
            inItem = false;
        } else if("title".equals(name) && inItem) {
            item.title = buf.toString();
        } else if("link".equals(name) && inItem) {
            item.link = buf.toString();
        } else if("description".equals(name) && inItem) {
            item.description = buf.toString();
        }

        buf = null;
    }
```

```
//Called with character data inside elements
@Override
public void characters(char ch[], int start, int length) {
    //Don't bother if buffer isn't initialized
    if(buf != null) {
        for (int i=start; i<start+length; i++) {
            buf.append(ch[i]);
        }
    }
}
}
}
```

The RSSHandler is notified at the beginning and end of each element via startElement() and endElement(). In between, the characters that make up the element's value are passed into the characters() callback.

1. When the parser encounters the first element, the list of items is initialized.

2. When each item element is encountered a new NewsItem model is initialized.

3. Inside of each item element, data elements are captured in a StringBuffer and inserted into the members of the NewsItem.

4. When the end of each item is reached, the NewsItem is added to the list.

5. When parsing is complete, feedItems is a complete list of all the items in the feed.

Let's look at this in action by using some of the tricks from the API example in Recipe 3–6 to download the latest Google News in RSS form (see Listing 3–22).

Listing 3–22. *Activity That Parses the XML and Displays the Items*

```
public class FeedActivity extends Activity {
    private static final String FEED_ACTION = "com.examples.rest.FEED";
    private static final String FEED_URI = "http://news.google.com/?output=rss";

    private ListView list;
    private ArrayAdapter<NewsItem> adapter;

    @Override
    public void onCreate(Bundle savedInstanceState) {
        super.onCreate(savedInstanceState);

        list = new ListView(this);
        adapter = new ArrayAdapter<NewsItem>(this, android.R.layout.simple_list_item_1,
            android.R.id.text1);
        list.setAdapter(adapter);
        list.setOnItemClickListener(new AdapterView.OnItemClickListener() {
            @Override
            public void onItemClick(AdapterView<?> parent, View v, int position,
            long id) {
```

```
            NewsItem item = adapter.getItem(position);
            //Launch the link in the browser
            Intent intent = new Intent(Intent.ACTION_VIEW);
            intent.setData(Uri.parse(item.link));
            startActivity(intent);
        }
    });

    setContentView(list);
}

@Override
public void onResume() {
    super.onResume();
    registerReceiver(receiver, new IntentFilter(FEED_ACTION));
    //Retrieve the RSS feed
    try{
        HttpGet feedRequest = new HttpGet( new URI(FEED_URI) );
        RestTask task = new RestTask(this,FEED_ACTION);
        task.execute(feedRequest);
    } catch (Exception e) {
        e.printStackTrace();
    }
}

@Override
public void onPause() {
    super.onPause();
    unregisterReceiver(receiver);
}

private BroadcastReceiver receiver = new BroadcastReceiver() {
    @Override
    public void onReceive(Context context, Intent intent) {
        String response = intent.getStringExtra(RestTask.HTTP_RESPONSE);

        try {
            //Parse the response data using SAX
            SAXParserFactory factory = SAXParserFactory.newInstance();
            SAXParser p = factory.newSAXParser();
            RSSHandler parser = new RSSHandler();
            //Run the parsing operation
            p.parse(new InputSource(new StringReader(response)), parser);
            //Clear all current items from the list
            adapter.clear();
            //Add all items from the parsed XML
            for(NewsItem item : parser.getParsedItems()) {
                adapter.add(item);
            }
            //Tell adapter to update the view
            adapter.notifyDataSetChanged();
        } catch (Exception e) {
            e.printStackTrace();
        }
    }
};
}
```

The example has been modified to display a ListView, which will be populated by the parsed items from the RSS feed. In the example, we add an OnItemClickListener to the list that will launch the news item's link in the browser.

Once the data is returned from the API in the BroadcastReceiver, Android's built-in SAXParser handles the job of traversing the XML string. SAXParser.parse() uses an instance of our RSSHandler to process the XML, which results in the handler's feedItems list being populated. The receiver then iterates through all the parsed items and adds them to an ArrayAdapter for display in the ListView.

3–8. Receiving SMS

Problem

Your application must react to incoming SMS messages, commonly called text messages.

Solution

(API Level 1)

Register a BroadcastReceiver to listen for incoming messages, and process them in onReceive(). The operating system will fire a broadcast Intent with the android.provider.Telephony.SMS_RECEIVED action whenever there is an incoming SMS message. Your application can register a BroadcastReceiver to filter for this Intent and process the incoming data.

> **NOTE:** Receiving this broadcast does not prevent the rest of the system's applications from receiving it as well. The default messaging application will still receive and display any incoming SMS.

How It Works

In previous recipes, we have defined BroadcastReceivers as private internal members to an Activity. In this case, it is probably best to define the receiver separately and register it in AndroidManifest.xml using the <receiver> tag. This will allow your receiver to process the incoming events even when your application is not active. Listings 3–23 and 3–24 show an example receiver that monitors all incoming SMS, and raises a Toast when one arrives from the interesting party.

Listing 3–23. *Incoming SMS BroadcastReceiver*

```
public class SmsReceiver extends BroadcastReceiver {
    private static final String SHORTCODE = "55443";

    @Override
```

```
public void onReceive(Context context, Intent intent) {
    Bundle bundle = intent.getExtras();

    Object[] messages = (Object[])bundle.get("pdus");
    SmsMessage[] sms = new SmsMessage[messages.length];
    //Create messages for each incoming PDU
    for(int n=0; n < messages.length; n++) {
        sms[n] = SmsMessage.createFromPdu((byte[]) messages[n]);
    }
    for(SmsMessage msg : sms) {
        //Verify if the message came from our known sender
        if(TextUtils.equals(msg.getOriginatingAddress(), SHORTCODE)) {
            Toast.makeText(context,
                    "Received message from the mothership: "+msg.getMessageBody(),
                    Toast.LENGTH_SHORT).show();
        }
    }
}
```

Listing 3–24. *Partial AndroidManifest.xml*

```xml
<?xml version="1.0" encoding="utf-8"?>
<manifest …>
    <application …>
      <receiver android:name=".SmsReceiver">
        <intent-filter>
          <action android:name="android.provider.Telephony.SMS_RECEIVED" />
        </intent-filter>
      </receiver>
    </application>
    <uses-permission android:name="android.permission.RECEIVE_SMS" />
</manifest>
```

> **IMPORTANT:** Receiving SMS requires the `android.permission.RECEIVE_SMS` permission be declared in the manifest!

Incoming SMS messages are passed via the extras of the broadcast Intent as an Object array of byte arrays, each byte array representing an SMS packet data unit (PDU). `SmsMessage.createFromPdu()` is a convenience method allowing us to create `SmsMessage` objects from the raw PDU data. With the setup work complete, we can inspect each message to determine if there is something interesting to handle or process. In the example, we compare the originating address of each message against a known short code, and notify the user when one arrives.

At the point in the example where the Toast is raised, you may wish to provide something more useful to the user. Perhaps the SMS message includes an offer code for your application, and you could launch the appropriate Activity to display this information to the user within the application.

3–9. Sending an SMS Message

Problem

Your application must issue outgoing SMS messages.

Solution

(API Level 4)

Use the SMSManager to send text and data SMS messages. SMSManager is a system service that handles sending SMS and providing feedback to the application about the status of the operation. SMSManager provides methods to send text messages using SmsManager.sendTextMessage() and SmsManager.sendMultipartTextMessage(), or data messages using SmsManager.sendDataMessage(). Each of these methods takes PendingIntent parameters to deliver status for the send operation and the message delivery back to a requested destination.

How It Works

Let's take a look at a simple example Activity that sends an SMS message and monitors its status (see Listing 3–25).

Listing 3–25. *Activity to Send SMS Messages*

```
public class SmsActivity extends Activity {
    private static final String SHORTCODE = "55443";
    private static final String ACTION_SENT = "com.examples.sms.SENT";
    private static final String ACTION_DELIVERED = "com.examples.sms.DELIVERED";

    @Override
    public void onCreate(Bundle savedInstanceState) {
        super.onCreate(savedInstanceState);

        Button sendButton = new Button(this);
        sendButton.setText("Hail the Mothership");
        sendButton.setOnClickListener(new View.OnClickListener() {
            @Override
            public void onClick(View v) {
                sendSMS("Beam us up!");
            }
        });

        setContentView(sendButton);
    }

    private void sendSMS(String message) {
        PendingIntent sIntent = PendingIntent.getBroadcast(this, 0,
            new Intent(ACTION_SENT), 0);
        PendingIntent dIntent = PendingIntent.getBroadcast(this, 0,
            new Intent(ACTION_DELIVERED), 0);
         //Monitor status of the operation
```

```
        registerReceiver(sent, new IntentFilter(ACTION_SENT));
        registerReceiver(delivered, new IntentFilter(ACTION_DELIVERED));
        //Send the message
        SmsManager manager = SmsManager.getDefault();
        manager.sendTextMessage(SHORTCODE, null, message, sIntent, dIntent);
    }

    private BroadcastReceiver sent = new BroadcastReceiver(){
        @Override
        public void onReceive(Context context, Intent intent) {
            switch (getResultCode()) {
            case Activity.RESULT_OK:
                //Handle sent success
                break;
            case SmsManager.RESULT_ERROR_GENERIC_FAILURE:
            case SmsManager.RESULT_ERROR_NO_SERVICE:
            case SmsManager.RESULT_ERROR_NULL_PDU:
            case SmsManager.RESULT_ERROR_RADIO_OFF:
                //Handle sent error
                break;
            }

            unregisterReceiver(this);
        }
    };

    private BroadcastReceiver delivered = new BroadcastReceiver(){
        @Override
        public void onReceive(Context context, Intent intent) {
            switch (getResultCode()) {
            case Activity.RESULT_OK:
                //Handle delivery success
                break;
            case Activity.RESULT_CANCELED:
                //Handle delivery failure
                break;
            }

            unregisterReceiver(this);
        }
    };
}
```

IMPORTANT: Sending SMS messages requires the `android.permission.SEND_SMS` permission be declared in the manifest!

In the example, an SMS message is sent out via the SMSManager whenever the user taps the button. Because SMSManager is a system service, the static SMSManager.getDefault() method must be called to get a reference to it. sendTextMessage() takes the destination address (number), service center address, and message as parameters. The service center address should be null to allow SMSManager to use the system default.

Two BroadcastReceivers are registered to receive the callback Intents that will be sent: one for status of the send operation and the other for status of the delivery. The receivers are registered only while the operations are pending, and they unregister themselves as soon as the Intent is processed.

3–10. Communicating over Bluetooth

Problem

You want to leverage Bluetooth communication to transmit data between devices in your application.

Solution

(API Level 5)

Use the Bluetooth APIs introduced in API Level 5 to create a peer-to-peer connection. Bluetooth is a very popular wireless radio technology that is in almost all mobile devices today. Many users think of Bluetooth as a way for their mobile device to connect with a wireless headset or integrate with their vehicles stereo system. However, Bluetooth can also be a simple and effective way for developers to create peer-to-peer connections in their applications.

How It Works

IMPORTANT: Bluetooth is not currently supported in the Android emulator. In order to execute the code in this example, it must be run on an Android device. Furthermore, to appropriately test the functionality, two devices running the application simultaneously is required.

Bluetooth Peer-To-Peer

Listings 3–26 through 3–28 illustrate an example that uses Bluetooth to find other users nearby and quickly exchange contact information (in this case, just an email address). Connections are made over Bluetooth by discovering available "services" and connecting to them by referencing their unique 128-bit UUID value. This means that the UUID of the service you want to use must either be discovered or known ahead of time.

In this example, the same application is running on both devices on each end of the connection, so we have the freedom to define the UUID in code as a constant because both devices will have a reference to it.

NOTE: To ensure that the UUID you choose is unique, use one of the many free UUID generators available on the Web .

Listing 3–26. *AndroidManifest.xml*

```xml
<?xml version="1.0" encoding="utf-8"?>
<manifest xmlns:android="http://schemas.android.com/apk/res/android"
      android:versionCode="1"
      android:versionName="1.0" package="com.examples.bluetooth">
    <application android:icon="@drawable/icon" android:label="@string/app_name"
        <activity android:name=".ExchangeActivity"
                android:label="@string/app_name">
            <intent-filter>
                <action android:name="android.intent.action.MAIN" />
                <category android:name="android.intent.category.LAUNCHER" />
            </intent-filter>
        </activity>
    </application>
    <uses-sdk android:minSdkVersion="5" />

    <uses-permission android:name="android.permission.BLUETOOTH"/>
    <uses-permission android:name="android.permission.BLUETOOTH_ADMIN"/>
</manifest>
```

> **IMPORTANT:** Remember that `android.permission.BLUETOOTH` must be declared in the manifest to use these APIs. In addition, `android.permission.BLUETOOTH_ADMIN` must be declared to make changes to preferences like discoverability, and enable/disable the adapter.

Listing 3–27. *res/layout/main.xml*

```xml
<?xml version="1.0" encoding="utf-8"?>
<RelativeLayout xmlns:android="http://schemas.android.com/apk/res/android"
  android:layout_width="fill_parent"
  android:layout_height="fill_parent">
  <TextView
    android:id="@+id/label"
    android:layout_width="wrap_content"
    android:layout_height="wrap_content"
    android:textAppearance="?android:attr/textAppearanceLarge"
    android:text="Enter Your Email:"
  />
  <EditText
    android:id="@+id/emailField"
    android:layout_width="fill_parent"
    android:layout_height="wrap_content"
    android:layout_below="@id/label"
    android:singleLine="true"
    android:inputType="textEmailAddress"
  />
  <Button
    android:id="@+id/scanButton"
    android:layout_width="fill_parent"
    android:layout_height="wrap_content"
    android:layout_alignParentBottom="true"
    android:text="Connect and Share"
  />
  <Button
```

```
        android:id="@+id/listenButton"
        android:layout_width="fill_parent"
        android:layout_height="wrap_content"
        android:layout_above="@id/scanButton"
        android:text="Listen for Sharers"
    />
</RelativeLayout>
```

The user interface for this example consists of an EditText for the user to enter their email address, and two buttons to initiate communication. The button titled "Listen for Sharers" puts the device into Listen Mode. In this mode, the device will accept and communicate with any device that attempts to connect with it. The button titled "Connect and Share" puts the device into Search Mode. In this mode, the device searches for any device that is currently listening and makes a connection (see Listing 3–28).

Listing 3–28. *Bluetooth Exchange Activity*

```java
public class ExchangeActivity extends Activity {

    // Unique UUID for this application (generated from the web)
    private static final UUID MY_UUID =
        UUID.fromString("321cb8fa-9066-4f58-935e-ef55d1ae06ec");
    //Friendly name to match while discovering
    private static final String SEARCH_NAME = "bluetooth.recipe";

    BluetoothAdapter mBtAdapter;
    BluetoothSocket mBtSocket;
    Button listenButton, scanButton;
    EditText emailField;

    @Override
    public void onCreate(Bundle savedInstanceState) {
        super.onCreate(savedInstanceState);
        requestWindowFeature(Window.FEATURE_INDETERMINATE_PROGRESS);
        setContentView(R.layout.main);

        //Check the system status
        mBtAdapter = BluetoothAdapter.getDefaultAdapter();
        if(mBtAdapter == null) {
            Toast.makeText(this, "Bluetooth is not supported.",
                Toast.LENGTH_SHORT).show();
            finish();
            return;
        }
        if (!mBtAdapter.isEnabled()) {
            Intent enableIntent = new Intent(BluetoothAdapter.ACTION_REQUEST_ENABLE);
            startActivityForResult(enableIntent, REQUEST_ENABLE);
        }

        emailField = (EditText)findViewById(R.id.emailField);
        listenButton = (Button)findViewById(R.id.listenButton);
        listenButton.setOnClickListener(new View.OnClickListener() {
            @Override
            public void onClick(View v) {
                //Make sure the device is discoverable first
                if (mBtAdapter.getScanMode() !=
```

```
                          BluetoothAdapter.SCAN_MODE_CONNECTABLE_DISCOVERABLE) {
                    Intent discoverableIntent = new
                          Intent(BluetoothAdapter.ACTION_REQUEST_DISCOVERABLE);
                    discoverableIntent.putExtra(BluetoothAdapter.
                          EXTRA_DISCOVERABLE_DURATION, 300);
                    startActivityForResult(discoverableIntent, REQUEST_DISCOVERABLE);
                    return;
                }
                startListening();
            }
        });
        scanButton = (Button)findViewById(R.id.scanButton);
        scanButton.setOnClickListener(new View.OnClickListener() {
            @Override
            public void onClick(View v) {
                mBtAdapter.startDiscovery();
                setProgressBarIndeterminateVisibility(true);
            }
        });
    }

    @Override
    public void onResume() {
        super.onResume();
        //Register the activity for broadcast intents
        IntentFilter filter = new IntentFilter(BluetoothDevice.ACTION_FOUND);
        registerReceiver(mReceiver, filter);
        filter = new IntentFilter(BluetoothAdapter.ACTION_DISCOVERY_FINISHED);
        registerReceiver(mReceiver, filter);
    }

    @Override
    public void onPause() {
        super.onPause();
        unregisterReceiver(mReceiver);
    }

    @Override
    public void onDestroy() {
        super.onDestroy();
        try {
            if(mBtSocket != null) {
                mBtSocket.close();
            }
        } catch (IOException e) {
            e.printStackTrace();
        }
    }

    private static final int REQUEST_ENABLE = 1;
    private static final int REQUEST_DISCOVERABLE = 2;

    @Override
    protected void onActivityResult(int requestCode, int resultCode, Intent data) {
        switch(requestCode) {
        case REQUEST_ENABLE:
            if(resultCode != Activity.RESULT_OK) {
```

```java
                Toast.makeText(this, "Bluetooth Not Enabled.",
                    Toast.LENGTH_SHORT).show();
                finish();
            }
            break;
        case REQUEST_DISCOVERABLE:
            if(resultCode == Activity.RESULT_CANCELED) {
                Toast.makeText(this, "Must be discoverable.",
                    Toast.LENGTH_SHORT).show();
            } else {
                startListening();
            }
            break;
        default:
            break;
        }
    }

    //Start a server socket and listen
    private void startListening() {
        AcceptTask task = new AcceptTask();
        task.execute(MY_UUID);
        setProgressBarIndeterminateVisibility(true);
    }

    //AsyncTask to accept incoming connections
    private class AcceptTask extends AsyncTask<UUID,Void,BluetoothSocket> {

        @Override
        protected BluetoothSocket doInBackground(UUID... params) {
            String name = mBtAdapter.getName();
            try {
                //While listening, set the discovery name to a specific value
                mBtAdapter.setName(SEARCH_NAME);
                BluetoothServerSocket socket =
                    mBtAdapter.listenUsingRfcommWithServiceRecord("BluetoothRecipe",
                    params[0]);
                BluetoothSocket connected = socket.accept();
                //Reset the BT adapter name
                mBtAdapter.setName(name);
                return connected;
            } catch (IOException e) {
                e.printStackTrace();
                mBtAdapter.setName(name);
                return null;
            }
        }

        @Override
        protected void onPostExecute(BluetoothSocket socket) {
            if(socket == null) {
                return;
            }
            mBtSocket = socket;
            ConnectedTask task = new ConnectedTask();
            task.execute(mBtSocket);
        }
```

```
}

    //AsyncTask to receive a single line of data and post
    private class ConnectedTask extends AsyncTask<BluetoothSocket,Void,String> {

        @Override
        protected String doInBackground(BluetoothSocket... params) {
            InputStream in = null;
            OutputStream out = null;
            try {
                //Send your data
                out = params[0].getOutputStream();
                out.write(emailField.getText().toString().getBytes());
                //Receive the other's data
                in = params[0].getInputStream();
                byte[] buffer = new byte[1024];
                in.read(buffer);
                //Create a clean string from results
                String result = new String(buffer);
                //Close the connection
                mBtSocket.close();
                return result.trim();
            } catch (Exception exc) {
                return null;
            }
        }

        @Override
        protected void onPostExecute(String result) {
            Toast.makeText(ExchangeActivity.this, result, Toast.LENGTH_SHORT).show();
            setProgressBarIndeterminateVisibility(false);
        }
    }

    // The BroadcastReceiver that listens for discovered devices
    private BroadcastReceiver mReceiver = new BroadcastReceiver() {
        @Override
        public void onReceive(Context context, Intent intent) {
            String action = intent.getAction();

            // When discovery finds a device
            if (BluetoothDevice.ACTION_FOUND.equals(action)) {
                // Get the BluetoothDevice object from the Intent
                BluetoothDevice device =
                    intent.getParcelableExtra(BluetoothDevice.EXTRA_DEVICE);
                if(TextUtils.equals(device.getName(), SEARCH_NAME)) {
                    //Matching device found, connect
                    mBtAdapter.cancelDiscovery();
                    try {
                        mBtSocket = device.createRfcommSocketToServiceRecord(MY_UUID);
                        mBtSocket.connect();
                        ConnectedTask task = new ConnectedTask();
                        task.execute(mBtSocket);
                    } catch (IOException e) {
                        e.printStackTrace();
                    }
```

```
        }
    //When discovery is complete
    } else if (BluetoothAdapter.ACTION_DISCOVERY_FINISHED.equals(action)) {
        setProgressBarIndeterminateVisibility(false);
    }

        }
    };
}
```

When the application first starts up, it runs some basic checks on the Bluetooth status of the device. If BluetoothAdapter.getDefaultAdapter() returns null, it is an indication that the device does not have Bluetooth support and the application will go no further. Even with Bluetooth on the device, it must be enabled for the application to use it. If Bluetooth is disabled, the preferred method for enabling the adapter is to send an Intent to the system with BluetoothAdapter.ACTION_REQUEST_ENABLE as the action. This notifies the user of the issue, and allows them to enable Bluetooth. A BluetoothAdapter can be manually enabled with the enable() method, but we strongly discourage you from doing this unless you have requested the user's permission another way.

With Bluetooth validated, the application waits for user input. As mentioned previously, the example can be put into one of two modes on each device, Listen Mode or Search Mode. Let's look at the path each mode takes.

Listen Mode

Tapping the "Listen for Sharers" button starts the application listening for incoming connections. In order for a device to accept incoming connections from devices it may not know, it must be set as discoverable. The application verifies this by checking if the adapter's scan mode is equal to SCAN_MODE_CONNECTABLE_DISCOVERABLE. If the adapter does not meet this requirement, another Intent is sent to the system to notify the user that they should allow the device to be discoverable, similar to the method used to request Bluetooth be enabled. If the user accepts this request, the Activity will return a result equal to the length of time they allowed the device to be discoverable; if they cancel the request, the Activity will return Activity.RESULT_CANCELED. Our example monitors for a user canceling in onActivityResult(), and finishes under those conditions.

If the user allows discovery, or if the device was already discoverable, an AcceptTask is created and executed. This task creates a listener socket for the specified UUID of the service we defined, and blocks while waiting for an incoming connection request. Once a valid request is received, it is accepted and the application moves into Connected Mode.

During the period of time while the device is listening, its Bluetooth name is set to a known unique value (SEARCH_NAME) to speed up the discovery process (we'll see more about why in the "Search Mode" section). Once the connection is established, the default name given to the adapter is restored.

Search Mode

Tapping the "Connect and Share" button tells the application to begin searching for another device to connect with. It does this by starting a Bluetooth discovery process and handling the results in a BroadcastReceiver. When a discovery is started via `BluetoothAdapter.startDiscovery()`, Android will asynchronously call back with broadcasts under two conditions: when another device is found, and when the process is complete.

The private receiver `mReceiver` is registered at all times when the Activity is visible to the user, and will receive a broadcast with each new discovered device. Recall from the discussion on Listen Mode that the device name of a listening device was set to a unique value. Upon each discovery made, the receiver checks if the device name matches our known value, and attempts to connect when one is found. This is important to the speed of the discovery process because otherwise the only way to validate each device is to attempt a connection to the specific service UUID and see if the operation is successful. The Bluetooth connection process is heavyweight and slow, and should only be done when necessary to keep things performing well.

This method of matching devices also relieves the user of the need to select manually which device they want to connect to. The application is smart enough to find another device that is running the same application and in a listening mode to complete the transfer. Removing the user also means that this value should be unique and obscure so as to avoid finding other devices that may accidentally have the same name.

With a matching device found, we cancel the discovery process (as it is also heavyweight and will slow down the connection) and make a connection to the service's UUID. With a successful connection made, the application moves into Connected Mode.

Connected Mode

Once connected, the application on both devices will create a `ConnectedTask` to send and receive the user contact information. The connected `BluetoothSocket` has an `InputStream` and an `OutputStream` available to do data transfer. First, the current value of the email text field is packaged up and written to the `OutputStream`. Then, the `InputStream` is read to receive the remote device's information. Finally, each device takes the raw data it received and packages it into a clean String to display for the user.

The `ConnectedTask.onPostExecute()` method is tasked with displaying the results of the exchange to the user; currently, this is done by raising a Toast with the received contents. After the transaction, the connection is closed and both devices are in the same mode and ready to execute another exchange.

For more information on this topic, take a look at the BluetoothChat sample application provided with the Android SDK. This application provides a great demonstration of making a long-lived connection for users to send chat messages between devices.

Bluetooth Beyond Android

As we mentioned in the beginning of this section, Bluetooth is found in many wireless devices besides mobile phones and tablets. RFCOMM interfaces also exist in devices like Bluetooth modems and serial adapters. The same APIs that were used to create the peer-to-peer connection between Android devices can also be used to connect to other embedded Bluetooth devices for the purposes of monitoring and control.

The key to establishing a connection with these embedded devices is obtaining the UUID of the RFCOMM services they support. As with the previous example, with the proper UUID we can create a BluetoothSocket and transmit data. However, since the UUID is not known as it was in the last example, we must have a way to discover and obtain it.

The capability to do this exists in the SDK, although it is not documented and is subject to change in future versions.

Discover a UUID

A quick glance at the source code for BluetoothDevice (thanks to Android's open source roots) points out that there are a couple hidden methods that return UUID information for a remote device. The simplest to use is a synchronous (blocking) method called getUuids(), which returns an array of ParcelUuid objects referring to each service. However, since the method is currently hidden, it must be called using Java reflection. Here is an example method for reading the UUIDs of service records from a remote device using reflection:

```
public ParcelUuid servicesFromDevice(BluetoothDevice device) {
    try {
        Class cl = Class.forName("android.bluetooth.BluetoothDevice");
        Class[] par = {};
        Method method = cl.getMethod("getUuids", par);
        Object[] args = {};
        ParcelUuid[] retval = (ParcelUuid[])method.invoke(device, args);
        return retval;
    } catch (Exception e) {
        e.printStackTrace();
        return null;
    }
}
```

There is also an asynchronous version of this process named fetchUuidsWithSdp(), which can be called in the same fashion. Because it is asynchronous, the results are returned through a broadcast Intent. Register a BroadcastReceiver for android.bleutooth.device.action.UUID (note the misspelling of Bluetooth) to get a callback with the UUIDs discovered for that device. The ParcelUuid array obtained is an extra passed with the Intent referenced by android.bluetooth.device.extra.UUID, and it is the same as the result of the synchronous example.

3–11. Querying Network Reachability

Problem

Your application needs to be aware of changes in network connectivity.

Solution

(API Level 1)

Keep tabs on the device's connectivity with ConnectivityManager. One of the paramount issues to consider in mobile application design is that the network is not always available for use. As people move about, the speed and capabilities of the network are subject to change. Because of this, an application that uses network resources should always be able to detect if those resources are reachable, and notify the user when they are not.

In addition to reachability, ConnectivityManager can provide the application with information about the connection type. This allows you to make decisions like whether to download a large file because the user is currently roaming and it may cost them a fortune.

How It Works

Listing 3–29 creates a wrapper method you can place in your code to check for network connectivity.

Listing 3–29. *ConnectivityManager Wrapper*

```
public boolean isNetworkReachable() {
    ConnectivityManager mManager =
            (ConnectivityManager)context.getSystemService(Context.CONNECTIVITY_SERVICE);
    NetworkInfo current = mManager.getActiveNetworkInfo();
    if(current == null) {
        return false;
    }
    return (current.getState() == NetworkInfo.State.CONNECTED);
}
```

ConnectivityManager does pretty much all of the work in checking the network status, and this wrapper method is more to simplify having to check all possible network paths each time. Note that ConnectivityManager.getActiveNetworkInfo() will return null if there is no active data connection available, so we must check for that case first. If there is an active network, we can inspect its state, which will return one of the following:

- DISCONNECTED

- CONNECTING

- CONNECTED

- DISCONNECTING

When the state returns as CONNECTED, the network is considered stable and we can utilize it to access remote resources.

It is considered good practice to call a reachability check whenever a network request fails, and notify the user that their request failed due to a lack of connectivity. Listing 3–30 is an example of doing this when a network access fails.

Listing 3–30. *Notify User of Connectivity Failure*

```
try {
    //Attempt to access network resource
    //May throw HttpResponseException or some other IOException on failure
} catch (Exception e) {
    if( !isNetworkReachable() ) {
        AlertDialog.Builder builder = new AlertDialog.Builder(context);
        builder.setTitle("No Network Connection");
        builder.setMessage("The Network is unavailable. Please try your request again later.");
        builder.setPositiveButton("OK",null);
        builder.create().show();
    }
}
```

Determining Connection Type

In cases where it is also essential to know whether the user is connected to a network that charges for bandwidth, we can call NetworkInfo.getType() on the active network connection (see Listing 3–31).

Listing 3–31. *ConnectivityManager Bandwidth Checking*

```
public boolean isWifiReachable() {
    ConnectivityManager mManager =
            (ConnectivityManager)context.getSystemService(Context.CONNECTIVITY_SERVICE);
    NetworkInfo current = mManager.getActiveNetworkInfo();
    if(current == null) {
        return false;
    }
    return (current.getType() == ConnectivityManager.TYPE_WIFI);
}
```

This modified version of the reachability check determines if the users is attached to a WiFi connection, typically indicating that they have a faster connection where bandwidth isn't tariffed.

Summary

Connecting an Android application to the Web and web services is a great way to add user value in today's connected world. Android's framework for connecting to the Web and other remote hosts makes adding this functionality straightforward. We've explored how to bring the standards of the Web into your application, using HTML and JavaScript to interact with the user, but within a native context. You also saw how to use Android to download content from remote servers and consume it in your application. We also exposed that a web server is not the only host worth connecting to, using Bluetooth and SMS to communicate directly from one device to another. In the next chapter, we will look at using the tools Android provides to interact with a device's hardware resources.

Chapter 4

Interacting with Device Hardware and Media

Integrating application software with device hardware presents opportunities to create unique user experiences that only the mobile platform can provide. Capturing media using the microphone and camera allows applications to incorporate a personal touch through a photo or recorded greeting. Integration of sensor and location data can help you develop applications to answer relevant questions such as, "Where am I?" and, "What am I looking at?"

In this chapter, we are going to investigate how the location, media, and sensor APIs provided by Android can be used to add that unique value the mobile brings into your applications.

4–1. Integrating Device Location

Problem

You want to leverage the device's ability to report its current physical position in an application.

Solution

(API Level 1)

Utilize the background services provided by the Android LocationManager. One of the most powerful benefits that a mobile application can often provide to the user is the ability to add context by including information based on where they are currently located. Applications may ask the LocationManager to provide updates of a device's location either regularly, or just when it is detected that the device has moved a significant distance.

When working with the Android location services, some care should be taken to respect both the device battery and the user's wishes. Obtaining a fine-grained location fix using a device's GPS is a power-intensive process, and can quickly drain the battery in the user's device if left on continuously. For this reason, among others, Android allows the user to disable certain sources of location data, such as the device's GPS. These settings must be observed when your application decides how it will obtain location.

Each location source also comes with a tradeoff degree of accuracy. The GPS will return a more exact location (within a few meters), but take longer to fix and use more power; whereas the Network location will usually be accurate to a few kilometers, but is returned much faster and uses less power. Consider the requirements of the application when deciding which sources to access; if your application only wishes to display information about the local city, perhaps GPS fixes are not necessary.

> **IMPORTANT:** When using location services in an application, keep in mind that `android.permission.ACCESS_COARSE_LOCATION` or `android.permission.ACCESS_FINE_LOCATION` must be declared in the application manifest. If you declare `android.permission.ACCESS_FINE_LOCATION`, you do not need both as it includes coarse permissions as well.

How It Works

When creating a simple monitor for user location in an Activity or Service, there are a few actions that we need to consider:

1. Determine if the source we want to use is enabled. If it's not, decide whether to ask the user to enable it or try another source.

2. Register for updates using reasonable values for minimum distance and update interval.

3. Unregister for updates when they are no longer needed to conserve device power.

In Listing 4–1, we register an Activity to listen for location updates while it is visible to the user, and display that location onscreen.

Listing 4–1. *Activity Monitoring Location Updates*

```
public class MyActivity extends Activity {

    LocationManager manager;
    Location currentLocation;

    TextView locationView;

    @Override
    public void onCreate(Bundle savedInstanceState) {
        super.onCreate(savedInstanceState);
```

```java
        locationView = new TextView(this);
        setContentView(locationView);

        manager = (LocationManager)getSystemService(Context.LOCATION_SERVICE);
    }

    @Override
    public void onResume() {
        super.onResume();
        if(!manager.isProviderEnabled(LocationManager.GPS_PROVIDER)) {
            //Ask the user to enable GPS
            AlertDialog.Builder builder = new AlertDialog.Builder(this);
            builder.setTitle("Location Manager");
            builder.setMessage("We want to use your location, but GPS is currently disabled.\n"
                    +"Would you like to change these settings now?");
            builder.setPositiveButton("Yes", new DialogInterface.OnClickListener() {
                @Override
                public void onClick(DialogInterface dialog, int which) {
                    //Launch settings, allowing user to make a change
                    Intent i = new Intent(Settings.ACTION_LOCATION_SOURCE_SETTINGS);
                    startActivity(i);
                }
            });
            builder.setNegativeButton("No", new DialogInterface.OnClickListener() {
                @Override
                public void onClick(DialogInterface dialog, int which) {
                    //No location service, no Activity
                    finish();
                }
            });
            builder.create().show();
        }

        //Get a cached location, if it exists
        currentLocation = manager.getLastKnownLocation(LocationManager.GPS_PROVIDER);
        updateDisplay();
        //Register for updates
        int minTime = 5000;
        float minDistance = 0;
        manager.requestLocationUpdates(LocationManager.GPS_PROVIDER,
                minTime, minDistance, listener);
    }

    @Override
    public void onPause() {
        super.onPause();
        manager.removeUpdates(listener);
    }

    //Update text view
    private void updateDisplay() {
        if(currentLocation == null) {
            locationView.setText("Determining Your Location...");
        } else {
            locationView.setText(String.format("Your Location:\n%.2f, %.2f",
                    currentLocation.getLatitude(),
```

```
                    currentLocation.getLongitude()));
        }
    }

    //Handle location callback events
    private LocationListener listener = new LocationListener() {

        @Override
        public void onLocationChanged(Location location) {
            currentLocation = location;
            updateDisplay();
        }

        @Override
        public void onProviderDisabled(String provider) { }

        @Override
        public void onProviderEnabled(String provider) { }

        @Override
        public void onStatusChanged(String provider, int status, Bundle extras) { }

    };
}
```

This example chooses to work strictly with the device's GPS to get location updates. Because it is a key element to the functionality of this Activity, the first major task undertaken after each resume is to check if the LocationManager.GPS_PROVIDER is still enabled. If, for any reason, the user has disabled this feature, we give them the opportunity to rectify this by asking if they would like to enable GPS. An application does not have the ability to do this for the user, so if they agree we launch an Activity using the Intent action Settings.ACTION_LOCATION_SOURCE_SETTINGS, which brings up the device settings so the user may enable GPS.

Once GPS is active and available, the Activity registers a LocationListener to be notified of location updates. The LocationManager.requestLocationUpdates() method takes two major parameters of interest in addition to the provider type and destination listener:

- minTime

    - The minimum time interval between updates, in milliseconds.

    - Setting this to non-zero allows the location provider to rest for approximately the specified period before updating again.

    - This is a parameter to conserver power, and should not be set to a value any lower than the minimum acceptable update rate.

- minDistance

    - The distance the device must move before another update will be sent, in meters.

- Setting this to non-zero will block updates until it is determined that the device has moved at least this much.

In the example, we request that updates be sent no more often than every five seconds, with no regard for whether the location has changed significantly or not. When these updates arrive, the onLocationChanged() method of the registered listener is called. Notice that a LocationListener will also be notified when the status of different providers changes, although we are not utilizing those callbacks here.

> **NOTE:** If you are receiving updates in a Service or other background operation, Google recommends that the minimum time interval should be no less than 60,000 (60 seconds).

The example keeps a running reference to the latest location it received. Initially, this value is set to the last known location that the provider has cached by calling getLastKnownLocation(), which may return null if the provider does not have a cached location value. With each incoming update, the location value is reset and the user interface display is updated to reflect the new change.

4–2. Mapping Locations

Problem

You would like to display one or more locations on a map for the user.

Solution

(API Level 1)

The simplest way to show the user a map is to create an Intent with the location data and pass it to the Android system to launch in a mapping application. We'll look more in-depth at this method for doing a number of different tasks in a later chapter. In addition, maps can be embedded within your application using the MapView and MapActivity provided by the Google Maps API SDK add-on.

The Maps API is an add-on module to the core SDK, although they are still bundled together. If you do not already have the Google APIs SDK, open the SDK manager and you will find a package for each API level listed under "Third-party Add-ons."

In order to use the Maps API in your application, an API key must first be obtained from Google. This key is built using the private key that your application is signed with. Without an API key, the mapping classes may be utilized, but no map tiles will be returned to the application.

> **NOTE:** For more information on the SDK, and to obtain an API key, visit
> http://code.google.com/android/add-ons/google-apis/mapkey.html.
> Notice also that Android uses the same signing key for all applications run in debug mode (such
> as when they are run from the IDE), so one key can serve for all applications you develop while in
> the testing phase.

If you are running code in an emulator to test, that emulator must be built with an SDK target that includes the Google APIs for mapping to operate properly. If you create emulators from the command line, these targets are named "Google Inc.:Google APIs:X," where "X" is the API version indicator. If you create emulators from inside an IDE (such as Eclipse), the target has a similar naming convention of "Google APIs (Google Inc.) – X," where "X" is the API version indicator.

With the API key in hand and a suitable test platform in place, you are ready to begin.

How It Works

To display a map, simply create an instance of `MapView` inside a `MapActivity`. One of the required attributes that must be passed to the `MapView` in your XML layout is the API key that you obtained from Google. See Listing 4–2.

Listing 4–2. *Typical MapView in a Layout*

```
<com.google.android.maps.MapView
  android:layout_width="fill_parent"
  android:layout_height="fill_parent"
  android:enabled="true"
  android:clickable="true"
  android:apiKey="API_KEY_STRING_HERE"
/>
```

> **NOTE:** When adding `MapView` to an XML layout, the fully qualified package name must be
> included, because the class does not exist in `android.view` or `android.widget`.

Although, MapView may be instantiated from code as well, the API key is still required as a constructor parameter:

```
MapView map = new MapView(this, "API_KEY_STRING_HERE");
```

In addition, the application manifest must declare its use of the Maps library, which dually acts as an Android Market filter to remove the application from devices that don't have this capability.

Now, let's look at an example that puts the last known user location on a map and displays it. See Listing 4–3.

Listing 4–3. *AndroidManifest.xml*

```xml
<?xml version="1.0" encoding="utf-8"?>
<manifest xmlns:android="http://schemas.android.com/apk/res/android"
    package="com.examples.mapper"
    android:versionCode="1"
    android:versionName="1.0">
    <uses-sdk android:minSdkVersion="3" />
    <uses-permission android:name="android.permission.ACCESS_FINE_LOCATION" />
    <uses-permission android:name="android.permission.INTERNET" />

    <application android:icon="@drawable/icon" android:label="@string/app_name">
        <activity android:name=".MyActivity"
            android:label="@string/app_name">
            <intent-filter>
                <action android:name="android.intent.action.MAIN" />
                <category android:name="android.intent.category.LAUNCHER" />
            </intent-filter>
        </activity>

        <uses-library android:name="com.google.android.maps"></uses-library>

    </application>
</manifest>
```

Notice the permissions declared for INTERNET and ACCESS_FINE_LOCATION. The latter is only required because this example is hooking back up to the LocationManager to get the cached location value. The other key ingredient that must be present in the manifest is the <uses-library> tag referencing the Google Maps API. Android requires this item to properly link the external library into your application build, but it also serves another purpose. The library declaration is used by Android Market to filter out the application so it cannot be installed on devices that are not equipped with the proper mapping library. See Listing 4–4.

Listing 4–4. *res/layout/main.xml*

```xml
<?xml version="1.0" encoding="utf-8"?>
<LinearLayout xmlns:android="http://schemas.android.com/apk/res/android"
  android:orientation="vertical"
  android:layout_width="fill_parent"
  android:layout_height="fill_parent">
  <TextView
    android:layout_width="fill_parent"
    android:layout_height="wrap_content"
    android:gravity="center_horizontal"
    android:text="Map Of Your Location"
  />
  <com.google.android.maps.MapView
    android:id="@+id/map"
    android:layout_width="fill_parent"
    android:layout_height="fill_parent"
    android:enabled="true"
    android:clickable="true"
    android:apiKey="YOUR_API_KEY_HERE"
  />
</LinearLayout>
```

Note the location of the required API key that you must enter. Also, notice that the MapView does not have to be the only thing in the Activity layout, despite the fact that it must be inflated inside of a MapActivity. See Listing 4–5.

Listing 4–5. *MapActivity Displaying Cached Location*

```
public class MyActivity extends MapActivity {

    MapView map;
    MapController controller;

    @Override
    public void onCreate(Bundle savedInstanceState) {
        super.onCreate(savedInstanceState);
        setContentView(R.layout.main);

        map = (MapView)findViewById(R.id.map);
        controller = map.getController();

        LocationManager manager =
            (LocationManager)getSystemService(Context.LOCATION_SERVICE);
        Location location = manager.getLastKnownLocation(LocationManager.GPS_PROVIDER);
        int lat, lng;
        if(location != null) {
            //Convert to microdegrees
            lat = (int)(location.getLatitude() * 1000000);
            lng = (int)(location.getLongitude() * 1000000);
        } else {
            //Default to Google HQ
            lat = 37427222;
            lng = -122099167;
        }
        GeoPoint mapCenter = new GeoPoint(lat,lng);
        controller.setCenter(mapCenter);
        controller.setZoom(15);
    }

    //Required abstract method, return false
    @Override
    protected boolean isRouteDisplayed() {
        return false;
    }
}
```

This Activity takes the latest user location, and centers the map on that point. All control of the map is done through a MapController instance, which we obtain by calling MapView.getController(); the controller can be used to pan, zoom, and otherwise adjust the map on screen. In this example, we use the controller's setCenter() and setZoom() methods to adjust the map display.

MapController.setCenter() takes a GeoPoint as its parameter, which is slightly different than the Location we receive from the Android services. The primary difference is that GeoPoint expresses latitude and longitude in terms of microdegrees (or degrees * 1E6) instead of a decimal value representing whole degrees. Therefore, we must convert the Location values before applying them to the map.

`MapController.setZoom()` allows the map to be programmatically zoomed to a specified level, between 1 and 21. By default, the map will zoom to level 1, which the SDK documentation defines as being a global view, with each increasing level magnifying the map by two. See Figure 4–1.

Figure 4–1. *Map of user location*

The first thing you will probably notice is that the map doesn't display any indicator on the location point (such as a pin). In Recipe 4–3 we will create these annotations, and describe how to customize them.

4–3. Annotating Maps

Problem

In addition to displaying a map centered on a specific location, your application needs to put an annotation down to more visibly mark the location.

Solution

(API Level 1)

Create a custom `ItemizedOverlay` for the map, which includes all of the points to mark. `ItemizedOverlay` is an abstract base class that handles all the drawing of the individual items on a MapView. The items themselves are instances of OverlayItem, which is a model class that defines the name, subtitle, and drawable marker to describe the point on the map.

How It Works

Let's create an implementation of ItemizedOverlay that will take an array of GeoPoints and draw them on the map using the same drawable marker for each. See Listing 4–6.

Listing 4–6. *Basic ItemizedOverlay Implementation*

```
public class LocationOverlay extends ItemizedOverlay<OverlayItem> {
    private List<GeoPoint> mItems;

    public LocationOverlay(Drawable marker) {
        super( boundCenterBottom(marker) );
    }

    public void setItems(ArrayList<GeoPoint> items) {
        mItems = items;
        populate();
    }

    @Override
    protected OverlayItem createItem(int i) {
        return new OverlayItem(mItems.get(i), null, null);
    }

    @Override
    public int size() {
        return mItems.size();
    }

    @Override
    protected boolean onTap(int i) {
        //Handle a tap event here
        return true;
    }
}
```

In this implementation, the constructor takes a Drawable to represent the marker placed on the map at each location. Drawables that are used in overlays must have proper bounds applied to them, and boundCenterBottom() is a convenience method that handles this for us. Specifically, it applies bounds, such that the point on the Drawable that touches the map location will be in the center of the bottom row of pixels.

ItemizedOverlay has two abstract methods that must be overridden: createItem(), which must return an object of the declared type, and size(), which returns the number of items managed. This example takes a list of GeoPoints and wraps them all into OverlayItems. The populate() method should be called on the overlay as soon as all the data is present and ready for display, which in this case is at the end of setItems().

Let's apply this overlay to a map to draw three custom locations around Google HQ, using the default app icon as the marker. See Listing 4–7.

Listing 4–7. *Activity Using Custom Map Overlay*

```
public class MyActivity extends MapActivity {

    MapView map;
    MapController controller;

    @Override
    public void onCreate(Bundle savedInstanceState) {
        super.onCreate(savedInstanceState);
        setContentView(R.layout.main);

        map = (MapView)findViewById(R.id.map);
        controller = map.getController();

        ArrayList<GeoPoint> locations = new ArrayList<GeoPoint>();
        //Google HQ @ 37.427,-122.099
        locations.add(new GeoPoint(37427222,-122099167));
        //Subtract 0.01 degrees
        locations.add(new GeoPoint(37426222,-122089167));
        //Add 0.01 degrees
        locations.add(new GeoPoint(37428222,-122109167));

        LocationOverlay myOverlay =
            new LocationOverlay(getResources().getDrawable(R.drawable.icon));
        myOverlay.setItems(locations);
        map.getOverlays().add(myOverlay);
        controller.setCenter(locations.get(0));
        controller.setZoom(15);

    }
    //Required abstract method, return false
    @Override
    protected boolean isRouteDisplayed() {
        return false;
    }

}
```

When run, this Activity produces the display shown in Figure 4–2.

Figure 4–2. *Map with ItemizedOverlay*

Notice how the drawing of the drop shadow on the marker was handled for us by
MapView and the ItemizedOverlay.

But, what if we want to customize each item so it displays a different marker image?
How would we do that? By explicitly setting the item's marker, a custom Drawable can
be returned for each item. In this case, the Drawable provided to the ItemizedOverlay
constructor is just a default value to be used if no custom override exists. Consider a
modification to the implementation, shown in Listing 4–8.

Listing 4–8. *ItemizedOverlay with Custom Markers*

```
public class LocationOverlay extends ItemizedOverlay<OverlayItem> {
    private List<GeoPoint> mItems;
    private List<Drawable> mMarkers;

    public LocationOverlay(Drawable marker) {
        super( boundCenterBottom(marker) );
    }

    public void setItems(ArrayList<GeoPoint> items, ArrayList<Drawable> drawables) {
        mItems = items;
        mMarkers = drawables;
        populate();
    }

    @Override
    protected OverlayItem createItem(int i) {
        OverlayItem item = new OverlayItem(mItems.get(i), null, null);
```

```
            item.setMarker( boundCenterBottom(mMarkers.get(i)) );
            return item;
        }

        @Override
        public int size() {
            return mItems.size();
        }

        @Override
        protected boolean onTap(int i) {
            //Handle a tap event here
            return true;
        }
    }
}
```

With this modification, the OverlayItems created now receive a custom marker image in the form of a bounded Drawable matching the item's index in a list of images. If the Drawable that you set has states, the pressed and focused states will display when the item is selected or touched. Our example modified to use the new implementation looks like Listing 4–9.

Listing 4–9. *Example Activity Providing Custom Markers*

```
public class MyActivity extends MapActivity {

    MapView map;
    MapController controller;

    @Override
    public void onCreate(Bundle savedInstanceState) {
        super.onCreate(savedInstanceState);
        setContentView(R.layout.main);

        map = (MapView)findViewById(R.id.map);
        controller = map.getController();

        ArrayList<GeoPoint> locations = new ArrayList<GeoPoint>();
        ArrayList<Drawable> images = new ArrayList<Drawable>();

        //Google HQ 37.427,-122.099
        locations.add(new GeoPoint(37427222,-122099167));
        images.add(getResources().getDrawable(R.drawable.logo));
        //Subtract 0.01 degrees
        locations.add(new GeoPoint(37426222,-122089167));
        images.add(getResources().getDrawable(R.drawable.icon));
        //Add 0.01 degrees
        locations.add(new GeoPoint(37428222,-122109167));
        images.add(getResources().getDrawable(R.drawable.icon));

        LocationOverlay myOverlay =
            new LocationOverlay(getResources().getDrawable(R.drawable.icon));
        myOverlay.setItems(locations, images);
        map.getOverlays().add(myOverlay);
        controller.setCenter(locations.get(0));
        controller.setZoom(15);
```

```
    }

    //Required abstract method, return false
    @Override
    protected boolean isRouteDisplayed() {
        return false;
    }
}
```

Now our example provides a discrete image for each item it wants to display on the map. Specifically, we have decided to represent the actual Google HQ location by a version of the Google logo, while keeping the other two points with the same marker. See Figure 4–3.

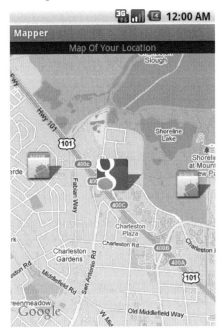

Figure 4–3. *Map overlay with custom markers*

Make Them Interactive

Perhaps you noticed the onTap() method that was defined in the LocationOverlay, but never mentioned. Another nice feature of the ItemizedOverlay base implementation is that it handles hit testing and has a convenience method when a specific item it tapped, referencing that item's index. From this method, you can raise a toast, show a dialog, start a new Activity, or any other action that fits the context of the user tapping on the annotation for more information.

What About Me?

The Maps API for Android also includes a special overlay to draw the user location, the MyLocationOverlay. This overlay is very straightforward to use, but it should only be enabled while the Activity it is present on is visible. Otherwise, unnecessary resource usage will cause poor performance and battery life on the device. See Listing 4–10.

Listing 4–10. *Adding a MyLocationOverlay*

```
public class MyActivity extends MapActivity {

    MapView map;
    MyLocationOverlay myOverlay;

    @Override
    public void onCreate(Bundle savedInstanceState) {
        super.onCreate(savedInstanceState);
        setContentView(R.layout.main);

        map = (MapView)findViewById(R.id.map);
        myOverlay = new MyLocationOverlay(this, map);
        map.getOverlays().add(myOverlay);
    }

    @Override
    public void onResume() {
        super.onResume();
        myOverlay.enableMyLocation();
    }

    @Override
    public void onPause() {
        super.onResume();
        myOverlay.disableMyLocation();
    }

    //Required abstract method, return false
    @Override
    protected boolean isRouteDisplayed() {
        return false;
    }
}
```

This will display a standard dot or arrow marker (depending on whether the compass is in use) on the user's latest location, and will track as the user moves as long as the overlay is enabled.

They key to using the MyLocationOverlay is to disable its features when they are not in use (when the Activity is not visible), and re-enable them when they are needed. Just as with using the LocationManager, this ensures these services are not draining unnecessary power.

4–4. Capturing Images and Video

Problem

Your application needs to make use of the device's camera in order to capture media, whether it be still images or short video clips.

Solution

(API Level 3)

Send an Intent to Android to transfer control to the Camera application, and return the image the user captured. Android does contain APIs for directly accessing the camera hardware, previewing, and taking snapshots or videos. However, if your only goal is to simply get the media content using the camera with an interface the user is familiar with, there is not better solution than a handoff.

How It Works

Let's take a look at how to use the Camera application to take both still images and video clips.

Image Capture

Let's take a look at an example Activity that will activate the camera application when the "Take a Picture" button is pressed, and receive the result of this operation as a Bitmap. See Listings 4–11 and 4–12.

Listing 4–11. *res/layout/main.xml*

```xml
<?xml version="1.0" encoding="utf-8"?>
<LinearLayout xmlns:android="http://schemas.android.com/apk/res/android"
  android:orientation="vertical"
  android:layout_width="fill_parent"
  android:layout_height="fill_parent">
  <Button
    android:id="@+id/capture"
    android:layout_width="fill_parent"
    android:layout_height="wrap_content"
    android:text="Take a Picture"
  />
  <ImageView
    android:id="@+id/image"
    android:layout_width="fill_parent"
    android:layout_height="fill_parent"
    android:scaleType="centerInside"
  />
</LinearLayout>
```

Listing 4–12. *Activity to Capture an Image*

```java
public class MyActivity extends Activity {

    private static final int REQUEST_IMAGE = 100;

    Button captureButton;
    ImageView imageView;

    @Override
    public void onCreate(Bundle savedInstanceState) {
        super.onCreate(savedInstanceState);
        setContentView(R.layout.main);

        captureButton = (Button)findViewById(R.id.capture);
        captureButton.setOnClickListener(listener);

        imageView = (ImageView)findViewById(R.id.image);
    }

    @Override
    protected void onActivityResult(int requestCode, int resultCode, Intent data) {
        if(requestCode == REQUEST_IMAGE && resultCode == Activity.RESULT_OK) {
            //Process and display the image
            Bitmap userImage = (Bitmap)data.getExtras().get("data");
            imageView.setImageBitmap(userImage);
        }
    }

    private View.OnClickListener listener = new View.OnClickListener() {
        @Override
        public void onClick(View v) {
            Intent intent = new Intent(MediaStore.ACTION_IMAGE_CAPTURE);
            startActivityForResult(intent, REQUEST_IMAGE);
        }
    };
}
```

This method captures the image and returns a scaled-down Bitmap as an extra in the "data" field. If you need to capture an image and need the full-sized image to be saved somewhere, insert a Uri for the image destination into the MediaStore.EXTRA_OUTPUT field of the Intent before starting the capture. See Listing 4–13.

Listing 4–13. *Full-Size Image Capture to File*

```java
public class MyActivity extends Activity {

    private static final int REQUEST_IMAGE = 100;

    Button captureButton;
    ImageView imageView;
    File destination;

    @Override
    public void onCreate(Bundle savedInstanceState) {
        super.onCreate(savedInstanceState);
        setContentView(R.layout.main);
```

```
        captureButton = (Button)findViewById(R.id.capture);
        captureButton.setOnClickListener(listener);

        imageView = (ImageView)findViewById(R.id.image);

        destination = new File(Environment.getExternalStorageDirectory(),"image.jpg");
    }

    @Override
    protected void onActivityResult(int requestCode, int resultCode, Intent data) {
        if(requestCode == REQUEST_IMAGE && resultCode == Activity.RESULT_OK) {
            try {
                FileInputStream in = new FileInputStream(destination);
                BitmapFactory.Options options = new BitmapFactory.Options();
                options.inSampleSize = 10; //Downsample by 10x

                Bitmap userImage = BitmapFactory.decodeStream(in, null, options);
                imageView.setImageBitmap(userImage);
            } catch (Exception e) {
                e.printStackTrace();
            }
        }
    }

    private View.OnClickListener listener = new View.OnClickListener() {
        @Override
        public void onClick(View v) {
            Intent intent = new Intent(MediaStore.ACTION_IMAGE_CAPTURE);
            //Add extra to save full-image somewhere
            intent.putExtra(MediaStore.EXTRA_OUTPUT, Uri.fromFile(destination));
            startActivityForResult(intent, REQUEST_IMAGE);
        }
    };
}
```

This method will instruct the camera application to store the image elsewhere (in this case, on the device's SD card as "image.jpg") and the result will not be scaled down. When going to retrieve the image after the operation returns, we now go directly to the file location where we told the camera to store.

Using `BitmapFactory.Options`, however, we do still scale the image down prior to displaying to the screen to avoid from loading the full-size Bitmap into memory at once. Also note that this example chose a file location that was on the device's external storage, which requires the `android.permission.WRITE_EXTERNAL_STORAGE` permission to be declared in API Levels 4 and above. If your final solution writes the file elsewhere, this may not be necessary.

Video Capture

Capturing video clips using this method is just as straightforward, although the results produced are slightly different. There is no case under which the actual video clip data is returned directly in the Intent extras, and it is always saved to a destination file location. The following two parameters may be passed along as extras:

1. MediaStore.EXTRA_VIDEO_QUALITY

    a. Integer value to describe the quality level used to capture the video.

    b. Allowed values are 0 for low quality and 1 for high quality.

2. MediaStore.EXTRA_OUTPUT

    a. Uri destination of where to save the video content.

    b. If this is not present, the video will be saved in a standard location for the device.

When the video recording is complete, the actual location where the data was saved is returned as a Uri in the data field of the result Intent. Let's take a look at a similar example that allows the user to record and save their video, and then displays the saved location back to the screen. See Listings 4–14 and 4–15.

Listing 4–14. *res/layout/main.xml*

```xml
<?xml version="1.0" encoding="utf-8"?>
<LinearLayout xmlns:android="http://schemas.android.com/apk/res/android"
  android:orientation="vertical"
  android:layout_width="fill_parent"
  android:layout_height="fill_parent">
  <Button
    android:id="@+id/capture"
    android:layout_width="fill_parent"
    android:layout_height="wrap_content"
    android:text="Take a Video"
  />
  <TextView
    android:id="@+id/file"
    android:layout_width="fill_parent"
    android:layout_height="fill_parent"
  />
</LinearLayout>
```

Listing 4–15. *Activity to Capture a Video Clip*

```java
public class MyActivity extends Activity {

    private static final int REQUEST_VIDEO = 100;

    Button captureButton;
    TextView text;
    File destination;

    @Override
    public void onCreate(Bundle savedInstanceState) {
        super.onCreate(savedInstanceState);
        setContentView(R.layout.main);

        captureButton = (Button)findViewById(R.id.capture);
        captureButton.setOnClickListener(listener);

        text = (TextView)findViewById(R.id.file);
```

```
            destination = new File(Environment.getExternalStorageDirectory(),"myVideo");
    }

    @Override
    protected void onActivityResult(int requestCode, int resultCode, Intent data) {
        if(requestCode == REQUEST_VIDEO && resultCode == Activity.RESULT_OK) {
            String location = data.getData().toString();
            text.setText(location);
        }
    }

    private View.OnClickListener listener = new View.OnClickListener() {
        @Override
        public void onClick(View v) {
            Intent intent = new Intent(MediaStore.ACTION_VIDEO_CAPTURE);
            //Add (optional) extra to save video to our file
            intent.putExtra(MediaStore.EXTRA_OUTPUT, Uri.fromFile(destination));
            //Optional extra to set video quality
            intent.putExtra(MediaStore.EXTRA_VIDEO_QUALITY, 0);
            startActivityForResult(intent, REQUEST_VIDEO);
        }
    };
}
```

This example, like the previous example saving an image, puts the recorded video on the device's SD card (which requires the android.permission.WRITE_EXTERNAL_STORAGE permission for API Levels 4+). To initiate the process, we send an Intent with the MediaStore.ACTION_VIDEO_CAPTURE action string to the system. Android will launch the default camera application to handle recording the video and return with an OK result when recording is complete. We retrieve the location where the data was stored as a Uri by calling Intent.getData() in the onActivityResult() callback method, and then display that location to the user.

This example requests explicitly that the video be shot using the low quality setting, but this parameter is optional. If MediaStore.EXTRA_VIDEO_QUALITY is not present in the request Intent, the device will usually choose to shoot using high quality.

In cases where MediaStore.EXTRA_OUTPUT is provided, the Uri returned should match the location you requested, unless an error occurs that keeps the application from writing to that location. If this parameter is not provided, the returned value will be a content:// Uri to retrieve the media from the system's MediaStore Content Provider.

Later on, in Recipe 4–8, we will look at practical ways to play this media back in your application.

4–5. Making a Custom Camera Overlay

Problem

Many applications need more direct access to the camera, either for the purposes of overlaying a custom UI for controls or to display metadata about what is visible through information based on location and direction sensors (augmented reality).

Solution

(API Level 5)

Attach directly to the camera hardware in a custom Activity. Android provides APIs to directly access the device's camera for the purposes of obtaining the preview feed and taking photos. We can access these when the needs of the application grow beyond simply snapping and returning a photo for display.

> **NOTE:** Because we are taking a more direct approach to the camera here, it is required that the android.permission.CAMERA permission be declared in the manifest.

How It Works

We start by creating a SurfaceView, a dedicated view for live drawing where we will attach the camera's preview stream. This provides us with a live preview inside a view that we can lay out any way we choose inside an Activity. From there, it's simply a matter of adding other views and controls that suit the context of the application. Let's take a look at the code (see Listings 4–16 and 4–17).

> **NOTE:** The Camera class used here is android.hardware.Camera, not to be confused with android.graphics.Camera. Ensure you have imported the correct reference in your application.

Listing 4–16. *res/layout/main.xml*

```xml
<?xml version="1.0" encoding="utf-8"?>
<RelativeLayout xmlns:android="http://schemas.android.com/apk/res/android"
  android:layout_width="fill_parent"
  android:layout_height="fill_parent">
  <SurfaceView
    android:id="@+id/preview"
    android:layout_width="fill_parent"
    android:layout_height="fill_parent"
  />
</RelativeLayout>
```

Listing 4–17. *Activity Displaying Live Camera Preview*

```java
import android.hardware.Camera;

public class PreviewActivity extends Activity implements SurfaceHolder.Callback {

    Camera mCamera;
    SurfaceView mPreview;

    @Override
    public void onCreate(Bundle savedInstanceState) {
        super.onCreate(savedInstanceState);
        setContentView(R.layout.main);

        mPreview = (SurfaceView)findViewById(R.id.preview);
        mPreview.getHolder().addCallback(this);
        mPreview.getHolder().setType(SurfaceHolder.SURFACE_TYPE_PUSH_BUFFERS);

        mCamera = Camera.open();
    }

    @Override
    public void onPause() {
        super.onPause();
        mCamera.stopPreview();
    }

    @Override
    public void onDestroy() {
        super.onDestroy();
        mCamera.release();
    }

    //Surface Callback Methods
    @Override
    public void surfaceChanged(SurfaceHolder holder, int format, int width, int height)
    {
        Camera.Parameters params = mCamera.getParameters();
        //Get all the devices's supported sizes and pick the first (largest)
        List<Camera.Size> sizes = params.getSupportedPreviewSizes();
        Camera.Size selected = sizes.get(0);
        params.setPreviewSize(selected.width,selected.height);
        mCamera.setParameters(params);

        mCamera.startPreview();
    }

    @Override
    public void surfaceCreated(SurfaceHolder holder) {
        try {
            mCamera.setPreviewDisplay(mPreview.getHolder());
        } catch (Exception e) {
            e.printStackTrace();
        }
    }

    @Override
    public void surfaceDestroyed(SurfaceHolder holder) { }
}
```

> **NOTE:** If you are testing on an emulator, there is no camera to preview. What the emulator displays to fake a preview depends on the version you are running. To verify that this code is working properly, open the Camera application on your specific emulator and take note of what the preview looks like. The same display should appear in this sample.

In the example, we create a `SurfaceView` that fills the window, and tell it that our Activity is to be notified of all the `SurfaceHolder` callbacks. The camera cannot begin displaying preview information on the surface until it is fully initialized, so we wait until `surfaceCreated()` gets called to attach the `SurfaceHolder` of our view to the `Camera` instance. Similarly, we wait to size the preview and start drawing until the surface has been given its size, which occurs when `surfaceChanged()` is called.

Calling `Parameters.getSupportedPreviewSizes()` returns a list of all the sizes the device will accept, and they are typically ordered largest to smallest. In the example, we pick the first (and, thus, largest) preview resolution and use it to set the size.

> **NOTE:** In versions earlier than 2.0 (API Level 5), it was acceptable to directly pass the height and width parameters from this method as to `Parameters.setPreviewSize()`; but in 2.0, and later, the Camera will only set its preview to one of the supported resolutions of the device. Attempts otherwise will result in an Exception.

`Camera.startPreview()` begins the live drawing of camera data on the surface. Notice that the preview always displays in a landscape orientation. Prior to Android 2.2 (API Level 8), there was no official way to adjust the rotation of the preview display. For that reason, it is recommended that an Activity using the camera preview have its orientation fixed with `android:screenOrientation="landscape"` in the manifest to match.

The Camera service can only be accessed by one application at a time. For this reason, it is important that you call `Camera.release()` as soon as the camera is no longer needed. In the example, we no longer need the camera when the Activity is finished, so this call takes place in `onDestroy()`.

Later Additions

There were two additions to later versions of the API that can also be made useful if your application targets them:

- `Camera.setDisplayOrientation(int degrees)`
  - Available with API Level 8 (Android 2.2).
  - Enables the live preview to be set to 0, 90, 180, or 270 degrees. 0 maps to the default landscape orientation.

- `Camera.open(int which)`
    - Available with API Level 9 (Android 2.3).
    - Enabled support of multiple cameras (mainly front and back-facing).
    - Takes a parameter from 0 to `getNumberOfCameras()-1`.

Photo Overlay

We can now add on to the previous example any controls or views that are appropriate to display on top of the camera preview. Let's modify the preview to include a Cancel and Snap Photo button. See Listings 4–18 and 4–19.

Listing 4–18. *res/layout/main.xml*

```xml
<?xml version="1.0" encoding="utf-8"?>
<RelativeLayout xmlns:android="http://schemas.android.com/apk/res/android"
  android:layout_width="fill_parent"
  android:layout_height="fill_parent">
  <SurfaceView
    android:id="@+id/preview"
    android:layout_width="fill_parent"
    android:layout_height="fill_parent"
  />
  <RelativeLayout
    android:layout_width="fill_parent"
    android:layout_height="100dip"
    android:layout_alignParentBottom="true"
    android:gravity="center_vertical"
    android:background="#A000">
    <Button
      android:layout_width="100dip"
      android:layout_height="wrap_content"
      android:text="Cancel"
      android:onClick="onCancelClick"
    />
    <Button
      android:layout_width="100dip"
      android:layout_height="wrap_content"
      android:layout_alignParentRight="true"
      android:text="Snap Photo"
      android:onClick="onSnapClick"
    />
  </RelativeLayout>
</RelativeLayout>
```

Listing 4–19. *Activity with Photo Controls Added*

```java
public class PreviewActivity extends Activity implements
                SurfaceHolder.Callback, Camera.ShutterCallback, Camera.PictureCallback {

    Camera mCamera;
    SurfaceView mPreview;

    @Override
```

```java
public void onCreate(Bundle savedInstanceState) {
    super.onCreate(savedInstanceState);
    setContentView(R.layout.main);

    mPreview = (SurfaceView)findViewById(R.id.preview);
    mPreview.getHolder().addCallback(this);
    mPreview.getHolder().setType(SurfaceHolder.SURFACE_TYPE_PUSH_BUFFERS);

    mCamera = Camera.open();
}

@Override
public void onPause() {
    super.onPause();
    mCamera.stopPreview();
}

@Override
public void onDestroy() {
    super.onDestroy();
    mCamera.release();
    Log.d("CAMERA","Destroy");
}

public void onCancelClick(View v) {
    finish();
}

public void onSnapClick(View v) {
    //Snap a photo
    mCamera.takePicture(this, null, null, this);
}

//Camera Callback Methods
@Override
public void onShutter() {
    Toast.makeText(this, "Click!", Toast.LENGTH_SHORT).show();
}

@Override
public void onPictureTaken(byte[] data, Camera camera) {

    //Store the picture off somewhere
    //Here, we chose to save to internal storage
    try {
        FileOutputStream out = openFileOutput("picture.jpg", Activity.MODE_PRIVATE);
        out.write(data);
        out.flush();
        out.close();
    } catch (FileNotFoundException e) {
        e.printStackTrace();
    } catch (IOException e) {
        e.printStackTrace();
    }

    //Must restart preview
    camera.startPreview();
```

```
        }

        //Surface Callback Methods
        @Override
        public void surfaceChanged(SurfaceHolder holder, int format, int width, int height) {
            Camera.Parameters params = mCamera.getParameters();
            List<Camera.Size> sizes = params.getSupportedPreviewSizes();
            Camera.Size selected = sizes.get(0);
            params.setPreviewSize(selected.width,selected.height);
            mCamera.setParameters(params);

            mCamera.setDisplayOrientation(90);
            mCamera.startPreview();
        }

        @Override
        public void surfaceCreated(SurfaceHolder holder) {
            try {
                mCamera.setPreviewDisplay(mPreview.getHolder());
            } catch (Exception e) {
                e.printStackTrace();
            }
        }

        @Override
        public void surfaceDestroyed(SurfaceHolder holder) { }
    }
```

Here we have added a simple, partially transparent overlay to include a pair of controls for camera operation. The action taken by cancel is nothing to speak of; we simply finish the Activity. However, Snap Photo introduces more of the Camera API in manually taking a returning a photo to the application. A user action will initiate the Camera.takePicture() method, which takes a series of callback pointers.

Notice that the Activity in this example implements two more interfaces: Camera.ShutterCallback and Camera.PictureCallback. The former is called as near as possible to the moment when the image is captured (when the "shutter" closes), while the latter can be called at multiple instances when different forms of the image are available.

The parameters of takePicture() are a single ShutterCallback, and up to three PictureCallback instances. The PictureCallbacks will be called at the following times (in the order they appear as parameters):

1. After the image is captured with RAW image data

    a. This may return null on devices with limited memory.

2. After the image is processed with scaled image data (known as the POSTVIEW image)

    a. This may return null on devices with limited memory.

3. After the image is compressed with JPEG image data

This example only cares to be notified when the JPEG is ready. Consequently, that is also the last callback made and the point in time when the preview must be started back up again. If startPreview() is not called again after a picture is taken, then preview on the surface will remain frozen at the captured image.

4–6. Recording Audio

Problem

You have an application that needs to make use of the device microphone to record audio input.

Solution

(API Level 1)

Use the MediaRecorder to capture the audio and store it out to a file.

How It Works

MediaRecorder is quite simple to use. All you need to provide is some basic information about the file format to use for encoding and where to store the data. Listings 4–20 and 4–21 provide an example that records an audio file to the device's SD card monitoring user actions for when to start and stop.

> **IMPORTANT:** In order to use MediaRecorder to record audio input, you must also declare the android.permission.RECORD_AUDIO permission in the application manifest.

Listing 4–20. *res/layout/main.xml*

```xml
<?xml version="1.0" encoding="utf-8"?>
<LinearLayout xmlns:android="http://schemas.android.com/apk/res/android"
  android:orientation="vertical"
  android:layout_width="fill_parent"
  android:layout_height="fill_parent">
  <Button
    android:id="@+id/startButton"
    android:layout_width="fill_parent"
    android:layout_height="wrap_content"
    android:text="Start Recording"
  />
  <Button
    android:id="@+id/stopButton"
    android:layout_width="fill_parent"
    android:layout_height="wrap_content"
    android:text="Stop Recording"
    android:enabled="false"
  />
</LinearLayout>
```

Listing 4–21. *Activity for Recording Audio*

```java
public class RecordActivity extends Activity {

    private MediaRecorder recorder;
    private Button start, stop;
    File path;

    @Override
    public void onCreate(Bundle savedInstanceState) {
        super.onCreate(savedInstanceState);
        setContentView(R.layout.main);

        start = (Button)findViewById(R.id.startButton);
        start.setOnClickListener(startListener);
        stop = (Button)findViewById(R.id.stopButton);
        stop.setOnClickListener(stopListener);

        recorder = new MediaRecorder();
        path = new File(Environment.getExternalStorageDirectory(),"myRecording.3gp");

        resetRecorder();
    }

    @Override
    public void onDestroy() {
        super.onDestroy();
        recorder.release();
    }

    private void resetRecorder() {
        recorder.setAudioSource(MediaRecorder.AudioSource.MIC);
        recorder.setOutputFormat(MediaRecorder.OutputFormat.THREE_GPP);
        recorder.setAudioEncoder(MediaRecorder.AudioEncoder.DEFAULT);
        recorder.setOutputFile(path.getAbsolutePath());
        try {
            recorder.prepare();
        } catch (Exception e) {
            e.printStackTrace();
        }
    }

    private View.OnClickListener startListener = new View.OnClickListener() {
        @Override
        public void onClick(View v) {
            try {
                recorder.start();

                start.setEnabled(false);
                stop.setEnabled(true);
            } catch (Exception e) {
                e.printStackTrace();
            }
        }
    };

    private View.OnClickListener stopListener = new View.OnClickListener() {
        @Override
```

```
        public void onClick(View v) {
            recorder.stop();
            resetRecorder();

            start.setEnabled(true);
            stop.setEnabled(false);
        }
    };
}
```

The user interface for this example is very basic. There are two buttons, which alternate which the user can access based on the recording state. When the user presses start, we enable the stop button and begin recording. When the user presses stop, we re-enable the start button and reset the recorder to run again.

MediaRecorder setup is just about as straightforward. We create a file on the SD card entitled "myRecording.3gp" and pass the path in setOutputFile(). The remaining setup methods tell the recorder to use the device microphone as input (AudioSource.MIC), and create a 3GP file format for the output using the default encoder.

For now, you could play this audio file using any of the device's file browser or media player application. Later on, in Recipe 4–8, we will point out how to play audio back through the application as well.

4–7. Adding Speech Recognition

Problem

Your application needs speech recognition technology to interpret voice input.

Solution

(API Level 3)

Use the classes of the android.speech package to leverage the built-in speech recognition technology of every Android device. Every Android device that is equipped with voice search (available since Android 1.5) provides applications the ability to use the built-in SpeechRecognizer to process voice input.

To activate this process, the application need only to send a RecognizerIntent to the system, where the recognition service will handle recording the voice input and processing it; returning to you a list of strings indicating what the recognizer thought it heard.

How It Works

Let's examine this technology in action. See Listing 4–22.

Listing 4–22. *Activity Launching and Processing Speech Recognition*

```java
public class RecognizeActivity extends Activity {

    private static final int REQUEST_RECOGNIZE = 100;

    TextView tv;

    @Override
    public void onCreate(Bundle savedInstanceState) {
        super.onCreate(savedInstanceState);
        tv = new TextView(this);
        setContentView(tv);

        Intent intent = new Intent(RecognizerIntent.ACTION_RECOGNIZE_SPEECH);
        intent.putExtra(RecognizerIntent.EXTRA_LANGUAGE_MODEL,
                        RecognizerIntent.LANGUAGE_MODEL_FREE_FORM);
        intent.putExtra(RecognizerIntent.EXTRA_PROMPT, "Tell Me Your Name");
        try {
            startActivityForResult(intent, REQUEST_RECOGNIZE);
        } catch (ActivityNotFoundException e) {
            //If no recognizer exists, download one from Android Market
            AlertDialog.Builder builder = new AlertDialog.Builder(this);
            builder.setTitle("Not Available");
            builder.setMessage("There is currently no recognition application installed. "
                +"  Would you like to download one?");
            builder.setPositiveButton("Yes", new DialogInterface.OnClickListener() {
                @Override
                public void onClick(DialogInterface dialog, int which) {
                    //Download, for example, Google Voice Search
                    Intent marketIntent = new Intent(Intent.ACTION_VIEW);
                    marketIntent.setData
                        (Uri.parse("market://details?id=com.google.android.voicesearch"));
                }
            });
            builder.setNegativeButton("No", null);
            builder.create().show();
        }
    }

    @Override
    protected void onActivityResult(int requestCode, int resultCode, Intent data) {
        if(requestCode == REQUEST_RECOGNIZE && resultCode == Activity.RESULT_OK) {
            ArrayList<String> matches =
                data.getStringArrayListExtra(RecognizerIntent.EXTRA_RESULTS);
            StringBuilder sb = new StringBuilder();
            for(String piece : matches) {
                sb.append(piece);
                sb.append('\n');
            }
            tv.setText(sb.toString());
        } else {
            Toast.makeText(this, "Operation Canceled", Toast.LENGTH_SHORT).show();
        }
    }
}
```

NOTE: If you are testing your application in the emulator, beware that neither Android Market nor any voice recognizers are likely installed. It is best to test the operation of this example on a device.

This example automatically starts the speech recognition Activity on launch of the application and asks the user to "Tell Me Your Name". Upon receiving speech from the user and processing the result, the Activity returns with a list of possible items the user could have said. This list is in order of probability, and so in many cases it would be prudent to simply call `matches.get(0)` as the best possible choice and move on. However, this activity takes all the returned values and displays them on the screen for entertainment purposes.

When starting up the `SpeechRecognizer`, there are a number of extras that can be passed in the Intent to customize the behavior. This example uses the two that are most common:

- EXTRA_LANGUAGE_MODEL

  - A value to help fine tune the results from the speech processor.

  - Typical speech-to-text queries should use the LANGUAGE_MODEL_FREE_FORM option.

  - If shorter request-type queries are being made, LANGUAGE_MODEL_WEB_SEARCH may produce better results.

- EXTRA_PROMPT

  - A string value that displays as the prompt for user speech.

In addition to these, a handful of other parameters may be useful to pass along:

- EXTRA_MAX_RESULTS

  - Integer to set the maximum number of returned results.

- EXTRA_LANGUAGE

  - Request that results be returned in a language other than the current system default.

  - String value of a valid IETF tag, such as "en-US" or "es"

4–8. Playing Back Audio/Video

Problem

An application needs to play audio or video content, either local or remote, on the device.

Solution

(API Level 1)

Use the MediaPlayer to play local or streamed media. Whether the content is audio or video, local or remote, MediaPlayer will connect, prepare, and play the associated media efficiently. In this recipe, we will also explore using MediaController and VideoView as simple ways to include interaction and video play into an Acitivity layout.

How It Works

> **NOTE:** Before expecting a specific media clip or stream to play, please read the "Android Supported Media Formats" section of the developer documentation to verify support.

Audio Playback

Let's look at a simple example of just using MediaPlayer to play a sound. See Listing 4–23.

Listing 4–23. *Activity Playing Local Sound*

```
public class PlayActivity extends Activity implements MediaPlayer.OnCompletionListener {

    Button mPlay;
    MediaPlayer mPlayer;

    @Override
    public void onCreate(Bundle savedInstanceState) {
        super.onCreate(savedInstanceState);

        mPlay = new Button(this);
        mPlay.setText("Play Sound");
        mPlay.setOnClickListener(playListener);

        setContentView(mPlay);
    }

    @Override
    public void onDestroy() {
        super.onDestroy();
        if(mPlayer != null) {
            mPlayer.release();
        }
    }

    private View.OnClickListener playListener = new View.OnClickListener() {

        @Override
        public void onClick(View v) {
            if(mPlayer == null) {
                try {
                    mPlayer = MediaPlayer.create(PlayActivity.this, R.raw.sound);
```

```
                    mPlayer.start();
                } catch (Exception e) {
                    e.printStackTrace();
                }
            } else {
                mPlayer.stop();
                mPlayer.release();
                mPlayer = null;
            }
        }
    };

    //OnCompletionListener Methods
    @Override
    public void onCompletion(MediaPlayer mp) {
        mPlayer.release();
        mPlayer = null;
    }

}
```

This example uses a Button to start and stop playback of a local sound file that is stored in the res/raw directory of a project. MediaPlayer.create() is a convenience method with several forms, intended to construct and prepare a player object in one step. The form used in this example takes a reference to a local resource ID, but create() can also be used to access and play a remote resource using

```
MediaPlayer.create(Context context, Uri uri);
```

Once created, the example starts playing the sound immediately. While the sound is playing, the user may press the button again to stop play. The Activity also implements the MediaPlayer.OnCompletionListener interface, so it receives a callback when the playing operation completes normally.

In either case, once play is stopped, the MediaPlayer instance is released. This method allows the resources to be retained only as long as they are in use, and the sound may be played multiple times. To be sure resources are not unnecessarily retained, the player is also released when the Activity is destroyed if it still exists.

If your application has a need to playing many different sounds, you may consider calling reset() instead of release() when playback is over. Remember, though, to still call release() when the player is no longer needed (or the Activity goes away).

Audio Player

Beyond just simple playback, what if the application needs to create an interactive experience for the user to be able to play, pause, and seek through the media? There are methods available on MediaPlayer to implement all these functions with custom UI elements, but Android also provides the MediaController view so you don't have to. See Listings 4–24 and 4–25.

Listing 4–24. *res/layout/main.xml*

```xml
<?xml version="1.0" encoding="utf-8"?>
<LinearLayout xmlns:android="http://schemas.android.com/apk/res/android"
  android:id="@+id/root"
  android:orientation="vertical"
  android:layout_width="fill_parent"
  android:layout_height="fill_parent">
  <TextView
    android:layout_width="wrap_content"
    android:layout_height="wrap_content"
    android:layout_gravity="center_horizontal"
    android:text="Now Playing..."
  />
  <ImageView
    android:id="@+id/coverImage"
    android:layout_width="fill_parent"
    android:layout_height="fill_parent"
    android:scaleType="centerInside"
  />
</LinearLayout>
```

Listing 4–25. *Activity Playing Audio with a MediaController*

```java
public class PlayerActivity extends Activity implements
            MediaController.MediaPlayerControl, MediaPlayer.OnBufferingUpdateListener {

    MediaController mController;
    MediaPlayer mPlayer;
    ImageView coverImage;

    int bufferPercent = 0;

    @Override
    public void onCreate(Bundle savedInstanceState) {
        super.onCreate(savedInstanceState);
        setContentView(R.layout.main);

        coverImage = (ImageView)findViewById(R.id.coverImage);

        mController = new MediaController(this);
        mController.setAnchorView(findViewById(R.id.root));
    }

    @Override
    public void onResume() {
        super.onResume();
        mPlayer = new MediaPlayer();
        //Set the audio data source
        try {
            mPlayer.setDataSource(this, Uri.parse("URI_TO_REMOTE_AUDIO"));
            mPlayer.prepare();
        } catch (Exception e) {
            e.printStackTrace();
        }
        //Set an image for the album cover
        coverImage.setImageResource(R.drawable.icon);
```

```java
        mController.setMediaPlayer(this);
        mController.setEnabled(true);
    }

    @Override
    public void onPause() {
        super.onPause();
        mPlayer.release();
        mPlayer = null;
    }

    @Override
    public boolean onTouchEvent(MotionEvent event) {
        mController.show();
        return super.onTouchEvent(event);
    }

    //MediaPlayerControl Methods
    @Override
    public int getBufferPercentage() {
        return bufferPercent;
    }

    @Override
    public int getCurrentPosition() {
        return mPlayer.getCurrentPosition();
    }

    @Override
    public int getDuration() {
        return mPlayer.getDuration();
    }

    @Override
    public boolean isPlaying() {
        return mPlayer.isPlaying();
    }

    @Override
    public void pause() {
        mPlayer.pause();
    }

    @Override
    public void seekTo(int pos) {
        mPlayer.seekTo(pos);
    }

    @Override
    public void start() {
        mPlayer.start();
    }

    //BufferUpdateListener Methods
    @Override
    public void onBufferingUpdate(MediaPlayer mp, int percent) {
        bufferPercent = percent;
```

```
    }

    //Android 2.0+ Target Callbacks
    public boolean canPause() {
        return true;
    }

    public boolean canSeekBackward() {
        return true;
    }

    public boolean canSeekForward() {
        return true;
    }
}
```

This example creates a simple audio player that displays an image for artist or cover art associated with the audio being played (we just set it to the application icon here). The example still uses a MediaPlayer instance, but this time we are not creating it using the `create()` convenience method. Instead we use `setDataSource()` after the instance is created to set the content. When attaching the content in this manner, the player is not automatically prepared so we must also call `prepare()` to ready the player for use.

At this point, the audio is ready to start. We would like the MediaController to handle all playback controls, but MediaController can only attach to objects that implement the MediaController.MediaPlayerControl interface. Strangely, MediaPlayer alone does not implement this interface so we appoint the Activity to do that job instead. Six of the seven method included in the interface are actually implemented by MediaPlayer, so we just call down to those directly.

> **LATE ADDITIONS:** If your application is targeting API Level 5 or later, there are three additional methods to implement in the MediaController.MediaPlayerControl interface:
>
> canPause()
>
> canSeekBackward()
>
> canSeekForward()
>
> These methods simply tell the system whether we want to allow these operations to occur inside of this control, so our example returns true for all three. These methods are not required if you target a lower API Level (which is why we didn't provide @Override annotations above them), but you may implement them for best results when running on later versions.

The final method required to use MediaController is getBufferPercentage(). To obtain this data, the Activity is also tasked with implementing MediaPlayer.OnBufferingUpdateListener, which updates the buffer percentage as it changes.

MediaController has one trick to its implementation. It is designed as a widget that floats above an active view in its own Window and is only visible for a few seconds at a time. As a result, we do not instantiate the widget in the XML layout of the content view, but rather in code. The link is made between the MediaController and the content view by calling setAnchorView(), which also determines where the controller will show up onscreen. In this example, we anchor it to the root layout object, so it will display at the bottom of the screen when visible. If the MediaController is anchored to a child view in the hierarchy, it will display next to that child instead.

Also, due to the controller's separate window, MediaController.show() must not be called from within onCreate(), and doing so will cause a fatal exception. MediaController is designed to be hidden by default and activated by the user. In this example, we override the onTouchEvent() method of the Activity to show the controller whenever the user taps the screen. Unless show() is called with a parameter of 0, it will fade out after the amount of time noted by the parameter. Calling show() without any parameter tells it to fade out after the default timeout, which is around three seconds. See Figure 4–4.

Figure 4–4. *Activity using MediaController*

Now all features of the audio playback are handled by the standard controller widget. The version of setDataSource() used in this example takes a Uri, making is suitable for loading audio from a ContentProvider or a remote location. Keep in mind that all of this works just as well with local audio files and resources using the alternate forms of setDataSource().

Video Player

When playing video, typically a full set of playback controls is required to play, pause, and seek the content. In addition, MediaPlayer must have a reference to a SurfaceHolder onto which it can draw the frames of the video. As we mentioned in the example previous, Android provides APIs to do all of this and create a custom video playing experience. However, in many cases the most efficient path forward is to let the classes provided with the SDK, namely MediaController and VideoView, do all the heavy lifting.

Let's take a look at an example of creating a video player in an Activity. See Listing 4–26.

Listing 4–26. *Activity to Play Video Content*

```
public class VideoActivity extends Activity {

    VideoView videoView;
    MediaController controller;

    @Override
    public void onCreate(Bundle savedInstanceState) {
        super.onCreate(savedInstanceState);
        videoView = new VideoView(this);

        videoView.setVideoURI( Uri.parse("URI_TO_REMOTE_VIDEO") );
        controller = new MediaController(this);
        videoView.setMediaController(controller);
        videoView.start();

        setContentView(videoView);
    }

    @Override
    public void onDestroy() {
        super.onDestroy();
        videoView.stopPlayback();
    }
}
```

This example passes the URI of a remote video location to VideoView and tells it to handle the rest. VideoView can be embedded in larger XML layout hierarchies as well, although often it is the only thing and is displayed full-screen, so setting is in code as the only view in the layout tree is not uncommon.

With VideoView, interaction with MediaController is much simpler. VideoView implements the MediaController.MediaPlayerControl interface, so no additional glue logic is required to make the controls functional. VideoView also internally handles the anchoring of the controller to itself, so it displays on screen in the proper location.

Handling Redirects

We have one final note about using the MediaPlayer classes to handle remote content. Many media content servers on the Web today do not publicly expose a direct URL to the video container. Either for the purposes of tracking or security, public media URLs can often redirect one or more times before ending up at the true media content.

MediaPlayer does not handle this redirect process, and will return an error when presented with a redirected URL.

If you are unable to directly retrieve locations of the content you want to display in an application, that application must trace the redirect path before handing the URL to MediaPlayer. Listing 4–27 is an example of a simple AsyncTask tracer that will do the job.

Listing 4–27. *RedirectTracerTask*

```java
public class RedirectTracerTask extends AsyncTask<Uri, Void, Uri> {

    private VideoView mVideo;
    private Uri initialUri;

    public RedirectTracerTask(VideoView video) {
        super();
        mVideo = video;
    }

    @Override
    protected Uri doInBackground(Uri... params) {
        initialUri = params[0];
        String redirected = null;
        try {
          URL url = new URL(initialUri.toString());
          HttpURLConnection connection = (HttpURLConnection)url.openConnection();
          //Once connected, see where you ended up
          redirected = connection.getHeaderField("Location");

          return Uri.parse(redirected);
        } catch (Exception e) {
          e.printStackTrace();
          return null;
        }
    }

    @Override
    protected void onPostExecute(Uri result) {
        if(result != null) {
            mVideo.setVideoURI(result);
        } else {
            mVideo.setVideoURI(initialUri);
        }
    }

}
```

This helper class tracks down the final location by retrieving it out of the HTTP headers. If there were no redirects in the supplied Uri, the background operation will end up returning null, in which case the original Uri is passed to the VideoView. With this helper class, you can now pass the locations to the view as follows:

```java
VideoView videoView = new VideoView(this);
RedirectTracerTask task = new RedirectTracerTask(videoView);
Uri location = Uri.parse("URI_TO_REMOTE_VIDEO");

task.execute(location);
```

4–9. Creating a Tilt Monitor

Problem

Your application requires feedback from the device's accelerometer that goes beyond just understanding whether the device is oriented in portrait or landscape.

Solution

(API Level 3)

Use SensorManager to receive constant feedback from the accelerometer sensor. SensorManager provides a generic abstracted interface for working with sensor hardware on Android devices. The accelerometer is just one of many sensors that an application can register to receive regular updates from.

How It Works

IMPORTANT: Device sensors, such as the accelerometer, do not exist in the emulator. If you cannot test SensorManager code on an Android device, you will need to use a tool such as SensorSimulator to inject sensor events into the system. SensorSimulator requires modifying this example to use a different SensorManager interface for testing; see "Useful Tools To Know: SensorSimulator" at the end of this chapter for more information.

This example Activity registers with SensorManager for accelerometer updates and displays the data on screen. The raw X/Y/Z data is displayed in a TextView at the bottom of the screen, but in addition the device's "tilt" is visualized through a simple graph of four views in a TableLayout. See Listings 4–28 and 4–29.

NOTE: It is also recommended that you add android:screenOrientation="portrait" or android:screenOrientation="landscape" to the application's manifest to keep the Activity from trying to rotate as you move and tilt the device.

Listing 4–28. *res/layout/main.xml*

```
<?xml version="1.0" encoding="utf-8"?>
<RelativeLayout xmlns:android="http://schemas.android.com/apk/res/android"
  android:layout_width="fill_parent"
  android:layout_height="fill_parent">
  <TableLayout
    android:layout_width="fill_parent"
    android:layout_height="fill_parent"
    android:stretchColumns="0,1,2">
    <TableRow
      android:layout_weight="1">
```

```
    <View
      android:id="@+id/top"
      android:layout_column="1"
    />
  </TableRow>
  <TableRow
    android:layout_weight="1">
    <View
      android:id="@+id/left"
      android:layout_column="0"
    />
    <View
      android:id="@+id/right"
      android:layout_column="2"
    />
  </TableRow>
  <TableRow
    android:layout_weight="1">
    <View
      android:id="@+id/bottom"
      android:layout_column="1"
    />
  </TableRow>
  </TableLayout>
  <TextView
    android:id="@+id/values"
    android:layout_width="fill_parent"
    android:layout_height="wrap_content"
    android:layout_alignParentBottom="true"
  />
</RelativeLayout>
```

Listing 4–29. *Tilt Monitoring Activity*

```
public class TiltActivity extends Activity implements SensorEventListener {

    private SensorManager mSensorManager;
    private Sensor mAccelerometer;
    private TextView valueView;
    private View mTop, mBottom, mLeft, mRight;

    public void onCreate(Bundle savedInstanceState) {
        super.onCreate(savedInstanceState);
        setContentView(R.layout.main);

        mSensorManager = (SensorManager)getSystemService(SENSOR_SERVICE);
        mAccelerometer = mSensorManager.getDefaultSensor(Sensor.TYPE_ACCELEROMETER);

        valueView = (TextView)findViewById(R.id.values);
        mTop = findViewById(R.id.top);
        mBottom = findViewById(R.id.bottom);
        mLeft = findViewById(R.id.left);
        mRight = findViewById(R.id.right);
    }

    protected void onResume() {
        super.onResume();
```

```
        mSensorManager.registerListener(this, mAccelerometer,
            SensorManager.SENSOR_DELAY_UI);
    }

    protected void onPause() {
        super.onPause();
        mSensorManager.unregisterListener(this);
    }

    public void onAccuracyChanged(Sensor sensor, int accuracy) { }

    public void onSensorChanged(SensorEvent event) {
        float[] values = event.values;
        float x = values[0] / 10;
        float y = values[1] / 10;
        int scaleFactor;

        if(x > 0) {
            scaleFactor = (int)Math.min(x * 255, 255);
            mRight.setBackgroundColor(Color.TRANSPARENT);
            mLeft.setBackgroundColor(Color.argb(scaleFactor, 255, 0, 0));
        } else {
            scaleFactor = (int)Math.min(Math.abs(x) * 255, 255);
            mRight.setBackgroundColor(Color.argb(scaleFactor, 255, 0, 0));
            mLeft.setBackgroundColor(Color.TRANSPARENT);
        }

        if(y > 0) {
            scaleFactor = (int)Math.min(y * 255, 255);
            mTop.setBackgroundColor(Color.TRANSPARENT);
            mBottom.setBackgroundColor(Color.argb(scaleFactor, 255, 0, 0));
        } else {
            scaleFactor = (int)Math.min(Math.abs(y) * 255, 255);
            mTop.setBackgroundColor(Color.argb(scaleFactor, 255, 0, 0));
            mBottom.setBackgroundColor(Color.TRANSPARENT);
        }
        //Display the raw values
        valueView.setText(String.format("X: %1$1.2f, Y: %2$1.2f, Z: %3$1.2f",
                values[0], values[1], values[2]));
    }
}
```

The orientation of the three axes on the device accelerometer are as follows, from the perspective of looking at the device screen, upright in portrait:

- X: Horizontal axis with positive pointing to the right

- Y: Vertical axis with positive pointing up

- Z: Perpendicular axis with positive pointing back at you

When the Activity is visible to the user (between onResume() and onPause()), it registers with SensorManager to receive updates about the acclerometer. When registering, the last parameter to registerListener() defines the update rate. The chosen value, SENSOR_DELAY_UI, is the fastest recommended rate to receive updates and still directly modify the user interface with each update.

With each new sensor value, the onSensorChanged() method of our registered listener is called with a SensorEvent value; this event contains the X/Y/Z acceleration values.

QUICK SCIENCE NOTE: An accelerometer measures the acceleration due to forces applied. When a device is at rest, the only force operating on it is the force of gravity (~9.8 m/s^2). The output value on each axis is the product of this force (pointing down to the ground), and each orientation vector. When the two are parallel, the value will be at its maximum (~9.8-10). When the two are perpendicular, the value will be at its minimum (~0.0). Therefore, a device laying flat on a table will read ~0.0 for both X and Y, and ~9.8 for Z.

The example application displays the raw acceleration values for each axis in the TextView at the bottom of the screen. In addition, there is a grid of four Views arranged in a top/bottom/left/right pattern, and we proportionally adjust the background color of this grid based on the orientation. When the device is perfectly flat, both X and Y should be close to zero and the entire screen will be black. As the device tilts, the squares on the low side of the tilt will start to glow red until they are completely red once the device orientation reaches upright in either position.

TIP: Try modifying this example with some of the other rate values, like SENSOR_DELAY_NORMAL. Notice how the change affects the update rate in the example.

In addition, you can shake the device and see alternating grid boxes highlight as the device accelerates in each direction.

4–10. Monitoring Compass Orientation

Problem

Your application wants to know which major direction the user is facing by monitoring the device's compass sensor.

Solution

(API Level 3)

SensorManager comes to the rescue once again. Android doesn't provide a "compass" sensor exactly, but rather includes the necessary methods to gather where the device is pointing based on other sensor data. In this case, the device's magnetic field sensor will be used in conjunction with the accelerometer to ascertain where the user is facing.

We can then ask SensorManager for the user's orientation with respect to the Earth using getOrientation().

How It Works

> **IMPORTANT:** Device sensors such as the accelerometer do not exist in the emulator. If you cannot test SensorManager code on an Android device, you will need to use a tool such as SensorSimulator to inject sensor events into the system. SensorSimulator requires modifying this example to use a different SensorManager interface for testing; see "Useful Tools to Know: SensorSimulator" at the end of this chapter for more information.

As with the previous accelerometer example, we use SensorManager to register for updates on all sensors of interest (in this case, there are two), and process the results in onSensorChanged(). This example calculates and displays the user orientation from the device camera's point-of-view, as it would be required for an application such as augmented reality. See Listings 4–30 and 4–31.

Listing 4–30. *res/layout/main.xml*

```xml
<?xml version="1.0" encoding="utf-8"?>
<RelativeLayout xmlns:android="http://schemas.android.com/apk/res/android"
  android:layout_width="fill_parent"
  android:layout_height="fill_parent">
  <TextView
    android:id="@+id/direction"
    android:layout_width="wrap_content"
    android:layout_height="wrap_content"
    android:layout_centerInParent="true"
    android:textSize="64dip"
    android:textStyle="bold"
  />
  <TextView
    android:id="@+id/values"
    android:layout_width="wrap_content"
    android:layout_height="wrap_content"
    android:layout_alignParentBottom="true"
  />
</RelativeLayout>
```

Listing 4–31. *Activity Monitoring User Orientation*

```java
public class CompassActivity extends Activity implements SensorEventListener {

    private SensorManager mSensorManager;
    private Sensor mAccelerometer, mField;
    private TextView valueView, directionView;

    private float[] mGravity;
    private float[] mMagnetic;

    public void onCreate(Bundle savedInstanceState) {
        super.onCreate(savedInstanceState);
        setContentView(R.layout.main);

        mSensorManager = (SensorManager)getSystemService(SENSOR_SERVICE);
        mAccelerometer = mSensorManager.getDefaultSensor(Sensor.TYPE_ACCELEROMETER);
```

```java
        mField = mSensorManager.getDefaultSensor(Sensor.TYPE_MAGNETIC_FIELD);

        valueView = (TextView)findViewById(R.id.values);
        directionView = (TextView)findViewById(R.id.direction);
    }

    protected void onResume() {
        super.onResume();
        mSensorManager.registerListener(this, mAccelerometer,
            SensorManager.SENSOR_DELAY_UI);
        mSensorManager.registerListener(this, mField, SensorManager.SENSOR_DELAY_UI);
    }

    protected void onPause() {
        super.onPause();
        mSensorManager.unregisterListener(this);
    }

    private void updateDirection() {
        float[] temp = new float[9];
        float[] R = new float[9];
        //Load rotation matrix into R
        SensorManager.getRotationMatrix(temp, null, mGravity, mMagnetic);
        //Map to camera's point-of-view
        SensorManager.remapCoordinateSystem(temp, SensorManager.AXIS_X,
            SensorManager.AXIS_Z, R);
        //Return the orientation values
        float[] values = new float[3];
        SensorManager.getOrientation(R, values);
        //Convert to degrees
        for (int i=0; i < values.length; i++) {
            Double degrees = (values[i] * 180) / Math.PI;
            values[i] = degrees.floatValue();
        }
        //Display the compass direction
        directionView.setText( getDirectionFromDegrees(values[0]) );
        //Display the raw values
        valueView.setText(String.format("Azimuth: %1$1.2f, Pitch: %2$1.2f, Roll: %3$1.2f",
                values[0], values[1], values[2]));
    }

private String getDirectionFromDegrees(float degrees) {
        if(degrees >= -22.5 && degrees < 22.5) { return "N"; }
        if(degrees >= 22.5 && degrees < 67.5) { return "NE"; }
        if(degrees >= 67.5 && degrees < 112.5) { return "E"; }
        if(degrees >= 112.5 && degrees < 157.5) { return "SE"; }
        if(degrees >= 157.5 || degrees < -157.5) { return "S"; }
        if(degrees >= -157.5 && degrees < -112.5) { return "SW"; }
        if(degrees >= -112.5 && degrees < -67.5) { return "W"; }
        if(degrees >= -67.5 && degrees < -22.5) { return "NW"; }

        return null;
    }

    public void onAccuracyChanged(Sensor sensor, int accuracy) { }
```

```
public void onSensorChanged(SensorEvent event) {
    switch(event.sensor.getType()) {
    case Sensor.TYPE_ACCELEROMETER:
        mGravity = event.values.clone();
        break;
    case Sensor.TYPE_MAGNETIC_FIELD:
        mMagnetic = event.values.clone();
        break;
    default:
        return;
    }

    if(mGravity != null && mMagnetic != null) {
        updateDirection();
    }
  }
}
```

This example Activity displays the three raw values returned by the sensor calculation at the bottom of the screen in real time. In addition, the compass direction associated with where the user is currently facing is converted and displayed center-stage. As updates are received from the sensors, local copies of the latest values from each is maintained. As soon as we have received at least one reading from both sensors of interest, we allow the UI to begin updating.

updateDirection() is where all the heavy lifting takes place. SensorManager.getOrientation() provides the output information we require to display direction. The method returns no data, and instead an empty float array is passed in for the method to fill in three angle values, and they represent (in order):

- Azimuth

  - Angle of rotation about an axis pointing directly into the Earth.

  - This is the value of interest to the example.

- Pitch

  - Angle of rotation about an axis pointing West.

- Roll

  - Angle of rotation about and axis pointing at magnetic North.

One of the parameters passed to getOrientation() is a float array representing a rotation matrix. The rotation matrix is a representation of how the current coordinate system of the devices is oriented, so the method may provide appropriate rotation angles based on its references coordinates. The rotation matrix for the device orientation is obtained using getRotationMatrix(), which takes the latest values from the accelerometer and magnetic field sensor as input. Like getOrientation(), it also returns void; and empty float array of length 9 or 16 (to represent a 3x3 or 4x4 matrix) must be passed in as the first parameter for the method to fill in.

Finally, we want the output of the orientation calculation to be specific to the camera's point-of-view. To further transform the obtained rotation, we use the remapCoordinateSystem() method. This method takes four parameters (in order):

1. Input array representing the matrix to transform

2. How to transform the device's X-axis with respect to world coordinates

3. How to transform the device's Y-axis with respect to world coordinates

4. Empty array to fill in the result

In our example, we want to leave the X-axis untouched, so we map X to X. However, we would like to align the device's Y-axis (vertical axis) to the world's Z-axis (the one pointing into the Earth). This orients the rotation matrix we receive to match up with the device being held vertically upright as if the user is using the camera and looking at the preview on the screen.

With the angular data calculated, we do some data conversion and display the result on the screen. The unit output of getOrientation() is radians, so we first have to convert each result to degrees before displaying it. In addition, we need to convert the azimuth value to a compass direction; getDirectionFromDegrees() is a helper method to return the proper direction based on the range the current reading falls within. Going full-circle clockwise, the azimuth will read from 0 to 180 degrees from North to South. Continuing around the circle, the azimuth will read -180 to 0 degrees rotating from South to North.

Useful Tools to Know: SensorSimulator

Google's Android emulator doesn't support sensors because most computers don't have compasses, accelerometers, or even light sensors that the emulator can leverage. Although this limitation is problematic for apps that need to interact with sensors, and where the emulator is the only viable testing option, it can be overcome by working with Sensor Simulator.

Sensor Simulator (http://code.google.com/p/openintents/wiki/SensorSimulator) is an open source tool that lets you simulate sensor data and make this data available to your apps for testing purposes. It currently supports accelerometer, magnetic field (compass), orientation, temperature, and barcode reader sensors; the behavior of these sensors can be customized through various configuration settings.

> **NOTE:** Sensor Simulator is one of several projects made available to Android developers by *OpenIntents* (http://code.google.com/p/openintents/wiki/OpenIntents), a Google-hosted project for creating reusable components and tools for the Android platform.

Obtaining Sensor Simulator

Sensor Simulator is distributed in a single ZIP archive. Point your browser to
http://code.google.com/p/openintents/downloads/list?q=sensorsimulator and click
the sensorsimulator-1.1.0-rc1.zip link followed by the sensorsimulator-1.1.0-
rc1.zip link on the subsequent page to download this 284Kb file.

After unzipping this archive, you'll discover a sensorsimulator-1.1.0-rc1 home
directory with the following subdirectories:

- **bin:** Contains the sensorsimulator-1.1.0-rc1.jar (Sensor Simulator
  standalone Java application that lets you generate test data) and
  SensorSimulatorSettings-1.1.0-rc1.apk (Android app to set default
  IP address/port settings and to test the connection to the Sensor
  Simulator Java application) executables along with readme files for
  these executables.

- **lib:** Contains the sensorsimulator-lib-1.1.0-rc1.jar library, which
  your Android apps use to access sensor settings from the Sensor
  Simulator Java application.

- **release:** Contains the Apache Ant build script to assemble the
  sensorsimulator-1.1.0-rc1.zip release.

- **samples:** Contains a SensorDemo Android app example on how to
  access Sensor Simulator from an Android app.

- **SensorSimulator:** Contains the source code for the Sensor Simulator
  Java application.

- **SensorSimulatorSettings:** Contains the source code for the Sensor
  Simulator Settings Android app and project settings for building its
  APK and the library file.

Launching Sensor Simulator Settings and Sensor Simulator

Now that you've downloaded and unarchived the Sensor Simulator distribution, you'll
want to launch this software. Complete the following steps to accomplish this task:

1. Start the Android emulator if not already running; for example, execute
   emulator -avd test_AVD at the command line. This example assumes
   that you've previously created test_AVD in Chapter 1.

2. Install SensorSimulatorSettings-1.1.0-rc1.apk on the emulator; for
   example, execute adb install SensorSimulatorSettings-1.1.0-
   rc1.apk. This example assumes that the adb tool is accessible via your
   PATH environment variable, and that the bin directory is current. It
   outputs a success message when the APK is successfully installed on
   the emulator.

3. Click the app launcher screen's Sensor Simulator icon to start the Sensor Simulator app.

4. Start the `bin` directory's Sensor Simulator Java application, which is located in `sensorsimulator-1.1.0-rc1.jar`. For example, under Windows, double-click this filename.

Figure 4–5 reveals the emulator's app launcher screen with the Sensor Simulator icon highlighted.

Figure 4–5. *The Sensor Simulator icon is highlighted on the app launcher screen.*

Click the Sensor Simulator icon. Figure 4–6 reveals the Sensor Simulator Settings screen divided into two activities: Settings and Testing.

Figure 4–6. *The default Settings activity prompts for the IP address and socket port.*

The Settings activity prompts you to enter the IP address and socket port number of the Sensor Simulator Java application, whose user interface appears in Figure 4–7.

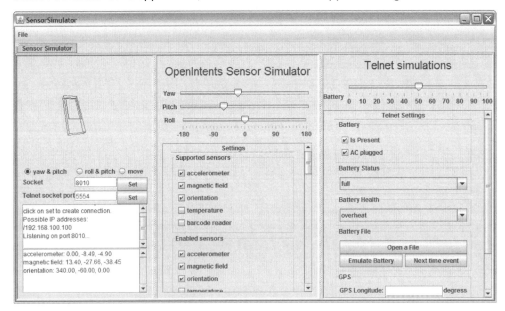

Figure 4–7. *Use the Sensor Simulator application's user interface to send sensor data to Sensor Simulator Settings and your own apps.*

Sensor Simulator presents a tabbed user interface, where each tab lets you send test data to a different emulator instance. At present, there is only a single default Sensor Simulator tab, but you can add more tabs and remove them by selecting the New Tab and Close Tab menu items from the File menu.

Each tab is divided into three panes:

- The left-hand pane displays a graphic of a device that shows its orientation and position. It also lets you select a socket port and Telnet socket port, displays connection information, and (by default) displays only accelerometer, magnetic field, and orientation sensor data.

- The middle pane lets you adjust the device's yaw, pitch, and roll, choose which sensors are supported, enable appropriate sensors for testing, and choose additional sensor data (such as choosing the current temperature value) as well as how often sensor data is sent to the emulator.

- The right-hand pane lets you communicate with the emulator instance via Telnet. You can communicate battery state (such as whether a battery is present and the battery's health – is it overheating?) along with GPS data to the emulator instance.

The left-hand pane displays the IP address (192.168.100.100 in this example) that's to be entered in the Settings activity's IP address textfield. Because Sensor Simulator uses the same port number (8010) as the number appearing in the Settings activity's Socket textfield, you don't need to change this field's value.

> **NOTE:** You might need to change the port number in both the Settings activity's Socket textfield and Sensor Simulator's Socket textfield if 8010 is being used by some other application running on your computer.

After entering this IP address in the Settings activity's IP address field (see Figure 4–6), select the Testing activity by clicking the Testing tab. Figure 4–8 shows the results.

Figure 4–8. *Click Connect to connect to the Sensor Simulator app and to start receiving test data.*

According to this screen, you must click the Connect button to establish a connection with the Sensor Simulator Java application, which must be running at this point. (You later click Disconnect to break the connection.)

After clicking Connect, the Testing tab reveals accelerometer, magnetic field, and orientation checkboxes with labels underneath to show test values. It doesn't show checkboxes for temperature and barcode reader because these sensors are not supported nor enabled (see the Sensor Simulator application's middle panel).

Check the acclerometer checkbox and, as Figure 4–9 shows, the label underneath the checkbox reveals to you the current yaw, pitch, and roll values obtained from Sensor Simulator.

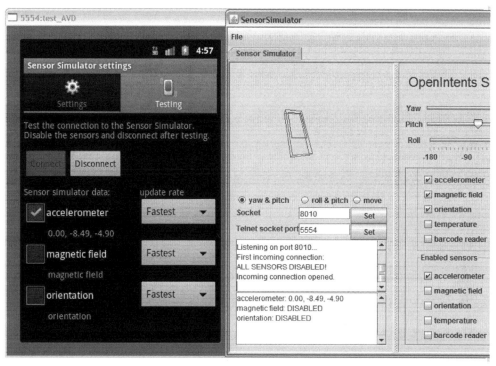

Figure 4–9. *The Sensor Simulator Settings app is now receiving accelerometer data from the Sensor Simulator application.*

Accessing Sensor Simulator from Your Apps

Although Sensor Simulator Settings helps you learn how to use Sensor Simulator to send test data to an app, it's no substitute for your own apps. At some point, you'll want to incorporate code into your activities that accesses this tool. Google provides the following guidelines for modifying your app to access Sensor Simulator:

1. Add the `lib` directory's JAR file (`sensorsimulator-lib-1.1.0-rc1.jar`, for example) to your project.

2. Import the following Sensor Simulator types from this library into your source code:

```
import org.openintents.sensorsimulator.hardware.Sensor;
import org.openintents.sensorsimulator.hardware.SensorEvent;
import org.openintents.sensorsimulator.hardware.SensorEventListener;
import org.openintents.sensorsimulator.hardware.SensorManagerSimulator;
```

3. Replace your activity's onCreate() method's existing
   SensorManager.getSystemService() method calls with equivalent
   SensorManagerSimulator.getSystemService() method calls. For
   example, you might replace mSensorManager = (SensorManager)
   getSystemService(SENSOR_SERVICE); with mSensorManager =
   SensorManagerSimulator.getSystemService(this, SENSOR_SERVICE);.

4. Connect to the Sensor Simulator Java application using the settings that
   have been set previously with SensorSimulatorSettings:
   mSensorManager.connectSimulator();, for example.

5. All other code remains untouched. However, remember to register the
   sensors in onResume() and unregister them in onStop():

```
@Override
protected void onResume()
{
    super.onResume();
    mSensorManager.registerListener(this,
        mSensorManager.getDefaultSensor(Sensor.TYPE_ACCELEROMETER),
        SensorManager.SENSOR_DELAY_FASTEST);
    mSensorManager.registerListener(this,
        mSensorManager.getDefaultSensor(Sensor.TYPE_MAGNETIC_FIELD),
        SensorManager.SENSOR_DELAY_FASTEST);
    mSensorManager.registerListener(this,
        mSensorManager.getDefaultSensor(Sensor.TYPE_ORIENTATION),
        SensorManager.SENSOR_DELAY_FASTEST);
    mSensorManager.registerListener(this,
        mSensorManager.getDefaultSensor(Sensor.TYPE_TEMPERATURE),
        SensorManager.SENSOR_DELAY_FASTEST);
}
@Override
protected void onStop()
{
    mSensorManager.unregisterListener(this);
    super.onStop();
}
```

6. Finally, you must implement the SensorEventListener interface:

```
class MySensorActivity extends Activity implements SensorEventListener
{
    public void onAccuracyChanged(Sensor sensor, int accuracy)
    {
    }

    public void onSensorChanged(SensorEvent event)
    {
        int sensor = event.type;
        float[] values = event.values;
        // do something with the sensor data
    }
}
```

NOTE: OpenIntents' `SensorManagerSimulator` class is derived from the Android `SensorManager` class, and implements exactly the same functions as `SensorManager`. For the callback, the new `SensorEventListener` interface has been implemented to resemble the standard Android `SensorEventListener` interface.

Whenever you are not connected to the Sensor Simulator Java application, you'll get real device sensor data: the `org.openintents.hardware.SensorManagerSimulator` class transparently calls the `SensorManager` instance that's returned by the system service to make this happen.

Summary

This collection of recipes exposed how to use Android to use maps, user location, and device sensor data to integrate information about the user's surroundings into your applications. We also discussed how to utilize the device's camera and microphone, allowing the user to capture, and sometimes interpret, what's around them. Finally, using the media APIs you learned how to take media content, either captured locally by the user or downloaded remotely from the Web, and play it back from within your applications. In the next chapter, we will discuss how to use Android's many persistence techniques to store nonvolatile data on the device.

Chapter 5

Persisting Data

Even in the midst of grand architectures put in place to shift as much user data into the cloud as possible, the transient nature of mobile applications will always require that at least some user data be persisted locally on the device. This data may range from cached responses from a web service guaranteeing offline access to preferences the user has set for specific application behaviors. Android provides a series of helpful frameworks to take the pain out of using files and databases to persist information.

5–1. Making a Preference Screen

Problem

You need to create a simple way to store, change, and display user preferences and settings within your application.

Solution

(API Level 1)

Use the PreferenceActivity and an XML Preference hierarchy to provide the user interface, key/value combinations, and persistence all at once. Using this method will create a user interface that is consistent with the Settings application on Android devices, keep the user's experience consistent with what they expect.

Within the XML, an entire set of one or more screens can be defined with the associated settings displayed and grouped into categories using the PreferenceScreen, PreferenceCategory, and associated Preference elements. The Activity can then load this hierarchy for the user using very little code.

How It Works

Listings 5–1 and 5–2 provide a sample of basic settings for an Android application. The XML defines two screens with a variety of all the common preference types that this framework supports. Notice that one screen is nested inside of the other; the internal screen will be displayed when the user clicks on its associated list item from the root screen.

Listing 5–1. *res/xml/settings.xml*

```xml
<?xml version="1.0" encoding="utf-8"?>
<PreferenceScreen xmlns:android="http://schemas.android.com/apk/res/android">
  <EditTextPreference
    android:key="namePref"
    android:title="Name"
    android:summary="Tell Us Your Name"
    android:defaultValue="Apress"
  />
  <CheckBoxPreference
      android:key="morePref"
      android:title="Enable More Settings"
      android:defaultValue="false"
  />
  <PreferenceScreen
    android:key="moreScreen"
    android:title="More Settings"
    android:dependency="morePref">
    <ListPreference
      android:key="colorPref"
      android:title="Favorite Color"
      android:summary="Choose your favorite color"
      android:entries="@array/color_names"
      android:entryValues="@array/color_values"
      android:defaultValue="GRN"
    />
    <PreferenceCategory
      android:title="Location Settings">
      <CheckBoxPreference
        android:key="gpsPref"
        android:title="Use GPS Location"
        android:summary="Use GPS to Find You"
        android:defaultValue="true"
      />
      <CheckBoxPreference
        android:key="networkPref"
        android:title="Use Network Location"
        android:summary="Use Network to Find You"
        android:defaultValue="true"
      />
    </PreferenceCategory>
  </PreferenceScreen>
</PreferenceScreen>
```

Listing 5–2. *res/values/arrays.xml*

```xml
<?xml version="1.0" encoding="utf-8"?>
<resources>
    <string-array name="color_names">
      <item>Black</item>
      <item>Red</item>
      <item>Green</item>
    </string-array>
```

```
    <string-array name="color_values">
      <item>BLK</item>
      <item>RED</item>
      <item>GRN</item>
    </string-array>
</resources>
```

Notice first the convention used to create the XML file. Although this resource could be inflated from any directory (such as res/layout), convention is to put them into a generic directory of the project titled simply "xml."

Also, notice that we provide an android:key attribute for each Preference object instead of android:id. When each stored value is referenced elsewhere in the application through a SharedPreferences object, it will be accessed using the key. In addition, PreferenceActivity includes the findPreference() method for obtaining a reference to an inflated Preference in Java code, which is more efficient than using findViewById(); and findPreference() also takes the key as a parameter.

When inflated, the root PreferenceScreen presents a list with the following three options (in order):

1. An item titled "Name"

    a. Instance of EditTextPreference, which stores a string value.

    b. Tapping this item will present a text box for the user to type a new preference value.

2. An item titled "Enable More Settings" with a checkbox beside it

    a. Instance of CheckBoxPreference, which stores a boolean value.

    b. Tapping this item will toggle the checked status of the checkbox.

3. An item titled "More Settings"

    a. Tapping this item will load another PreferenceScreen with more items.

When the user taps the "More Settings" item, a second screen is displayed with three more items: a ListPreference item and two more CheckBoxPreferences grouped together by a PreferenceCategory. PreferenceCategory is simply a way to create section breaks and headers in the list for grouping actual preference items.

The ListPreference is the final preference type used in the example. This item requires two array parameters (although they can both be set to the same array) that represent a set of choices the user may pick from. The android:entries array is the list of human-readable items to display, while the android:entryValues array represents the actual value to be stored.

All the preference items may optionally have a default value set for them as well. This value is not automatically loaded, however. It will load the first time this XML file is inflated when the PreferenceActivity is displayed OR when a call to PreferenceManager.setDefaultValues() is made.

Now let's take a look at how a PreferenceActivity would load and manage this. See Listing 5–3.

Listing 5–3. *PreferenceActivity in Action*

```
public class SettingsActivity extends PreferenceActivity {

    @Override
    public void onCreate(Bundle savedInstanceState) {
        super.onCreate(savedInstanceState);
        //Load preference data from XML
        addPreferencesFromResource(R.xml.settings);
    }
}
```

All that is required to display the preferences to the user and allow them to make changes is a call to addPreferencesFromResource(). There is no need to call setContentView() with PreferenceActivity, as addPreferencesFromResource() inflates the XML and displays it as well. However a custom layout may be provided as long as it contains a ListView with the android:id="@android:id/list" attribute set, which is where PreferenceActivity will load the preference items.

Preference items can also be placed in the list for the sole purpose of controlling access. In the example, we put the "Enable More Settings" item in the list just to allow the user to enable or disable access to the second PreferenceScreen. In order to accomplish this, our nested PreferenceScreen includes the android:dependency attribute, which links its enabled state to the state of another preference. Whenever the referenced preference is either not set or false, this preference will be disabled.

When this Activity loads, you see something like Figure 5–1.

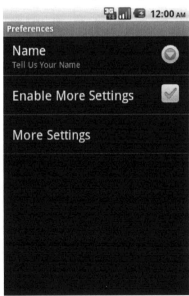

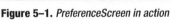
Figure 5–1. *PreferenceScreen in action*

The root `PreferenceScreen` (left) displays first. If the user taps on "More Settings," the secondary screen (right) displays.

Loading Defaults and Accessing Preferences

Typically, a `PreferenceActivity` such as this one is not the root of an application. Often, if default values are set they may need to be accessed by the rest of the application before the user ever visits Settings (the first case under which the defaults will load). Therefore, it can be helpful to put a call to the following method elsewhere in your application to ensure that the defaults are loaded prior to being used.

```
PreferenceManager.setDefaultValues(Context context, int resId, boolean readAgain);
```

This method may be called multiple times, and the defaults will not get loaded over again. It may be placed in the main Activity so it is called on first launch, or perhaps in a common place where it is called before any access to shared preferences.

Preferences stored using this mechanism are put into the default shared preferences object, which can be accessed with any `Context` pointer using

```
PreferenceManager.getDefaultSharedPreferences(Context context);
```

An example Activity that would load the defaults set in our previous example and access some of the current values stored would look like Listing 5–4.

Listing 5–4. *Activity Loading Preference Defaults*

```java
public class HomeActivity extends Activity {

    @Override
    public void onCreate(Bundle savedInstanceState) {
        super.onCreate(savedInstanceState);
        setContentView(R.layout.main);

        //Load the preference defaults
        PreferenceManager.setDefaultValues(this, R.xml.settings, false);
    }

    @Override
    public void onResume() {
        super.onResume();
        //Access the current settings
        SharedPreferences settings =
            PreferenceManager.getDefaultSharedPreferences(this);

        String name = settings.getString("namePref", "");
        boolean isMoreEnabled = settings.getBoolean("morePref", false);
    }
}
```

Calling `setDefaultValues()` will create a value in the preference store for any item in the XML file that includes an `android:defaultValue` attribute. This will make them accessible to the application, even if the user has not yet visited the settings screen.

These values can then be accessed using a set of typed accessor functions on the SharedPreferences object. Each of these accessor methods requires both the name of the preference key and a default value to be returned if a value for preference key does not yet exist.

5–2. Persisting Simple Data

Problem

Your application needs a simple, low-overhead method of storing basic data, such as numbers and strings, in persistent storage.

Solution

(API Level 1)

Using SharedPreferences objects, applications can quickly create one or more persistent stores where data can be saved and retrieved at a later time. Underneath the hood, these objects are actually stored as XML files in the application's user data area. However, unlike directly reading and writing data from files, SharedPreferences provide an efficient framework for persisting basic data types.

Creating multiple SharedPreferences as opposed to dumping all your data in the default object can be a good habit to get into, especially if the data you are storing has a shelf life. Keeping in mind that all preferences stored using the XML and PreferenceActivity framework are also stored in the default location – what if you wanted to store a group of items related to, say, a logged in user? When that user logs out, you will need to remove all the persisted data that goes along with that. If you store all that data in default preferences, you will most likely need to remove each item individually. However, if you create a preference object just for those settings, logging out can be as simple as calling SharedPreferences.clear().

How It Works

Let's look at a practical example of using SharedPreferences to persist simple data. Listings 5–5 and 5–6 create a data entry form for the user to send a simple message to a remote server. To aid the user, we will remember all the data they enter for each field until a successful request is made. This will allow the user to leave the screen (or be interrupted by a text message or phone call) without having to enter all their information again.

Listing 5–5. *res/layout/form.xml*

```xml
<?xml version="1.0" encoding="utf-8"?>
<LinearLayout xmlns:android="http://schemas.android.com/apk/res/android"
  android:orientation="vertical"
  android:layout_width="fill_parent"
  android:layout_height="fill_parent">
```

```xml
<TextView
  android:layout_width="fill_parent"
  android:layout_height="wrap_content"
  android:text="Email:"
  android:padding="5dip"
/>
<EditText
  android:id="@+id/email"
  android:layout_width="fill_parent"
  android:layout_height="wrap_content"
  android:singleLine="true"
/>
<CheckBox
  android:id="@+id/age"
  android:layout_width="fill_parent"
  android:layout_height="wrap_content"
  android:text="Are You Over 18?"
/>
<TextView
  android:layout_width="fill_parent"
  android:layout_height="wrap_content"
  android:text="Message:"
  android:padding="5dip"
/>
<EditText
  android:id="@+id/message"
  android:layout_width="fill_parent"
  android:layout_height="wrap_content"
  android:minLines="3"
  android:maxLines="3"
/>
<Button
  android:id="@+id/submit"
  android:layout_width="fill_parent"
  android:layout_height="wrap_content"
  android:text="Submit"
/>
</LinearLayout>
```

Listing 5–6. *Entry Form with Persistence*

```java
public class FormActivity extends Activity implements View.OnClickListener {

    EditText email, message;
    CheckBox age;
    Button submit;

    SharedPreferences formStore;

    boolean submitSuccess = false;

    @Override
    public void onCreate(Bundle savedInstanceState) {
        super.onCreate(savedInstanceState);
        setContentView(R.layout.form);

        email = (EditText)findViewById(R.id.email);
        message = (EditText)findViewById(R.id.message);
```

```java
        age = (CheckBox)findViewById(R.id.age);

        submit = (Button)findViewById(R.id.submit);
        submit.setOnClickListener(this);

        //Retrieve or create the preferences object
        formStore = getPreferences(Activity.MODE_PRIVATE);
    }

    @Override
    public void onResume() {
        super.onResume();
        //Restore the form data
        email.setText(formStore.getString("email", ""));
        message.setText(formStore.getString("message", ""));
        age.setChecked(formStore.getBoolean("age", false));
    }

    @Override
    public void onPause() {
        super.onPause();
        if(submitSuccess) {
            //Editor calls can be chained together
            formStore.edit().clear().commit();
        } else {
            //Store the form data
            SharedPreferences.Editor editor = formStore.edit();
            editor.putString("email", email.getText().toString());
            editor.putString("message", message.getText().toString());
            editor.putBoolean("age", age.isChecked());
            editor.commit();
        }
    }

    @Override
    public void onClick(View v) {

        //DO SOME WORK SUBMITTING A MESSAGE

        //Mark the operation successful
        submitSuccess = true;
        //Close
        finish();
    }
}
```

We start with a typical user form, two simple EditText entry fields and a CheckBox. When the Activity is created, we gather a SharedPreferences object using Activity.getPreferences(), and this is where all the persisted data will be stored. If at any time the Activity is paused for a reason other than a successful submission (controlled by the boolean member), the current state of the form will be quickly loaded into the preferences and persisted.

> **NOTE:** When saving data into SharedPreferences using an Editor, always remember to call commit() or apply() after the changes are made. Otherwise your changes will not be saved.

Conversely, whenever the Activity becomes visible, onResume() loads the user interface with the latest information stored in the preferences object. If no preferences exist, either because they were cleared or never created (first launch), then the form is set to blank.

When a user presses Submit and the fake form submits successfully, the subsequent call to onPause() will clear any stored form data in preferences. Because all these operations were done on a private preferences object, clearing the data does not affect any user settings that may have been stored using other means.

> **NOTE:** Methods called from an Editor always return the same Editor object, allowing them to be chained together in places where doing so makes your code more readable.

Sharing SharedPreferences

The previous example illustrated using a single SharedPreferences object within the context of a single Activity with an object obtained from Activity.getPreferences(). Truth be told, this method is really just a convenience wrapper for Context.getSharedPreferences(), in which it passes the Activity name as the preference store name. If the data you are storing is best shared between two or more Activity instances, it might make sense to call getSharedPreferences() instead and pass a more common name so it can be accessed easily from different places in code. See Listing 5–7.

Listing 5–7. *Two Activities Using the Same Preferences*

```
public class ActivityOne extends Activity {
    public static final String PREF_NAME = "myPreferences";
    private SharedPreferences mPreferences;

    @Override
    public void onCreate(Bundle savedInstanceState) {
        super.onCreate(savedInstanceState);
        mPreferences = getSharedPreferences(PREF_NAME, Activity.MODE_PRIVATE);
    }
}

public class ActivityTwo extends Activity {

    private SharedPreferences mPreferences;

    @Override
    public void onCreate(Bundle savedInstanceState) {
        super.onCreate(savedInstanceState);
        mPreferences = getSharedPreferences(ActivityOne.PREF_NAME,
            Activity.MODE_PRIVATE);
    }

}
```

In this example, both Activity classes retrieve the `SharedPreferences` object using the same name (defined as a constant string), thus they will be accessing the same set of preference data. Furthermore, both references are even pointing at the same *instance* of preferences, as the framework creates a singleton object for each set of `SharedPreferences` (a set being defined by its name). This means that changes made on one side will immediately be reflected on the other.

A Note About Mode

`Context.getSharedPreferences()` also takes a mode parameter. Passing 0 or `MODE_PRIVATE` provides the default behavior of allowing only the application that created the preferences (or another application with the same user ID) to gain read and write access. This method supports two more mode parameters; `MODE_WORLD_READABLE` and `MODE_WORLD_WRITEABLE`. These modes allow other applications to gain access to these preferences by setting the user permissions on the file it creates appropriately. However, the external application still requires a valid Context pointing back to the package where the preference file was created.

For example, let's say you created `SharedPreferences` with `world readable` permission in an application with the package `com.examples.myfirstapplication`. In order to access those preferences from a second application, the second application would obtain them using the following code:

```
Context otherContext = createPackageContext("com.examples.myfirstapplication", 0);
SharedPreferences externalPreferences = otherContext.getSharedPreferences(PREF_NAME, 0);
```

> **CAUTION:** If you choose to use the mode parameter to allow external access, be sure that you are consistent in the mode you provide everywhere `getSharedPreferences()` is called. This mode is only used the first time the preference file gets created, so calling up `SharedPreferences` with different mode parameters at different times will only lead to confusion on your part.

5–3. Reading and Writing Files

Problem

Your application needs to read data in from an external file or write more complex data out for persistence.

Solution

(API Level 1)

Sometimes, there is no substitute for working with a file system. Android supports all the standard Java File I/O for create, read, update, and delete (CRUD) operations, along with some additional helpers to make accessing those files in specific locations a little more convenient. There are three main locations in which an application can work with files:

- Internal storage
  - Protected directory space to read and write file data.
- External storage
  - Externally mountable space to read and write file data.
  - Requires the WRITE_EXTERNAL_STORAGE permission in API Level 4+.
  - Often, this is a physical SD Card in the device.
- Assets
  - Protected read-only space inside the APK bundle.
  - Good for local resources that can't/shouldn't be compiled.

While the underlying mechanism to work with file data remains the same, we will look at the details that make working with each destination slightly different.

How It Works

As we stated earlier, the traditional Java FileInputStream and FileOutputStream classes constitute the primary method of accessing file data. In fact, you can create a File instance at any time with an absolute path location and start streaming data. However, with root paths varying on different devices and certain directories being protected from your application, we recommend some slightly more efficient ways to work with files.

Internal Storage

In order to create or modify a file's location on internal storage, utilize the Context.openFileInput() and Context.openFileOutput() methods. These methods require only the name of the file as parameters, instead of the entire path, and will reference the file in relation to the application's protected directory space, regardless of the exact path on the specific device. See Listing 5–8.

Listing 5–8. *CRUD a File on Internal Storage*

```
public class InternalActivity extends Activity {

    private static final String FILENAME = "data.txt";

    @Override
    public void onCreate(Bundle savedInstanceState) {
        super.onCreate(savedInstanceState);
        TextView tv = new TextView(this);
        setContentView(tv);

        //Create a new file and write some data
```

```
        try {
            FileOutputStream mOutput = openFileOutput(FILENAME, Activity.MODE_PRIVATE);
            String data = "THIS DATA WRITTEN TO A FILE";
            mOutput.write(data.getBytes());
            mOutput.close();
        } catch (FileNotFoundException e) {
            e.printStackTrace();
        } catch (IOException e) {
            e.printStackTrace();
        }

        //Read the created file and display to the screen
        try {
            FileInputStream mInput = openFileInput(FILENAME);
            byte[] data = new byte[128];
            mInput.read(data);
            mInput.close();

            String display = new String(data);
            tv.setText(display.trim());
        } catch (FileNotFoundException e) {
            e.printStackTrace();
        } catch (IOException e) {
            e.printStackTrace();
        }

        //Delete the created file
        deleteFile(FILENAME);
    }
}
```

This example uses `Context.openFileOutput()` to write some simple string data out to a file. When using this method, the file will be created if it does not already exist. It takes two parameters, a file name and an operating mode. In this case, we use the default operation by defining the mode as `MODE_PRIVATE`. This mode will overwrite the file with each new write operation; use `MODE_APPEND` if you prefer that each write tack on to the end of the existing file.

After the write is complete, the example uses `Context.openFileInput()`, which only requires the file name again as a parameter, to open an InputStream and read the file data. The data is read into a byte array and displayed to the user interface through a TextView. Upon completing the operation, `Context.deleteFile()` is used to remove the file from storage.

> **NOTE:** Data is written to the file streams as bytes, so higher level data (even strings) must be converted into and out of this format.

This example leaves no traces of the file behind, but we encourage you to try the same example without running `deleteFile()` at the end to keep the file in storage. Using DDMS with an emulator or unlocked device, you may view the file system and can find the file this application creates in its respective application data folder.

Because these methods are a part of `Context`, and not bound to Activity, this type of file access can occur anywhere in an application that you require, such as a `BroadcastReceiver` or even a custom class. Many system constructs either are a subclass of `Context`, or pass a reference to one in their callbacks. This allows the same open/close/delete operations to take place anywhere.

External Storage

The key differentiator between internal and external storage lies in the fact that external storage is mountable. This means that the user can connect their device to a computer and have the option of mounting that external storage as a removable disk on the PC. Often, the storage itself is physically removable (such as an SD card), but this is not a requirement of the platform.

> **IMPORTANT:** Writing to the external storage of the device will require that you add a declaration for `android.permission.WRITE_EXTERNAL_STORAGE` to the application manifest.

During periods where the device's external storage is either mounted externally or physically removed, it is not accessible to an application. Because of this, it is always prudent to check whether or not external storage is ready by checking `Environment.getExternalStorageState()`.

Let's modify the file example to do the same operation with the device's external storage. See Listing 5–9.

Listing 5–9. *CRUD a File on External Storage*

```java
public class ExternalActivity extends Activity {

    private static final String FILENAME = "data.txt";

    @Override
    public void onCreate(Bundle savedInstanceState) {
        super.onCreate(savedInstanceState);
        TextView tv = new TextView(this);
        setContentView(tv);

        //Create the file reference
        File dataFile = new File(Environment.getExternalStorageDirectory(), FILENAME);

        //Check if external storage is usable
        if(!Environment.getExternalStorageState().equals(Environment.MEDIA_MOUNTED)) {
            Toast.makeText(this, "Cannot use storage.", Toast.LENGTH_SHORT).show();
            finish();
            return;
        }

        //Create a new file and write some data
        try {
            FileOutputStream mOutput = new FileOutputStream(dataFile, false);
            String data = "THIS DATA WRITTEN TO A FILE";
            mOutput.write(data.getBytes());
```

```
        mOutput.close();
    } catch (FileNotFoundException e) {
        e.printStackTrace();
    } catch (IOException e) {
        e.printStackTrace();
    }

    //Read the created file and display to the screen
    try {
        FileInputStream mInput = new FileInputStream(dataFile);
        byte[] data = new byte[128];
        mInput.read(data);
        mInput.close();

        String display = new String(data);
        tv.setText(display.trim());
    } catch (FileNotFoundException e) {
        e.printStackTrace();
    } catch (IOException e) {
        e.printStackTrace();
    }

    //Delete the created file
    dataFile.delete();
    }
}
```

With external storage, we utilize a little more of the traditional Java File I/O. The key to working with external storage is calling `Environment.getExternalStorageDirectory()` to retrieve the root path to the device's external storage location.

Before any operations can take place, the status of the device's external storage is first checked with `Environment.getExternalStorageState()`. If the value returned is anything other than `Environment.MEDIA_MOUNTED`, we wil not proceed because the storage cannot be written to, so the Activity is closed. Otherwise, a new file can be created and the operations may commence.

The input and output streams must now use default Java constructors, as opposed to the `Context` convenience methods. The default behavior of the output stream will be to overwrite the current file, or create it if it does not exist. If your application must append to the end of the exiting file with each write, change the boolean parameter in the `FileOutputStream` constructor to true.

Often, it makes sense to create a special directory on the external storage for your application's files. We can accomplish this simply using more of Java's File API. See Listing 5–10.

Listing 5–10. *CRUD a File Inside New Directory*

```
public class ExternalActivity extends Activity {

    private static final String FILENAME = "data.txt";
    private static final String DNAME = "myfiles";

    @Override
    public void onCreate(Bundle savedInstanceState) {
```

```
super.onCreate(savedInstanceState);
TextView tv = new TextView(this);
setContentView(tv);

//Create a new directory on external storage
File rootPath = new File(Environment.getExternalStorageDirectory(), DNAME);
if(!rootPath.exists()) {
    rootPath.mkdirs();
}
//Create the file reference
File dataFile = new File(rootPath, FILENAME);

//Create a new file and write some data
try {
    FileOutputStream mOutput = new FileOutputStream(dataFile, false);
    String data = "THIS DATA WRITTEN TO A FILE";
    mOutput.write(data.getBytes());
    mOutput.close();
} catch (FileNotFoundException e) {
    e.printStackTrace();
} catch (IOException e) {
    e.printStackTrace();
}

//Read the created file and display to the screen
try {
    FileInputStream mInput = new FileInputStream(dataFile);
    byte[] data = new byte[128];
    mInput.read(data);
    mInput.close();

    String display = new String(data);
    tv.setText(display.trim());
} catch (FileNotFoundException e) {
    e.printStackTrace();
} catch (IOException e) {
    e.printStackTrace();
}

//Delete the created file
dataFile.delete();
    }
}
```

In this example we create a new directory path within the external storage directory and use that new location as the root location for the data file. Once the file reference is created using the new directory location, the remainder of the example is the same.

5–4. Using Files as Resources

Problem

Your application must utilize resource files that are in a format Android cannot compile into a resource ID.

Solution

(API Level 1)

Use the Assets directory to house files your application needs to read from, such as local HTML, CSV, or proprietary data. The assets directory is a protected resource location for files in an Android application. The files placed in this directory will be bundled with the final APK, but will not be processed or compiled. Like all other application resources, the files in Assets are read-only.

How It Works

There are a few specific instances that we've seen already in this book where Assets can be used to load content directly into widgets, like `WebView` and `MediaPlayer`. However, in most cases, Assets is best accessed using a traditional `InputStream`. Listings 5–11 and 5–12 provide an example in which a private Comma Separated Values (CSV) file is read from Assets and displayed onscreen.

Listing 5–11. *assets/data.csv*

```
John,38,Red
Sally,42,Blue
Rudy,31,Yellow
```

Listing 5–12. *Reading from an Asset File*

```java
public class AssetActivity extends Activity {

    @Override
    public void onCreate(Bundle savedInstanceState) {
        super.onCreate(savedInstanceState);
        TextView tv = new TextView(this);
        setContentView(tv);

        try {
            //Access application assets
            AssetManager manager = getAssets();
            //Open our data file
            InputStream mInput = manager.open("data.csv");
            //Read data in
            byte[] data = new byte[128];
            mInput.read(data);
            mInput.close();

            //Parse the CSV data and display
            String raw = new String(data);
            ArrayList<Person> cooked = parse(raw.trim());
            StringBuilder builder = new StringBuilder();
            for(Person piece : cooked) {
              builder.append(String.format("%s is %s years old, and likes the color %s",
                        piece.name, piece.age, piece.color));
              builder.append('\n');
            }
            tv.setText(builder.toString());
```

```java
        } catch (FileNotFoundException e) {
            e.printStackTrace();
        } catch (IOException e) {
            e.printStackTrace();
        }

    }

    /* Simple CSV Parser */
    private static final int COL_NAME = 0;
    private static final int COL_AGE = 1;
    private static final int COL_COLOR = 2;

    private ArrayList<Person> parse(String raw) {
        ArrayList<Person> results = new ArrayList<Person>();
        Person current = null;

        StringTokenizer st = new StringTokenizer(raw,",\n");
        int state = COL_NAME;
        while(st.hasMoreTokens()) {
            switch(state) {
            case COL_NAME:
                current = new Person();
                current.name = st.nextToken();
                state = COL_AGE;
                break;
            case COL_AGE:
                current.age = st.nextToken();
                state = COL_COLOR;
                break;
            case COL_COLOR:
                current.color = st.nextToken();
                results.add(current);
                state = COL_NAME;
                break;
            }
        }

        return results;
    }

    private class Person {
        public String name;
        public String age;
        public String color;

        public Person() { }
    }
}
```

The key to accessing files in Assets lies in using `AssetManager`, which will allow the application to open any resource currently residing in the Assets directory. Passing the name of the file we are interested in to `AssetManager.open()` returns an InputStream for us to read the file data. Once the stream is read into memory, the example passes the raw data off to a parsing routine and displays the results to the user interface.

Parsing the CSV

This example also illustrates a simple method of taking data from a CSV file and parsing it into a model object (called Person in this case). The method used here takes the entire file and reads it into a byte array for processing as a single string. This method is not the most memory efficient when the amount of data to be read is quite large, but for small files like this one it works just fine.

The raw string is passed into a StringTokenizer instance, along with the required characters to use as breakpoints for the tokens: comma and new line. At this point, each individual chunk of the file can be processed in order. Using a basic state machine approach, the data from each line is inserted into new Person instances and loaded into the resulting list.

5–5. Managing a Database

Problem

Your application needs to persist data that can later be queried or modified later as subsets or individual records.

Solution

(API Level 1)

Create an SQLiteDatabase with the assistance of an SQLiteOpenHelper to manage your data store. SQLite is a fast and lightweight database technology that utilizes SQL syntax to build queries and manage data. Support for SQLite is baked in to the Android SDK, making it very easy to set up and use in your applications.

How It Works

Customizing SQLiteOpenHelper allows you to manage the creation and modification of the database schema itself. It is also an excellent place to insert any initial or default values you may want into the database while it is created. Listing 5–13 is an example customizing the helper to create a database with a single table to store basic information about people.

Listing 5–13. *Custom SQLiteOpenHelper*

```
public class MyDbHelper extends SQLiteOpenHelper {

    private static final String DB_NAME = "mydb";
    private static final int DB_VERSION = 1;

    public static final String TABLE_NAME = "people";
    public static final String COL_NAME = "pName";
    public static final String COL_DATE = "pDate";
    private static final String STRING_CREATE =
```

```
                    "CREATE TABLE "+TABLE_NAME+" (_id INTEGER PRIMARY KEY AUTOINCREMENT, "
                    +COL_NAME+" TEXT, "+COL_DATE+" DATE);";

    public MyDbHelper(Context context) {
        super(context, DB_NAME, null, DB_VERSION);
    }

    @Override
    public void onCreate(SQLiteDatabase db) {
        //Create the database table
        db.execSQL(STRING_CREATE);

        //You may also load initial values into the database here
        ContentValues cv = new ContentValues(2);
        cv.put(COL_NAME, "John Doe");
        //Create a formatter for SQL date format
        SimpleDateFormat dateFormat = new SimpleDateFormat("yyyy-MM-dd HH:mm:ss");
        cv.put(COL_DATE, dateFormat.format(new Date())); //Insert 'now' as the date
        db.insert(TABLE_NAME, null, cv);
    }

    @Override
    public void onUpgrade(SQLiteDatabase db, int oldVersion, int newVersion) {
        //For now, clear the database and re-create
        db.execSQL("DROP TABLE IF EXISTS "+TABLE_NAME);
        onCreate(db);
    }
}
```

They key pieces of information you will need for your database are a name and version number. Creating and upgrading an SQLiteDatabase does require a light knowledge of SQL, so we recommend glancing at an SQL reference briefly if you are unfamiliar with some of the syntax. The helper will call onCreate() any time this particular database is accessed, using either SQLiteOpenHelper.getReadableDatabase() or SQLiteOpenHelper.getWritableDatabase(), if it does not already exist.

The example abstracts the table and column names as constants for external use (a good practice to get into). Here is the actual SQL create string that is used in onCreate() to make our table:

```
CREATE TABLE people (_id INTEGER PRIMARY KEY AUTOINCREMENT, pName TEXT, pAge INTEGER,
pDate DATE);
```

When using SQLite in Android, there is a small amount of formatting that the database must have in order for it to work properly with the framework. Most of it is created for you, but one piece that the tables you create must have is a column for _id. The remainder of this string creates two more columns for each record in the table:

- A text field for the person's name

- A date field for the date this record was entered

Data is inserted into the database using ContentValues objects. The example illustrates how to use ContentValues to insert some default data into the database when it is created. SQLiteDatabase.insert() takes a table name, null column hack, and ContentValues representing the record to insert as parameters.

The null column hack is not used here, but serves a purpose that may be vital to your application. SQL cannot insert an entirely empty value into the database, and attempting to do so will cause an error. If there is a chance that your implementation may pass an empty ContentValues to insert(), the null column hack is used to instead insert a record where the value of the referenced column is NULL.

A Note About Upgrading

SQLiteOpenHelper also does a great job of assisting you with migrating your database schema in future versions of the application. Whenever the database is accessed, but the version on disk does not match the current version (meaning the version passed in the constructor), onUpgrade() will be called.

In our example, we took the lazy man's way out and simply dropped the existing database and recreated it. In practice, this may not be a suitable method if the database contains user entered data; they probably won't be too happy to see it disappear. So let's digress for a moment and look at an example of onUpgrade() that may be more useful. Take, for example, the following three databases used throughout the lifetime of an application:

- Version 1: First release of the application
- Version 2: Application upgrade to include phone number field
- Version 3: Application upgrade to include date entry inserted

We can leverage onUpgrade() to alter the existing database instead of erasing all the current information in place. See Listing 5–14.

Listing 5–14. *Sample of onUpgrade()*

```
@Override
public void onUpgrade(SQLiteDatabase db, int oldVersion, int newVersion) {
    //Upgrade from v1. Adding phone number
    if(oldVersion <= 1) {
        db.execSQL("ALTER TABLE "+TABLE_NAME+" ADD COLUMN phone_number INTEGER;");
    }
    //Upgrade from v2. Add entry date
    if(oldVersion <= 2) {
        db.execSQL("ALTER TABLE "+TABLE_NAME+" ADD COLUMN entry_date DATE;");
    }
}
```

In this example, if the user's existing database version is 1, both statements will be called to add columns to the database. If they already have version 2, just the latter statement is called to add the entry date column. In both cases, any existing data in the application database is preserved.

Using the Database

Looking back to our original sample, let's take a look at how an Activity would utilize the database we've created. See Listings 5–15 and 5–16.

Listing 5–15. *res/layout/main.xml*

```xml
<?xml version="1.0" encoding="utf-8"?>
<LinearLayout xmlns:android="http://schemas.android.com/apk/res/android"
  android:orientation="vertical"
  android:layout_width="fill_parent"
  android:layout_height="fill_parent">
  <EditText
    android:id="@+id/name"
    android:layout_width="fill_parent"
    android:layout_height="wrap_content"
  />
  <Button
    android:id="@+id/add"
    android:layout_width="fill_parent"
    android:layout_height="wrap_content"
    android:text="Add New Person"
  />
  <ListView
    android:id="@+id/list"
    android:layout_width="fill_parent"
    android:layout_height="fill_parent"
  />
</LinearLayout>
```

Listing 5–16. *Activity to View and Manage Database*

```java
public class DbActivity extends Activity implements View.OnClickListener,
        AdapterView.OnItemClickListener {

    EditText mText;
    Button mAdd;
    ListView mList;

    MyDbHelper mHelper;
    SQLiteDatabase mDb;
    Cursor mCursor;
    SimpleCursorAdapter mAdapter;

    @Override
    public void onCreate(Bundle savedInstanceState) {
        super.onCreate(savedInstanceState);
        setContentView(R.layout.main);

        mText = (EditText)findViewById(R.id.name);
        mAdd = (Button)findViewById(R.id.add);
        mAdd.setOnClickListener(this);
        mList = (ListView)findViewById(R.id.list);
        mList.setOnItemClickListener(this);

        mHelper = new MyDbHelper(this);
    }

    @Override
    public void onResume() {
        super.onResume();
        //Open connections to the database
        mDb = mHelper.getWritableDatabase();
```

```java
        String[] columns = new String[] {"_id", MyDbHelper.COL_NAME, MyDbHelper.COL_DATE};
        mCursor = mDb.query(MyDbHelper.TABLE_NAME, columns, null, null, null, null, null);
        //Refresh the list
        String[] headers = new String[] {MyDbHelper.COL_NAME, MyDbHelper.COL_DATE};
        mAdapter = new SimpleCursorAdapter(this, android.R.layout.two_line_list_item,
                mCursor, headers, new int[]{android.R.id.text1, android.R.id.text2});
        mList.setAdapter(mAdapter);
    }

    @Override
    public void onPause() {
        super.onPause();
        //Close all connections
        mDb.close();
        mCursor.close();
    }

    @Override
    public void onClick(View v) {
        //Add a new value to the database
        ContentValues cv = new ContentValues(2);
        cv.put(MyDbHelper.COL_NAME, mText.getText().toString());
        //Create a formatter for SQL date format
        SimpleDateFormat dateFormat = new SimpleDateFormat("yyyy-MM-dd HH:mm:ss");
        cv.put(MyDbHelper.COL_DATE, dateFormat.format(new Date())); //Insert 'now' as the date
        mDb.insert(MyDbHelper.TABLE_NAME, null, cv);
        //Refresh the list
        mCursor.requery();
        mAdapter.notifyDataSetChanged();
        //Clear the edit field
        mText.setText(null);
    }

    @Override
    public void onItemClick(AdapterView<?> parent, View v, int position, long id) {
        //Delete the item from the database
        mCursor.moveToPosition(position);
         //Get the id value of this row
        String rowId = mCursor.getString(0); //Column 0 of the cursor is the id
        mDb.delete(MyDbHelper.TABLE_NAME, "_id = ?", new String[]{rowId});
        //Refresh the list
        mCursor.requery();
        mAdapter.notifyDataSetChanged();
    }
}
```

In this example, we utilize our custom SQLiteOpenHelper to give us access to a database instance, and display each record in that database as a list to the user interface. Information from the database if returned in the form of a Cursor, an interface designed to read, write, and traverse the results of a query.

When the Activity becomes visible, a database query is made to return all records in the "people" table. An array of column names must be passed to the query to tell the database which values to return. The remaining parameters of query() are designed to narrow the selection data set, and we will investigate this further in the next recipe. It is important to close all database and cursor connections when they are no longer needed. In the example, we do this in onPause(), when the Activity is no longer in the foreground.

SimpleCursorAdapter is used to map the data from the database to the standard Android two-line list item view. The string and int array parameters constitute the mapping; the data from each item in the string array will be inserted into the view with the corresponding id value in the int array. Notice that the list of column names passed here is slightly different than the array passed to the query. This is because we will need to know the record id for other operations, but it is not necessary in mapping the data to the user interface.

The user may enter a name in the text field and then press the "Add New Person" button to create new ContentValues and insert it into the database. At that point, in order for the UI to display the change we call Cursor.requery() and ListAdapter.notifyDataSetChanged().

Conversely, tapping on an item in the list will remove that specified item from the database. In order to accomplish this, we must construct a simple SQL statement telling the database to remove only records where the _id value matches this selection. At that point, the cursor and list adapter are refreshed again.

The _id value of the selection is obtained by moving the cursor to the selected position and calling getString(0) to get the value of column index zero. This request returns the _id because the first parameter (index 0) passed in the columns list to the query was "_id." The delete statement is comprised of two parameters: the statement string and the arguments. An argument from the passed array will be inserted in the statement for each question mark that appears in the string.

5–6. Querying a Database

Problem

Your application uses an SQLiteDatabase, and you need to return specific subsets of the data contained therein.

Solution

(API Level 1)

Using fully structured SQL queries, it is very simple to create filters for specific data and return those subsets from the database. There are several overloaded forms of SQLiteDatabase.query() to gather information from the database. We'll examine the most verbose of them here.

```
public Cursor query(String table, String[] columns, String selection, String[]
selectionArgs, String groupBy, String having, String orderBy, String limit)
```

The first two parameters simply define the table in which to query data, and the columns for each record that we would like to have access to. The remaining parameters define how we will narrow the scope of the results.

- selection
    - SQL WHERE clause for the given query.
- selectionArgs
    - If question marks are in selection, these items fill in those fields.
- groupBy
    - SQL GROUP BY clause for the given query.
- having
    - SQL ORDER BY clause for the given query.
- orderBy
    - SQL ORDER BY clause for the given query.
- limit
    - Maximum number of results returned from the query.

As you can see, all of these parameters are designed to provide the full power of SQL to the database queries.

How It Works

Let's look at some example queries that can be constructed to accomplish some common practical queries.

- Return all rows where the value matches a given parameter.

```
String[] COLUMNS = new String[] {COL_NAME, COL_DATE};
String selection = COL_NAME+" = ?";
String[] args = new String[] {"NAME_TO_MATCH"};
Cursor result = db.query(TABLE_NAME, COLUMNS, selection, args, null, null, null, null);
```

This query is fairly straightforward. The selection statement just tells the database to match any data in the name column with the argument supplied (which is inserted in place of "?" in the selection string).

- Return the last 10 rows inserted into the database.

```
String orderBy = "_id DESC";
String limit = "10";
Cursor result = db.query(TABLE_NAME, COLUMNS, null, null, null, null, orderBy, limit);
```

This query has no special selection criteria, but instead tells the database to order the results by the auto-incrementing _id value, with the newest (highest _id) records first. The limit clause sets the maximum number of returned results to ten.

- Return rows where a date field is within a specified range (within the year 2000, in this example).

```
String[] COLUMNS = new String[] {COL_NAME, COL_DATE};
String selection = "datetime("+COL_DATE+") > datetime(?)"+
        " AND datetime("+COL_DATE+") < datetime(?)";
String[] args = new String[] {"2000-1-1 00:00:00","2000-12-31 23:59:59"};
Cursor result = db.query(TABLE_NAME, COLUMNS, selection, args, null, null, null, null);
```

SQLite does not reserve a specific data type for dates, although they allow DATE as a declaration type when creating a table. However, the standard SQL date and time functions can be used to create representations of the data as TEXT, INTEGER, or REAL. Here, we compare the return values of datetime() for both the value in the database and a formatted string for the start and end dates of the range.

- Return rows where an integer field is within a specified range (between 7 and 10 in the example).

```
String[] COLUMNS = new String[] {COL_NAME, COL_AGE};
String selection = COL_AGE+" > ? AND "+COL_AGE+" < ?";
String[] args = new String[] {"7","10"};
Cursor result = db.query(TABLE_NAME, COLUMNS, selection, args, null, null, null, null);
```

This is similar to the previous example, but much less verbose. Here, we simply have to create the selection statement to return values greater than the low limit, but less than the high limit. Both limits are provided as arguments to be inserted so they can be dynamically set in the application.

5–7. Backing Up Data

Problem

Your application persists data on the device, and you need to provide the user with a way to back up and restore this data in cases where they change devices or are forced to reinstall the application.

Solution

(API Level 1)

Use the device's external storage as a safe location to copy databases and other files. External storage is often physically removable, allowing the user to place it in another device and do a restore. Even in cases where this is not possible, external storage can always be mounted when the user connects their device to a computer, allowing data transfer to take place.

How It Works

Listing 5–17 shows an implementation of AsyncTask that copies a database file back and forth between the device's external storage and its location in the application's data directory. It also defines an interface for an Activity to implement to get notified when the operation is complete.

Listing 5–17. *AsyncTask for Backup and Restore*

```java
public class BackupTask extends AsyncTask<String,Void,Integer> {

    public interface CompletionListener {
        void onBackupComplete();
        void onRestoreComplete();
        void onError(int errorCode);
    }

    public static final int BACKUP_SUCCESS = 1;
    public static final int RESTORE_SUCCESS = 2;
    public static final int BACKUP_ERROR = 3;
    public static final int RESTORE_NOFILEERROR = 4;

    public static final String COMMAND_BACKUP = "backupDatabase";
    public static final String COMMAND_RESTORE = "restoreDatabase";

    private Context mContext;
    private CompletionListener listener;

    public BackupTask(Context context) {
        super();
        mContext = context;
    }

    public void setCompletionListener(CompletionListener aListener) {
        listener = aListener;
    }

    @Override
    protected Integer doInBackground(String... params) {

        //Get a reference to the database
        File dbFile = mContext.getDatabasePath("mydb");
        //Get a reference to the directory location for the backup
        File exportDir = new File(Environment.getExternalStorageDirectory(), "myAppBackups");
        if (!exportDir.exists()) {
            exportDir.mkdirs();
        }
        File backup = new File(exportDir, dbFile.getName());

        //Check the required operation
        String command = params[0];
        if(command.equals(COMMAND_BACKUP)) {
            //Attempt file copy
            try {
                backup.createNewFile();
                fileCopy(dbFile, backup);
```

```
                return BACKUP_SUCCESS;
            } catch (IOException e) {
                return BACKUP_ERROR;
            }
        } else if(command.equals(COMMAND_RESTORE)) {
            //Attempt file copy
            try {
                if(!backup.exists()) {
                    return RESTORE_NOFILEERROR;
                }
                dbFile.createNewFile();
                fileCopy(backup, dbFile);
                return RESTORE_SUCCESS;
            } catch (IOException e) {
                return BACKUP_ERROR;
            }
        } else {
            return BACKUP_ERROR;
        }
    }

    @Override
    protected void onPostExecute(Integer result) {

        switch(result) {
        case BACKUP_SUCCESS:
            if(listener != null) {
                listener.onBackupComplete();
            }
            break;
        case RESTORE_SUCCESS:
            if(listener != null) {
                listener.onRestoreComplete();
            }
            break;
        case RESTORE_NOFILEERROR:
            if(listener != null) {
                listener.onError(RESTORE_NOFILEERROR);
            }
            break;
        default:
            if(listener != null) {
                listener.onError(BACKUP_ERROR);
            }
        }
    }

    private void fileCopy(File source, File dest) throws IOException {
        FileChannel inChannel = new FileInputStream(source).getChannel();
        FileChannel outChannel = new FileOutputStream(dest).getChannel();
        try {
            inChannel.transferTo(0, inChannel.size(), outChannel);
        } finally {
            if (inChannel != null)
                inChannel.close();
            if (outChannel != null)
                outChannel.close();
```

```
        }
      }
    }
```

As you can see, BackupTask operates by copying the current version of a named database to a specific directory in external storage when `COMMAND_BACKUP` is passed to `execute()`, and copies the file back when `COMMAND_RESTORE` is passed.

Once executed, the task uses `Context.getDatabasePath()` to retrieve a reference to the database file we need to backup. This line could easily be replaced with a call to `Context.getFilesDir()`, accessing a file on the system's internal storage to back up instead. A reference to a backup directory we've created on external storage is also obtained.

The files are copied using traditional Java File I/O, and if all is successful the registered listener is notified. During the process, any exceptions thrown are caught and an error is returned to the listener instead. Now let's take a look at an Activity that utilizes this task to back up a database – see Listing 5–18.

Listing 5–18. *Activity Using BackupTask*

```java
public class BackupActivity extends Activity implements BackupTask.CompletionListener {

    @Override
    public void onCreate(Bundle savedInstanceState) {
        super.onCreate(savedInstanceState);
        setContentView(R.layout.main);
        //Dummy example database
        SQLiteDatabase db = openOrCreateDatabase("mydb", Activity.MODE_PRIVATE, null);
        db.close();
    }

    @Override
    public void onResume() {
        super.onResume();
        if( Environment.getExternalStorageState().equals(Environment.MEDIA_MOUNTED) ) {
            BackupTask task = new BackupTask(this);
            task.setCompletionListener(this);
            task.execute(BackupTask.COMMAND_RESTORE);
        }
    }

    @Override
    public void onPause() {
        super.onPause();
        if( Environment.getExternalStorageState().equals(Environment.MEDIA_MOUNTED) ) {
            BackupTask task = new BackupTask(this);
            task.execute(BackupTask.COMMAND_BACKUP);
        }
    }

    @Override
    public void onBackupComplete() {
        Toast.makeText(this, "Backup Successful", Toast.LENGTH_SHORT).show();
    }
```

```
    @Override
    public void onError(int errorCode) {
        if(errorCode == BackupTask.RESTORE_NOFILEERROR) {
            Toast.makeText(this, "No Backup Found to Restore",
                Toast.LENGTH_SHORT).show();
        } else {
            Toast.makeText(this, "Error During Operation: "+errorCode,
                Toast.LENGTH_SHORT).show();
        }
    }

    @Override
    public void onRestoreComplete() {
        Toast.makeText(this, "Restore Successful", Toast.LENGTH_SHORT).show();
    }
}
```

The Activity implements the CompletionListener defined by BackupTask, so it may be notified when operations are finished or an error occurs. For the purposes of the example, a dummy database is created in the application's database directory. We call openOrCreateDatabase() only to allow a file to be created, so the connection is immediately closed afterward. Under normal circumstances, this database would already exist and these lines would not be necessary.

The example does a restore operation each time the Activity is resumed, registering itself with the task so it can be notified and raise a toast to the user of the status result. Notice that the task of checking whether external storage is usable falls to the Activity as well, and no tasks are executed if external storage is not accessible. When the Activity is paused a backup operation is executed, this time without registering for callbacks. This is because the Activity is no longer interesting to the user, so we won't need to raise a toast to point out the operation results.

Extra Credit

This background task could be extended to save the data to a cloud-based service for maximum safety and data portability. There are many options available to accomplish this, including Google's own set of web APIs, and we recommend you give this a try.

Android, as of API Level 8, also includes an API for backing up data to a cloud-based service. This API may suit your purposes, however we will not discuss it here. The Android framework cannot guarantee that this service will be available on all Android devices, and there is no API as of this writing to determine whether the device the user has will support the Android backup, so it is not recommended for critical data.

5–8. Sharing Your Database

Problem

Your application would like to provide the database content it maintains to other applications on the device.

Solution

(API Level 1)

Create a ContentProvider to act as an external interface for your application's data. ContentProvider exposes an arbitrary set of data to external requests through a database-like interface of query(), insert(), update(), and delete(); though the implementer is free to design how the interface maps to the actual data model. Creating a ContentProvider to expose the data from an SQLiteDatabase is straightforward and simple. With some minor exceptions, the developer needs only to pass calls from the provider down to the database.

Arguments about which data set to operate on are typically encoded in the Uri passed to the ContentProvider. For example, sending a query Uri such as

content://com.examples.myprovider/friends

would tell the provider to return information from the "friends" table within its data set, while

content://com.examples.myprovider/friends/15

would instruct just the record id 15 to return from the query. It should be noted that these are only the conventions used by the rest of the system, and that you are responsible for making the ContentProvider you create behave in this manner. There is nothing inherent about ContentProvider that provide this functionality for you.

How It Works

First of all, to create a ContentProvider that interacts with a database, we must have a database in place to interact with. Listing 5–19 is a sample SQLiteOpenHelper implementation that we will use to create and access the database itself.

Listing 5–19. *Sample SQLiteOpenHelper*

```
public class ShareDbHelper extends SQLiteOpenHelper {

    private static final String DB_NAME = "frienddb";
    private static final int DB_VERSION = 1;

    public static final String TABLE_NAME = "friends";
    public static final String COL_FIRST = "firstName";
    public static final String COL_LAST = "lastName";
    public static final String COL_PHONE = "phoneNumber";
```

```
private static final String STRING_CREATE =
    "CREATE TABLE "+TABLE_NAME+" (_id INTEGER PRIMARY KEY AUTOINCREMENT, "
    +COL_FIRST+" TEXT, "+COL_LAST+" TEXT, "+COL_PHONE+" TEXT);";

public ShareDbHelper(Context context) {
    super(context, DB_NAME, null, DB_VERSION);
}

@Override
public void onCreate(SQLiteDatabase db) {
    //Create the database table
    db.execSQL(STRING_CREATE);

    //Inserting example values into database
    ContentValues cv = new ContentValues(3);
    cv.put(COL_FIRST, "John");
    cv.put(COL_LAST, "Doe");
    cv.put(COL_PHONE, "8885551234");
    db.insert(TABLE_NAME, null, cv);
    cv = new ContentValues(3);
    cv.put(COL_FIRST, "Jane");
    cv.put(COL_LAST, "Doe");
    cv.put(COL_PHONE, "8885552345");
    db.insert(TABLE_NAME, null, cv);
    cv = new ContentValues(3);
    cv.put(COL_FIRST, "Jill");
    cv.put(COL_LAST, "Doe");
    cv.put(COL_PHONE, "8885553456");
    db.insert(TABLE_NAME, null, cv);
}

@Override
public void onUpgrade(SQLiteDatabase db, int oldVersion, int newVersion) {
    //For now, clear the database and re-create
    db.execSQL("DROP TABLE IF EXISTS "+TABLE_NAME);
    onCreate(db);
}
}
```

Overall this helper is fairly simple, creating a single table to keep a list of our friends with just three columns for housing text data. For the purposes of this example, three row values are inserted. Now let's take a look at a ContentProvider that will expose this database to other applications – see Listings 5–20 and 5–21.

Listing 5–20. *Manifest Declaration for ContentProvider*

```
<manifest xmlns:android="http://schemas.android.com/apk/res/android" …>
    <application …>
        <provider android:name=".FriendProvider"
            android:authorities="com.examples.sharedb.friendprovider">
        </provider>
    </application>
</manifest>
```

Listing 5–20. *ContentProvider for a Database*

```java
public class FriendProvider extends ContentProvider {

    public static final Uri CONTENT_URI =
            Uri.parse("content://com.examples.sharedb.friendprovider/friends");

    public static final class Columns {
        public static final String _ID = "_id";
        public static final String FIRST = "firstName";
        public static final String LAST = "lastName";
        public static final String PHONE = "phoneNumber";
    }

    /* Uri Matching */
    private static final int FRIEND = 1;
    private static final int FRIEND_ID = 2;

    private static final UriMatcher matcher = new UriMatcher(UriMatcher.NO_MATCH);
    static {
        matcher.addURI(CONTENT_URI.getAuthority(), "friends", FRIEND);
        matcher.addURI(CONTENT_URI.getAuthority(), "friends/#", FRIEND_ID);
    }

    SQLiteDatabase db;

    @Override
    public int delete(Uri uri, String selection, String[] selectionArgs) {
        int result = matcher.match(uri);
        switch(result) {
        case FRIEND:
            return db.delete(ShareDbHelper.TABLE_NAME, selection, selectionArgs);
        case FRIEND_ID:
            return db.delete(ShareDbHelper.TABLE_NAME, "_ID = ?",
                    new String[]{uri.getLastPathSegment()});
        default:
            return 0;
        }
    }

    @Override
    public String getType(Uri uri) {
        return null;
    }

    @Override
    public Uri insert(Uri uri, ContentValues values) {
        long id = db.insert(ShareDbHelper.TABLE_NAME, null, values);
        if(id >= 0) {
            return Uri.withAppendedPath(uri, String.valueOf(id));
        } else {
            return null;
        }
    }

    @Override
    public boolean onCreate() {
        ShareDbHelper helper = new ShareDbHelper(getContext());
```

```
            db = helper.getWritableDatabase();
            return true;
    }

    @Override
    public Cursor query(Uri uri, String[] projection, String selection,
            String[] selectionArgs, String sortOrder) {
        int result = matcher.match(uri);
        switch(result) {
        case FRIEND:
            return db.query(ShareDbHelper.TABLE_NAME, projection, selection,
                    selectionArgs, null, null, sortOrder);
        case FRIEND_ID:
            return db.query(ShareDbHelper.TABLE_NAME, projection, "_ID = ?",
                    new String[]{uri.getLastPathSegment()}, null, null, sortOrder);
        default:
            return null;
        }
    }

    @Override
    public int update(Uri uri, ContentValues values, String selection,
            String[] selectionArgs) {
        int result = matcher.match(uri);
        switch(result) {
        case FRIEND:
            return db.update(ShareDbHelper.TABLE_NAME, values, selection,
                    selectionArgs);
        case FRIEND_ID:
            return db.update(ShareDbHelper.TABLE_NAME, values, "_ID = ?",
                    new String[]{uri.getLastPathSegment()});
        default:
            return 0;
        }
    }

}
```

A ContentProvider must be declared in the application's manifest with the authority string that it represents. This allows the provider to be accessed from external applications, but is still required even if you only use the provider internally within your application. The authority is what Android uses to match Uri requests to the provider, so it should match the authority portion of the public CONTENT_URI.

The six required methods to override when extending ContentProvider are query(), insert(), update(), delete(), getType(), and onCreate(). The first four of these methods have direct counterparts in SQLiteDatabase, so the database method is simply called with the appropriate parameters. The primary difference between the two is that the ContentProvider method passes in a Uri, which the provider should inspect to determine which portion of the database to operate on.

These four primary CRUD methods are called on the provider when an Activity or other system component calls the corresponding method on its internal ContentResolver (you see this in action in Listing 5–21) or, in the case of Activity, when managedQuery() is called.

To adhere to the `Uri` convention mentioned in the first part of this recipe, `insert()` returns a `Uri` object created by appending the newly created record id onto the end of the path. This `Uri` should be considered by its requester to be a direct reference back to the record that was just created.

The remaining methods (`query()`, `update()`, and `delete()`) adhere to the convention by inspecting the incoming `Uri` to see if it refers to a specific record, or the whole table. This task is accomplished with the help of the `UriMatcher` convenience class. The `UriMatcher.match()` method compares a `Uri` to a set of supplied patterns and returns the matching pattern as an int, or `UriMatcher.NO_MATCH` if one is not found. If a `Uri` is supplied with a record id appended, the call to the database is modified to affect only that specific row.

A `UriMatcher` should be initialized by supplying a set of patterns with `UriMatcher.addURI()`; Google recommends that this all be done in a static context within the `ContentProvider`. Each pattern added is also given a constant identifier that will be the return value when matches are made. There are two wildcard characters that may be placed in the supplied patterns: the pound (#) character will match any number, and the asterisk (*) will match any text.

Our example has created two patterns to match. The initial pattern matches the supplied `CONTENT_URI` directly, and is taken to reference the entire database table. The second pattern looks for an appended number to the path, which will be taken to reference just the record at that id.

Access to the database is obtained through a reference given by the `ShareDbHelper` in `onCreate()`. The size of the database used should be considered when deciding if this method is applicable to your application. Our database is quite small when it is created, but larger databases may take a long time to create, in which case the main thread should not be tied up while this operation is taking place; `getWritableDatabase()` may need to be wrapped in an AsyncTask and done in the background in these cases. Now let's take a look at a sample Activity accessing the data – see Listings 5–23 and 5–24.

Listing 5–23. *AndroidManifest.xml*

```xml
<?xml version="1.0" encoding="utf-8"?>
<manifest xmlns:android="http://schemas.android.com/apk/res/android"
    package="com.examples.sharedb" android:versionCode="1" android:versionName="1.0">
    <uses-sdk android:minSdkVersion="1" />
    <application android:icon="@drawable/icon" android:label="@string/app_name">
        <activity android:name=".ShareActivity" android:label="@string/app_name">
            <intent-filter>
                <action android:name="android.intent.action.MAIN" />
                <category android:name="android.intent.category.LAUNCHER" />
            </intent-filter>
        </activity>
        <provider android:name=".FriendProvider"
            android:authorities="com.examples.sharedb.friendprovider">
        </provider>
    </application>
</manifest>
```

Listing 5–24. *Activity Accessing the ContentProvider*

```java
public class ShareActivity extends ListActivity implements
AdapterView.OnItemClickListener {

    Cursor mCursor;

    @Override
    public void onCreate(Bundle savedInstanceState) {
        super.onCreate(savedInstanceState);

        //List of column names to return from the query for each record
        String[] projection = new String[]{FriendProvider.Columns._ID,
            FriendProvider.Columns.FIRST};
        mCursor = managedQuery(FriendProvider.CONTENT_URI, projection, null, null,
            null);

        SimpleCursorAdapter adapter = new SimpleCursorAdapter(this,
                android.R.layout.simple_list_item_1,
                mCursor,
                new String[]{FriendProvider.Columns.FIRST},
                new int[]{android.R.id.text1});

        ListView list = getListView();
        list.setOnItemClickListener(this);
        list.setAdapter(adapter);
    }

    @Override
    public void onItemClick(AdapterView<?> parent, View v, int position, long id) {
        mCursor.moveToPosition(position);

        Uri uri = Uri.withAppendedPath(FriendProvider.CONTENT_URI,
            mCursor.getString(0));
        String[] projection = new String[]{FriendProvider.Columns.FIRST,
                FriendProvider.Columns.LAST,
                FriendProvider.Columns.PHONE};
        //Get the full record
        Cursor cursor = getContentResolver().query(uri, projection, null, null, null);
        cursor.moveToFirst();

        String message = String.format("%s %s, %s", cursor.getString(0),
            cursor.getString(1), cursor.getString(2));
        Toast.makeText(this, message, Toast.LENGTH_SHORT).show();
    }
}
```

This example queries the FriendsProvider for all its records and places them into a list, displaying only the first name column. In order for the Cursor to adapt properly into a list, our projection must include the ID column, even though it is not displayed.

If the user taps any of the items in the list, another query is made of the provider using a Uri constructed with the record ID appended to the end, forcing the provider to only return that one record. In addition, an expanded projection is provided to get all the column data about this friend.

The returned data is placed into a Toast and raised for the user to see. Individual fields from the cursor are accessed by their *column index*, corresponding to the index in the projection passed to the query. The Cursor.getColumnIndex() method may also be used to query the cursor for the index associated with a given column name.

A Cursor should always be closed when it is no longer needed, as we do with the Cursor created on user click. The member mCursor is never closed explicitly because it is managed by the Activity. Whenever a Cursor is created using managedQuery(), the Activity will open, close, and refresh the data along with its own normal lifecycle.

Figure 5–2 shows the result of running this sample to display the provider content.

Figure 5–2. *Information from a ContentProvider*

5–9. Sharing Your Other Data

Problem

You would like your application to provide the files or other data it maintains to other applications on the device.

Solution

(API Level 3)

Create a `ContentProvider` to act as an external interface for your application's data. `ContentProvider` exposes an arbitrary set of data to external requests through a database-like interface of `query()`, `insert()`, `update()`, and `delete()`, though the implementation is free to design how the data passes to the actual model from these methods.

`ContentProvider` can be used to expose any type of application data, including the application's resources and assets, to external requests.

How It Works

Let's take a look at a `ContentProvider` implementation that exposes two data sources: an array of strings located in memory, and a series of image files stored in the application's assets directory. As before, we must declare our provider to the Android system using a `<provider>` tag in the manifest. See Listings 5–25 and 5–26.

Listing 5–25. *Manifest Declaration for ContentProvider*

```xml
<?xml version="1.0" encoding="utf-8"?>
<manifest xmlns:android="http://schemas.android.com/apk/res/android" …>
    <application …>
      <provider android:name=".ImageProvider"
          android:authorities="com.examples.share.imageprovider">
      </provider>
    </application>
</manifest>
```

Listing 5–26. *Custom ContentProvider Exposing Assets*

```java
public class ImageProvider extends ContentProvider {

    public static final Uri CONTENT_URI =
        Uri.parse("content://com.examples.share.imageprovider");

    public static final String COLUMN_NAME = "nameString";
    public static final String COLUMN_IMAGE = "imageUri";

    private String[] mNames;

    @Override
    public int delete(Uri uri, String selection, String[] selectionArgs) {
        throw new UnsupportedOperationException("This ContentProvider is read-only");
    }

    @Override
    public String getType(Uri uri) {
        return null;
    }

    @Override
```

```java
public Uri insert(Uri uri, ContentValues values) {
    throw new UnsupportedOperationException("This ContentProvider is read-only");
}

@Override
public boolean onCreate() {
    mNames = new String[] {"John Doe", "Jane Doe", "Jill Doe"};
    return true;
}

@Override
public Cursor query(Uri uri, String[] projection, String selection,
    String[] selectionArgs, String sortOrder) {
    MatrixCursor cursor = new MatrixCursor(projection);
    for(int i = 0; i < mNames.length; i++) {
        //Insert only the columns they requested
        MatrixCursor.RowBuilder builder = cursor.newRow();
        for(String column : projection) {
            if(column.equals("_id")) {
                //Use the array index as a unique id
                builder.add(i);
            }
            if(column.equals(COLUMN_NAME)) {
                builder.add(mNames[i]);
            }
            if(column.equals(COLUMN_IMAGE)) {
                builder.add(Uri.withAppendedPath(CONTENT_URI, String.valueOf(i)));
            }
        }
    }
    return cursor;
}

@Override
public int update(Uri uri, ContentValues values, String selection,
    String[] selectionArgs) {
    throw new UnsupportedOperationException("This ContentProvider is read-only");
}

@Override
public AssetFileDescriptor openAssetFile(Uri uri, String mode) throws
    FileNotFoundException {
    int requested = Integer.parseInt(uri.getLastPathSegment());
    AssetFileDescriptor afd;
    AssetManager manager = getContext().getAssets();
    //Return the appropriate asset for the requested item
    try {
        switch(requested) {
        case 0:
            afd = manager.openFd("logo1.png");
            break;
        case 1:
            afd = manager.openFd("logo2.png");
            break;
        case 2:
            afd = manager.openFd("logo3.png");
            break;
```

```
            default:
                afd = manager.openFd("logo1.png");
            }
            return afd;
        } catch (IOException e) {
            e.printStackTrace();
            return null;
        }
    }
}
```

As you may have guessed, the example exposes three logo image assets. The images we have chosen for this example are shown in Figure 5–3.

Figure 5–3. *Example logo1.png (left), logo2.png (center), and logo3.png (right) stored in assets*

Notice first that, because we are exposing read-only content in the assets directory, there is no need to support the inherited methods insert(), update(), or delete(), so we have these methods simply throw an UnsupportedOperationException.

When the provider is created, the string array that holds people's names is created and onCreate() returns true; this signals to the system that the provider was created successfully. The provider exposes constants for its Uri and all readable column names. These values will be used by external applications to make requests for data.

This provider only supports a query for all the data within it. To support conditional queries for specific records or a subset of all the content, an application can process the values passed in to query() for selection and selectionArgs. In this example, any call to query() will build a cursor with all three elements contained within.

The cursor implementation used in this provider is a MatrixCursor, which is a cursor designed to be built around data not held inside a database. The example iterates through the list of columns requested (the projection) and builds each row according to these columns it contains. Each row is created by calling MatrixCursor.newRow(), which also returns a Builder instance that will be used to add the column data. Care should always be taken to match the order of the column data is added to the order of the requested projection. They should always match.

The value in the name column is the respective string in the local array, and the _id value, which Android requires to utilize the returned cursor with most ListAdapters, is simply returned as the array index. The data presented in the image column for each row is actually a content Uri representing the image file for each row, created with the provider's content Uri as the base, with the array index appended to it.

When an external application actually goes to retrieve this content, through ContentResolver.openInputStream(), a call will be made to openAssetFile(), which has been overridden to return an AssetFileDescriptor pointing to one of the image files in the assets directory. This implementation determines which image file to return by deconstructing the content Uri once again and retrieving the appended index value from the end.

Usage Example

Let's take a look at how this provider should be implemented and accessed in the context of the Android application. See Listing 5–27.

Listing 5–27. *AndroidManifest.xml*

```xml
<?xml version="1.0" encoding="utf-8"?>
<manifest xmlns:android="http://schemas.android.com/apk/res/android"
     package="com.examples.share"
     android:versionCode="1"
     android:versionName="1.0">
  <uses-sdk android:minSdkVersion="3" />

  <application android:icon="@drawable/icon" android:label="@string/app_name">
     <activity android:name=".ShareActivity"
               android:label="@string/app_name">
        <intent-filter>
           <action android:name="android.intent.action.MAIN" />
           <category android:name="android.intent.category.LAUNCHER" />
        </intent-filter>
     </activity>
     <provider android:name=".ImageProvider"
        android:authorities="com.examples.share.imageprovider">
     </provider>
  </application>
</manifest>
```

To implement this provider, the manifest of the application that owns the content must declare a <provider> tag pointing out the ContentProvider name and the authority to match when requests are made. The authority value should match the base portion of the exposed content Uri. The provider must be declared in the manifest so the system can instantiate and run it, even when the owning application is not running. See Listings 5–28 and 5–29.

Listing 5–28. *res/layout/main.xml*

```xml
<?xml version="1.0" encoding="utf-8"?>
<LinearLayout xmlns:android="http://schemas.android.com/apk/res/android"
  android:orientation="vertical"
  android:layout_width="fill_parent"
  android:layout_height="fill_parent">
  <TextView
    android:id="@+id/name"
    android:layout_width="wrap_content"
    android:layout_height="20dip"
    android:layout_gravity="center_horizontal"
  />
  <ImageView
    android:id="@+id/image"
    android:layout_width="wrap_content"
    android:layout_height="50dip"
```

```
      android:layout_gravity="center_horizontal"
  />
  <ListView
    android:id="@+id/list"
    android:layout_width="fill_parent"
    android:layout_height="fill_parent"
  />
</LinearLayout>
```

Listing 5–29. *Activity Reading from ImageProvider*

```java
public class ShareActivity extends Activity implements AdapterView.OnItemClickListener {

    Cursor mCursor;

    @Override
    public void onCreate(Bundle savedInstanceState) {
        super.onCreate(savedInstanceState);
        setContentView(R.layout.main);

        String[] projection = new String[]{"_id", ImageProvider.COLUMN_NAME,
            ImageProvider.COLUMN_IMAGE};
        mCursor = managedQuery(ImageProvider.CONTENT_URI, projection, null, null, null);

        SimpleCursorAdapter adapter = new SimpleCursorAdapter(this,
            android.R.layout.simple_list_item_1, mCursor, new String[]{ImageProvider.COLUMN_NAME},
            new int[]{android.R.id.text1});

        ListView list = (ListView)findViewById(R.id.list);
        list.setOnItemClickListener(this);
        list.setAdapter(adapter);
    }

    @Override
    public void onItemClick(AdapterView<?> parent, View v, int position, long id) {
        //Seek the cursor to the selection
        mCursor.moveToPosition(position);

        //Load the name column into the TextView
        TextView tv = (TextView)findViewById(R.id.name);
        tv.setText(mCursor.getString(1));

        ImageView iv = (ImageView)findViewById(R.id.image);
        try {
            //Load the content from the image column into the ImageView
            InputStream in =
                getContentResolver().openInputStream(Uri.parse(mCursor.getString(2)));
            Bitmap image = BitmapFactory.decodeStream(in);
            iv.setImageBitmap(image);
        } catch (FileNotFoundException e) {
            e.printStackTrace();
        }

    }

}
```

In this example a managed cursor is obtained from the custom `ContentProvider`, referencing the exposed Uri and column names for the data. The data is then connected to a `ListView` using a `SimpleCursorAdapter` to display only the name value.

When the user taps any of the items in the list, the cursor is moved to that position and the respective name and image are displayed above. This is where the Activity calls `ContentResolver.openInputStream()` to access the asset images through the Uri that was stored in the column field.

Figure 5–4 displays the result of running this application and selecting the last item in the list (Jill Doe).

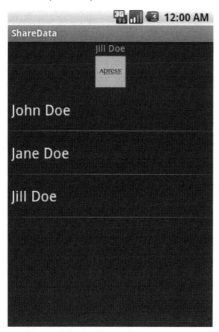

Figure 5–4. *Activity drawing resources from ContentProvider*

Note that the connection to the `Cursor` is not closed explicitly because it was created using `managedQuery()`, which means the Activity will manage the cursor as part of its normal lifecycle, including closing it when the Activity leaves the foreground.

Useful Tools to Know: SQLite3

Android provides the `sqlite3` tool (in the `tools` subdirectory of the Android SDK's home directory) for creating new databases and managing existing databases on your hosting platform or (when used in conjunction with adb, the Android Debug Bridge tool) on an Android device. If you're not familiar with `sqlite3`, point your browser to `http://sqlite.org/sqlite.html` and read the short tutorial on this command-line tool.

You can specify `sqlite3` with a database filename argument (`sqlite3 employees`, for example) to create the database file if it doesn't exist or open the existing file, and enter this tool's shell from where you can execute `sqlite3`-specific dot-prefixed commands and SQL statements. As Figure 5–5 shows, you can also specify `sqlite3` without an argument and enter the shell.

```
C:\WINDOWS\system32\cmd.exe

C:\>sqlite3
SQLite version 3.6.22
Enter ".help" for instructions
Enter SQL statements terminated with a ";"
sqlite> .help
.backup ?DB? FILE      Backup DB (default "main") to FILE
.bail ON|OFF           Stop after hitting an error.  Default OFF
.databases             List names and files of attached databases
.dump ?TABLE? ...      Dump the database in an SQL text format
                           If TABLE specified, only dump tables matching
                           LIKE pattern TABLE.
.echo ON|OFF           Turn command echo on or off
.exit                  Exit this program
.explain ?ON|OFF?      Turn output mode suitable for EXPLAIN on or off.
                           With no args, it turns EXPLAIN on.
.genfkey ?OPTIONS?     Options are:
                           --no-drop: Do not drop old fkey triggers.
                           --ignore-errors: Ignore tables with fkey errors
                           --exec: Execute generated SQL immediately
                       See file tool/genfkey.README in the source
                       distribution for further information.
.header(s) ON|OFF      Turn display of headers on or off
.help                  Show this message
.import FILE TABLE     Import data from FILE into TABLE
```

Figure 5–5. *Invoking* `sqlite3` *without a database filename argument*

Figure 5–5 reveals the prologue that greets you after entering the `sqlite3` shell, which is indicated by the `sqlite>` prompt from where you enter commands. It also reveals part of the help text that's presented when you type the `sqlite3`-specific ".help" command.

> **TIP:** You can create a database after specifying `sqlite3` without an argument by entering the appropriate SQL statements to create and populate desired tables (and possibly create indexes) and then invoking `.backup filename` (where `filename` identifies the file that stores the database) before exiting `sqlite3`.

After you've created the database on your hosting platform, you'll want to upload it to your Android device. You can accomplish this task by invoking the adb tool with its push command according to the following command-line syntax:

```
adb [-s <serialNumber>] push local.db /data/data/<application
package>/databases/remote.db
```

This command pushes the locally hosted database identified as *local*.db to a file named *remote*.db that's located in the /data/data/<application package>/databases directory on the connected Android device.

> **NOTE:** *Local* and *remote* are placeholders for the actual database filenames. By convention, the filename is associated with a .db file extension (although an extension isn't mandatory). Also, /data/data/*<application package>* refers to the application's own private storage area, and *application package* refers to an application's unique package name.

If only one device is connected to the hosting platform, -s *<serialNumber>* isn't required, and the local database is pushed onto that device. If multiple devices are connected, -s *<serialNumber>* is required to identify a specific device (-s emulator-5556, for example).

Alternatively, you might want to download a device's database to your hosting platform, perhaps to use with a desktop version of the device's application. You can accomplish this task by invoking adb with its pull command according to the following syntax:

```
adb [-s <serialNumber>] pull /data/data/<application package>/databases/remote.db
local.db
```

If you want to use sqlite3 to manage SQLite databases that are stored on a device, you'll need to invoke this tool from within an adb remote shell for that device. You can accomplish this task by invoking adb and sqlite3 according to the following syntax:

```
adb [-s <serialNumber>] shell
# sqlite3 /data/data/<application package>/databases/remote.db
```

The adb shell is indicated by the # prompt. Enter sqlite3 followed by the path and name of the existing device-hosted database file to manipulate the database, or of the new database to create. Alternatively, you can enter sqlite3 without an argument.

The sqlite3 command presents the same prologue that you saw in Figure 5–1. Enter sqlite3 commands and issue SQL statements to manage *remote*.db (or create a new database), and then exit sqlite3 (.exit or .quit) followed by the adb shell (exit).

SQLite3 and UC

Chapter 1 introduced you to an application named UC. This units-conversion application lets you perform conversions between various units (degrees Fahrenheit to degrees Celsius, for example).

Although useful, UC is flawed in that it must be rebuilt each time a new conversion is added to its list of conversions. We can eliminate this flaw by storing UC's conversions in a database, and that is what we'll do in this section.

We'll first create a database for storing the list of conversions. The database will consist of a single conversions table with conversion and multiplier columns. Furthermore, the database will be stored in a conversions.db file.

Table 5–1 lists the values that will be stored in the conversion and multiplier columns.

Table 5-1. *Values for the* Conversion *and* Multiplier *Columns*

Conversion	Multiplier
Acres to Square Miles	0.0015625
Atmospheres to Pascals	101325.0
Bars to Pascals	100000.0
Degrees Celsius to Degrees Fahrenheit	0 (placeholder)
Degrees Fahrenheit to Degrees Celsius	0 (placeholder)
Dynes to Newtons	0.00001
Feet/Second to Meters/Second	0.3048
Fluid Ounces (UK) to Liters	0.0284130625
Fluid Ounces (US) to Liters	0.0295735295625
Horsepower (electric) to Watts	746.0
Horsepower (metric) to Watts	735.499
Kilograms to Tons (UK or long)	1/1016.0469088
Kilograms to Tons (US or short)	1/907.18474
Liters to Fluid Ounces (UK)	1/0.0284130625
Liters to Fluid Ounces (US)	1/0.0295735295625
Mach Number to Meters/Second	331.5
Meters/Second to Feet/Second	1/0.3048
Meters/Second to Mach Number	1/331.5
Miles/Gallon (UK) to Miles/Gallon (US)	0.833
Miles/Gallon (US) to Miles/Gallon (UK)	1/0.833
Newtons to Dynes	100000.0
Pascals to Atmospheres	1/101325.0
Pascals to Bars	0.00001
Square Miles to Acres	640.0
Tons (UK or long) to Kilograms	1016.0469088
Tons (US or short) to Kilograms	907.18474
Watts to Horsepower (electic)	1/746.0
Watts to Horsepower (metric)	1/735.499

At the command line, execute `sqlite3 conversions.db` to create `conversions.db` and enter the shell, and then execute SQL statement `create table conversions(conversion varchar(50), mutliplier float);` to create this database's conversions table.

Continuing, enter a sequence of insert statements to insert Table 5–1's rows of values into conversions. For example, SQL statement `insert into conversions values('Acres to square miles', 0.0015625);` inserts the first row's values into the table.

> **CAUTION:** You must insert the rows in the same order as they appear in Table 5–1, because `Degrees Celsius to Degrees Fahrenheit` and `Degrees Fahrenheit to Degrees Celsius` must appear at zero-based positions 3 and 4 due to hardcoding these positions in `UC2.java`.

We'll next create a UC2 application that's similar to UC but obtains its conversions from `conversions.db`. Accomplish this task by following the instructions that are presented in Chapter 1's Recipe 1-10 (Developing UC with Eclipse), but with the following changes (see Listing 5–30):

- Change the package name from `com.apress.uc` to `com.apress.uc2`.

- Ignore the `arrays.xml` file. UC2 doesn't need this file.

- Replace the skeletal `UC2.java` source code with Listing 5–26.

Listing 5–30. *Activity for Performing Unit conversions Obtained from* `Conversions.db`

```java
public class UC2 extends Activity {
    private int position = 0;
    private String[] conversions;
    private double[] multipliers;

    private class DBHelper extends SQLiteOpenHelper
    {
        private final static String DB_PATH = "data/data/com.apress.uc2/databases/";
        private final static String DB_NAME = "conversions.db";
        private final static int CONVERSIONS_COLUMN_ID = 0;
        private final static int MULTIPLIERS_COLUMN_ID = 1;

        private SQLiteDatabase db;

        public DBHelper(Context context)
        {
            super(context, DB_NAME, null, 1);
        }

        @Override
        public void onCreate(SQLiteDatabase db)
        {
            // Do nothing ... we don't create a new database.
        }

        @Override
        public void onUpgrade(SQLiteDatabase db, int oldver, int newver)
```

```
    {
        // Do nothing ... we don't upgrade a database.
    }

    public boolean populateArrays()
    {
        try
        {
            String path = DB_PATH+DB_NAME;
                db = SQLiteDatabase.openDatabase(path, null, SQLiteDatabase.OPEN_READONLY|
                                                SQLiteDatabase.NO_LOCALIZED_COLLATORS);
                Cursor cur = db.query("conversions", null, null, null, null, null, null);
                if (cur.getCount() == 0)
                {
                    Toast.makeText(UC2.this, "conversions table is empty",
                                   Toast.LENGTH_LONG).show();
                    return false;
                }
                conversions = new String[cur.getCount()];
                multipliers = new double[cur.getCount()];
                int i = 0;
                while (cur.moveToNext())
                {
                    conversions[i] = cur.getString(CONVERSIONS_COLUMN_ID);
                    multipliers[i++] = cur.getFloat(MULTIPLIERS_COLUMN_ID);
                }
                return true;
        }
        catch (SQLException sqle)
        {
            Toast.makeText(UC2.this, sqle.getMessage(), Toast.LENGTH_LONG).show();
        }
        finally
        {
            if (db != null)
                db.close();
        }
        return false;
    }
}

@Override
public void onCreate(Bundle savedInstanceState)
{
    super.onCreate(savedInstanceState);
    setContentView(R.layout.main);

    DBHelper dbh = new DBHelper(this);
    if (!dbh.populateArrays())
        finish();

    final EditText etUnits = (EditText) findViewById(R.id.units);

    final Spinner spnConversions = (Spinner) findViewById(R.id.conversions);
    ArrayAdapter<CharSequence> aa;
    aa = new ArrayAdapter<CharSequence>(this, android.R.layout.simple_spinner_item,
                                        conversions);
```

```java
        aa.setDropDownViewResource(android.R.layout.simple_spinner_item);
        spnConversions.setAdapter(aa);

        AdapterView.OnItemSelectedListener oisl;
        oisl = new AdapterView.OnItemSelectedListener()
        {
            @Override
            public void onItemSelected(AdapterView<?> parent, View view,
                                       int position, long id)
            {
                UC2.this.position = position;
            }

            @Override
            public void onNothingSelected(AdapterView<?> parent)
            {
                System.out.println("nothing");
            }
        };
        spnConversions.setOnItemSelectedListener(oisl);

        final Button btnClear = (Button) findViewById(R.id.clear);
        AdapterView.OnClickListener ocl;
        ocl = new AdapterView.OnClickListener()
        {
            @Override
            public void onClick(View v)
            {
                etUnits.setText("");
            }
        };
        btnClear.setOnClickListener(ocl);
        btnClear.setEnabled(false);

        final Button btnConvert = (Button) findViewById(R.id.convert);
        ocl = new AdapterView.OnClickListener()
        {
            @Override
            public void onClick(View v)
            {
                String text = etUnits.getText().toString();
                double input = Double.parseDouble(text);
                double result = 0;
                if (position == 3)
                    result = input*9.0/5.0+32; // Celsius to Fahrenheit
                else
                if (position == 4)
                    result = (input-32)*5.0/9.0; // Fahrenheit to Celsius
                else
                    result = input*multipliers[position];
                etUnits.setText(""+result);
            }
        };
        btnConvert.setOnClickListener(ocl);
        btnConvert.setEnabled(false);

        Button btnClose = (Button) findViewById(R.id.close);
```

```
      ocl = new AdapterView.OnClickListener()
      {
         @Override
         public void onClick(View v)
         {
            finish();
         }
      };
      btnClose.setOnClickListener(ocl);

      TextWatcher tw;
      tw = new TextWatcher()
      {
         public void afterTextChanged(Editable s)
         {
         }
         public void beforeTextChanged(CharSequence s, int start, int count,
                                       int after)
         {
         }
         public void onTextChanged(CharSequence s, int start, int before,
                                   int count)
         {
            if (etUnits.getText().length() == 0)
            {
               btnClear.setEnabled(false);
               btnConvert.setEnabled(false);
            }
            else
            {
               btnClear.setEnabled(true);
               btnConvert.setEnabled(true);
            }
         }
      };
      etUnits.addTextChangedListener(tw);
   }
}
```

UC2 differs from UC mainly by relying on the DBHelper inner class to obtain the values for its conversions and multipliers arrays from the conversion and multiplier columns in the conversions.db database's conversions table.

DBHelper extends android.database.sqlite.SQLiteOpenHelper and overrides its abstract onCreate() and onUpgrade() methods. The overriding methods do nothing; all that's important is whether or not the database can be opened.

The database is opened in the populateArrays() method. If successfully opened, the conversions table is queried to return all rows. If the returned android.database.Cursor object contains at least one row, the arrays are populated from Cursor values.

If something goes wrong, a toast message is displayed. Although convenient for this simple example, you probably would want to display a dialog box and store its strings in a resources file. The database is closed whether or not a toast message is displayed.

UC2 also differs from UC in that it directly instantiates android.widget.ArrayAdapter instead of invoking this class's createFromResource() method. It does this so that it can pass the conversions array of string names to the ArrayAdapter instance.

Assuming that you've built this application, launch it from Eclipse. UC2 will briefly present a blank screen and then display a toast message before finishing. Figure 5–6 reveals that this toast appears on the app launcher screen.

Figure 5–6. *A toast is displayed because the* conversions.db *database is not yet present on the device.*

The toast appears because no conversions.db database exists in the /data/data/com.apress.uc2/databases/ path. We can rectify this situation by uploading the previously created conversions.db file to this path, as follows:

adb push conversions.db /data/data/com.apress.uc2/databases/conversions.db

This time, when you launch this application, you should see the screen that appears in Figure 5–7.

Figure 5–7. *Units Converter's solitary screen lets you perform various kinds of unit conversions.*

UC2.java suffers from the following pair of flaws – consider fixing these flaws to be exercises to accomplish:

- The Degrees Celsius to Degrees Fahrenheit and Degrees Fahrenheit to Degrees Celsius conversions must appear at zero-based positions 3 and 4, due to hardcoding these positions in UC2.java. This hardcoding is located in the following excerpt from the onClick() method in the click listener assigned to the click button in Lising 5–30:

```
if (position == 3)
    result = input*9.0/5.0+32; // Celsius to Fahrenheit
else
if (position == 4)
    result = (input-32)*5.0/9.0; // Fahrenheit to Celsius
else
    result = input*multipliers[position];
```

- DBHelper's populateArrays() method populates the conversions and multipliers arrays on the application's main thread. This shouldn't be a problem, because the conversions table contains only 28 rows. However, if you add many more rows to this table, it's possible that the main thread would be tied up long enough for the dreaded *Application Not Responding* dialog box to appear (see Appendix C). Furthermore, this is the reason why the Android documentation states that SQLiteOpenHelper's getReadableDatabase() and getWritableDatabase() methods shouldn't be called on the main thread. However, for small databases, calling these methods on the main thread shouldn't be a problem.

Summary

In this chapter, you have investigated a number of practical methods to persist data on Android devices. You learned how to quickly create a preferences screen as well as use preferences and a simple method for persisting basic data types. You saw how and where files can be placed, for reference as well as storage. You even learned how to share your persisted data with other applications. In the next chapter, we will investigate how to leverage the operating system's services to do background operations and communicate between applications.

Chapter 6

Interacting with the System

The Android operating system provides a number of useful services that applications can leverage. Many of these services are designed to allow your application to function within the mobile system in ways beyond just interacting briefly with a user. Applications can schedule themselves for alarms, run background services, and send messages to each other; all of which allows an Android application to integrate to the fullest extent with the mobile device. In addition, Android provides a set of standard interfaces designed to expose all the data collected by its core applications to your software. Through these interfaces, any application may integrate with, add to, and improve upon the core functionality of the platform, thereby enhancing the experience for the user.

6–1. Notifying from the Background

Problem

Your application is running in the background, with no currently visible interface to the user, but must notify the user of an important event that has occurred.

Solution

(API Level 1)

Use NotificationManager to post a status bar notification. Notifications are an unobtrusive way of telling the user that you want their attention. Perhaps new messages have arrived, an update is available, or a long-running job is complete; Notifications are perfect for accomplishing all of these tasks.

How It Works

A Notification can be posted to the NotificationManager from just about any system component, such as a Service, BroadcastReceiver, or Activity. In this example, we'll look at an Activity that uses a delay to simulate a long-running operation, resulting in a Notification when it is complete.

Listing 6–1. *Activity Firing a Notification*

```
public class NotificationActivity extends Activity implements View.OnClickListener {

    private static final int NOTE_ID = 100;

    @Override
    public void onCreate(Bundle savedInstanceState) {
        super.onCreate(savedInstanceState);
        Button button = new Button(this);
        button.setText("Post New Notification");
        button.setOnClickListener(this);
        setContentView(button);
    }

    @Override
    public void onClick(View v) {
        //Run 10 seconds after click
        handler.postDelayed(task, 10000);
        Toast.makeText(this, "Notification will post in 10 seconds",
            Toast.LENGTH_SHORT).show();
    }

    private Handler handler = new Handler();
    private Runnable task = new Runnable() {
        @Override
        public void run() {
            NotificationManager manager =
                    (NotificationManager)getSystemService(Context.NOTIFICATION_SERVICE);
            Intent launchIntent = new Intent(getApplicationContext(),
                NotificationActivity.class);
            PendingIntent contentIntent =
                PendingIntent.getActivity(getApplicationContext(), 0, launchIntent, 0);

            //Create notification with the time it was fired
            Notification note = new Notification(R.drawable.icon, "Something Happened",
                    System.currentTimeMillis());
            //Set notification information
            note.setLatestEventInfo(getApplicationContext(), "We're Finished!",
                "Click Here!", contentIntent);
            note.defaults |= Notification.DEFAULT_SOUND;
            note.flags |= Notification.FLAG_AUTO_CANCEL;

            manager.notify(NOTE_ID, note);
        }
    };
}
```

This example makes use of a Handler to schedule a task to post the Notification ten seconds after the button is clicked by calling Handler.postDelayed() in the button listener. This task will execute regardless of whether the Activity is in the foreground, so if the user gets bored and leaves the application, they will still get notified.

When the scheduled task executes, a new Notification is created. An icon resource and title string may be provided, and these items will display in the status bar at the time the notification occurs. In addition, we pass a time value (in milliseconds) to display in the notification list as the event time. Here, we are setting that value to the time the notification fired, but it may take on a different meaning in your application.

Once the Notification is created, we fill it out with some useful parameters. Using Notification.setLatestEventInfo(), we provide more detailed text to be displayed in the Notifications list when the user pulls down the status bar.

One of the parameters passed to this method is a PendingIntent that points back to our Activity. This Intent makes the Notification interactive, allowing the user to tap the Notification in the list and have the Activity launched.

> **NOTE:** This Intent will launch a new Activity with each event. If you would rather an existing instance of the Activity respond to the launch, if one exists in the stack, be sure to include Intent flags and manifest parameters appropriately to accomplish this, such as Intent.FLAG_ACTIVITY_CLEAR_TOP and android:launchMode="singleTop."

To enhance the Notification beyond the visual animation in the status bar, the Notification.defaults bitmask is modified to include that the system's default notification sound be played when the Notification fires. Values such as Notification.DEFAULT_VIBRATION and Notification.DEFAULT_LIGHTS may also be added.

> **TIP:** If you would like to customize the sound played with a Notification, set the Notification.sound parameter to a Uri that references a file or ContentProvider to read from.

Adding a series of flags to the Notification.flags bitmask allows further customization of a Notification. This example enables Notification.FLAG_AUTO_CANCEL to signify that the notification should be canceled, or removed from the list, as soon as the user selects it. Without this flag, the notification remains in the list until manually canceled by calling NotificationManager.cancel() or NotificationManager.cancelAll().

The following are some other useful flags to apply:

- FLAG_INSISTENT
    - Repeats the Notification sounds until the user responds.
- FLAG_NO_CLEAR
    - Does not allow the Notification to be cleared with the user's "Clear Notifications" button; only through a call to cancel().

Once the Notification is prepared, it is posted to the user with
NotificationManager.notify(), which takes an ID parameter as well. Each
Notification type in your application should have a unique ID. The manager will only
allow one Notification with the same ID in the list at a time, and new instances with the
same ID will take the place of those existing. In addition, the ID is required to cancel a
specific Notification manually.

When we run this example, an Activity like Figure 6–1 displays a Button to the user.
Upon pressing the button, you can see the Notification post some time later, even if the
Activity is no longer visible (see Figure 6–2).

Figure 6–1. *Notification Posted from button press*

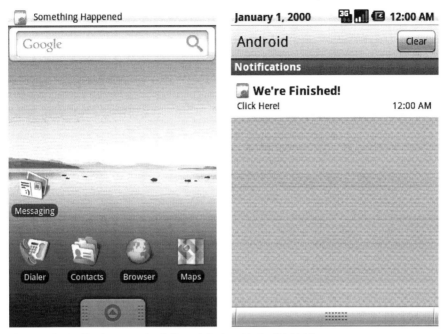

Figure 6–2. *Notification occurring (left), and displayed in the list (right)*

6–2. Creating Timed and Periodic Tasks

Problem

Your application needs to run an operation on a timer, such as updating the UI on a scheduled basis.

Solution

(API Level 1)

Use the timed operations provided by a Handler. With Handler, operations can efficiently be scheduled to occur at a specific time, or after a specified delay.

How It Works

Let's look at an example Activity that displays the current time in a TextView. See Listing 6–2.

Listing 6–2. *Activity Updated with a Handler*

```
public class TimingActivity extends Activity {

    TextView mClock;
```

```java
@Override
public void onCreate(Bundle savedInstanceState) {
    super.onCreate(savedInstanceState);
    mClock = new TextView(this);
    setContentView(mClock);
}

private Handler mHandler = new Handler();
private Runnable timerTask = new Runnable() {
    @Override
    public void run() {
        Calendar now = Calendar.getInstance();
        mClock.setText(String.format("%02d:%02d:%02d",
                now.get(Calendar.HOUR),
                now.get(Calendar.MINUTE),
                now.get(Calendar.SECOND)) );
        //Schedule the next update in one second
        mHandler.postDelayed(timerTask,1000);
    }
};

@Override
public void onResume() {
    super.onResume();
    mHandler.post(timerTask);
}

@Override
public void onPause() {
    super.onPause();
    mHandler.removeCallbacks(timerTask);
}
}
```

Here we've wrapped up the operation of reading the current time and updating the UI into a Runnable named timerTask, which will be triggered by the Handler that has also been created. When the Activity becomes visible, the task is executed as soon as possible with a call to Handler.post(). After the TextView has been updated, the final operation of timerTask is to invoke the Handler to schedule another execution one second (1,000 milliseconds) from now using Handler.postDelayed().

As long as the Activity remains uninterrupted, this cycle will continue, with the UI being updated every second. As soon as the Activity is paused (the user leaves or something else grabs their attention), Handler.removeCallbacks() removes all pending operations and ensures the task will not be called further until the Activity becomes visible once more.

> **TIP:** In this example, we are safe to update the UI because the Handler was created on the main thread. Operations will always execute on the same thread as the Handler that posted them is attached to.

6–3. Scheduling a Periodic Task

Problem

Your application needs to register to run a task periodically, such as checking a server for updates or reminding the user to do something.

Solution

(API Level 1)

Utilize the `AlarmManager` to manage and execute your task. `AlarmManager` is useful for scheduling future single or repeated operations that need to occur even if your application is not running. `AlarmManager` is handed a `PendingIntent` to fire whenever an alarm is scheduled. This Intent can point to any system component, such as an `Activity`, `BroadcastReceiver`, or `Service`, to be executed when the alarm triggers.

It should be noted that this method is best suited to operations that need to occur even when the application code may not be running. The `AlarmManager` requires too much overhead to be useful for simple timing operations that may be needed while an application is in use. These are better handled using the `postAtTime()` and `postDelayed()` methods of a `Handler`.

How It Works

Let's take a look at how `AlarmManager` can be used to trigger a BroadcastReceiver on a regular basis. See Listings 6–3 through 6–5.

Listing 6–3. *BroadcastReceiver to Be Triggered*

```
public class AlarmReceiver extends BroadcastReceiver {
    @Override
    public void onReceive(Context context, Intent intent) {
        //Perform an interesting operation, we'll just display the current time
        Calendar now = Calendar.getInstance();
        DateFormat formatter = SimpleDateFormat.getTimeInstance();
        Toast.makeText(context, formatter.format(now.getTime()),
            Toast.LENGTH_SHORT).show();
    }
}
```

> **REMINDER:** A BroadcastReceiver (`AlarmReceiver`, in this case) must be declared in the manifest
> with a `<receiver>` tag in order for AlarmManager to be able to trigger it. Be sure to include one
> within your `<application>` tag like so:
>
> ```
> <application>
>
>     ...
>
>     <receiver android:name=".AlarmReceiver"></receiver>
> </application>
> ```

Listing 6–4. *res/layout/main.xml*

```xml
<?xml version="1.0" encoding="utf-8"?>
<LinearLayout xmlns:android="http://schemas.android.com/apk/res/android"
  android:orientation="vertical"
  android:layout_width="fill_parent"
  android:layout_height="fill_parent">
  <Button
    android:id="@+id/start"
    android:layout_width="fill_parent"
    android:layout_height="wrap_content"
    android:text="Start Alarm"
  />
  <Button
    android:id="@+id/stop"
    android:layout_width="fill_parent"
    android:layout_height="wrap_content"
    android:text="Cancel Alarm"
  />
</LinearLayout>
```

Listing 6–5. *Activity to Register/Unregister Alarms*

```java
public class AlarmActivity extends Activity implements View.OnClickListener {

    private PendingIntent mAlarmIntent;

    @Override
    public void onCreate(Bundle savedInstanceState) {
        super.onCreate(savedInstanceState);
        setContentView(R.layout.main);
        //Attach the listener to both buttons
        findViewById(R.id.start).setOnClickListener(this);
        findViewById(R.id.stop).setOnClickListener(this);
        //Create the launch sender
        Intent launchIntent = new Intent(this, AlarmReceiver.class);
        mAlarmIntent = PendingIntent.getBroadcast(this, 0, launchIntent, 0);
    }

    @Override
    public void onClick(View v) {
        AlarmManager manager = (AlarmManager)getSystemService(Context.ALARM_SERVICE);
        long interval = 5*1000; //5 seconds

        switch(v.getId()) {
        case R.id.start:
```

```
            Toast.makeText(this, "Scheduled", Toast.LENGTH_SHORT).show();
            manager.setRepeating(AlarmManager.ELAPSED_REALTIME,
                    SystemClock.elapsedRealtime()+interval,
                    interval,
                    mAlarmIntent);
            break;
        case R.id.stop:
            Toast.makeText(this, "Canceled", Toast.LENGTH_SHORT).show();
            manager.cancel(mAlarmIntent);
            break;
        default:
            break;
        }
    }
}
```

In this example, we have provided a very basic BroadcastReceiver that, when triggered, will simply display the current time as a Toast. That receiver must be registered in the application's manifest with a `<receiver>` tag. Otherwise, AlarmManager—which is external to your application—will not be aware of how to trigger it. The sample Activity presents two buttons: one to begin firing regular alarms, and the other to cancel them.

The operation to trigger is referenced by a PendingIntent, which will be used to both set and cancel the alarms. We create an Intent referencing the application's BroadcastReceiver directly, and then a PendingIntent from that using getBroadcast() (since we are creating a reference to a BroadcastReceiver).

> **REMINDER:** PendingIntent has creator methods getActivity() and getService() as well. Be sure to reference the correct application component you are triggering when creating this piece.

When the start button is pressed, the Activity registers a repeating alarm using AlarmManager.setRepeating(). In addition to the PendingIntent, this method takes some parameters to determine when to trigger the alarms. The first parameter defines the alarm type, in terms of the units of time to use and whether or not the alarm should occur when the device is in sleep mode. In the example, we chose ELAPSED_REALTIME, which indicates a value (in milliseconds) since the last device boot. In addition, there are three other modes that may be used:

- ELAPSED_REALTIME_WAKEUP

  - Alarms times referenced to time elapsed, and will wake the device to trigger if it is asleep.

- RTC

  - Alarm times referenced to UTC time.

- RTC_WAKEUP

  - Alarm times referenced to UTC time, and will wake the device to trigger if it is asleep.

The following parameters (respectively) refer to the first time the alarm will trigger and the interval on which it should repeat. Since the chosen alarm type is ELAPSED_REALTIME, the start time must also be relative to elapsed time; SystemClock.elapsedRealtime() provides the current time in this format.

The alarm in the example is registered to trigger five seconds after the button is pressed, and then every five seconds after that. Every five seconds, a Toast will come onscreen with the current time value, even if the application is no longer running or in front of the user. When the user displays the Activity and presses the stop button, any pending alarms matching our PendingIntent are immediately canceled... stopping the flow of Toasts.

A More Precise Example

What if we wanted to schedule an alarm to occur at a specific time? Perhaps once per day at 9:00AM? Setting AlarmManager with some slightly different parameters could accomplish this. See Listing 6–6.

Listing 6–6. *Precision Alarm*

```
long oneDay = 24*3600*1000; //24 hours
long firstTime;

//Get a Calendar (defaults to today)
//Set the time to 09:00:00
Calendar startTime = Calendar.getInstance();
startTime.set(Calendar.HOUR_OF_DAY, 9);
startTime.set(Calendar.MINUTE, 0);
startTime.set(Calendar.SECOND, 0);

//Get a Calendar at the current time
Calendar now = Calendar.getInstance();

if(now.before(startTime)) {
    //It's not 9AM yet, start today
    firstTime = startTime.getTimeInMillis();
} else {
    //Start 9AM tomorrow
    startTime.add(Calendar.DATE, 1);
    firstTime = startTime.getTimeInMillis();
}

//Set the alarm
 manager.setRepeating(AlarmManager.RTC_WAKEUP,
              firstTime,
              oneDay,
              mAlarmIntent);
```

This example uses an alarm that is referenced to real time. A determination is made whether the next occurrence of 9:00AM will be today or tomorrow, and that value is returned as the initial trigger time for the alarm. The calculated value of 24 hours in terms of milliseconds is then passed as the interval so that the alarm triggers once per day from that point forward.

IMPORTANT: Alarms do not persist through a device reboot. If a device is powered off and then back on, any previously registered alarms must be rescheduled.

6–4. Creating Sticky Operations

Problem

Your application needs to execute one or more background operations that will run to completion even if the user suspends the application.

Solution

(API Level 3)

Create an Implementation of IntentService to handle the work. IntentService is a wrapper around Android's base Service implementation, the key component to doing work in the background without interaction from the user. IntentService queues incoming work (expressed using Intents), processing each request in turn, and then stops itself when the queue is empty.

IntentService also handles creation of the worker thread needed to do the work in the background, so it is not necessary to use AsyncTask or Java Threads to ensure the operation is properly in the background.

This recipe examines an example of using IntentService to create a central manager of background operations. In the example, the manager will be invoked externally with calls to Context.startService(). The manager will queue up all requests received, and process them individually with a call to onHandleIntent().

How It Works

Let's take a look at how to construct a simple IntentService implementation to handle a series of background operations. See Listing 6–7.

Listing 6–7. *IntentService Handling Operations*

```
public class OperationsManager extends IntentService {

    public static final String ACTION_EVENT = "ACTION_EVENT";
    public static final String ACTION_WARNING = "ACTION_WARNING";
    public static final String ACTION_ERROR = "ACTION_ERROR";
    public static final String EXTRA_NAME = "eventName";

    private static final String LOGTAG = "EventLogger";

    private IntentFilter matcher;
```

```java
public OperationsManager() {
    super("OperationsManager");
    //Create the filter for matching incoming requests
    matcher = new IntentFilter();
    matcher.addAction(ACTION_EVENT);
    matcher.addAction(ACTION_WARNING);
    matcher.addAction(ACTION_ERROR);
}

@Override
protected void onHandleIntent(Intent intent) {
    //Check for a valid request
    if(!matcher.matchAction(intent.getAction())) {
        Toast.makeText(this, "OperationsManager: Invalid Request", Toast.LENGTH_SHORT).show();
        return;
    }

    //Handle each request directly in this method. Don't create more threads.
    if(TextUtils.equals(intent.getAction(), ACTION_EVENT)) {
        logEvent(intent.getStringExtra(EXTRA_NAME));
    }
    if(TextUtils.equals(intent.getAction(), ACTION_WARNING)) {
        logWarning(intent.getStringExtra(EXTRA_NAME));
    }
    if(TextUtils.equals(intent.getAction(), ACTION_ERROR)) {
        logError(intent.getStringExtra(EXTRA_NAME));
    }
}

private void logEvent(String name) {
    try {
        //Simulate a long network operation by sleeping
        Thread.sleep(5000);
        Log.i(LOGTAG, name);
    } catch (InterruptedException e) {
        e.printStackTrace();
    }
}

private void logWarning(String name) {
    try {
        //Simulate a long network operation by sleeping
        Thread.sleep(5000);
        Log.w(LOGTAG, name);
    } catch (InterruptedException e) {
        e.printStackTrace();
    }
}

private void logError(String name) {
    try {
        //Simulate a long network operation by sleeping
        Thread.sleep(5000);
        Log.e(LOGTAG, name);
    } catch (InterruptedException e) {
        e.printStackTrace();
```

```
        }
    }
}
```

Notice that `IntentService` does not have a default constructor (one that takes no parameters), so a custom implementation must implement a constructor that calls through to super with a service name. This name is of little technical importance, as it is only useful for debugging; Android uses the name provided to name the worker thread that it creates.

All requests are processed by the service through the `onHandleIntent()` method. This method is called on the provided worker thread, so all work should be done directly here; no new threads or operations should be created. When `onHandleIntent()` returns, this is the signal to the IntentService to begin processing the next request in the queue.

This example provides three logging operations that can be requested using different action strings on the request Intents. For demonstration purposes, each operation writes the provided message out to the device log using a specific logging level (INFO, WARNING, or ERROR). Note that the message itself is passed as an extra of the request Intent. Use the data and extra fields of each Intent to hold any parameters for the operation, leaving the action field to define the operation type.

The example service maintains an IntentFilter, which is used for convenience to determine whether a valid request has been made. All of the valid actions are added to the filter when the service is created, allowing us to call `IntentFilter.matchAction()` on any incoming request to determine if it includes an action we can process here.

Listing 6–8 is an example of an Activity calling into this service to perform work.

Listing 6–8. *AndroidManifest.xml*

```xml
<?xml version="1.0" encoding="utf-8"?>
<manifest xmlns:android="http://schemas.android.com/apk/res/android"
      package="com.examples.sticky"
      android:versionCode="1"
      android:versionName="1.0">
    <uses-sdk android:minSdkVersion="3" />

    <application android:icon="@drawable/icon" android:label="@string/app_name">
        <activity android:name=".ReportActivity"
                android:label="@string/app_name">
            <intent-filter>
                <action android:name="android.intent.action.MAIN" />
                <category android:name="android.intent.category.LAUNCHER" />
            </intent-filter>
        </activity>
        <service android:name=".OperationsManager"></service>
    </application>
</manifest>
```

> **REMINDER:** The package attribute in AndroidManifest.xml must match the package you have chosen for your application; "com.examples.sticky" is simply the chosen package for our example here.

> **NOTE:** Since IntentService is invoked as a Service, it must be declared in the application manifest using a <service> tag.

Listing 6–9. *Activity Calling IntentService*

```java
public class ReportActivity extends Activity {

    @Override
    public void onCreate(Bundle savedInstanceState) {
        super.onCreate(savedInstanceState);
        logEvent("CREATE");
    }

    @Override
    public void onStart() {
        super.onStart();
        logEvent("START");
    }

    @Override
    public void onResume() {
        super.onResume();
        logEvent("RESUME");
    }

    @Override
    public void onPause() {
        super.onPause();
        logWarning("PAUSE");
    }

    @Override
    public void onStop() {
        super.onStop();
        logWarning("STOP");
    }

    @Override
    public void onDestroy() {
        super.onDestroy();
        logWarning("DESTROY");
    }

    private void logEvent(String event) {
        Intent intent = new Intent(this, OperationsManager.class);
        intent.setAction(OperationsManager.ACTION_EVENT);
```

```
        intent.putExtra(OperationsManager.EXTRA_NAME, event);

        startService(intent);
    }

    private void logWarning(String event) {
        Intent intent = new Intent(this, OperationsManager.class);
        intent.setAction(OperationsManager.ACTION_WARNING);
        intent.putExtra(OperationsManager.EXTRA_NAME, event);

        startService(intent);
    }
}
```

This Activity isn't much to look at, as all the interesting events are sent out through the device log instead of to the user interface. Nevertheless, it helps illustrate the queue processing behavior of the service we created in the previous example. As the Activity becomes visible, it will call through all of its normal life-cycle methods, resulting in three requests made of the logging service. As each request is processed, a line will output to the log and the service will move on.

> **TIP**: These log statements are visible through the `logcat` tool provided with the SDK. The `logcat` output from a device or emulator is visible from within most development environments (including Eclipse), or from the command line by typing adb `logcat`.

Notice also that when the service is finished with all three requests, a notification is sent out the log by the system that the service has been stopped. `IntentServices` are only around in memory for as long as is required to complete the job; a very useful feature for your services to have, making them a good citizen of the system.

Pressing either the HOME or BACK buttons will cause more of the life-cycle methods to generate requests of the service, and notice that the Pause/Stop/Destroy portion calls a separate operation in the service, causing their messages to be logged as warnings; simply setting the action string of the request intent to a different value controls this.

Notice that messages continue to be output to the log, even after the application is no longer visible (or even if another application is opened instead). This is the power of the Android Service component at work. These operations are protected from the system until they are complete, regardless of user behavior.

Possible Drawback

In each of the operation methods, a five-second delay has been placed to simulate the time required for an actual request to be made of a remote API or some similar operation. When running this example, it also helps to illustrate that `IntentService` handles all requests sent to it in a serial fashion with a single worker thread. The example queues multiple requests in succession from each life-cycle method, however the result will still be a log message every five seconds, since IntentService does not start a new request until the current one is complete (essentially, when onHandleIntent() returns).

If your application requires concurrency from sticky background tasks, you may need to create a more customized Service implementation that uses a pool of threads to execute work. The beauty of Android being open source is that you can go directly to the source code for IntentService and use it as a starting point for such an implementation if it is required, minimizing the amount of time and custom code required.

6–5. Running Persistent Background Operations

Problem

Your application has a component that must be running in the background indefinitely, performing some operation or monitoring certain events to occur.

Solution

(API Level 1)

Build the component into a Service. Services are designed as background components that an application may start and leave running for an indefinite amount of time. Services are also given elevated status above other background processes in terms of protection from being killed in low memory conditions.

Services may be started and stopped explicitly for operations that do not require a direct connection to another component (like an Activity). However, if the application must interact directly with the Service, a binding interface is provided to pass data. In these instances, the service may be started and stopped implicitly by the system as is required to fulfill its requested bindings.

The key thing to remember with Service implementations is to always be user-friendly. An indefinite operation most likely should not be started unless the user explicitly requests it. The overall application should probably contain an interface or setting that allows the user to control enabling or disabling such a Service.

How It Works

Listing 6–10 is an example of a persisted service that is used to track and log the user's location over a certain period.

Listing 6–10. *Persistent Tracking Service*

```
public class TrackerService extends Service implements LocationListener {

    private static final String LOGTAG = "TrackerService";

    private LocationManager manager;
    private ArrayList<Location> storedLocations;
```

```
private boolean isTracking = false;

/* Service Setup Methods */
@Override
public void onCreate() {
    manager = (LocationManager)getSystemService(LOCATION_SERVICE);
    storedLocations = new ArrayList<Location>();
    Log.i(LOGTAG, "Tracking Service Running...");
}

@Override
public void onDestroy() {
    manager.removeUpdates(this);
    Log.i(LOGTAG, "Tracking Service Stopped...");
}

public void startTracking() {
    if(!manager.isProviderEnabled(LocationManager.GPS_PROVIDER)) {
        return;
    }
    Toast.makeText(this, "Starting Tracker", Toast.LENGTH_SHORT).show();
    manager.requestLocationUpdates(LocationManager.GPS_PROVIDER, 30000, 0, this);

    isTracking = true;
}

public void stopTracking() {
    Toast.makeText(this, "Stopping Tracker", Toast.LENGTH_SHORT).show();
    manager.removeUpdates(this);
    isTracking = false;
}

public boolean isTracking() {
    return isTracking;
}

/* Service Access Methods */
public class TrackerBinder extends Binder {
    TrackerService getService() {
        return TrackerService.this;
    }
}

private final IBinder binder = new TrackerBinder();

@Override
public IBinder onBind(Intent intent) {
    return binder;
}

public int getLocationsCount() {
    return storedLocations.size();
}

public ArrayList<Location> getLocations() {
    return storedLocations;
```

```
    }

    /* LocationListener Methods */
    @Override
    public void onLocationChanged(Location location) {
        Log.i("TrackerService", "Adding new location");
        storedLocations.add(location);
    }

    @Override
    public void onProviderDisabled(String provider) { }

    @Override
    public void onProviderEnabled(String provider) { }

    @Override
    public void onStatusChanged(String provider, int status, Bundle extras) { }
}
```

This Service's job is to monitor and track the updates it receives from the LocationManager. When the Service is created, it prepares a blank list of Location items and waits to begin tracking. An external component, such as an Activity, can call startTracking() and stopTracking() to enable and disable the flow of location updates to the Service. In addition, methods are exposed to access the list of locations that the Service has logged.

Because this Service requires direct interaction from an Activity or other component, a Binder interface is required. The Binder concept can get complex when Services have to communicate across process boundaries, but for instances like this, where everything is local to the same process, a very simple Binder is created with one method, getService(), to return the Service instance itself to the caller. We'll look at this in more detail from the Activity's perspective in a moment.

When tracking is enabled on the service, it registers for updates with LocationManager, and stores every update received in its locations list. Notice that requestLocationUpdates() was called with a minimum time of 30 seconds. Since this Service is expected to be running for a long time, it is prudent to space out the updates to give the GPS (and consequently the battery) a little rest.

Now let's take a look at a simple Activity that allows the user access into this Service. See Listings 6–11 through 6–13.

Listing 6–11. *AndroidManifest.xml*

```xml
<?xml version="1.0" encoding="utf-8"?>
<manifest xmlns:android="http://schemas.android.com/apk/res/android"
    package="com.examples.service"
    android:versionCode="1"
    android:versionName="1.0">
    <uses-sdk android:minSdkVersion="1" />
    <application android:icon="@drawable/icon" android:label="@string/app_name">
        <activity android:name=".ServiceActivity"
                android:label="@string/app_name">
            <intent-filter>
                <action android:name="android.intent.action.MAIN" />
```

```
            <category android:name="android.intent.category.LAUNCHER" />
        </intent-filter>
    </activity>
    <service android:name=".TrackerService"></service>
</application>
<uses-permission android:name="android.permission.ACCESS_FINE_LOCATION"/>
</manifest>
```

> **REMINDER:** The Service must be declared in the application manifest using a `<service>` tag
> so Android knows how and where to call on it. Also, for this example the permission
> `android.permission.ACCESS_FINE_LOCATION` is required since we are working with the
> GPS.

Listing 6–12. *res/layout/main.xml*

```xml
<?xml version="1.0" encoding="utf-8"?>
<LinearLayout xmlns:android="http://schemas.android.com/apk/res/android"
  android:orientation="vertical"
  android:layout_width="fill_parent"
  android:layout_height="fill_parent">
  <Button
    android:id="@+id/enable"
    android:layout_width="fill_parent"
    android:layout_height="wrap_content"
    android:text="Start Tracking"
  />
  <Button
    android:id="@+id/disable"
    android:layout_width="fill_parent"
    android:layout_height="wrap_content"
    android:text="Stop Tracking"
  />
  <TextView
    android:id="@+id/status"
    android:layout_width="fill_parent"
    android:layout_height="wrap_content"
  />
</LinearLayout>
```

Listing 6–13. *Activity Interacting with Service*

```java
public class ServiceActivity extends Activity implements View.OnClickListener {

    Button enableButton, disableButton;
    TextView statusView;

    TrackerService trackerService;
    Intent serviceIntent;

    @Override
    public void onCreate(Bundle savedInstanceState) {
        super.onCreate(savedInstanceState);
        setContentView(R.layout.main);
```

```
        enableButton = (Button)findViewById(R.id.enable);
        enableButton.setOnClickListener(this);
        disableButton = (Button)findViewById(R.id.disable);
        disableButton.setOnClickListener(this);
        statusView = (TextView)findViewById(R.id.status);

        serviceIntent = new Intent(this, TrackerService.class);
    }

    @Override
    public void onResume() {
        super.onResume();
        //Starting the service makes it stick, regardless of bindings
        startService(serviceIntent);
        //Bind to the service
        bindService(serviceIntent, serviceConnection, Context.BIND_AUTO_CREATE);
    }

    @Override
    public void onPause() {
        super.onPause();
        if(!trackerService.isTracking()) {
            //Stopping the service let's it die once unbound
            stopService(serviceIntent);
        }
        //Unbind from the service
        unbindService(serviceConnection);
    }

    @Override
    public void onClick(View v) {
        switch(v.getId()) {
        case R.id.enable:
            trackerService.startTracking();
            break;
        case R.id.disable:
            trackerService.stopTracking();
            break;
        default:
            break;
        }
        updateStatus();
    }

    private void updateStatus() {
        if(trackerService.isTracking()) {
            statusView.setText(
                String.format("Tracking enabled. %d locations
                    logged.",trackerService.getLocationsCount()));
        } else {
            statusView.setText("Tracking not currently enabled.");
        }
    }

    private ServiceConnection serviceConnection = new ServiceConnection() {
        public void onServiceConnected(ComponentName className, IBinder service) {
            trackerService = ((TrackerService.TrackerBinder)service).getService();
```

```
            updateStatus();
        }

        public void onServiceDisconnected(ComponentName className) {
            trackerService = null;
        }
    };
}
```

Figure 6–3 displays the basic Activity with two buttons for the user to enable and disable location tracking behavior, and a text display for the current service status.

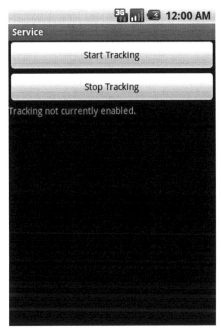

Figure 6–3. *ServiceActivity Layout*

While the Activity is visible, it is bound to the TrackerService. This is done with the help of the ServiceConnection interface, which provides callback methods when the binding and unbinding operations are complete. With the Service bound to the Activity, we can now make direct calls on all the public methods exposed by the Service.

However, bindings alone will not allow the Service to stay running long-term; accessing the Service solely through its Binder interface causes it to be created and destroyed automatically along with the lifecycle of this Activity. In this case, we want the Service to persist beyond when this Activity is in memory. In order to accomplish this, the Service is explicitly started via startService() before it is bound. There is no harm in sending start commands to a service that is already running, so we can safely do this in onResume() as well.

The Service will now continue running in memory, even after the Activity unbinds itself. In onPause() the example always checks whether the user has activated tracking, and if not it stops the service first. This allows the Service to die if it is not required for tracking, which keeps the Service from perpetually hanging out in memory if it has no real work to do.

Running this example, and pressing the Start Tracking button will spin up the persisted service and the LocationManager. The user may leave the application at this point and the service will remain running, all the while logging all incoming location updates from the GPS. When the user returns to this application, they can see that the Service is still running and the current number of stored location points is displayed. Pressing Stop Tracking will end the process and allow the Service to die as soon as the user leaves the Activity once more.

6–6. Launching Other Applications

Problem

Your application requires a specific function that another application on the device is already programmed to do. Instead of overlapping functionality, you would like to launch the other application for the job instead.

Solution

(API Level 1)

Use an implicit Intent to tell the system what you are looking to do, and determine if any applications exist to meet the need. Most often, developers use Intents in an explicit fashion to start another Activity or Service, like so:

```
Intent intent = new Intent(this, NewActivity.class);
startActivity(intent);
```

By declaring the specific component we want to launch, the Intent is very explicit in its delivery. We also have the power to define an Intent in terms of its action, category, data, and type to define a more implicit requirement of what task we want to accomplish.

External applications are always launched within the same Android task as your application when fired in this fashion, so once the operation is complete (or if the user backs out) the user is returned to your application. This keeps the experience seamless, allowing multiple applications to act as one from the user's perspective.

How It Works

When defining Intents in this fashion, it can be unclear what information you must include, because there is no published standard and it is possible for two applications offering the same service (reading a PDF file, for example) to define slightly different filters to listen for incoming Intents. You want to make sure and provide enough information for the system (or the user) to pick the best application to handle the required task.

The core piece of data to define on almost any implicit Intent is the action; a string value passed either in the constructor or via `Intent.setAction()`. This value tells Android what you want to do, whether it is to view a piece of content, send a message, select a choice, or what have you. From there, the fields provided are scenario specific, and often multiple combinations can arrive at the same result. Let's take a look at some useful examples.

Read a PDF File

Components to display PDF documents are not included in the core SDK, although almost every consumer Android device on the market today ships with a PDF reader application, and many more are available on Android Market. Because of this, it may not make sense to go through the trouble of embedding PDF display capabilities in your application.

Instead, the following Listing 6–14 illustrates how to find and launch another app to view the PDF.

Listing 6–14. *Method to View PDF*

```java
private void viewPdf(Uri file) {
    Intent intent;
    intent = new Intent(Intent.ACTION_VIEW);
    intent.setDataAndType(file, "application/pdf");
    try {
        startActivity(intent);
    } catch (ActivityNotFoundException e) {
        //No application to view, ask to download one
        AlertDialog.Builder builder = new AlertDialog.Builder(this);
        builder.setTitle("No Application Found");
        builder.setMessage("We could not find an application to view PDFs."
            +"  Would you like to download one from Android Market?");
        builder.setPositiveButton("Yes, Please",
            new DialogInterface.OnClickListener() {
            @Override
            public void onClick(DialogInterface dialog, int which) {
                Intent marketIntent = new Intent(Intent.ACTION_VIEW);
                marketIntent.setData(Uri.parse("market://details?id=com.adobe.reader"));
                startActivity(marketIntent);
            }
        });
        builder.setNegativeButton("No, Thanks", null);
        builder.create().show();
    }
}
```

This example method will open any local PDF file on the device (internal or external storage) using the best application found. If no application is found on the device to view PDFs, we encourage the user to go to Android Market and download one.

The Intent we create for this is constructed using the generic `Intent.ACTION_VIEW` action string, telling the system we want to view the data provided in the Intent. The data file itself, and its MIME type are also set to tell the system what kind of data we want to view.

> **TIP:** `Intent.setData()` and `Intent.setType()` clear each other's previous values when used. If you need to set both simultaneously, use `Intent.setDataAndType()`, as in the example.

If `startActivity()` fails with an `ActivityNotFoundException`, it means the user does not have an application installed on their device that can view PDFs. We want our users to have the full experience, so if this happens, we present a dialog telling them the problem, and asking if they would like to go to Market and get a reader. If the user presses Yes, we use another implicit Intent to request that Android Market be opened directly to the application page for Adobe Reader, a free application the user may download to view PDF files. We'll discuss the `Uri` scheme used for this Intent in the next recipe.

Notice that the example method takes a `Uri` parameter to the local file. Here is an example of how to retrieve a `Uri` for files located on internal storage:

```
String filename = NAME_OF_YOUR_FILE;
File internalFile = getFileStreamPath(filename);
Uri internal = Uri.fromFile(internalFile);
```

The method `getFileStreamPath()` is called from a `Context`, so if this code is not in an Activity you must have reference to a `Context` object to call on. Here's how to create a `Uri` for files located on external storage:

```
String filename = NAME_OF_YOUR_FILE;
File externalFile = new File(Environment.getExternalStorageDirectory(), filename);
Uri external = Uri.fromFile(externalFile);
```

This same example will work for any other document type as well by simply changing the MIME type attached to the Intent.

Share with Friends

Another popular feature for developers to include in their applications is a method of sharing the application content with others; through e-mail, text messaging, and prominent social networks. All Android devices include applications for e-mail and text messaging, and most users who wish to share via a social network (like Facebook or Twitter) also have those mobile applications on their device.

As it turns out, this task can also be accomplished using an implicit Intent because most all of these applications respond to the `Intent.ACTION_SEND` action string in some way.

Listing 6–15 is an example of allowing a user to post to any medium they wish with a single Intent request.

Listing 6–15. *Sharing Intent*

```
private void shareContent(String update) {
        Intent intent = new Intent(Intent.ACTION_SEND);
        intent.setType("text/plain");
        intent.putExtra(Intent.EXTRA_TEXT, update);
        startActivity(Intent.createChooser(intent, "Share..."));
    }
```

Here, we tell the system that we have a piece of text that we would like to send, passed in as an extra. This is a very generic request, and we expect more than one application to be able to handle it. By default, Android will present the user with a list of applications to select which they'd like to open. In addition, some devices provide the user with a checkbox to set their selection as a default so the list is never shown again!

We would prefer to have a little more control over this process because we also expect multiple results every time. Therefore, instead of passing the Intent directly to startActivity(), we first pass it through Intent.createChooser(), which allows us to customize the title and guarantee the selection list will always be displayed.

When the user selects a choice, that specific application will launch with the EXTRA_TEXT prepopulated into the message entry box, ready for sharing!

6–7. Launching System Applications

Problem

Your application requires a specific function that one of the system applications on the device is already programmed to do. Instead of overlapping functionality, you would like to launch the system application for the job instead.

Solution

(API Level 1)

Use an implicit Intent to tell the system which application you are interested in. Each system application subscribes to a custom Uri scheme that can be inserted as data into an implicit Intent to signify the specific application you need to launch.

External applications are always launched in the same task as your application when fired in this fashion, so once the task is complete (or if the user backs out) the user is returned to your application. This keeps the experience seamless, allowing multiple applications to act as one from the user's perspective.

How It Works

All of the following examples will construct Intents that can be used to launch system applications in various states. Once constructed, you should launch these applications by passing said Intent to `startActivity()`.

Browser

The browser application may be launched to display a web page or run a web search.

To display a web page, construct and launch the following Intent:

```
Intent pageIntent = new Intent();
pageIntent.setAction(Intent.ACTION_VIEW);
pageIntent.setData(Uri.parse("http://WEB_ADDRESS_TO_VIEW"));
```

This replaces the Uri in the data field with the page you would like to view. To launch a web search inside the browser, construct and launch the following Intent:

```
Intent searchIntent = new Intent();
searchIntent.setAction(Intent.ACTION_WEB_SEARCH);
searchIntent.putExtra(SearchManager.QUERY, STRING_TO_SEARCH);
```

This places the search query you want to execute as an extra in the Intent.

Phone Dialer

The dialer application may be launched to place a call to a specific number using the following Intent:

```
Intent dialIntent = new Intent();
dialIntent.setAction(Intent.ACTION_DIAL);
dialIntent.setData(Uri.Parse("tel:8885551234"));
```

This replaces the phone number in the data Uri with the number to call.

> **NOTE:** This action just brings up the dialer; it does not actually place the call.
> `Intent.ACTION_CALL` can be used to actually place the call directly, although Google discourages using this in most cases. Using `ACTION_CALL` will also require that the `android.permission.CALL_PHONE` permission be declared in the manifest.

Maps

The maps application on the device can be launched to display a location or to provide directions between two points. If you know the latitude and longitude of the location you want to map, then create the following Intent:

```
Intent mapIntent = new Intent();
mapIntent.setAction(Intent.ACTION_VIEW);
mapIntent.setData(Uri.parse("geo:latitude,longitude"));
```

This replaces the coordinates for latitude and longitude of your location. For example, the Uri

"geo:37.422,122.084"

would map the location of Google headquarters. If you know the address of the location to display, then create the following Intent:

```
Intent mapIntent = new Intent();
mapIntent.setAction(Intent.ACTION_VIEW);
mapIntent.setData(Uri.parse("geo:0,0?q=ADDRESS"));
```

This inserts the address you would like to map. For example, the Uri

"geo:0,0?q=1600 Amphitheatre Parkway, Mountain View, CA 94043"

would map the address of Google headquarters.

> **TIP:** The Maps application will also accept a Uri where spaces in the Address query are replaced with the "+" character. If you are having trouble encoding a String with spaces in it, try replacing them with "+" instead.

If you would like to display directions between to locations, create the following Intent:

```
Intent mapIntent = new Intent();
mapIntent.setAction(Intent.ACTION_VIEW);
mapIntent.setData(Uri.parse("http://maps.google.com/maps?saddr=lat,lng&daddr=lat,lng"));
```

This inserts the locations for the start and end address.

It is also allowed for only one of the parameters to be included if you would like to open the maps application with one address open ended. For example, the Uri

"http://maps.google.com/maps?&daddr=37.422,122.084"

would display the maps application with the destination location prepopulated, but allowing the user to enter their own start address.

E-mail

Any e-mail application on the device can be launched into compose mode using the following Intent:

```
Intent mailIntent = new Intent();
mailIntent.setAction(Intent.ACTION_SEND);
mailIntent.setType("message/rfc822");
mailIntent.putExtra(Intent.EXTRA_EMAIL, new String[] {"recipient@gmail.com"});
mailIntent.putExtra(Intent.EXTRA_CC, new String[] {"carbon@gmail.com"});
mailIntent.putExtra(Intent.EXTRA_BCC, new String[] {"blind@gmail.com"});
mailIntent.putExtra(Intent.EXTRA_SUBJECT, "Email Subject");
mailIntent.putExtra(Intent.EXTRA_TEXT, "Body Text");
mailIntent.putExtra(Intent.EXTRA_STREAM, URI_TO_FILE);
```

In this scenario, the action and type fields are the only required pieces to bring up a blank e-mail message. All the remaining extras prepopulate specific fields of the e-mail message. Notice that EXTRA_EMAIL (which fills the To: field), EXTRA_CC, and EXTRA_BCC are passed String arrays, even if there is only one recipient to be placed there. File attachments may also be specified in the Intent using EXTRA_STREAM. The value passed here should be a Uri pointing to the local file to be attached.

If you need to attach more than one file to an e-mail, the requirements change slightly to the following:

```
Intent mailIntent = new Intent();
mailIntent.setAction(Intent.ACTION_SEND_MULTIPLE);
mailIntent.setType("message/rfc822");
mailIntent.putExtra(Intent.EXTRA_EMAIL, new String[] {"recipient@gmail.com"});
mailIntent.putExtra(Intent.EXTRA_CC, new String[] {"carbon@gmail.com"});
mailIntent.putExtra(Intent.EXTRA_BCC, new String[] {"blind@gmail.com"});
mailIntent.putExtra(Intent.EXTRA_SUBJECT, "Email Subject");
mailIntent.putExtra(Intent.EXTRA_TEXT, "Body Text");

ArrayList<Uri> files = new ArrayList<Uri>();
files.add(URI_TO_FIRST_FILE);
files.add(URI_TO_SECOND_FILE);
//...Repeat add() as often as necessary to add all the files you need
mailIntent.putParcelableArrayListExtra(Intent.EXTRA_STREAM, files);
```

Notice that the Intent's action string is now ACTION_SEND_MULTIPLE. All the primary fields remain the same as before, except for the data that gets added as the EXTRA_STREAM. This example creates a list of Uris pointing to the files you want to attach and adds them using putParcelableArrayListExtra().

It is not uncommon for users to have multiple applications on their device that can handle this content, so it is usually prudent to wrap either of these constructed Intents with Intent.createChooser() before passing it on to startActivity().

SMS (Messages)

The messages application can be launched into compose mode for a new SMS message using the following Intent:

```
Intent smsIntent = new Intent();
smsIntent.setAction(Intent.ACTION_VIEW);
smsIntent.setType("vnd.android-dir/mms-sms");
smsIntent.putExtra("address", "8885551234");
smsIntent.putExtra("sms_body", "Body Text");
```

As with composing e-mail, you must set the action and type at a minimum to launch the application with a blank message. Including the address and sms_body extras allows the application to prepopulate the recipient (address) and body text (sms_body) of the message.

Notice that neither of these keys has a constant defined in the Android framework, which means that they are subject to change in the future. However, as of this writing, the keys behave as expected on all versions of Android.

Contact Picker

An application may launch the default contact picker for the user to make a selection from their contacts database using the following Intent:

```
Intent pickIntent = new Intent();
pickIntent.setAction(Intent.ACTION_PICK);
pickIntent.setData(URI_TO_CONTACT_TABLE);
```

This Intent requires the CONTENT_URI of the Contacts table you are interested in to be passed in the data field. Because of the major changes to the Contacts API in API Level 5 (Android 2.0) and later, this may not be the same Uri if you are supporting versions across that boundary.

For example, to pick a person from the contacts list on a device previous to 2.0, we would pass

```
android.provider.Contacts.People.CONTENT_URI
```

However, in 2.0 and later, similar data would be gathered by passing

```
android.provider.ContactsContract.Contacts.CONTENT_URI
```

Be sure to consult the API documentation with regards to the contact data you need to access.

Android Market

Android Market can be launched from within an application to display a specific application's details page or to run a search for specific keywords. To launch a specific applications market page, use the following Intent:

```
Intent marketIntent = new Intent();
marketIntent.setAction(Intent.ACTION_VIEW);
marketIntent.setData(Uri.parse("market://details?id=PACKAGE_NAME_HERE"));
```

This inserts the unique package name (such as "com.adobe.reader") of the application you want to display. If you would like to open the market with a search query, use this Intent:

```
Intent marketIntent = new Intent();
marketIntent.setAction(Intent.ACTION_VIEW);
marketIntent.setData(Uri.parse("market://search?q=SEARCH_QUERY"));
```

Inserting the query string you would like to search on. The search query itself can take one of three main forms:

- q=<simple text string here>
    - In this case, the search will be a keyword style search of the market.
- q=pname:<package name here>
    - In this case, the package names will be searched, and only exact matches will return.
- q=pub:<developer name here>

■   In this case, the developer name field will be searched, and only exact matches will return.

6–8. Letting Other Applications Launch Yours

Problem

You've created an application that is absolutely the best at doing a specific task, and you would like to expose an interface for other applications on the device to be able to run your application.

Solution

(API Level 1)

Create an `IntentFilter` on the Activity or Service you would like to expose, then publicly document the actions, data types, and extras required to access it properly. Recall that the action, category and data/type of an Intent can all be used as criteria to match requests to your application. Any additional required or optional parameters should be passed in as extras.

How It Works

Let's say that you have created an application that includes an Activity to play a video and marquee the video's title at the top of the screen during playback. You want to allow other applications to play video using your application, so we need to define a useful Intent structure for applications to pass in the required data and then create an `IntentFilter` on the Activity in the applications manifest to match.

This hypothetical Activity requires two pieces of data to do its job:

1.   The `Uri` of a video, either local or remote

2.   A `String` representing the video's title

If the application specializes in a certain type of video, we could define that a generic action (such as ACTION_VIEW) be used and filter more specifically on the data type of the video content we want to handle. Listing 6–16 is an example of how the Activity would be defined in the manifest to filter Intents in this manner.

Listing 6–16. *AndroidManifest.xml <activity> Element with Data Type Filter*

```
<activity android:name=".PlayerActivity">
    <intent-filter>
        <action android:name="android.intent.action.VIEW" />
        <category android:name="android.intent.category.DEFAULT" />
        <data android:mimeType="video/h264" />
    </intent-filter>
</activity>
```

This filter will match any Intent with Uri data that is either explicitly declared as an H.264 video clip, or determined to be H.264 upon inspecting the Uri file. An external application would then be able to call on this Activity to play a video using the following lines of code:

```
Uri videoFile = A_URI_OF_VIDEO_CONTENT;
Intent playIntent = new Intent(Intent.ACTION_VIEW);
playIntent.setDataAndType(videoFile, "video/h264");
playIntent.putExtra(Intent.EXTRA_TITLE, "My Video");
startActivity(playIntent);
```

In some cases, it may be more useful for an external application to directly reference this player as the target, regardless of the type of video they want to pass in. In this case, we would create a unique custom action string for Intents to implement. The filter attached to the Activity in the manifest would then only need to match the custom action string. See Listing 6–17.

Listing 6–17. *AndroidManifest.xml <activity> Element with Custom Action Filter*

```
<activity android:name=".PlayerActivity">
    <intent-filter>
      <action android:name="com.examples.myplayer.PLAY" />
      <category android:name="android.intent.category.DEFAULT" />
    </intent-filter>
</activity>
```

An external application could call on this Activity to play a video using the following code:

```
Uri videoFile = A_URI_OF_VIDEO_CONTENT;
Intent playIntent = new Intent("com.examples.myplayer.PLAY");
playIntent.setData(videoFile);
playIntent.putExtra(Intent.EXTRA_TITLE, "My Video");
startActivity(playIntent);
```

Processing a Successful Launch

Regardless of how the Intent is matched to the Activity, once it is launched, we want to inspect the incoming Intent for the two pieces of data the Activity needs to complete its intended purpose. See Listing 6–18.

Listing 6–18. *Activity Inspecting Intent*

```
public class PlayerActivity extends Activity {

    public static final String ACTION_PLAY = "com.examples.myplayer.PLAY";

    @Override
    public void onCreate(Bundle savedInstanceState) {
        super.onCreate(savedInstanceState);
        setContentView(R.layout.main);

        //Inspect the Intent that launched us
        Intent incoming = getIntent();
        //Get the video URI from the data field
        Uri videoUri = incoming.getData();
```

```
        //Get the optional title extra, if it exists
        String title;
        if(incoming.hasExtra(Intent.EXTRA_TITLE)) {
            title = incoming.getStringExtra(Intent.EXTRA_TITLE);
        } else {
            title = "";
        }

        /* Begin playing the video and displaying the title */
    }

    /* Remainder of the Activity Code */

}
```

When the Activity is launched, the calling Intent can be retrieved with `Activity.getIntent()`. Since the `Uri` for the video content is passed in the data field of the Intent, it is unpacked by calling `Intent.getData()`. We have determined that the video's title is an optional value for calling Intents, so we check the extras bundle to first see if the caller decided to pass it in; if it exists, that value is unpacked from the Intent as well.

Notice that the `PlayerActivity` in this example did define the custom action string as a constant, but it was not referenced in the sample Intent we constructed above to launch the Activity. Since this call is coming from an external application, it does not have access to the shared public constants defined in this application.

For this reason, it is also a good idea to reuse the Intent extra keys already in the SDK whenever possible, as opposed to defining new constants. In this example, we chose the standard Intent.EXTRA_TITLE to define the optional extra to be passed instead of creating a custom key for this value.

6–9. Interacting with Contacts

Problem

Your application needs to interact directly with the `ContentProvider` exposed by Android to the user's contacts to add, view, change, or remove information from the database.

Solution

(API Level 5)

Use the interface exposed by `ContactsContract` to access the data. `ContactsContract` is a vast `ContentProvider` API that attempts to aggregate the contact information stored in the system from multiple user accounts into a single data store. The result is a maze of `Uris`, tables, and columns, from which data may be accessed and modified.

The Contact structure is a hierarchy with three tiers: Contacts, RawContacts, and Data.

- A Contact conceptually represents a person, and is an aggregation of all RawContacts believed by Android to represent that same person.

- A RawContacts represents a collection of Data stored in the device from a specific device account, such as the user's e-mail address book, Facebook account, or otherwise.

- Data elements are the specific pieces of information attached to each RawContacts, such as an e-mail address, phone number, or postal address.

The complete API has too many combinations and options for us to cover them all here, so consult the SDK documentation for all the possibilities. We will investigate how to construct the basic building blocks for performing queries and making changes to the contacts data set.

How It Works

The Android Contacts API boils down to a complex database with multiple tables and joins. Therefore, the methods for accessing the data are no different than those used to access any other SQLite database from an application.

Listing/Viewing Contacts

Let's look at an example Activity that lists all contact entries in the database, and the displays more detail when an item is selected. See Listing 6–19.

> **IMPORTANT:** In order to display information from the Contacts API in your application, you will need to declare android.permission.READ_CONTACTS in the application manifest.

Listing 6–19. *Activity Displaying Contacts*

```
public class ContactsActivity extends ListActivity implements
AdapterView.OnItemClickListener {

    Cursor mContacts;

    @Override
    public void onCreate(Bundle savedInstanceState) {
        super.onCreate(savedInstanceState);
        // Return all contacts, ordered by name
        String[] projection = new String[] { ContactsContract.Contacts._ID,
                ContactsContract.Contacts.DISPLAY_NAME };
        mContacts = managedQuery(ContactsContract.Contacts.CONTENT_URI,
                projection, null, null, ContactsContract.Contacts.DISPLAY_NAME);

        // Display all contacts in a ListView
        SimpleCursorAdapter mAdapter = new SimpleCursorAdapter(this,
                android.R.layout.simple_list_item_1, mContacts,
                new String[] { ContactsContract.Contacts.DISPLAY_NAME },
                new int[] { android.R.id.text1 });
        setListAdapter(mAdapter);
```

```java
        // Listen for item selections
        getListView().setOnItemClickListener(this);
}

@Override
public void onItemClick(AdapterView<?> parent, View v, int position, long id) {
    if (mContacts.moveToPosition(position)) {
        int selectedId = mContacts.getInt(0); // _ID column
        // Gather email data from email table
        Cursor email = getContentResolver().query(
                CommonDataKinds.Email.CONTENT_URI,
                new String[] { CommonDataKinds.Email.DATA },
                ContactsContract.Data.CONTACT_ID + " = " + selectedId, null, null);
        // Gather phone data from phone table
        Cursor phone = getContentResolver().query(
                CommonDataKinds.Phone.CONTENT_URI,
                new String[] { CommonDataKinds.Phone.NUMBER },
                ContactsContract.Data.CONTACT_ID + " = " + selectedId, null, null);
        // Gather addresses from address table
        Cursor address = getContentResolver().query(
                CommonDataKinds.StructuredPostal.CONTENT_URI,
                new String[] { CommonDataKinds.StructuredPostal.FORMATTED_ADDRESS },
                ContactsContract.Data.CONTACT_ID + " = " + selectedId, null, null);

        //Build the dialog message
        StringBuilder sb = new StringBuilder();
        sb.append(email.getCount() + " Emails\n");
        if (email.moveToFirst()) {
            do {
                sb.append("Email: " + email.getString(0));
                sb.append('\n');
            } while (email.moveToNext());
            sb.append('\n');
        }
        sb.append(phone.getCount() + " Phone Numbers\n");
        if (phone.moveToFirst()) {
            do {
                sb.append("Phone: " + phone.getString(0));
                sb.append('\n');
            } while (phone.moveToNext());
            sb.append('\n');
        }
        sb.append(address.getCount() + " Addresses\n");
        if (address.moveToFirst()) {
            do {
                sb.append("Address:\n" + address.getString(0));
            } while (address.moveToNext());
            sb.append('\n');
        }

        AlertDialog.Builder builder = new AlertDialog.Builder(this);
        builder.setTitle(mContacts.getString(1)); // Display name
        builder.setMessage(sb.toString());
        builder.setPositiveButton("OK", null);
        builder.create().show();

        // Finish temporary cursors
```

```
                email.close();
                phone.close();
                address.close();
            }
        }
    }
```

As you can see, referencing all the tables and columns in this API can result in very verbose code. All of the references to Uris, tables, and columns in this example are inner classes stemming off of ContactsContract. It is important to verify when interacting with the Contacts API that you are referencing the proper classes, as any Contacts classes not stemming from ContactsContract are deprecated and incompatible.

When the Activity is created, we make a simple query on the core Contacts table by calling Activity.managedQuery() with Contacts.CONTENT_URI, requesting only the columns we need to wrap the cursor in a ListAdapter. The resulting cursor is displayed in a list on the user interface. The example leverages the convenience behavior of ListActivity to provide a ListView as the content view so that we do not have to manage these components.

At this point, the user may scroll through all the contact entries on the device, and tap on one to get more information. When a list item is selected, the _ID value of that particular contact is recorded and the application goes out to the other ContactsContract.Data tables to gather more detailed information. Notice that the data for this single contact is spread across multiple tables (e-mails in an e-mail table, phone numbers in a phone table, and so on), requiring multiple queries to obtain.

Each CommonDataKinds table has a unique CONTENT_URI for the query to reference, and a unique set of column aliases for requesting the data. All of the rows in these data tables are linked to the specific contact through the Data.CONTACT_ID, so each cursor asks to only return rows where the values match.

With all the data collected for the selected contact, we iterate through the results to display in a dialog to the user. Since the data in these tables is an aggregation of multiple sources, it is not uncommon for all of these queries to return multiple results. With each cursor, we display the number of results, and then append each value included. When all the data is composed, the dialog is created and shown to the user.

As a final step, all temporary and unmanaged cursors are closed as soon as they are no longer required.

Running the Application

The first thing that you may notice when running this application on a device that has any number of accounts set up is that the list seems insurmountably long, certainly much longer than what shows up when running the Contacts application bundled with the device. The Contacts API allows for storage of grouped entries that may be hidden from the user and are used for internal purposes. Gmail often uses this to store incoming e-mail addresses for quick access, even if the address is not associated with a true contact.

In the next example, we will show how to filter this list, but for now marvel at the amount of data truly stored in the Contacts table.

Changing/Adding Contacts

Now let's look at an example Activity that manipulates the data for a specific contact. See Listing 6–20.

> **IMPORTANT:** In order to interact with the Contacts API in your application, you must declare `android.permission.READ_CONTACTS` and `android.permission.WRITE_CONTACTS` in the application manifest.

Listing 6–20. *Activity Writing to Contacts API*

```java
public class ContactsEditActivity extends ListActivity implements
        AdapterView.OnItemClickListener, DialogInterface.OnClickListener {

    private static final String TEST_EMAIL = "test@email.com";

    private Cursor mContacts, mEmail;
    private int selectedContactId;

    @Override
    public void onCreate(Bundle savedInstanceState) {
        super.onCreate(savedInstanceState);
        // Return all contacts, ordered by name
        String[] projection = new String[] { ContactsContract.Contacts._ID,
                ContactsContract.Contacts.DISPLAY_NAME };
        //List only contacts visible to the user
        mContacts = managedQuery(ContactsContract.Contacts.CONTENT_URI,
                projection,
                ContactsContract.Contacts.IN_VISIBLE_GROUP+" = 1",
                null, ContactsContract.Contacts.DISPLAY_NAME);

        // Display all contacts in a ListView
        SimpleCursorAdapter mAdapter = new SimpleCursorAdapter(this,
                android.R.layout.simple_list_item_1, mContacts,
                new String[] { ContactsContract.Contacts.DISPLAY_NAME },
                new int[] { android.R.id.text1 });

        setListAdapter(mAdapter);
        // Listen for item selections
        getListView().setOnItemClickListener(this);
    }

    @Override
    public void onItemClick(AdapterView<?> parent, View v, int position, long id) {
        if (mContacts.moveToPosition(position)) {
            selectedContactId = mContacts.getInt(0); // _ID column
            // Gather email data from email table
            String[] projection = new String[] { ContactsContract.Data._ID,
                    ContactsContract.CommonDataKinds.Email.DATA };
            mEmail = getContentResolver().query(
```

```
                    ContactsContract.CommonDataKinds.Email.CONTENT_URI,
                    projection,
                    ContactsContract.Data.CONTACT_ID+" = "+selectedContactId, null, null);
            AlertDialog.Builder builder = new AlertDialog.Builder(this);
            builder.setTitle("Email Addresses");
            builder.setCursor(mEmail, this, ContactsContract.CommonDataKinds.Email.DATA);
            builder.setPositiveButton("Add", this);
            builder.setNegativeButton("Cancel", null);
            builder.create().show();
        }
    }

    @Override
    public void onClick(DialogInterface dialog, int which) {
        //Data must be associated with a RAW contact, retrieve the first raw ID
        Cursor raw = getContentResolver().query(
                ContactsContract.RawContacts.CONTENT_URI,
                new String[] { ContactsContract.Contacts._ID },
                ContactsContract.Data.CONTACT_ID+" = "+selectedContactId, null, null);
        if(!raw.moveToFirst()) {
            return;
        }

        int rawContactId = raw.getInt(0);
        ContentValues values = new ContentValues();
        switch(which) {
        case DialogInterface.BUTTON_POSITIVE:
            //User wants to add a new email
            values.put(ContactsContract.CommonDataKinds.Email.RAW_CONTACT_ID, rawContactId);
            values.put(ContactsContract.Data.MIMETYPE,
                    ContactsContract.CommonDataKinds.Email.CONTENT_ITEM_TYPE);
            values.put(ContactsContract.CommonDataKinds.Email.DATA, TEST_EMAIL);
            values.put(ContactsContract.CommonDataKinds.Email.TYPE,
                    ContactsContract.CommonDataKinds.Email.TYPE_OTHER);
            getContentResolver().insert(ContactsContract.Data.CONTENT_URI, values);
            break;
        default:
            //User wants to edit selection
            values.put(ContactsContract.CommonDataKinds.Email.DATA, TEST_EMAIL);
            values.put(ContactsContract.CommonDataKinds.Email.TYPE,
                    ContactsContract.CommonDataKinds.Email.TYPE_OTHER);
            getContentResolver().update(ContactsContract.Data.CONTENT_URI, values,
                    ContactsContract.Data._ID+" = "+mEmail.getInt(0), null);
            break;
        }

        //Don't need the email cursor anymore
        mEmail.close();
    }
}
```

In this example, we start out as before, performing a query for all entries in the Contacts database. This time, we provide a single piece of selection criteria:

```
ContactsContract.Contacts.IN_VISIBLE_GROUP+" = 1"
```

The effect of this line is to limit the returned entries to only those that include entries visible to the user through the Contacts user interface. This will (drastically, in some cases) reduce the size of the list displayed in the Activity, and make it more closely match the list displayed in the Contacts application.

When the user selects a contact from this list, a dialog is displayed with a list of all the e-mail entries attached to that contact. If a specific address is selected from the list, that entry is edited; and if the add button is pressed a new e-mail address entry is added. For the purposes of simplifying the example, we do not provide an interface to enter a new e-mail address. Instead, a constant value is inserted, either as a new record or an update to the selected one.

Data elements, such as e-mail addresses, can only be associated with a RawContact. Therefore, when we want to add a new e-mail address, we must obtain the ID of one of the RawContacts represented by the higher-level contact that the user selected. For the purposes of the example we aren't terribly interested in which one, so we retrieve the ID of the first RawContact that matches. This value is only required for doing an insert, since the update references the distinct row ID of the e-mail record already present in the table.

Notice also that the Uri provided in CommonDataKinds that was used as an alias to read this data cannot be used to make updates and changes. Inserts and updates must be called directly on the ContactsContract.Data Uri. What this means (besides referencing a different Uri in the operation method) is that an extra piece of metadata, the MIMETYPE, must also be specified. Without setting the MIMETYPE field for inserted data, subsequent queries made may not recognize it as a Contact's e-mail address.

Aggregation at Work

Because this example updates records by adding or editing e-mail addresses with the same value, it offers a unique opportunity to see Android's aggregation operations in real-time. As you run this example application you may take notice of the fact that adding or editing contacts to give them the same e-mail address often triggers Android to start thinking that previously separate Contacts are now the same person. Even in this sample application, as the managed query attached to the core Contacts table updates, notice that certain contacts will disappear as they become aggregated together.

> **NOTE:** Contact aggregation behavior is not fully implemented on the Android emulator. To see this effect in full you will need to run the code on a real device.

Maintaining a Reference

The Android Contacts API introduces one more concept that can be important depending on the scope of the application. Because of this aggregation process that occurs, the distinct row ID that refers to a contact becomes quite volatile; a certain contact may receive a new _ID when it is aggregated together with another one.

If your application requires a long-standing reference to a specific contact, it is recommended that your application persist the ContactsContract.Contacts.LOOKUP_KEY, instead of the row ID. When querying for a Contact using this key, a special Uri is also provided as the ContactsContract.Contacts.CONTENT_LOOKUP_URI. Using these values to query records long-term will protect your application from getting confused by the automatic aggregation process.

6–10. Picking Device Media

Problem

Your application needs to import a user-selected media item (audio, video, or image) for display or playback.

Solution

(API Level 1)

Use an implicit Intent targeted with Intent.ACTION_GET_CONTENT to bring up a system media picker interface. Firing this Intent with a matching content type for the media of interest (audio, video, or image) will present the user with a picker interface to select an item, and the Intent result will include a Uri pointing to the selection they made.

How It Works

Let's take a look at this technique used in the context of an example Activity. See Listings 6–21 and 6–22.

Listing 6–21. *res/layout/main.xml*

```xml
<?xml version="1.0" encoding="utf-8"?>
<LinearLayout xmlns:android="http://schemas.android.com/apk/res/android"
  android:orientation="vertical"
  android:layout_width="fill_parent"
  android:layout_height="fill_parent">
  <Button
    android:id="@+id/imageButton"
    android:layout_width="fill_parent"
    android:layout_height="wrap_content"
    android:text="Images"
  />
  <Button
    android:id="@+id/videoButton"
    android:layout_width="fill_parent"
    android:layout_height="wrap_content"
    android:text="Video"
  />
```

```
  <Button
    android:id="@+id/audioButton"
    android:layout_width="fill_parent"
    android:layout_height="wrap_content"
    android:text="Audio"
  />
</LinearLayout>
```

Listing 6–22. *Activity to Pick Media*

```java
public class MediaActivity extends Activity implements View.OnClickListener {

    private static final int REQUEST_AUDIO = 1;
    private static final int REQUEST_VIDEO = 2;
    private static final int REQUEST_IMAGE = 3;

    @Override
    public void onCreate(Bundle savedInstanceState) {
        super.onCreate(savedInstanceState);
        setContentView(R.layout.main);

        Button images = (Button)findViewById(R.id.imageButton);
        images.setOnClickListener(this);
        Button videos = (Button)findViewById(R.id.videoButton);
        videos.setOnClickListener(this);
        Button audio = (Button)findViewById(R.id.audioButton);
        audio.setOnClickListener(this);

    }

    @Override
    protected void onActivityResult(int requestCode, int resultCode, Intent data) {

        if(resultCode == Activity.RESULT_OK) {
            //Uri to user selection returned in the Intent
            Uri selectedContent = data.getData();

            if(requestCode == REQUEST_IMAGE) {
                //Display the image
            }
            if(requestCode == REQUEST_VIDEO) {
                //Play the video clip
            }
            if(requestCode == REQUEST_AUDIO) {
                //Play the audio clip
            }
        }
    }

    @Override
    public void onClick(View v) {
        Intent intent = new Intent();
        intent.setAction(Intent.ACTION_GET_CONTENT);
        switch(v.getId()) {
        case R.id.imageButton:
            intent.setType("image/*");
            startActivityForResult(intent, REQUEST_IMAGE);
            return;
```

```
        case R.id.videoButton:
            intent.setType("video/*");
            startActivityForResult(intent, REQUEST_VIDEO);
            return;
        case R.id.audioButton:
            intent.setType("audio/*");
            startActivityForResult(intent, REQUEST_AUDIO);
            return;
        default:
            return;
        }
    }
}
```

This example has three buttons for the user to press, each targeting a specific type of media. When the user presses any one of these buttons, an Intent with the Intent.ACTION_GET_CONTENT action string is fired to the system, launching the proper picker Activity. If the user selects a valid item, a content Uri pointing to that item is returned in the result Intent with a status of RESULT_OK. If the user cancels or otherwise backs out of the picker, the status will be RESULT_CANCELED and the Intent's data field will be null.

With the Uri of the media received, the application is now free to play or display the content as is deemed appropriate. Classes like MediaPlayer and VideoView will take a Uri directly to play media content, and the Uri.getPath() method will return a file path for images that can be passed to BitmapFactory.decodeFile().

6–11. Saving to the MediaStore

Problem

Your application would like to store media and insert it into the device's global MediaStore so that it is visible to all applications.

Solution

(API Level 1)

Utilize the ContentProvider interface exposed by MediaStore to perform inserts. In addition to the media content itself, this interface allows you to insert metadata to tag each item, such as a title, description, or time created. The result of the ContentProvider insert operation is a Uri that the application may use as a destination for the new media.

How It Works

Let's take a look at an example of inserting an image or video clip into MediaStore. See Listings 6–23 and 6–24.

Listing 6–23. *res/layout/main.xml*

```xml
<?xml version="1.0" encoding="utf-8"?>
<LinearLayout xmlns:android="http://schemas.android.com/apk/res/android"
  android:orientation="vertical"
  android:layout_width="fill_parent"
  android:layout_height="fill_parent">
  <Button
    android:id="@+id/imageButton"
    android:layout_width="fill_parent"
    android:layout_height="wrap_content"
    android:text="Images"
  />
  <Button
    android:id="@+id/videoButton"
    android:layout_width="fill_parent"
    android:layout_height="wrap_content"
    android:text="Video"
  />
</LinearLayout>
```

Listing 6–24. *Activity Saving Data in the MediaStore*

```java
public class StoreActivity extends Activity implements View.OnClickListener {

    private static final int REQUEST_CAPTURE = 100;

    @Override
    public void onCreate(Bundle savedInstanceState) {
        super.onCreate(savedInstanceState);
        setContentView(R.layout.main);

        Button images = (Button)findViewById(R.id.imageButton);
        images.setOnClickListener(this);
        Button videos = (Button)findViewById(R.id.videoButton);
        videos.setOnClickListener(this);
    }

    @Override
    protected void onActivityResult(int requestCode, int resultCode, Intent data) {
        if(requestCode == REQUEST_CAPTURE && resultCode == Activity.RESULT_OK) {
            Toast.makeText(this, "All Done!", Toast.LENGTH_SHORT).show();
        }
    }

    @Override
    public void onClick(View v) {
        ContentValues values;
        Intent intent;
        Uri storeLocation;

        switch(v.getId()) {
        case R.id.imageButton:
            //Create any metadata for image
            values = new ContentValues(2);
            values.put(MediaStore.Images.ImageColumns.DATE_TAKEN, System.currentTimeMillis());
            values.put(MediaStore.Images.ImageColumns.DESCRIPTION, "Sample Image");
            //Insert metadata and retrieve Uri location for file
```

```
            storeLocation = getContentResolver().insert(
                    MediaStore.Images.Media.EXTERNAL_CONTENT_URI, values);
            //Start capture with new location as destination
            intent = new Intent(MediaStore.ACTION_IMAGE_CAPTURE);
            intent.putExtra(MediaStore.EXTRA_OUTPUT, storeLocation);
            startActivityForResult(intent, REQUEST_CAPTURE);
            return;
        case R.id.videoButton:
            //Create any metadata for video
            values = new ContentValues(2);
            values.put(MediaStore.Video.VideoColumns.ARTIST, "Yours Truly");
            values.put(MediaStore.Video.VideoColumns.DESCRIPTION, "Sample Video Clip");
            //Insert metadata and retrieve Uri location for file
            storeLocation = getContentResolver().insert(
                    MediaStore.Video.Media.EXTERNAL_CONTENT_URI, values);
            //Start capture with new location as destination
            intent = new Intent(MediaStore.ACTION_VIDEO_CAPTURE);
            intent.putExtra(MediaStore.EXTRA_OUTPUT, storeLocation);
            startActivityForResult(intent, REQUEST_CAPTURE);
            return;
        default:
            return;
        }
    }
}
```

> **NOTE:** Since this example interacts with the Camera hardware, you should run it on a real device to get the full effect. In fact, there is a known bug in emulators running Android 2.2 or later that will cause this example to crash if the Camera is accessed. Earlier emulators will execute the code appropriately, but without real hardware the example is less interesting.

In this example, when the user clicks on either button, metadata that is to be associated with the media itself is inserted into a ContentValues instance. Some of the more common metadata columns that are common to both image and video are:

- TITLE: String value for the content title

- DESCRIPTION: String value for the content description

- DATE_TAKEN: Integer value describing the date the media was captured. Fill this field with System.currentTimeMillis() to indicate a time of "now"

The ContentValues are then inserted into the MediaStore using the appropriate CONTENT_URI reference. Notice that the metadata is inserted before the media itself is actually captured. The return value from a successful insert is a fully qualified Uri that the application may use as the destination for the media content.

In the previous example, we are using the simplified methods from Chapter 4 of capturing audio and video by requesting that the system applications handle this process. Recall from Chapter 4 that both the audio and video capture Intent can be passed with an extra declaring the destination for the result. This is where we pass the Uri that was returned from insert.

Upon a successful return from the capture Activity, there is nothing more for the application to do. The external application has saved the captured image or video into the location referenced by our MediaStore insert. This data is now visible to all applications, including the system's Gallery application.

Summary

In this chapter, you learned how your application can interact directly with the Android operating system. We discussed several methods of placing operations into the background for various lengths of time. You learned how applications can share responsibility, launching each other to best accomplish the task at hand. Finally, we presented how the system exposes the content gathered by its core application suite for your application's use. In the next and final chapter, we will look at how you can leverage the wide array of publicly available Java libraries to further enhance your application.

Chapter 7

Working with Libraries

Smart Android developers deliver their apps to market faster by taking advantage of libraries, which reduce development time by providing previously created and tested code. Developers may create and use their own libraries, use libraries created by others, or do both.

This chapter's initial recipes introduce you to creating and using your own libraries. Subsequent recipes introduce you to Kidroid's kiChart charting library for presenting bar charts and line charts, and to IBM's MQTT library for implementing lightweight push messaging in your apps.

TIP: OpenIntents.org publishes a list of libraries from various vendors that you might find helpful in your app development (`www.openintents.org/en/libraries`).

7–1. Creating Java Library JARs

Problem

You want to create a library that stores Android-agnostic code, and which can be used in your Android and non-Android projects.

Solution

Create a JAR-based library that accesses only Java 5 (and earlier) APIs via JDK command-line tools or Eclipse.

How It Works

Suppose you plan to create a simple library of math-oriented utilities. This library will consist of a single MathUtils class with various `static` methods. Listing 7–1 presents an early version of this class.

Listing 7–1. *MathUtils Implementing Math-Oriented Utilities via* `static` *Methods*

```
// MathUtils.java

package com.apress.mathutils;

public class MathUtils
{
   public static long factorial(long n)
   {
      if (n <= 0)
         return 1;
      else
         return n*factorial(n-1);
   }
}
```

MathUtils currently consists of a single `static factorial()` method for computing and returning factorials (perhaps for use in calculating permutations and combinations). You might eventually expand this class to support fast Fourier transforms and other math operations not supported by the java.lang.Math class.

> **CAUTION:** When creating a library that stores Android-agnostic code, make sure to access only standard Java APIs (such as the collections framework) that are supported by Android – don't access unsupported Java APIs (such as Swing) or Android-specific APIs (such as Android widgets). Also, don't access any standard Java APIs more recent than Java version 5.

Creating MathUtils with the JDK

Developing a JAR-based library with the JDK is trivial. Perform the following steps to create a `mathutils.jar` file that contains the MathUtils class:

1. Within the current directory, create a package directory structure consisting of a com subdirectory that contains an apress subdirectory that contains a mathutils subdirectory.

2. Copy Listing 7–1's MathUtils.java source code to a MathUtils.java file stored in mathutils.

3. Assuming that the current directory contains the com subdirectory, execute javac com/apress/mathutils/MathUtils.java to compile MathUtils.java. A MathUtils.class file is stored in com/apress/mathutils.

4. Create `mathutils.jar` by executing `jar cf mathutils.jar com/apress/mathutils/*.class`. The resulting `mathutils.jar` file contains a `com/apress/mathutils/MathUtils.class` entry.

Creating MathUtils with Eclipse

Developing a JAR-based library with Eclipse is a bit more involved. Perform the following steps to create a `mathutils.jar` file that contains the `MathUtils` class:

1. Assuming that you've installed the Eclipse version discussed in Chapter 1, start this IDE if not already running.

2. Select New from the File menu and Java Project from the resulting pop-up menu.

3. On the resulting *New Java Project* dialog box, enter `mathutils` into the Project name textfield and click the Finish button.

4. Expand Package Explorer's mathutils node.

5. Right-click the src node (underneath mathutils) and select New, followed by Package from the resulting pop-up menus.

6. On the resulting *New Java Package* dialog box, enter `com.apress.mathutils` into the Name field and click Finish.

7. Right-click the resulting com.apress.mathutils node and select New, followed by Class on the resulting pop-up menus.

8. On the resulting *New Java Class* dialog box, enter `MathUtils` into the Name field and click Finish.

9. Replace the skeletal contents in the resulting MathUtils.java editor window with Listing 7–1.

10. Right-click the mathutils project node and select Build Project from the resulting pop-up menu. (You might have to deselect Build Automatically from the project menu first.)

11. Right-click the mathutils project node and select Export from the resulting pop-up menu.

12. On the resulting *Export* dialog box, select JAR file under the Java node and click the Next button.

13. On the resulting JAR Export pane, keep the defaults but enter `mathutils.jar` in the JAR file textfield. Click Finish. The resulting `mathutils.jar` file is created in your Eclipse workspace's root directory.

7–2. Using Java Library JARs

Problem

You've successfully built mathutils.jar and want to learn how to integrate this JAR file into your Eclipse-based Android projects.

Solution

You'll create your Eclipse-based Android project with a libs directory and copy mathutils.jar into this directory.

> **NOTE:** It's common practice to store libraries (.jar files and Linux shared object libraries, .so files) in a libs subdirectory of the Android project directory. The Android build system automatically takes files found in libs and integrates them into APKs. If the library is a shared object library, it is stored in the .apk file with an entry starting with lib (not libs).

How It Works

Now that you've created mathutils.jar, you'll need an Android app to try out this library. Listing 7–2 presents the source code to a UseMathUtils single-activity-based app that computes 5-factorial, which the activity subsequently outputs.

Listing 7–2. *UseMathUtils Invoking* MathUtil's factorial() *Method to Compute 5-factorial*

```java
// UseMathUtils.java

package com.apress.usemathutils;

import android.app.Activity;

import android.os.Bundle;

import android.widget.TextView;

import com.apress.mathutils.MathUtils;

public class UseMathUtils extends Activity
{
    @Override
    public void onCreate(Bundle savedInstanceState)
    {
        super.onCreate(savedInstanceState);
        TextView tv = new TextView(this);
        tv.setText("5! = "+MathUtils.factorial(5));
        setContentView(tv);
    }
}
```

Assuming that Eclipse is running, complete the following steps to create a `UseMathUtils` project:

1. Select New from the File menu, and select Project from the resulting pop-up menu.

2. On the *New Project* dialog box, expand the Android node in the wizard tree, select the Android Project branch below this node, and click the Next button.

3. On the resulting *New Android Project* dialog box, enter **UseMathUtils** into the Project name textfield. This entered name identifies the folder/directory in which the `UseMathUtils` project is stored.

4. Select the "Create new project in workspace" radio button if it's not selected.

5. Under Build Target, check the checkbox of the appropriate Android target to be used as `UseMathUtils`'s build target. This target specifies which Android platform you'd like your application to be built against. Assuming that you've installed only the Android 2.3 platform, only this build target should appear and should already be checked.

6. Under Properties, enter **Use MathUtils** into the Application name textfield. This human-readable title will appear on the Android device. Continuing, enter **com.apress.usemathutils** into the Package name textfield. This value is the package namespace (following the same rules as for packages in the Java programming language) where all your source code will reside. Check the Create Activity checkbox if it's not checked, and enter **UseMathUtils** as the name of the app's starting activity in the textfield that appears beside this checkbox. The textfield is disabled when this checkbox is not checked. Finally, enter integer **9** into the Min SDK Version textfield to identify the minimum API Level required to properly run `UseMathUtils` on the Android 2.3 platform.

7. Click Finish.

Eclipse creates a UseMathUtils node in the Package Explorer window. Complete the following steps to set up all files:

1. Expand the UseMathUtils node, followed by the src node, followed by the com.apress.usemathutils node.

2. Double-click the UseMathUtils.java node (underneath com.apress.usemathutils) and replace the skeletal contents in the resulting window with Listing 7–2.

3. Right-click the UseMathUtils node and select New followed by Folder on the resulting pop-up menu. On the resulting *New Folder* dialog box, enter libs into the Folder name textfield and click the Finish button.

4. Use your platform's file manager program (such as Windows XP's Windows Explorer) to select and drag the previously created mathutils.jar file to the libs node. If a *File Operation* dialog box appears, keep the Copy files radio button selected and click the OK button.

5. Right-click mathutils.jar and select Build Path followed by Configure Build Path on the resulting pop-up menus.

6. On the resulting *Properties for UseMathUtils* dialog box, select the Libraries tab and click the Add Jars button.

7. On the resulting *JAR Selection* dialog box, expand the UseMathUtils node followed by the libs node. Select mathutils.jar and click OK to close *JAR Selection*. Click OK a second time to close *Properties for UseMathUtils*.

You're now ready to run this project. Select Run from the menubar followed by Run from the dropdown menu. If a *Run As* dialog box appears, select Android Application and click OK. Eclipse starts the emulator, installs this project's APK, and runs the app, whose output appears in Figure 7–1.

Figure 7–1. *UseMathUtils's simple user interface could be expanded to let the user enter an arbitrary number.*

NOTE: Examine this application's UseMathUtils.apk file (jar tvf UseMathUtils.apk), and you won't find a mathutils.jar entry. Instead, you'll find classes.dex, which contains the app's Dalvik-executable bytecode. classes.dex also contains the Dalvik equivalent of the MathUtils classfile, because the Android build system unpacks JAR files, processes their contents with the dx tool to convert their Java bytecodes to Dalvik bytecodes, and merges the equivalent Dalvik code into classes.dex.

7–3. Creating Android Library Projects

Problem

You want to create a library that stores Android-specific code, such as custom widgets or activities with or without resources.

Solution

Android 2.2 and successors let you create *Android library projects*, which are Eclipse projects describing libraries that incorporate Android-specific code and even resources.

How It Works

Suppose you want to create a library that contains a single reusable custom widget describing a game board (for playing chess, checkers, or even tic-tac-toe). Listing 7–3 reveals this library's GameBoard class.

Listing 7–3. *GameBoard Describing a Reusable Custom Widget for Drawing Different Game Boards*

```java
// GameBoard.java

package com.apress.gameboard;

import android.content.Context;

import android.graphics.Canvas;
import android.graphics.Paint;

import android.view.View;

public class GameBoard extends View
{
    private int nSquares, colorA, colorB;

    private Paint paint;
    private int squareDim;

    public GameBoard(Context context, int nSquares, int colorA, int colorB)
    {
        super(context);
        this.nSquares = nSquares;
        this.colorA = colorA;
        this.colorB = colorB;
        paint = new Paint();
    }

    @Override
    protected void onDraw(Canvas canvas)
    {
        for (int row = 0; row < nSquares; row++)
        {
```

```
      paint.setColor(((row & 1) == 0) ? colorA : colorB);
      for (int col = 0; col < nSquares; col++)
      {
         int a = col*squareDim;
         int b = row*squareDim;
         canvas.drawRect(a, b, a+squareDim, b+squareDim, paint);
         paint.setColor((paint.getColor() == colorA) ? colorB : colorA);
      }
   }
}

@Override
protected void onMeasure(int widthMeasuredSpec, int heightMeasuredSpec)
{
   // keep the view squared
   int width = MeasureSpec.getSize(widthMeasuredSpec);
   int height = MeasureSpec.getSize(heightMeasuredSpec);
   int d = (width == 0) ? height : (height == 0) ? width :
           (width < height) ? width : height;
   setMeasuredDimension(d, d);
   squareDim = width/nSquares;
}
}
```

Android custom widgets are based on views that subclass android.view.View or one of its subclasses (such as android.widget.TextView). GameBoard subclasses View directly because it doesn't need any subclass functionality.

GameBoard provides several fields, including the following:

- nSquares stores the number of squares on each side of the game board. Typical values include 3 (for a 3-by-3 board) and 8 (for an 8-by-8 board).

- colorA stores the color of even-numbered squares on even-numbered rows, and the color of odd-numbered squares on odd-numbered rows – row and column numbering starts at 0.

- colorB stores the color of odd-numbered squares on even-numbered rows, and the color of even-numbered squares on odd-numbered rows.

- paint stores a reference to an android.graphics.Paint object that is used to specify the square color (colorA or colorB) when the game board is drawn.

- squareDim stores the dimension of a square – the number of pixels on each side.

GameBoard's constructor initializes this widget by storing its nSquares, colorA, and colorB arguments in same-named fields, and also instantiates the Paint class. Before doing so, however, it passes its context argument to its View superclass.

NOTE: View subclasses are required to pass an android.content.Context instance to their View superclass. Doing so identifies the context (an activity, for example) in which the custom widget is running. Custom widget subclasses can subsequently call View's Context getContext() method to return this Context object, so that they can call Context methods to access the current theme, resources, and so on.

Android tells a custom widget to draw itself by calling the widget's overriding protected void onDraw(Canvas canvas) method. GameBoard's onDraw(Canvas) method responds by invoking android.graphics.Canvas's void drawRect(float left, float top, float right, float bottom, Paint paint) method to paint each square for each row/column intersection. The final paint argument determines the color of that square.

Before Android invokes onDraw(Canvas), it must measure the widget. It accomplishes this task by invoking the widget's overriding protected void onMeasure(int widthMeasureSpec, int heightMeasureSpec) method, where the passed arguments specify the horizontal and vertical space requirements that are imposed by the parent view. The widget typically passes these arguments to the View.MeasureSpec nested class's static int getSize(int measureSpec) method to return the exact width or height of the widget based on the passed measureSpec argument. The returned values or a modified version of these values must then be passed to View's void setMeasuredDimension(int measuredWidth, int measuredHeight) method to store the measured width and height. Failure to call this method results in a thrown exception at runtime. Because game boards should be square, GameBoard's onMeasure(int, int) method passes the minimum of the width and height to setMeasuredDimension(int, int) to ensure a square game board.

Now that you know how GameBoard works, you're ready to create a library that stores this class. You'll create this library by creating an Android library project. The nice thing about such a project is that it's a standard Android project, so you can create a new Android library project in the same way as you would create a new app project.

Complete the following steps to create the GameBoard project:

1. Select New from the File menu, and select Project from the resulting pop-up menu.

2. On the *New Project* dialog box, expand the Android node in the wizard tree, select the Android Project branch below this node, and click the Next button.

3. On the resulting *New Android Project* dialog box, enter **GameBoard** into the Project name textfield. This entered name identifies the folder in which the GameBoard project is stored.

4. Select the "Create new project in workspace" radio button if it's not selected.

5. Under Build Target, check the checkbox of the appropriate Android target to be used as the GameBoard build target. This target specifies which Android platform you'd like your application to be built against. Assuming that you've installed only the Android 2.3 platform, only this build target should appear and it should already be checked.

6. Under Properties, leave the Application name textfield blank – the library isn't an app, so there's no point in entering a value in this field. Continuing, enter **com.apress.gameboard** into the Package name textfield. This value is the package namespace (following the same rules as for packages in the Java programming language) where all your library source code will reside. Uncheck the Create Activity checkbox if it's checked. The textfield is disabled when this checkbox is not checked. Finally, enter integer **9** into the Min SDK Version textfield to identify the minimum API Level required to properly run GameBoard on the Android 2.3 platform.

7. Click Finish.

Although you create an Android library project in the same fashion as creating a regular app project, you must adjust some of GameBoard's project properties to indicate that it is a library project:

1. In Package Explorer, right-click GameBoard and select Properties from the pop-up menu.

2. On the resulting Properties for GameBoard dialog box, select the Android properties group and check the Is Library check box.

3. Click the Apply button, followed by OK.

The new GameBoard project is now marked as an Android library project. However, it doesn't yet contain a GameBoard.java source file containing Listing 7–3's contents. Create this source file under Package Explorer's GameBoard/src/com/apress/gameboard node.

You can build this library if you want to (right-click the GameBoard node and select Build Project from the pop-up menu, for example). However, it isn't necessary to do so. The project will be built automatically when you build a project that uses this library. You'll learn how to do this in the next recipe.

> **NOTE:** If you build the GameBoard library, you'll discover a com/apress/gameboard directory structure where gameboard contains GameBoard.class and several resource-oriented classfiles (even though GameBoard.java doesn't reference resources). This is the essence of what constitutes a library based on an Android library project.

7–4. Using Android Library Projects

Problem

You've successfully built the GameBoard library and want to learn how to integrate this library into your Eclipse-based Android projects.

Solution

Identify the GameBoard library to Eclipse in the properties of the app project being built, and build the app.

How It Works

Now that you've created GameBoard, you'll need an Android app to try out this library. Listing 7–4 presents the source code to a UseGameBoard single-activity-based app that instantiates this library's GameBoard class and places it in the activity's view hierarchy.

Listing 7–4. *UseGameBoard Placing the GameBoard Widget into the Activity's View Hierarchy*

```java
// UseGameBoard.java

package com.apress.usegameboard;

import android.app.Activity;

import android.graphics.Color;

import android.os.Bundle;

import com.apress.gameboard.GameBoard;

public class UseGameBoard extends Activity
{
    @Override
    public void onCreate(Bundle savedInstanceState)
    {
        super.onCreate(savedInstanceState);
        GameBoard gb = new GameBoard(this, 8, Color.BLUE, Color.WHITE);
        setContentView(gb);
    }
}
```

Assuming that Eclipse is running, complete the following steps to create a UseGameBoard project:

1. Select New from the File menu, and select Project from the resulting pop-up menu.

2. On the *New Project* dialog box, expand the Android node in the wizard tree, select the Android Project branch below this node, and click the Next button.

3. On the resulting *New Android Project* dialog box, enter **UseGameBoard** into the Project name textfield. This entered name identifies the folder in which the UseGameBoard project is stored.

4. Select the "Create new project in workspace" radio button if it's not selected.

5. Under Build Target, check the checkbox of the appropriate Android target to be used as UseGameBoard's build target. This target specifies which Android platform you'd like your app to be built against. Assuming that you've installed only the Android 2.3 platform, only this build target should appear and it should already be checked.

6. Under Properties, enter **Use GameBoard** into the Application name textfield. This human-readable title will appear on the Android device. Continuing, enter **com.apress.usegameboard** into the Package name textfield. This value is the package namespace (following the same rules as for packages in the Java programming language) where all your source code will reside. Check the Create Activity checkbox if it's not checked, and enter **UseGameBoard** as the name of the app's starting activity in the textfield that appears beside this checkbox. The textfield is disabled when this checkbox is not checked. Finally, enter integer **9** into the Min SDK Version textfield to identify the minimum API Level required to properly run UseGameBoard on the Android 2.3 platform.

7. Click Finish.

Eclipse creates a UseGameBoard node in the Package Explorer window. Complete the following steps to set up all files:

1. Expand the UseGameBoard node, followed by the src node, followed by the com.apress.usegameboard node.

2. Double-click the UseGameBoard.java node (underneath com.apress.usegameboard) and replace the skeletal contents in the resulting window with Listing 7–4.

3. Right-click the UseGameBoard node and select Properties from the resulting pop-up menu.

4. On the resulting *Properties for UseGameBoard* dialog box, select the Android category and click the Add button.

5. On the resulting *Project Selection* dialog box, select GameBoard and click OK.

6. Click Apply, and then OK to close *Properties for UseGameBoard*.

You're now ready to run this project. Select Run from the menubar, followed by Run from the dropdown menu. If a *Run As* dialog box appears, select Android Application and click OK. Eclipse starts the emulator, installs this project's APK, and runs the app, whose output appears in Figure 7–2.

Figure 7–2. *UseGameBoard reveals a blue-and-white checkered game board that could be used as the background for a game such as checkers or chess.*

NOTE: If you're interested in creating and using an Android library project-based library that incorporates an activity, check out Google's `TicTacToe` example library project (http://developer.android.com/guide/developing/projects/projects-eclipse.html#SettingUpLibraryProject).

7–5. Charting

Problem

You're looking for a simple library that lets your app generate bar charts or line charts.

Solution

Although several Android libraries exist for generating charts, you might prefer the simplicity of Kidroid.com's kiChart product (`www.kidroid.com/kichart/`). Version 0.1 supports bar charts and line charts, and Kidroid promises to add new chart types in subsequent releases.

The link to kiChart's home page presents links for downloading `kiChart-0.1.jar` (the library) and `kiChart-Help.pdf` (documentation describing the library).

How It Works

kiChart's documentation states that bar and line charts support multiple series of data. Furthermore, it states that charts can be exported to image files, and that you can define chart parameters (such as font color, font size, margin, and so on).

The documentation then presents a pair of screenshots to the sample line and bar charts rendered by a demo app. These screenshots are followed by a code exert from this demo – specifically, the `LineChart` chart activity class.

`LineChart`'s source code reveals the basics of establishing a chart, explained here:

1. Create an activity that extends the `com.kidroid.kichart.ChartActivity` class. This activity renders either a bar chart or a line chart.

2. Within the activity's `onCreate(Bundle)` method, create a `String` array of horizontal axis labels, and create a floating-point array of data for each set of bars or each line.

3. Create an array of `com.kidroid.kichart.model.Aitem` (axis item) instances and populate this array with `Aitem` objects that store the data arrays. Each `Aitem` constructor call requires you to pass an `android.graphics.Color` value to identify the color associated with the data array (whose displayed values and bars or lines are displayed in that color), a `String` value that associates a label with the color and data array, and the data array itself.

4. Instantiate the `com.kidroid.kichart.view.BarView` class if you want to display a bar chart, or the `com.kidroid.kichart.view.LineView` class if you want to display a line chart.

5. Call the class's public void setTitle(String title) method to specify a title for the chart.

6. Call the class's public void setAxisValueX(String[] labels) method to specify the chart's horizontal labels.

7. Call the class's public void setItems(Aitem[] items) method to specify the chart's arrays of data items.

8. Call setContentView() with the chart instance as its argument to display the chart.

9. You don't have to worry about selecting a range of values for the vertical axis because kiChart takes care of this task on your behalf.

A class diagram that presents kiChart's classes and shows their relationships follows the source code. For example, com.kidroid.kichart.view.ChartView is the superclass of com.kidroid.kichart.view.AxisView, which superclasses BarView and LineView.

Each class's properties and ChartView's public boolean exportImage(String filename) method are then documented. This method lets you output a chart to a file, returning true if successful and false if unsuccessful.

> **TIP:** To influence the range of values displayed on the vertical axis, you will need to work with AxisView's intervalCount, intervalValue, and valueGenerate properties.

In practice, you'll find kiChart easy to use. For example, consider a ChartDemo app whose main activity (also named ChartDemo) presents a user interface that lets the user enter quarterly sales figures for each of the years 2010 and 2011 via its eight textfields. The main activity also presents a pair of buttons that let the user view this data in the context of a bar chart or in the context of a line chart via separate BarChart and LineChart activities.

Listing 7–5 presents ChartDemo's source code.

Listing 7–5. *ChartDemo Describing an Activity for Entering Chart Data Values and Launching the Bar Chart or Line Chart Activity*

```
// ChartDemo.java

package com.apress.chartdemo;

import android.app.Activity;

import android.content.Intent;

import android.os.Bundle;

import android.view.View;

import android.widget.AdapterView;
import android.widget.Button;
```

```java
import android.widget.EditText;

public class ChartDemo extends Activity
{
    @Override
    public void onCreate(Bundle savedInstanceState)
    {
        super.onCreate(savedInstanceState);
        setContentView(R.layout.main);

        Button btnViewBC = (Button) findViewById(R.id.viewbc);
        AdapterView.OnClickListener ocl;
        ocl = new AdapterView.OnClickListener()
        {
            @Override
            public void onClick(View v)
            {
                final float[] data2010 = new float[4];
                int[] ids = { R.id.data2010_1, R.id.data2010_2, R.id.data2010_3,
                              R.id.data2010_4 };
                for (int i = 0; i < ids.length; i++)
                {
                    EditText et = (EditText) findViewById(ids[i]);
                    String s = et.getText().toString();
                    try
                    {
                        float input = Float.parseFloat(s);
                        data2010[i] = input;
                    }
                    catch (NumberFormatException nfe)
                    {
                        data2010[i] = 0;
                    }
                }
                final float[] data2011 = new float[4];
                ids = new int[] { R.id.data2011_1, R.id.data2011_2,
                                  R.id.data2011_3, R.id.data2011_4 };
                for (int i = 0; i < ids.length; i++)
                {
                    EditText et = (EditText) findViewById(ids[i]);
                    String s = et.getText().toString();
                    try
                    {
                        float input = Float.parseFloat(s);
                        data2011[i] = input;
                    }
                    catch (NumberFormatException nfe)
                    {
                        data2011[i] = 0;
                    }
                }
                Intent intent = new Intent(ChartDemo.this, BarChart.class);
                intent.putExtra("2010", data2010);
                intent.putExtra("2011", data2011);
                startActivity(intent);
            }
        };
```

```
        btnViewBC.setOnClickListener(ocl);

        Button btnViewLC = (Button) findViewById(R.id.viewlc);
        ocl = new AdapterView.OnClickListener()
        {
            @Override
            public void onClick(View v)
            {
                final float[] data2010 = new float[4];
                int[] ids = { R.id.data2010_1, R.id.data2010_2, R.id.data2010_3,
                            R.id.data2010_4 };
                for (int i = 0; i < ids.length; i++)
                {
                    EditText et = (EditText) findViewById(ids[i]);
                    String s = et.getText().toString();
                    try
                    {
                        float input = Float.parseFloat(s);
                        data2010[i] = input;
                    }
                    catch (NumberFormatException nfe)
                    {
                        data2010[i] = 0;
                    }
                }
                final float[] data2011 = new float[4];
                ids = new int[] { R.id.data2011_1, R.id.data2011_2,
                                R.id.data2011_3, R.id.data2011_4 };
                for (int i = 0; i < ids.length; i++)
                {
                    EditText et = (EditText) findViewById(ids[i]);
                    String s = et.getText().toString();
                    try
                    {
                        float input = Float.parseFloat(s);
                        data2011[i] = input;
                    }
                    catch (NumberFormatException nfe)
                    {
                        data2011[i] = 0;
                    }
                }
                Intent intent = new Intent(ChartDemo.this, LineChart.class);
                intent.putExtra("2010", data2010);
                intent.putExtra("2011", data2011);
                startActivity(intent);
            }
        };
        btnViewLC.setOnClickListener(ocl);
    }
}
```

ChartDemo implements all of its logic in its onCreate(Bundle) method. This method largely concerns itself with setting its content view and attaching a click listener to each of the view's two buttons.

Because these listeners are nearly identical, we'll consider only the code for the listener attached to the viewbc (view bar chart) button. In response to this button being clicked, the listener's onClick(View) method is called to perform the following tasks:

1. Populate a data2010 floating-point array with the values from the four textfields corresponding to 2010 data.

2. Populate a data2011 floating-point array with the values from the four textfields corresponding to 2011 data.

3. Create an Intent object that specifies BarChart.class as the classfile of the activity to launch.

4. Store the data2010 and data2011 arrays in this object so that they can be accessed from the BarChart activity.

5. Launch the BarChart activity.

Listing 7–6 presents BarChart's source code.

Listing 7–6. *BarChart Describing the Bar Chart Activity*

```
// BarChart.java

package com.apress.chartdemo;

import com.kidroid.kichart.ChartActivity;

import com.kidroid.kichart.model.Aitem;

import com.kidroid.kichart.view.BarView;

import android.graphics.Color;

import android.os.Bundle;

public class BarChart extends ChartActivity
{
   @Override
   public void onCreate(Bundle savedInstanceState)
   {
      super.onCreate(savedInstanceState);
      Bundle bundle = getIntent().getExtras();
      float[] data2010 = bundle.getFloatArray("2010");
      float[] data2011 = bundle.getFloatArray("2011");
      String[] arrX = new String[4];
      arrX[0] = "2010.1";
      arrX[1] = "2010.2";
      arrX[2] = "2010.3";
      arrX[3] = "2010.4";
      Aitem[] items = new Aitem[2];
      items[0] = new Aitem(Color.RED, "2010", data2010);
      items[1] = new Aitem(Color.GREEN, "2011", data2011);
      BarView bv = new BarView(this);
      bv.setTitle("Quarterly Sales (Billions)");
      bv.setAxisValueX(arrX);
```

```
        bv.setItems(items);
        setContentView(bv);
    }
}
```

BarChart first obtains a reference to the Intent object passed to it by calling its inherited Intent getIntent() method. It then uses this method to retrieve a reference to the Intent object's Bundle object, which stores the floating-point arrays of data items. Each array is retrieved by invoking Bundle's float[] getFloatArray(String key) method.

BarChart next builds a String array of labels for the chart's X-axis and creates an Aitem array populated with two Aitem objects. The first object stores the 2010 data values and associates these values with the color red and 2010 as the legend value; the second object stores 2011 data values with color green and legend value 2011.

After instantiating BarView, BarChart calls this object's setTitle(String) method to establish the chart's title, setAxisValueX(String[]) method to pass the array of X-axis labels to the object, and setItems(Aitem[]) method to pass the Aitem array to the object. The BarView object is then passed to setContentView() to display the bar chart.

> **NOTE:** Because LineChart is nearly identical to BarChart, this class's source code isn't presented in this chapter. You can easily create LineChart by changing the line that reads BarView bv = new BarView(this); to LineView bv = new LineView(this); Also, you should probably rename the variable bv to lv for best practices. And don't forget to change import com.kidroid.kichart.view.BarView; to import com.kidroid.kichart.view.LineView;.

Listing 7–7 presents main.xml, which describes the layout and widgets that comprise ChartDemo's user interface.

Listing 7–7. *main.xml Describing the Chart Demo Activity's Layout*

```xml
<?xml version="1.0" encoding="utf-8"?>
<TableLayout xmlns:android="http://schemas.android.com/apk/res/android"
            android:layout_width = "fill_parent"
            android:layout_height="fill_parent"
            android:stretchColumns="*">
  <TableRow>
    <TextView android:text=""/>
    <TextView android:text="2010"
            android:layout_gravity="center"/>
    <TextView android:text="2011"
            android:layout_gravity="center"/>
  </TableRow>

  <TableRow>
    <TextView android:text="1st Quarter"/>
    <EditText android:id="@+id/data2010_1"
            android:inputType="numberDecimal"
            android:maxLines="1"/>
```

```
        <EditText android:id="@+id/data2011_1"
                android:inputType="numberDecimal"
                android:maxLines="1"/>
    </TableRow>

    <TableRow>
        <TextView android:text="2nd Quarter"/>
        <EditText android:id="@+id/data2010_2"
                android:inputType="numberDecimal"
                android:maxLines="1"/>
        <EditText android:id="@+id/data2011_2"
                android:inputType="numberDecimal"
                android:maxLines="1"/>
    </TableRow>

    <TableRow>
        <TextView android:text="3rd Quarter"/>
        <EditText android:id="@+id/data2010_3"
                android:inputType="numberDecimal"
                android:maxLines="1"/>
        <EditText android:id="@+id/data2011_3"
                android:inputType="numberDecimal"
                android:maxLines="1"/>
    </TableRow>

    <TableRow>
        <TextView android:text="4th Quarter"/>
        <EditText android:id="@+id/data2010_4"
                android:inputType="numberDecimal"
                android:maxLines="1"/>
        <EditText android:id="@+id/data2011_4"
                android:inputType="numberDecimal"
                android:maxLines="1"/>
    </TableRow>

    <TableRow>
        <TextView android:text=""/>
        <Button android:id="@+id/viewbc"
                android:text="View Barchart"/>
        <Button android:id="@+id/viewlc"
                android:text="View Linechart"/>
    </TableRow>
</TableLayout>
```

main.xml describes a tabular layout via the <TableLayout> tag, where the user interface is laid out in six rows and three columns. The "fill_parent" assignment to each of this tag's layout_width and layout_height attributes tells this layout to occupy the activity's entire screen. The "*" assignment to this tag's stretchColumns attribute tells this layout to give each column an identical width.

> **NOTE:** A *stretchable column* is a column that can expand in width to fit any available space. To specify which columns are stretchable, assign a comma-delimited list of 0-based integers to `stretchColumns`. For example, `"0, 1"` specifies that column 0 (the leftmost column) and column 1 are stretchable. The `"*"` assignment indicates that all columns are equally stretchable, which gives them identical widths.

Nested inside `<TableLayout>` and its `</TableLayout>` partner are a series of `<TableRow>` tags. Each `<TableRow>` tag describes the contents of a single row in the tabular layout, and these contents are a variety of zero or more views (such as `TextView` and `EditText`), where each view constitutes one column.

> **NOTE**: For brevity, string values are stored directly in `main.xml` instead of being stored in a separate `strings.xml` file. Consider it an exercise to introduce `strings.xml` and replace these literal strings with references to strings stored in `strings.xml`.

Listing 7–8 presents this app's `AndroidManifest.xml` file, which describes the app and its activities.

Listing 7–8. *AndroidManifest.xml Pulling Everything Together for the* ChartDemo *App*

```xml
<?xml version="1.0" encoding="utf-8"?>
<manifest xmlns:android="http://schemas.android.com/apk/res/android"
          package="com.apress.chartdemo"
          android:versionCode="1"
          android:versionName="1.0">
   <application android:icon="@drawable/icon" android:label="@string/app_name">
      <activity android:name=".ChartDemo"
                android:label="@string/app_name">
         <intent-filter>
            <action android:name="android.intent.action.MAIN" />
            <category android:name="android.intent.category.LAUNCHER" />
         </intent-filter>
      </activity>
      <activity android:name=".BarChart"/>
      <activity android:name=".LineChart"/>
   </application>
   <uses-sdk android:minSdkVersion="9" />
</manifest>
```

It's important to include `<activity>` tags for each of the `BarChart` and `LineChart` activities in the manifest. Failure to do so results in a runtime dialog box that displays the following message: "The application Chart Demo (process com.apress.chartdemo) has stopped unexpectedly. Please try again."

Figure 7–3 reveals `ChartDemo`'s main activity with sample values entered for each quarter.

Figure 7–3. *ChartDemo lets you enter eight data values and choose to display these values via a bar chart or a line chart.*

Clicking the View Barchart button after entering the aforementioned data values launches the BarChart activity, which displays the bar chart shown in Figure 7–4.

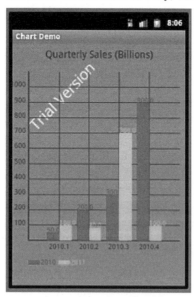

Figure 7–4. *BarChart displays each array's data values via a series of colored bars.*

In addition to presenting a barchart, Figure 7–4 reveals that a trial version of kiChart is being used. You'll need to contact Kidroid.com and find out about licensing and how to obtain a version of kiChart that doesn't display this message.

7–6. Practical Push Messaging

Problem

Google's Cloud-To-Device Messaging (C2DM) framework (http://code.google.com/android/c2dm/index.html), which is designed to implement push messaging to the device, has a number of drawbacks that can impact it as a practical solution for push messaging. Your app needs a more universal push solution.

THE LIMITATIONS OF GOOGLE'S C2DM

C2DM is a technology fostered by Google to run on Android devices over the Extensible Messaging and Presence Protocol (XMPP), a common implementation for chat clients. Upon further inspection, there are a number of required attributes for C2DM that often diminish its usefulness in apps:

- **Requires a minimum of API Level 8:** While this restriction will not remain a significant limitation forever, apps looking to support push messaging now on Android devices running versions earlier than 2.2 will not be able to use C2DM.

- **Requires a Google account and Google APIs on the device:** C2DM runs over the XMPP channel created by the GTalk chat service. If the user is running on an Android device that does not include the Google APIs (and, thus, the GTalk application), or if they have not entered a valid Google account into the device, your app will be unable to register for C2DM messaging on that device.

- **Utilizes HTTP POST for transactions between host app and C2DM servers:** From the server side of the app, messages that are to be sent down to devices are handed over to the C2DM servers using individual HTTP POST requests for each message. As the required number of messages to be sent increases, this mechanism becomes increasingly slow, to the point where C2DM may not be a viable option in certain time-critical apps.

Solution

Utilize IBM's MQTT library to implement lightweight push messaging in your apps. The MQTT client library is offered from IBM in a pure Java implementation, meaning it can be utilized on any Android device, without limitation on specific API Levels.

An MQTT system consists of three main components:

- **Client app:** Runs on the device, and registers with the message broker for a given set of "topics" on which to receive messages.

- **Message broker:** Handles registration of clients, and distributes incoming messages from the server app to each client based on its "topic."

- **Server application:** Responsible for publishing messages to the broker.

Messages are filtered by topic. Topics are defined in a tree format, represented by a path string. Clients may subscribe to specific topics, or sub-topic groups by providing the appropriate path. For example, suppose we define two topics for our app like so:

```
examples/one
examples/two
```

A client may subscribe to either topic by subscribing to the exact full path string. However, if the client prefers to subscribe to both topics (and any others that may be created later in this group), it may conveniently do so by subscribing as follows:

```
examples/#
```

The '#' wildcard character indicates that all topics in the examples group are of interest to this client.

In this recipe we'll focus on implementing the client app using the MQTT library on the Android device. IBM provides excellent tools for development and testing of the other components, which we'll expose here as well.

How It Works

The MQTT Java library may be freely downloaded from IBM at the following location: www-01.ibm.com/support/docview.wss?uid=swg24006006. The download archive contains sample code, API Javadoc, and usage documentation, in addition to the library JAR.

Locate the wmqtt.jar file from within the download archive. This is the library that must be included into the Android project. By convention, this means a /libs directory should be created in your project directory, and this JAR should be inserted there.

For testing your client implementation, IBM provides the Really Small Message Broker (RSMB). RSMB may be downloaded at the following location: www.alphaworks.ibm.com/tech/rsmb.

RSMB is a multi-platform download that includes command-line tools for both the message broker and an application to publish messages. The license provided by IBM for this tool forbids it from being used in a production environment; at that point you will need to roll your own or use one of the many open source implementations available. However, for development of the mobile client, RSMB couldn't be more perfect.

Client Sample

Since monitoring for incoming push messages is an indefinite, long-standing operation, let's take a look at an example that puts the basic functionality into a service.

Listing 7–9 presents the source code to an example MQTT service.

Listing 7–9. *MQTT Example Service*

```java
//ClientService.java
package com.apress.pushclient;

import android.app.AlarmManager;
import android.app.PendingIntent;
import android.app.Service;
import android.content.BroadcastReceiver;
import android.content.Context;
import android.content.Intent;
import android.content.IntentFilter;
import android.os.Handler;
import android.os.IBinder;
import android.os.Message;
import android.widget.Toast;
//Imports required from the MQTT Library JAR
import com.ibm.mqtt.IMqttClient;
import com.ibm.mqtt.MqttClient;
import com.ibm.mqtt.MqttException;
import com.ibm.mqtt.MqttPersistenceException;
import com.ibm.mqtt.MqttSimpleCallback;

public class ClientService extends Service implements MqttSimpleCallback {

    //Location where broker is running
    private static final String HOST = HOSTNAME_STRING_HERE;
    private static final String PORT = "1883";
    //30 minute keep-alive ping
    private static final short KEEP_ALIVE = 60 * 30;
    //Unique identifier of this device
    private static final String CLIENT_ID = "apress/"+System.currentTimeMillis();
    //Topic we want to watch for
    private static final String TOPIC = "apress/examples";

    private static final String ACTION_KEEPALIVE =
"com.examples.pushclient.ACTION_KEEPALIVE";

    private IMqttClient mClient;
    private AlarmManager mManager;
    private PendingIntent alarmIntent;

    @Override
    public void onCreate() {
        super.onCreate();
        mManager = (AlarmManager)getSystemService(Context.ALARM_SERVICE);

        Intent intent = new Intent(ACTION_KEEPALIVE);
        alarmIntent = PendingIntent.getBroadcast(this, 0, intent, 0);
```

```java
        registerReceiver(mReceiver, new IntentFilter(ACTION_KEEPALIVE));

        try {
            //Format: tcp://hostname@port
            String connectionString = String.format("%s%s@%s", MqttClient.TCP_ID, HOST,
PORT);

            mClient = MqttClient.createMqttClient(connectionString, null);
        } catch (MqttException e) {
            e.printStackTrace();
            //Can't continue without a client
            stopSelf();
        }
    }

    @Override
    public void onStart(Intent intent, int startId) {
        //Callback on Android devices prior to 2.0
        handleCommand(intent);
    }

    @Override
    public int onStartCommand(Intent intent, int flags, int startId) {
        //Callback on Android devices 2.0 and later
        handleCommand(intent);
        //If Android kills this service, we want it back when possible
        return START_STICKY;
    }

    private void handleCommand(Intent intent) {
        try {
            //Make a connection
            mClient.connect(CLIENT_ID, true, KEEP_ALIVE);
            //Target MQTT callbacks here
            mClient.registerSimpleHandler(this);
            //Subscribe to a topic
            String[] topics = new String[] { TOPIC };
            //QoS of 0 indicates fire once and forget
            int[] qos = new int[] { 0 };
            mClient.subscribe(topics, qos);

            //Schedule a ping
            scheduleKeepAlive();
        } catch (MqttException e) {
            e.printStackTrace();
        }
    }

    @Override
    public void onDestroy() {
        super.onDestroy();
        unregisterReceiver(mReceiver);
        unscheduleKeepAlive();

        if(mClient != null) {
            try {
                mClient.disconnect();
                mClient.terminate();
```

```java
        } catch (MqttPersistenceException e) {
            e.printStackTrace();
        }
        mClient = null;
    }
}

//Handle incoming message from remote
private Handler mHandler = new Handler() {
    @Override
    public void handleMessage(Message msg) {
        String incoming = (String)msg.obj;
        Toast.makeText(ClientService.this, incoming, Toast.LENGTH_SHORT).show();
    }
};

//Handle ping alarms to keep the connection alive
private BroadcastReceiver mReceiver = new BroadcastReceiver() {
    @Override
    public void onReceive(Context context, Intent intent) {
        if(mClient == null) {
            return;
        }
        //Ping the MQTT service
        try {
            mClient.ping();
        } catch (MqttException e) {
            e.printStackTrace();
        }
        //Schedule the next alarm
        scheduleKeepAlive();
    }
};

private void scheduleKeepAlive() {
    long nextWakeup = System.currentTimeMillis() + (KEEP_ALIVE * 1000);
    mManager.set(AlarmManager.RTC_WAKEUP, nextWakeup, alarmIntent);
}

private void unscheduleKeepAlive() {
    mManager.cancel(alarmIntent);
}

/* MqttSimpleCallback Methods */

@Override
public void connectionLost() throws Exception {
    mClient.terminate();
    mClient = null;
    stopSelf();
}

@Override
public void publishArrived(String topicName, byte[] payload, int qos, boolean
retained) throws Exception {
    //Be wary of UI related code here!
    //Best to use a Handler for UI or Context operations
```

```
        StringBuilder builder = new StringBuilder();
        builder.append(topicName);
        builder.append('\n');
        builder.append(new String(payload));
        //Pass the message up to our handler
        Message receipt = Message.obtain(mHandler, 0, builder.toString());
        receipt.sendToTarget();
    }

    /*Unused method*/
    //We are not using this service as bound
    //It is explicitly started and stopped with no direct connection
    @Override
    public IBinder onBind(Intent intent) { return null; }
}
```

> **IMPORTANT:** This Service will most likely be communicating with a remote server, so you must declare android.permission.INTERNET in the application manifest, as well as the Service itself with a <service> tag.

In order to subclass Service, an implementation of onBind() must be provided. In this case, our example does not need to provide a Binder interface because activities will never need to hook directly into call methods. Therefore, this required method simply returns null. This Service is designed to receive explicit instructions to start and stop, running for an indeterminate amount of time in between.

When the Service is created, an MqttClient object is also instantiated using createMqttClient(); this client takes the location of the message broker host as a string. The connection string is in the format of tcp://hostname@port. In the example, the chosen port number is 1883, which is the default port number for MQTT communication. If you choose a different port number, you should verify that your server implementation is running on a port to match.

From this point forward, the Service remains idle until a start command is issued. Upon receipt of a start command (issued externally by a call to Context.startService()), either onStart() or onStartCommand() will be called (depending on the version of Android running on the device). In the latter case, the service returns START_STICKY, a constant telling the system that it should leave this service running, and restart it if it's prematurely killed for memory reasons.

Once started, the service will register with the MQTT message broker, passing a unique client ID and a keep-alive time. For simplicity, this example defines the client ID in terms of the current time when the service was created. In production, a more unique identifier such as the Wi-Fi MAC Address or TelephonyManager.getDeviceId() might be more appropriate, keeping in mind that neither of those choices is guaranteed to appear on all devices.

The keep-alive parameter is the time (in seconds) that the broker should use to time-out the connection to this client. In order to avoid this time-out, clients should post a message or regularly ping the broker. We will shortly discuss this task more fully.

During startup, the client is also subscribed to a single topic. Notice that the `subscribe()` method takes arrays as parameters; a client may subscribe to multiple topics within a single method call. Each topic is also subscribed with a requested quality of service (QoS) value. The most tactful value to request for mobile devices is zero, telling the broker to only send a message once without requiring confirmation. Doing so reduces the amount of handshaking required between the broker and the device.

With the connection live and registered, any incoming messages from the remote broker will result in a call to `publishArrived()`, with the data about the message passed in. This method may be called on any of the background threads that `MqttClient` creates and maintains, so it's important to not do anything related to the main thread directly here. In the example's case, all incoming messages are passed to a local `Handler`, to guarantee that the resulting `Toast` is posted on the main thread for display.

There's one upkeep task required when implementing an MQTT client, and that is pinging the broker to keep the connection alive. To accomplish this task, the `Service` registers with the `AlarmManager` to trigger a broadcast on a schedule matching the keep-alive parameter. This task must be done even if the device is currently asleep, so the alarm is set each time with `AlarmManager.RTC_WAKEUP`. When each alarm triggers, the `Service` simply calls `MqttClient.ping()` and schedules the next keep-alive update.

Due to the persistent nature of this requirement, it is prudent to select a low-frequency interval for the keep-alive timer; we chose 30 minutes in this example. This timer value represents a balance between reducing the frequency of required updates on the device (to save power and bandwidth), and the latency before the remote broker becomes aware that a remote device is no longer there and times it out.

When the push service is no longer required, an external call to `Context.stopService()` will result in a call to `onDestroy()`. Here, the `Service` tears down the MQTT connection, removes any pending alarms, and releases all resources. The second callback implemented as part of the `MqttSimpleCallback` interface is `onConnectionLost()`, indicating an unexpected disconnect. In these cases, the `Service` stops itself much in the same way as a manual stop request.

Testing the Client

In order to test messaging with the device, you will need to start up an instance of RSMB on your machine. From the command line, navigate into the location where you unarchived the download, and then into the directory that matches your computer's platform (Windows, Linux, Mac OS X). From here, simply execute the `broker` command and the broker service will begin running on your machine, located at `localhost:1883`:

```
CWNAN9999I Really Small Message Broker
CWNAN9997I Licensed Materials - Property of IBM
CWNAN9996I Copyright IBM Corp. 2007, 2010 All Rights Reserved
...
```

```
CWNAN0014I MQTT protocol starting, listening on port 1883
```

At this point, you may connect to the service and publish messages or register to receive messages. To put this Service to the test, Listings 7–10 and 7–11 create a simple Activity that may be used to start and stop the service.

Listing 7–10. *res/menu/home.xml*

```xml
<?xml version="1.0" encoding="utf-8"?>
<menu xmlns:android="http://schemas.android.com/apk/res/android">
  <item
    android:id="@+id/menu_start"
    android:title="Start Service" />
  <item
    android:id="@+id/menu_stop"
    android:title="Stop Service" />
</menu>
```

Listing 7–11. *Activity Controlling MQTT Service*

```java
//ClientActivity.java
package com.apress.pushclient;

import android.app.Activity;
import android.content.Intent;
import android.os.Bundle;
import android.view.Menu;
import android.view.MenuItem;

public class ClientActivity extends Activity {

    private Intent serviceIntent;

    @Override
    public void onCreate(Bundle savedInstanceState) {
        super.onCreate(savedInstanceState);

        serviceIntent = new Intent(this, ClientService.class);
    }

    @Override
    public boolean onCreateOptionsMenu(Menu menu) {
        getMenuInflater().inflate(R.menu.home, menu);
        return true;
    }

    @Override
    public boolean onOptionsItemSelected(MenuItem item) {
        switch(item.getItemId()) {
        case R.id.menu_start:
            startService(serviceIntent);
            return true;
        case R.id.menu_stop:
            stopService(serviceIntent);
            return true;
        }
```

```
        return super.onOptionsItemSelected(item);
    }
}
```

Listing 7–11 creates an `Intent` that will be used by two menu options to start and stop the service at will (see Figure 7–5). By pressing the MENU button and selecting "Start Service," the MQTT connection will start up and register the device for messages with the topic "apress/examples."

Figure 7–5. *Activity to Control Service*

> **NOTE:** The HOST value in the example service needs to point to the machine where your RSMB instance is running. Even if you are testing in the emulator on the same machine, this value is **NOT** `localhost`! At the very least, you must point the emulator or device to the IP address of the machine where your broker is running.

With the Android device successfully registered for push messages from the broker, open up another command line window and navigate to the same directory from where `broker` was executed. Another command, `stdinpub`, can be used to connect to the broker instance and publish messages down to the device. From the command line type the following command:

```
stdinpub apress/examples
```

This command will register a client to publish messages with a topic matching our example. You will see the following as a result:

```
Using topic apress/examples
Connecting
```

Now you may type any message you like, followed by Enter. Upon pressing Enter, the message will be sent to the broker, and pushed out to the registered device. Do this as many times as you like, and then use CTRL-C to break out of the program. CTRL-C will also work to terminate the broker service.

> **TIP:** RSMB also includes a third command, `stdoutsub`, to subscribe to a set of topics with your local broker service. This command lets you completely close the loop, and test whether problems are occurring in the test suite or in your Android app.

Summary

Smart Android developers deliver their apps to market faster by taking advantage of libraries, which reduce development time by providing previously created and tested code.

This chapter's initial recipes introduced you to the topics of creating and using your own libraries. Specifically, you learned how to create and use Java library JARs whose code was restricted to Java 5 (or earlier) APIs, and Android library projects.

Although you'll probably create your own libraries to save yourself from reinventing the wheel, you might also need to use someone else's library. For example, if you need a simple charting library, you might want to look at kiChart, which facilitates the display of bar and line charts.

If you're working with the cloud, you might decide to use Google's C2DM framework. However, because this framework has a number of drawbacks (such as requiring a minimum of API level 8), you might consider utilizing IBM's MQTT library to implement lightweight push messaging in your apps.

Scripting Layer for Android

Scripting Layer for Android (SL4A), which was previously known as Android Scripting Environment, is a platform for installing scripting language interpreters on Android devices and running scripts via these interpreters. Scripts can access many of the APIs that are available to Android apps, but with a greatly simplified interface that makes it easier to get things done.

> **NOTE:** SL4A currently supports only the Python, Perl, JRuby, Lua, BeanShell, Rhino JavaScript, and Tcl scripting languages.
>
> You can run scripts interactively in a *terminal window* (command window), in the background, or via Locale (www.twofortyfouram.com/). *Locale* is an Android app that lets you run scripts at predetermined times, or when other criteria are met (running a script to change your phone's ringer mode to vibrate when you enter a theater or a courtroom, for example).

Installing SL4A

Before you can use SL4A, you must install it. You can download the latest release's APK file (sl4a_r3.apk at time of writing) from its Google-hosted project website (http://code.google.com/p/android-scripting) to your device. Do so by using your barcode reader app to scan the website's displayed barcode image.

If you're using the Android emulator, click the barcode image to download sl4a_r3.apk. Then execute adb install sl4a_r3.apk to install this app on the currently running emulated device. (You might have to make several attempts if you receive a device offline message.) Figure A–1 reveals SL4A's icon on the app launcher screen.

Figure A–1. *Click the SL4A icon to start exploring the Scripting Layer for Android app.*

Exploring SL4A

Now that you've installed SL4A, you'll want to learn how to use this app. Click the SL4A icon, and you'll be taken to a Scripts screen that presents a list of installed scripts (and other items). Click the MENU button and SL4A will reveal the Scripts menu. Figure A–2 shows you an initially empty list and this menu's choices.

Figure A–2. *SL4A's Scripts screen shows that no scripts have yet been installed.*

The Scripts menu is organized into the following six categories:

- **Add:** Add folders (for organizing scripts and other items), HTML pages with embedded JavaScript code, shell scripts, and scripts obtained by scanning barcode images to the Scripts screen. Folders and other items are stored in the device's /sdcard/sl4a/scripts directory.

- **View:** View installed interpreters (such as the Python interpreter), *triggers* (a kind of intent for running scripts repeatedly whether or not the device is sleeping, or for running scripts conditionally based on ringer mode changes), and *logcat* (a tool for viewing system debug output). SL4A comes with only the shell interpreter and HTML and JavaScript. Also, the Android emulator doesn't appear to support triggers.

- **Search:** Create and display a list of only those scripts and other items that match entered search text. The search logic outputs "No matches found" when there are no matches.

- **Preferences:** Configure general, script manager, script editor, and terminal options.

- **Refresh:** Redisplay the Scripts screen to reveal any changes; perhaps a script running in the background has updated this list.

- **Help:** Get help on using SL4A from SL4A's wiki documentation (`http://code.google.com/p/android-scripting/wiki/TableOfContents?tm=6`), YouTube screencasts, and terminal help documentation.

Adding a Shell Script

Let's add a simple shell script to the Scripts screen. Accomplish this task by completing the following steps:

1. Click the MENU button in the phone controls.

2. Click the Add menu item in the menu that appears at the bottom of the screen.

3. Click Shell from the pop-up Add menu.

4. Enter **hw.sh** into the single-line textfield at the top of the resulting script editor screen; this is the shell script's filename.

5. Enter **#! /system/bin/sh** followed by **echo "hello, world"** into the multiline textfield on separate lines. The former line tells Android where to find sh (the shell program), but doesn't appear to be essential; and the second line tells Android to output some text to the standard output device.

6. Click the MENU button in the phone controls.

7. Click the Save & Exit menu item from the resulting menu.

Figure A–3 shows you what the edit screen looks like prior to clicking Save & Exit.

Figure A–3. *SL4A's script editor screen prompts for a filename and a script.*

The Scripts screen should now present a single hw.sh item. Click this item and you'll see the icon menu that appears in Figure A–4.

Figure A–4. *The icon menu lets you run a script in a terminal window, run a script in the background, edit the script, rename the script, or delete the script.*

You have the option of running the script in a terminal window (the leftmost icon) or in the background (the next-to-leftmost "gear" icon). Click either icon to run this shell script. However, it's possible that you won't see any output should you run this script on a Windows platform with the Android emulator (possibly due to a bug in SL4A itself).

Accessing the Linux Shell

If you cannot observe hw.sh's output by running this script in the previously mentioned fashion, you can still observe its output by running this script via the Linux shell. Follow these steps to accomplish this task:

1. Select View from the Scripts screen's menu.

2. Select Interpreters from the pop-up list of viewables.

3. Select Shell from the Interpreters screen to present a terminal window.

4. Execute cd /sdcard/sl4a/scripts at the terminal window's $ prompt to switch to the directory containing hw.sh.

5. Execute sh hw.sh at the $ prompt to run hw.sh.

Figure A–5 shows you how to run hw.sh from the shell. It also reveals what happens when you click the BACK button in the phone controls.

Figure A–5. *Click the BACK button to get a "Confirm exit. Kill process?" message, and click the Yes button to exit the shell.*

Installing the Python Interpreter

Although you can't do much with SL4A, you can use this special app to install Python or another scripting language. Complete the following steps to install Python:

1. Select View from the main menu.

2. Select Interpreters from the pop-up list of viewables.

3. Press the MENU phone control button.

4. Select Add from the menu. Figure A–6 reveals the Add interpreters list.

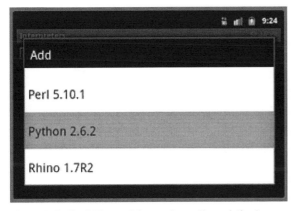

Figure A–6. *The Add menu lets you choose the scripting language interpreter that you want to install.*

5. Click Python 2.6.2. SL4A will start to download this interpreter from the SL4A website. When the download finishes, SL4A presents Figure A–7's notification.

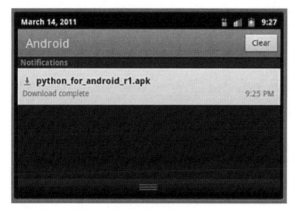

Figure A–7. *Click the notification to tell SL4A that you want to install Python.*

Click the notification and SL4A responds by presenting a dialog box (see Figure A–8) that asks you if you really want to install the Python app.

Figure A–8. *Click Install to begin installation.*

Click the Install button. SL4A presents Figure A–9's installing screen.

Figure A–9. *The installing screen keeps you entertained during the install.*

Finally, when installation finishes, SL4A presents the application-installed screen shown in Figure A–10.

Figure A–10. *Click the Open button to download supporting files.*

Although the Python app is installed, supporting archives containing items such as sample scripts have not been installed. Click the Open button to download these archives. Figure A–11 reveals part of the resulting screen, which contains only a single Install button.

Figure A–11. *Click the Install button to begin downloading and installing supporting files.*

After clicking Install, SL4A begins the task of downloading these archives and extracting their files. For example, Figure A–12 reveals the contents of the python_r7.zip file being extracted.

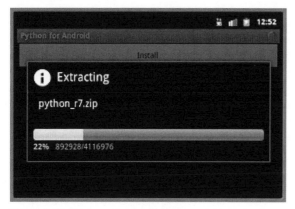

Figure A–12. *It takes a couple of minutes to download and extract all of the supporting files on the Android emulator.*

When this process finishes, you will see a screen similar to that shown in Figure A–11, but with an Uninstall button. Don't click Uninstall at this point. However, if you click the BACK button, you should now see Python 2.6.2 appearing in the Interpreters list, as in Figure A–13.

Figure A–13. *Click Python 2.6.2 to run the Python interpreter.*

If you now click Python 2.6.2, you can run the Python interpreter. Figure A–14 reveals the introductory screen.

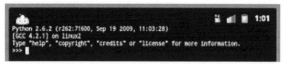

Figure A–14. *Go ahead and enter some Python code. Type **help** if you're new to Python.*

INSTALLING INTERPRETERS INDEPENDENTLY OF SL4A

When you visit SL4A's project website (http://code.google.com/p/android-scripting), you'll discover several standalone interpreter APKs, such as PythonForAndroid_r4.apk. These APKs contain newer versions of their respective interpreters than what you obtain when you install interpreters from within SL4A.

For example, click the PythonForAndroid_r4.apk link if you want to install the latest Python release (at the time of writing). On the resulting web page, scan the barcode with your Android device, or (for the Android emulator) click the PythonForAndroid_r4.apk link to save this APK to your hard drive, and then execute adb install PythonForAndroid_r4.apk to install this APK on the emulated device. Figure A–15 shows the resulting icon.

Figure A–15. *Click the Python for Android icon to install supporting files and perform other operations.*

Click the Python for Android icon and this app presents buttons for installing supporting files and performing other tasks (see Figure A–16).

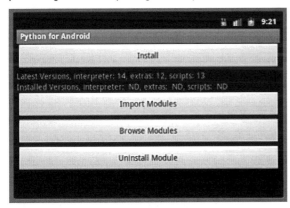

Figure A–16. *Python for Android's screen lets you install supporting files and perform other operations. It also presents version information and more.*

You can install the other standalone interpreter APKs in a similar manner.

Scripting with Python

Now that you've installed Python 2.6.2, you'll want to try out this interpreter. Figure A–17 reveals a sample session with Python, which consists of printing the version number (obtained from the sys module's version member), printing the math module's pi constant, and executing the exit() function to terminate the Python interpreter.

Figure A–17. *One way to terminate the Python interpreter is to execute Python's* exit() *function.*

You'll also want to access the Android API from this interpreter. You can accomplish this task by importing the android module, instantiating this module's Android class, and invoking this class's methods. Figure A–18 presents a session that follows this approach in order to present a toast message.

Figure A–18. *Android methods return* Result *objects with identifier, result, and error information.*

The Android class's methods return Result objects. Each object provides id, result, and error fields: id uniquely identifies the object, result contains the method's return value (or None if the method doesn't return a value), and error identifies any error that may have occurred (or None if no error occurred).

If you're interested in a more ambitious Python script, you'll want to check out the sample scripts that are installed with the Python interpreter, and which can be accessed from the Scripts screen (see Figure A–2). For example, the say_time.py script, whose code is shown in the following code, uses Android's ttsSpeak() function to speak the current time:

```
import android; import time
droid = android.Android()
droid.ttsSpeak(time.strftime("%_I %M %p on %A, %B %_e, %Y "))
```

Android NDK

The Android Native Development Kit (NDK) helps you boost an app's performance by converting C/C++ source code (in which you write the app's performance-critical sections) to native code libraries that run on Android devices. The NDK provides headers and libraries for building activities, handling user input, using hardware sensors, and more. Your app's files (including any native code libraries that you create) are packaged into APKs; they execute inside of an Android device's Dalvik virtual machine.

NOTE: Think carefully about whether you need to integrate native code into your app. Basing even part of an app on native code increases its complexity and makes it harder to debug. Also, not every app experiences a performance boost (apart from that already provided by Dalvik's Just-In-Time compiler, introduced in Android 2.2). Native code is often best used with processor-intensive apps, but only where performance profiling has revealed a bottleneck that could be solved by recoding that portion of the app in native code. For example, a game app with a computationally intensive physics simulation that profiling shows to run poorly would benefit from having these computations carried out natively.

Installing the NDK

If you believe that your app can benefit from being partly expressed in C/C++, you'll need to install the NDK. Before doing so, complete the following preparatory tasks:

- Verify that your development platform is one of Windows XP (32-bit) or Vista (32- or 64-bit), Mac OS X 10.4.8 or later (x86 only), or Linux (32- or 64-bit, tested on Linux Ubuntu Dapper Drake). The NDK officially supports only these development platforms.

- Install the Android SDK (version 1.5 or later is supported by the NDK) if this software isn't already installed.

■ Verify that your platform contains GNU Make 3.81 or later and a recent version of GNU Awk. To run Make and Awk on a Windows platform, you must first install *Cygwin*, which is a command-line-based and Unix-like shell tool for running Linux-like programs on Windows.

INSTALLING CYGWIN

Cygwin 1.7 or higher must be installed to run Make and Awk on Windows platforms. Complete the following steps to install Cygwin:

1. Point your browser to http://cygwin.com/.

2. Click the setup.exe link and save this file to your harddrive.

3. Run this program on your Windows platform to begin installing Cygwin version 1.7.8-1 (the latest version at time of writing). If you choose a different install location, make sure that the directory path contains no spaces.

4. When you reach the Select Packages screen, select the Devel category and look for an entry in this category whose Package column presents make: The GNU version of the 'make' utility. In the entry's New column, click the word Skip; this word should change to 3.81-2. Also, the Bin? column's checkbox should be checked – see Figure B–1.

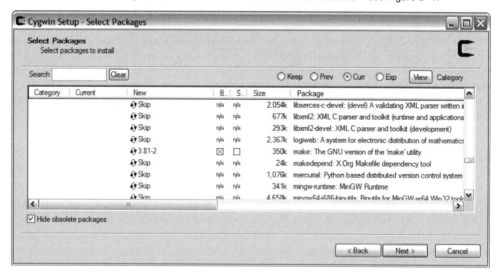

Figure B–1. *Make sure that 3.81-2 appears in the New column and that the check box in the Bin? column is checked before clicking Next.*

5. Click the Next button and continue the installation.

Cygwin installs an entry in the start menu and an icon on the desktop. Click this icon and you'll see the Cygwin console (which is based on the Bash shell) shown in Figure B–2.

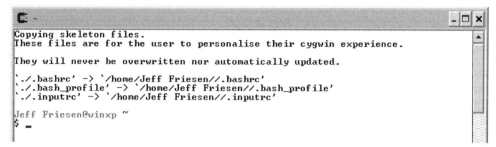

Figure B–2. *Cygwin's console displays initialization messages the first time it starts running.*

If you want to verify that Cygwin provides access to GNU Make 3.81 or later and GNU Awk, accomplish this task by entering the commands shown in Figure B–3.

```
Jeff Friesen@winxp ~
$ make -v
GNU Make 3.81
Copyright (C) 2006  Free Software Foundation, Inc.
This is free software; see the source for copying conditions.
There is NO warranty; not even for MERCHANTABILITY or FITNESS FOR A
PARTICULAR PURPOSE.

This program built for i686-pc-cygwin

Jeff Friesen@winxp ~
$ awk
Usage: awk [POSIX or GNU style options] -f progfile [--] file ...
Usage: awk [POSIX or GNU style options] [--] 'program' file ...
POSIX options:          GNU long options:
        -f progfile             --file=progfile
        -F fs                   --field-separator=fs
        -v var=val              --assign=var=val
        -m[fr] val
```

Figure B–3. *The awk tool doesn't display a version number.*

You can learn more about Cygwin by checking out cygwin.com as well as Wikipedia's Cygwin entry (http://en.wikipedia.org/wiki/Cygwin).

Continuing, point your browser to http://developer.android.com/sdk/ndk/index.html and download one of the following NDK packages for your platform – Revision 5b (January 2011) is the latest version at time of writing:

- android-ndk-r5B-windows.zip (Windows)

- android-ndk-r5B-darwin-x86.tar.bz2 (Mac OS X: Intel)

- android-ndk-r5B-linux-x86.tar.bz2 (Linux 32/64-bit: x86)

After downloading your chosen package, unarchive it and move its android-ndk-r5b home directory to a more suitable location, perhaps to the same directory that contains the Android SDK's home directory.

Exploring the NDK

Now that you've installed the NDK on your platform, you might want to explore its home directory to discover what the NDK offers. The following list describes those directories and files that are located in the home directory for the Windows-based NDK:

- build contains the files that comprise the NDK's build system.

- docs contains the NDK's HTML-based documentation files.

- Platforms contains subdirectories that contain header files and shared libraries for each of the Android SDK's installed Android platforms.

- samples contains various sample apps that demonstrate different aspects of the NDK.

- sources contains the source code and prebuilt binaries for various shared libraries, such as cpufeatures (detect the target device's CPU family and the optional features it supports) and stlport (multiplatform C++ standard library). Android NDK 1.5 required that developers organize their native code library projects under this directory. Starting with Android NDK 1.6, native code libraries are stored in jni subdirectories of their Android SDK project directories.

- tests contains scripts and sources to perform automated testing of the NDK. They are useful for testing a custom-built NDK.

- toolchains contains compilers, linkers, and other tools for generating native ARM (Advanced Risc Machine, the CPU used by Android, see http://en.wikipedia.org/wiki/ARM_architecture) binaries on Linux, OS X, and Windows (with Cygwin) platforms.

- documentation.html is the entry-point into the NDK's documentation.

- GNUmakefile is the default make file used by GNU Make.

- ndk-build is a shell script that simplifies building machine code.

- ndk-gdb is a shell script for easily launching a native debugging session for your NDK-generated machine code.

- README.TXT welcomes you to the NDK, and identifies various documentation files that inform you about changes in the current release, provide an overview of the NDK, and so on.

- RELEASE.TXT contains the NDK's release number.

Each of the platforms directory's subdirectories contains header files and shared libraries that target stable native APIs. Google guarantees that the following APIs will be supported in all later releases of the platform:

- Android logging (liblog)

- Android native app APIs

- C library (`libc`)

- C++ minimal support (`stlport`)

- JNI interface APIs

- Math library (`libm`)

- OpenGL ES 1.1 and OpenGL ES 2.0 (3D graphics libraries) APIs

- OpenSL ES native audio library APIs

- Pixel buffer access for Android 2.2 and above (`libjnigraphics`)

- Zlib compression (`libz`)

> **CAUTION:** Native system libraries not present in this list are not stable and may change in future versions of the Android platform. Do not use them.

Greetings from the NDK

Perhaps the easiest way to become familiar with NDK programming is to create a small app that calls a native function that returns a Java `String` object. For example, Listing B–1's NDKGreetings single-activity-based app calls a native `getGreetingMessage()` method to return a greeting message, which it displays via a dialog box.

Listing B–1. *NDKGreetings.java*

```java
// NDKGreetings.java

package com.apress.ndkgreetings;

import android.app.Activity;
import android.app.AlertDialog;

import android.os.Bundle;

public class NDKGreetings extends Activity
{
    static
    {
        System.loadLibrary("NDKGreetings");
    }
    private native String getGreetingMessage();
    @Override
    public void onCreate(Bundle savedInstanceState)
    {
        super.onCreate(savedInstanceState);
        setContentView(R.layout.main);
        String greeting = getGreetingMessage();
        new AlertDialog.Builder(this).setMessage(greeting).show();
    }
}
```

Listing B–1's NDKGreetings class reveals the following three important features of every app that incorporates native code:

■ Native code is stored in an external library that must be loaded before its code can be invoked. Libraries are typically loaded at class-loading time via a call to the System.loadLibrary() method. This method takes a single String argument that identifies the library without its lib prefix and .so suffix. In this example, the actual library file is named libNDKGreetings.so.

■ One or more native methods are declared that correspond to functions located within the library. A native method is identified to Java by prefixing its return type with keyword native.

■ A native method is invoked like any other Java method. Behind the scenes, Dalvik makes sure that the corresponding native function (expressed in C/C++) is invoked in the library.

Listing B–2 presents the C source code to a native code library that implements getGreetingMessage() via the Java Native Interface (JNI).

Listing B–2. *NDKGreetings.c*

```
// NDKGreetings.c

#include <jni.h>

jstring
  Java_com_apress_ndkgreetings_NDKGreetings_getGreetingMessage(JNIEnv* env,
                                                                jobject this)
{
  return (*env)->NewStringUTF(env, "Greetings from the NDK!");
}
```

This listing first specifies an #include preprocessor directive that includes the contents of the jni.h header file when the source code is compiled.

The listing then declares the native function equivalent of Java's getGreetingMessage() method. This native function's header reveals several important items:

■ The native function's return type is specified as jstring. This type is defined in jni.h and represents Java's String object type at the native code level.

■ The function's name must begin with the Java package and class names that identify where the associated native method is declared.

■ The type of the function's first parameter, env, is specified as a JNIEnv pointer. JNIEnv, which is defined in jni.h, is a C struct that identifies JNI functions that can be called to interact with Java.

- The type of the function's second parameter, this, is specified as jobject. This type, which is defined in jni.h, identifies an arbitrary Java object at the native code level. The argument passed to this parameter is the implicit this instance that the JVM passes to any Java instance method.

The function's single line of code dereferences its env parameter in order to call the NewStringUTF() JNI function. NewStringUTF() converts it second argument, a C string, to its jstring equivalent (where the string is encoded via the Unicode UTF encoding standard), and returns this equivalent Java string, which is then returned to Java.

> **NOTE:** When working with the JNI in the context of the C language, you must dereference the JNIEnv parameter (*env, for example) in order to call a JNI function. Also, you must pass the JNIEnv parameter as the first argument to the JNI function. In contrast, C++ doesn't require this verbosity: you don't have to dereference the JNIEnv parameter, and you don't have to pass this parameter as the first argument to the JNI function. For example, Listing B–2's C-based (*env)->NewStringUTF(env, "Greetings from the NDK!") function call is expressed as env->NewStringUTF("Greetings from the NDK!") in C++.

Building and Running NDKGreetings with the Android SDK

To build NDKGreetings with the Android SDK, first use the SDK's android tool to create an NDKGreetings project. Assuming a Windows XP platform, a C:\prj\dev hierarchy in which the NDKGreetings project is to be stored (in C:\prj\dev\NDKGreetings), and that the Android 2.3 platform target corresponds to integer ID 1, invoke the following command (split across two lines for readability) from anywhere in the filesystem to create NDKGreetings:

```
android create project -t 1 -p C:\prj\dev\NDKGreetings -a NDKGreetings
                       -k com.apress.ndkgreetings
```

This command creates various directories and files within C:\prj\dev\NDKGreetings. For example, the src directory contains the com\apress\ndkgreetings directory structure, and the final ndkgreetings directory contains a skeletal NDKGreetings.java source file. Replace this skeletal file's contents with Listing B–1.

Continuing, create a jni directory within C:\prj\dev\NDKGreetings, and copy Listing B–2 to C:\prj\dev\NDKGreetings\jni. Also, copy Listing B–3 to C:\prj\dev\NDKGreetings\jni\Android.mk, which is a GNU make file (explained in the NDK documentation) that's used to create the libNDKGreetings.so library.

Listing B–3. *Android.mk*

```
LOCAL_PATH := ./jni

include $(CLEAR_VARS)

LOCAL_MODULE    := NDKGreetings
```

```
LOCAL_SRC_FILES := NDKGreetings.c
```

```
include $(BUILD_SHARED_LIBRARY)
```

If you're working on a Windows platform, run Cygwin (if not running) and, from within Cygwin, set the current directory to C:\prj\dev\NDKGreetings. See Figure B–4.

```
C /cygdrive/c/prj/dev/NDKGreetings                                      _ □ ×

Jeff Friesen@winxp ~
$ cd /cygdrive/c/prj/dev/NDKGreetings

Jeff Friesen@winxp /cygdrive/c/prj/dev/NDKGreetings
$ ls -l
total 18
-rwx------+ 1 Jeff Friesen None   660 Mar  7 11:21 AndroidManifest.xml
drwx------+ 1 Jeff Friesen None     0 Mar  7 11:21 bin
-rwx------+ 1 Jeff Friesen None   696 Mar  7 11:21 build.properties
-rwx------+ 1 Jeff Friesen None  3290 Mar  7 11:21 build.xml
-rwx------+ 1 Jeff Friesen None   362 Mar  7 11:21 default.properties
drwx------+ 1 Jeff Friesen None     0 Mar  7 11:31 jni
drwx------+ 1 Jeff Friesen None     0 Mar  7 11:21 libs
-rwx------+ 1 Jeff Friesen None   415 Mar  7 11:21 local.properties
-rwx------+ 1 Jeff Friesen None  1195 Mar  7 11:21 proguard.cfg
drwx------+ 1 Jeff Friesen None     0 Mar  7 11:21 res
drwx------+ 1 Jeff Friesen None     0 Mar  7 11:21 src

Jeff Friesen@winxp /cygdrive/c/prj/dev/NDKGreetings
$
```

Figure B–4. *The path to* /prj/dev/NDKGreetings *begins with a* /cygdrive/c *prefix.*

Assuming that the NDK home directory is android-ndk-r5b, and that it's located in the root directory of drive C, execute the following command to build the library:

```
../../../android-ndk-r5b/ndk-build
```

If Cygwin succeeds in building the library, it displays the following messages:

```
Compile thumb  : NDKGreetings <= NDKGreetings.c
SharedLibrary  : libNDKGreetings.so
Install        : libNDKGreetings.so => libs/armeabi/libNDKGreetings.so
```

This output indicates that libNDKGreetings.so is located in the armeabi subdirectory of your NDKGreetings project directory's libs subdirectory.

> **TIP:** If this command outputs a message that includes the phrase No rule to make target, edit Android.mk to remove extraneous space characters and try again.

Assuming that C:\prj\dev\NDKGreetings is current, execute ant debug (from Cygwin's shell or the normal Windows command window) to create NDKGreetings-debug.apk.

This APK file is placed in the NDKGreetings project directory's bin subdirectory. To verify that libNDKGreetings.so is part of this APK, run the following command from bin:

```
jar tvf NDKGreetings-debug.apk
```

You should observe a line containing lib/armeabi/libNDKGreetings.so among the jar command's output.

To verify that the app works, start the emulator, which you can accomplish at the command line by executing the following command:

```
emulator -avd test_AVD
```

This command assumes that you've created the test_AVD device configuration as specified in Chapter 1.

Continuing, install NDKGreetings-debug.apk on the emulated device via the following command:

```
adb install NDKGreetings-debug.apk
```

This command assumes that adb is located in your path. It also assumes that bin is the current directory.

When adb indicates that NDKGreetings-debug.apk has been installed, navigate to the app launcher screen and click the NDKGreetings icon. Figure B–5 shows you the result.

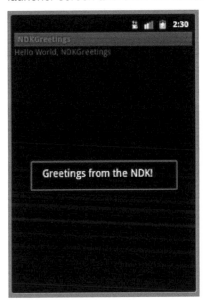

Figure B–5. *Press the Esc key (on Windows) to make the dialog box go away.*

The dialog box displays the "Greetings from the NDK!" message that was obtained by calling the native function in the native code library. It also reveals a faint "Hello World, NDKGreetings" message near the top of the screen. This message originates in the project's default main.xml file that's created by the android tool.

Building and Running NDKGreetings with Eclipse

To build NDKGreetings with Eclipse, first create a new Android project as described in Chapter 1's Recipe 1-10. For your convenience, the steps that you need to follow to accomplish this task are presented in the following:

1. Select New from the File menu, and select Project from the resulting pop-up menu.

2. On the *New Project* dialog box, expand the Android node in the wizard tree, select the Android Project branch below this node, and click the Next button.

3. On the resulting *New Android Project* dialog box, enter **NDKGreetings** into the Project name textfield, uncheck Use Default Location, and enter a path without spaces into the Location textfield; **C:\prj\dev\NDKGreetings** (assuming Windows), for example. This entered name identifies the folder in which the NDKGreetings project is stored.

4. Select the Create new project in workspace radio button if not selected.

5. Under Build Target, check the checkbox of the appropriate Android target to be used as NDGreetings's build target. This target specifies which Android platform you'd like your application to be built against. Assuming that you've installed only the Android 2.3 platform, only this build target should appear and should already be checked.

6. Under Properties, enter **NDK Greetings** into the Application name textfield. This human-readable title will appear on the Android device. Continuing, enter **com.apress.ndkgreetings** into the Package name textfield. This value is the package namespace (following the same rules as for packages in the Java programming language) where all your source code will reside. Check the Create Activity checkbox if not checked and enter **NDKGreetings** as the name of the app's starting activity in the textfield that appears beside this check box. The textfield is disabled when this checkbox is not checked. Finally, enter integer **9** into the Min SDK Version textfield to identify the minimum API Level required to properly run NDKGreetings on the Android 2.3 platform.

7. Click Finish.

Continuing, use Eclipse's Package Explorer to locate the NDKGreetings.java source file node. Double-click this node and replace the skeletal contents shown in the resulting edit window with Listing B–1.

Using Package Explorer, create a jni node below the NDKGreetings project node, add an NDKGreetings.c subnode of jni, replace this node's empty contents with Listing B–2, add a new Android.mk subnode of jni, and replace its empty contents with Listing B–3.

Launch Cygwin and use the cd command to change to the project's folder; for example, cd /cygdrive/c/prj/dev/NDKGreetings. Then, execute ndk-build as demonstrated in the previous section; for example, ../../../android-ndk-r5b/ndk-build. If all goes well, the NDKGreetings project directory's libs subdirectory should contain an armeabi subdirectory, which should contain a libNDKGreetings.so library file.

Finally, select Build Project from the Project menu; the bin subdirectory should contain an NDKGreetings.apk file (if successful). You might want to execute jar tvf NDKGreetings.apk to verify that this file contains lib/armeabi/libNDKGreetings.so.

To run NDKGreetings from Eclipse, select Run from the menubar, and Run from the dropdown menu. If a *Run As* dialog box appears, select Android Application and click OK. Eclipse launches emulator with the test_AVD device, installs NDKGreetings.apk, and runs this app, whose output appears in Figure B–5.

Sampling the NDK

The samples subdirectory of the NDK installation's home directory contains several sample apps that demonstrate different aspects of the NDK:

- bitmap-plasma: An app that demonstrates how to access the pixel buffers of Android android.graphics.Bitmap objects from native code, and uses this capability to generate an old-school "plasma" effect.

- hello-gl2: An app that renders a triangle using OpenGL ES 2.0 vertex and fragment shaders. (If you run this app on the Android emulator, you'll probably receive an error message stating that the app has stopped unexpectedly, because the emulator doesn't support OpenGL ES 2.0 hardware emulation.)

- hello-jni: An app that loads a string from a native method implemented in a shared library and then displays it in the app's user interface. This app is very similar to NDKGreetings.

- hello-neon: An app that shows how to use the cpufeatures library to check CPU capabilities at runtime, and then uses NEON (a marketing name of a SIMD instruction set for the ARM architecture) intrinsics if supported by the CPU. Specifically, the app implements two versions of a tiny benchmark for a FIR filter loop (http://en.wikipedia.org/wiki/Finite_impulse_response), a C version and a NEON-optimized version for devices that support it.

- native-activity: An app that demonstrates how to use the native-app-glue static library to create a *native activity* (an activity implemented entirely in native code).

- `native-audio`: An app that demonstrates how to use native methods to play sounds via OpenSL ES.

- `native-plasma`: A version of `bitmap-plasma` implemented with a native activity.

- `san-angeles`: An app that renders 3D graphics through the native OpenGL ES APIs, while managing activity lifecycle with an `android.opengl.GLSurfaceView` object.

- `two-libs`: An app that loads a shared library dynamically and calls a native method provided by the library. In this case, the method is implemented in a static library imported by the shared library.

You can use Eclipse to build these apps in a similar manner to `NDKGreetings`. For example, carry out the following steps to build `san-angeles`:

1. Select New from the File menu, and select Project from the resulting pop-up menu.

2. On the *New Project* dialog box, expand the Android node in the wizard tree, select the Android Project branch below this node, and click the Next button.

3. On the resulting *New Android Project* dialog box, enter **san-angeles** into the Project name textfield, and select the Create project from existing source radio button.

4. Click the Browse button beside the Location field and, via the *Browse For Folder* dialog box, select the `san-angeles` subdirectory under the `samples` subdirectory of the NDK installation's home directory. Click Ok.

5. Check the Android 2.3 target checkbox (or the Android 2.3.1 or 2.3.3 checkbox, if this is your version) in the Build Target area. Click Finish.

Eclipse responds by creating a `DemoActivity` project that incorporates this sample app's files and displays this project name in its Package Explorer.

Launch Cygwin and change to the project's folder; for example, `cd /cygdrive/c/android-ndk-r5b/samples/san-angeles`. Then, execute `ndk-build`; for example, `../../ndk-build`. If all goes well, the `san-angeles` project directory's `libs` subdirectory should contain an `armeabi` subdirectory containing `libsanangeles.so`.

Finally, select `DemoActivity` from Package Explorer and select Build Project from the Project menu; the `bin` subdirectory should contain a `DemoActivity.apk` file (if successful). You might want to execute `jar tvf DemoActivity.apk` to verify that this file contains `lib/armeabi/libsanangeles.so`.

Select Run from the menubar, and Run from the dropdown menu. If a *Run As* dialog box appears, select Android Application and click OK. Eclipse launches `emulator` with the `test_AVD` device, installs `DemoActivity.apk`, and runs this app. If successful, you should see a screen similar to that shown in Figure B–6.

Figure B–6. *DemoActivity* takes you on a tour of a three-dimensional city.

App Design Guidelines

This book focuses on the mechanics of developing apps using various Android technologies. However, knowing how to create an app is not enough if you want to succeed as an Android developer. You must also know how to design apps that are only available to users with compatible devices, that perform well, that are responsive to their users, and that interact properly with other apps. This appendix's recipes give you the necessary design knowledge so your apps shine.

C–1. Designing Filtered Apps

Problem

When you publish your app to Google's Android Market, you don't want the app to be visible to incompatible devices. You want Android Market to filter your app so that users of these incompatible devices cannot download the app.

Solution

Android runs on many devices, which gives developers a huge potential market. However, not all devices contain the same features (for example, some devices have cameras, whereas other devices don't), so certain apps might not run properly on some devices.

Recognizing this problem, Google provides various market filters that are triggered whenever a user visits Android Market via an Android device. If an app doesn't satisfy a filter, the app isn't made visible to the user. Table C–1 identifies three market filters that are triggered when specific elements are present in an app's manifest file.

Table C–1. *Market Filters Based on Manifest Elements*

Filter Name	Manifest Element	How the Filter Works
Minimum Framework Version	`<uses-sdk>`	An app requires a minimum API level. Devices that don't support that level won't be able to run the app.
		API levels are expressed as integers. For example, integer 9 corresponds to Android 2.3 (API Level 9).
		Example: `<uses-sdk android:minSdkVersion="9"/>` tells Android Market that the app only supports Android 2.3 and later.
		If you don't declare this attribute, Android Market assumes a default value of "1," which indicates that the app is compatible with all versions of Android.
Device Features	`<uses-feature>`	An app can require certain device features to be present on the device. This functionality was introduced in Android 2.0 (API Level 5).
		Example: `<uses-feature android:name="android.hardware.sensor.compass"/>` tells Android Market that the device must have a compass.
		The abstract `android.content.pm.PackageManager` class defines Java constants for `"android.hardware.sensor.compass"` and other feature IDs.
Screen Size	`<supports-screens>`	An app indicates the screen sizes that it's capable of supporting by setting attributes of the `<supports-screens>` element. When the app is published, Android Market uses those attributes to determine whether to show the app to users, based on the screen sizes of their devices.
		Example: `<supports-screens android:smallScreens="false"/>` tells Android Market that the app won't run on devices with QVGA (240-by-320-pixel) screens.
		Apps using API Level 4 or higher default `smallScreens` to `"true;"` previous levels default this attribute to `"false."`
		Android Market generally assumes that the device can adapt smaller layouts to larger screens, but cannot adapt larger layouts to smaller screens. As a result, if an app declares support for "normal" screen size only, Android Market makes the app available to normal- and large-screen devices, but filters the app so that it's not available to small-screen devices.

Android Market also uses other app characteristics (such as the country in which the user with the device is currently located) to determine whether to show or hide an app. Table C–2 identifies three market filters that are triggered when some of these additional characteristics are present.

Table C–2. *Market Filters Based on Manifest Elements*

Filter Name	How the Filter Works
Publishing Status	Only published apps will appear in searches within Android Market. Even if an app is unpublished, it can be installed if users can see it in their Downloads area among their purchased, installed, or recently uninstalled apps. If an app has been suspended, users won't be able to reinstall or update it, even if it appears in their Downloads.
Priced Status	Not all users can see paid apps. To show paid apps, a device must have a SIM card and be running Android 1.1 or later, and it must be in a country (as determined by the SIM carrier) in which paid apps are available.
Country / Carrier Targeting	When you upload your app to Android Market, you can select specific countries to target. The app will only be visible to the countries (carriers) that you select, as follows: ■ A device's carrier (when available) determines its country. If no carrier can be determined, Android Market tries to determine the country based on IP. ■ The carrier is determined based on the device's SIM (for GSM devices), not the current roaming carrier.

C–2. Designing High-Performance Apps

Problem

Apps should perform well, especially on devices with limited amounts of memory. Furthermore, better-performing apps provide less drain on battery power. You want to know how to design your app to have good performance.

Solution

Android devices differ in significant ways. Some devices may have a faster processor than others, some devices may have more memory than others, and some devices may include a Just-In-Time (JIT) compiler, whereas other devices don't have this technology for speeding up executable code by converting sequences of bytecode instructions to equivalent native code sequences on the fly. The following list identifies some things to consider when writing code so that your apps will perform well on any device:

■ **Optimize your code carefully:** Strive to write apps with a solid architecture that doesn't impede performance before thinking about optimizing the code. Once the app is running correctly, profile its code on various devices and look for bottlenecks that slow the app down. Keep in mind that the emulator will give you a false impression of your app's performance. For example, its network connection is based on your development platform's network connection, which is much faster than what you'll probably encounter on many Android devices.

■ **Minimize object creation:** Object creation impacts performance, especially where garbage collection is concerned. You should try to reuse existing objects as much as possible to minimize garbage collection cycles that can temporarily slow down an app. For example, use a `java.lang.StringBuilder` object (or a `java.lang.StringBuffer` object when multiple threads might access this object) to build strings instead of using the string concatenation operator in a loop, which results in unnecessary intermediate `String` objects being created.

■ **Minimize floating-point operations:** Floating-point operations are about twice as slow as integer operations on Android devices; for example, the floating-point-unit-less and JIT-less G1 device. Also, keep in mind that some devices lack a hardware-based integer division instruction, which means that integer division is performed in software. The resulting slowness is especially bothersome where hashtables (that rely on the remainder operator) are concerned.

■ **Use System.arraycopy() wherever you need to perform a copy:** The `java.lang.System` class's `static void arraycopy(Object src, int srcPos, Object dest, int destPos, int length)` method is around nine times faster than a hand-coded loop on a Nexus One with the JIT.

■ **Avoid enums:** Although convenient, enums add to the size of a .dex file and can impact speed. For example, `public enum Directions { UP, DOWN, LEFT, RIGHT }` adds several hundred bytes to a .dex file, compared to the equivalent class with four `public static final ints`.

■ **Use the enhanced for loop syntax:** In general, the enhanced for loop (such as `for (String s: strings) {}`) is faster than the regular for loop (such as `for (int i = 0; i < strings.length; i++)`) on a device without a JIT and no slower then a regular for loop when a JIT is involved. Because the enhanced for loop tends to be slower when iterating over a `java.util.ArrayList` instance, however, a regular for loop should be used instead for arraylist traversal.

You'll also want to choose algorithms and data structures carefully. For example, the linear search algorithm (which searches a sequence of items from start to finish, comparing each item to a search value) examines half of the items on average, whereas the binary search algorithm uses a recursive division technique to locate the search value with few comparisons. For example, where a linear search of 4 billion items averages 2 billion comparisons, binary search performs 32 comparisons at most.

C–3. Designing Responsive Apps

Problem

Apps that are slow to respond to users, or that appear to hang or freeze, risk triggering the *Application Not Responding* dialog box (see Figure C–1), which gives the user the opportunity to kill the app (and probably uninstall it) or keep waiting in the hope that the app will eventually respond.

Figure C–1. *The dreaded Application Not Responding dialog box may result in users uninstalling the app.*

You want to know how to design responsive apps so that you can avoid this dialog box (and quite likely a bad reputation from unimpressed users).

Solution

Android displays the *Application Not Responding* dialog box when an app cannot respond to user input. For example, an app blocking on an I/O operation (often a network access) prevents the main app thread from processing incoming user input events. After an Android-determined length of time, Android concludes that the app is frozen, and displays this dialog box to give the user the option to kill the app.

Similarly, when an app spends too much time building an elaborate in-memory data structure, or perhaps the app is performing an intensive computation (such as calculating the next move in chess or some other game), Android concludes that the app has hung. Therefore, it's always important to make sure these computations are efficient by using techniques such as those described in Recipe C–2.

In these situations, the app should create another thread and perform most of its work on that thread. This is especially true for activities, which should do as little work as possible in key lifecycle callback methods, such as onCreate(Bundle) and onResume(). As a result, the main thread (which drives the user interface event loop) keeps running and Android doesn't conclude that the app has frozen.

NOTE: The activity manager and window manager (see Chapter 1, Figure 1-1) monitor app responsiveness. When they detect no response to an input event (a key press or a screen touch, for example) within 5 seconds, or that a broadcast receiver has not finished executing within 10 seconds, they conclude that the app has frozen and display the *Application Not Responding* dialog box.

C–4. Designing Seamless Apps

Problem

You want to know how to design your apps to interact properly with other apps. Specifically, you want to know what things your app should avoid doing so that it doesn't cause problems for the user (and face the possibility of being uninstalled).

Solution

Your apps must play fair with other apps so that they don't disrupt the user by doing something such as popping up a dialog box when the user is interacting with some activity. Also, you don't want one of your app's activities to lose state when it's paused, leaving the user confused as to why previously entered data is missing when the user returns to the activity. In other words, you want your app to work well with other apps so that it doesn't disrupt the user's experience.

An app that achieves a seamless experience must take the following rules into account:

- **Don't drop data:** Because Android is a mobile platform, another activity can pop up over your app's activity (perhaps an incoming phone call has triggered the Phone app). When this happens, your activity's void `onSaveInstanceState(Bundle outState)` and `onPause()` callback methods are called, and your app will probably be killed. If the user was editing data at the time, the data will be lost unless saved via `onSaveInstanceState()`. The data is later restored in the `onCreate()` or void `onRestoreInstanceState(Bundle savedInstanceState)` method.

- **Don't expose raw data:** It's not a good idea to expose raw data, because other apps must understand your data format. If you change the format, these other apps will break unless updated to take the format changes into account. Instead, you should create a `ContentProvider` instance that exposes the data via a carefully designed API.

- **Don't interrupt the user:** When the user is interacting with an activity, the user won't be happy when interrupted by a pop-up dialog box (perhaps activated via a background service as a result of a `startActivity(Intent)` method call). The preferred way to notify the user is to send a message via the `android.app.NotificationManager` class. The message appears on the status bar and the user can view the message at the user's convenience.

- **Use threads for lengthy activities:** Components that perform lengthy computations or are involved with other time-consuming activities should move this work to another thread. Doing so prevents the *Application Not Responding* dialog box from appearing, and reduces the chance of the user uninstalling your app from the device.

- **Don't overload a single activity screen:** Apps with complex user interfaces should present their user interfaces via multiple activities. That way, the user is not overwhelmed with many items appearing on the screen. Furthermore, your code becomes more maintainable and it also plays nicely with Android's activity stack model.

- **Design your user interfaces to support multiple screen resolutions:** Different Android devices often support different screen resolutions. Some devices can even change screen resolutions on the fly, such as switching to landscape mode. It's therefore important to make sure your layouts and drawables have the flexibility to display themselves properly on various device screens. This task can be accomplished by providing different versions of your artwork (if you use any) for key screen resolutions, and then designing your layout to accommodate various dimensions. (For example, avoid using hard-coded positions and instead use relative layouts.) Do this much and the system handles other tasks; the result is an app that looks great on any device.

- **Assume a slow network:** Android devices come with a variety of network-connectivity options, and some devices are faster than others. However, the lowest common denominator is GPRS (the non-3G data service for GSM networks). Even 3G-capable devices spend lots of time on non3G networks so slow networks will remain a reality for a long time to come. For this reason, always code your apps to minimize network accesses and bandwidth. Don't assume that the network is fast; plan for it to be slow. If your users happen to be on faster networks, their experience only improves.

- **Don't assume a touchscreen or a keyboard:** Android supports various kinds of input devices: some Android devices have full "QWERTY" keyboards, whereas other devices have 40-key, 12-key, or other key configurations. Similarly, some devices have touchscreens, but many won't. Keep these differences in mind when designing your apps. Don't assume specific keyboard layouts unless you want to restrict your app for use only on certain devices.

- **Conserve the device's battery:** Mobile devices are battery powered, and it's important to minimize battery drain. Two of the biggest battery power consumers are the processor and the radio, which is why it's important to write apps that use as few processor cycles, and as little network activity, as possible. Minimizing the amount of processor time occupied by an app comes down to writing efficient code. Minimizing the power drain from using the radio comes down to handling error conditions gracefully and fetching only the data that's needed. For example, don't constantly retry a network operation if one attempt failed. If it failed once, another immediate attempt is likely to fail because the user has no reception; all you'll accomplish is to waste battery power. Keep in mind that users will notice a power-hungry app and most likely uninstall the app.

Index

B

▪T

V

W

X, Y

Z

Made in the USA
San Bernardino, CA
04 January 2013